CLYMER MANUALS

HONDA
CR250R • 1997-2001

WHAT'S IN YOUR TOOLBOX?

More information available at haynes.com
Phone: 805-498-6703

Haynes Group Limited
Haynes North America, Inc.

ISBN-10: 0-89287-789-8
ISBN-13: 978-0-89287-789-8
Library of Congress: 2002106385

Author: Jay Bogart
Technical Photography: Ron Wright, CR250R courtesy of Clawson Motorsports, Fresno, California
Technical Illustrations: Mike Rose
Cover: Mark Clifford Photography, CR250R courtesy of Rice Motorsports, La Puente, California

Common spark plug conditions

NORMAL

Symptoms: Brown to grayish-tan color and slight electrode wear. Correct heat range for engine and operating conditions.
Recommendation: When new spark plugs are installed, replace with plugs of the same heat range.

WORN

Symptoms: Rounded electrodes with a small amount of deposits on the firing end. Normal color. Causes hard starting in damp or cold weather and poor fuel economy.
Recommendation: Plugs have been left in the engine too long. Replace with new plugs of the same heat range. Follow the recommended maintenance schedule.

TOO HOT

Symptoms: Blistered, white insulator, eroded electrode and absence of deposits. Results in shortened plug life.
Recommendation: Check for the correct plug heat range, over-advanced ignition timing, lean fuel mixture, intake manifold vacuum leaks, sticking valves and insufficient engine cooling.

CARBON DEPOSITS

Symptoms: Dry sooty deposits indicate a rich mixture or weak ignition. Causes misfiring, hard starting and hesitation.
Recommendation: Make sure the plug has the correct heat range. Check for a clogged air filter or problem in the fuel system or engine management system. Also check for ignition system problems.

PREIGNITION

Symptoms: Melted electrodes. Insulators are white, but may be dirty due to misfiring or flying debris in the combustion chamber. Can lead to engine damage.
Recommendation: Check for the correct plug heat range, over-advanced ignition timing, lean fuel mixture, insufficient engine cooling and lack of lubrication.

ASH DEPOSITS

Symptoms: Light brown deposits encrusted on the side or center electrodes or both. Derived from oil and/or fuel additives. Excessive amounts may mask the spark, causing misfiring and hesitation during acceleration.
Recommendation: If excessive deposits accumulate over a short time or low mileage, install new valve guide seals to prevent seepage of oil into the combustion chambers. Also try changing gasoline brands.

HIGH SPEED GLAZING

Symptoms: Insulator has yellowish, glazed appearance. Indicates that combustion chamber temperatures have risen suddenly during hard acceleration. Normal deposits melt to form a conductive coating. Causes misfiring at high speeds.
Recommendation: Install new plugs. Consider using a colder plug if driving habits warrant.

OIL DEPOSITS

Symptoms: Oily coating caused by poor oil control. Oil is leaking past worn valve guides or piston rings into the combustion chamber. Causes hard starting, misfiring and hesitation.
Recommendation: Correct the mechanical condition with necessary repairs and install new plugs.

DETONATION

Symptoms: Insulators may be cracked or chipped. Improper gap setting techniques can also result in a fractured insulator tip. Can lead to piston damage.
Recommendation: Make sure the fuel anti-knock values meet engine requirements. Use care when setting the gaps on new plugs. Avoid lugging the engine.

GAP BRIDGING

Symptoms: Combustion deposits lodge between the electrodes. Heavy deposits accumulate and bridge the electrode gap. The plug ceases to fire, resulting in a dead cylinder.
Recommendation: Locate the faulty plug and remove the deposits from between the electrodes.

MECHANICAL DAMAGE

Symptoms: May be caused by a foreign object in the combustion chamber or the piston striking an incorrect reach (too long) plug. Causes a dead cylinder and could result in piston damage.
Recommendation: Repair the mechanical damage. Remove the foreign object from the engine and/or install the correct reach plug.

CONTENTS

QUICK REFERENCE DATA

Table 1 MOTORCYCLE INFORMATION

MODEL:_____ YEAR:_____

VIN NUMBER:_____

ENGINE SERIAL NUMBER:_____

CARBURETOR SERIAL NUMBER OR I.D. MARK:_____

Table 2 FUEL, LUBRICANTS AND FLUIDS

Fuel type	Unleaded gasoline; 92 octane minimum
Fuel tank capacity	7.5 liters (2 U.S. gal.)
Engine oil	Pro Honda HP-2, 2-Stroke Oil or equivalent
Engine oil mixing ratio	32:1
Transmission oil type	Pro Honda HP transmission oil or Pro Honda GN4 4-stroke 10W-40 SF/SG engine oil or equivalent
Transmission oil capacity	
Overhaul capacity	0.85 L (0.9 U.S. qt.)
Change capacity	0.75 L (0.8 U.S. qt.)
Coolant type	Ethylene glycol containing silicate-free corrosion inhibitors for aluminum engines
Coolant mixture	50/50 (antifreeze/distilled water)
Cooling system capacity	
1997-1999	
At change	1.26 liters (1.32 U.S. qt.)
At disassembly	1.28 liters (1.35 U.S. qt.)
2000-2001	
At change	1.22 liters (1.29 U.S. qt.)
At disassembly	1.35 liters (1.43 U.S. qt.)
Fork oil grade	Pro-Honda HP fork oil 5W or equivalent
Fork oil capacity (standard)	Refer to Chapter 12 for minimum/maximum capacities
1997	369 cc (12.5 U.S. oz.)
1998	375 cc (12.7 U.S. oz.)
1999	373 cc (12.6 U.S. oz.)
2000	386 cc (13.6 U.S. oz.)
2001	383 cc (13.0 U.S. oz.)
Air filter	Foam air filter oil
Brake fluid type	DOT 4
Control cable pivots	Cable lube
Drive chain	Pro Honda chain lubricant or equivalent

Table 3 TUNE-UP SPECIFICATIONS

Pilot air screw turns out	
1997-1999	2
2000	1 1/2
2001	1 3/4
Spark plug	
Standard	Denso W24ESR-V or NGK BR8EG
Optional	Denso W24ESR-G or NGK BR8EV
Spark plug gap	0.5-0.6 mm (0.020-0.024 in.)
Ignition timing	
1997	18° at 3000 rpm
1998-2001	18° ± 2° at 3000 rpm

Table 4 ROUTINE CHECK AND ADJUSTMENT SPECIFICATIONS

Drive chain
Slack	25-35 mm (1.0-1.4 in.)
Length wear limit (16 pitch/17 pins)	259 mm (10.2 in.)
Slider thickness wear limit	5.0 mm (0.2 in.)
Tensioner roller diameter wear limit	
1997	25 mm (1.00 in.)
1998	
Upper	25 mm (1.00 in.)
Lower	35 mm (1.38 in.)
1999	
Upper	25 mm (1.00 in.)
Lower	39 mm (1.54 in.)
2000-2001	
Upper and lower	25 mm (0.98 in.)

Wheels
Axle runout (front/rear)	0.20 mm (0.008 in.)
Rim runout (radial and lateral)	2.0 mm (0.08 in.)
Tire Pressure (front/rear)	100 kPa (15 psi)
Radiator cap relief pressure	108-137 kPa (16-20 psi)
Throttle grip free play	3-5 mm (1/8-1/4 in.)
Clutch lever free play	10-20 mm (3/8-3/4 in.)

Table 5 MAINTENANCE TORQUE SPECIFICATIONS

	N•m	in.-lb.	ft.-lb.
Axle nut (front)	88	–	65
Axle nut (rear)			
1997	93	–	69
1998-1999	108	–	80
2000-2001	127	–	94
Coolant drain bolt	10	88	–
Clutch lever pivot bolt	2	18	–
Clutch lever pivot nut	10	88	–
Drive chain adjusting nut	27	–	20
Drive chain guide mounting nut	12	106	–
Drive chain roller bolt			
1997-2000	22	–	16
2001	12	106	–
Drive sprocket bolt	26	–	20
Driven sprocket nuts	32	–	24
Rim lock	13	115	–
Shift lever bolt	12	88	–
Spark plug	18	–	13
Spokes	3.8	33	–
Throttle housing bolts	9	80	–
Throttle housing cover screw	1.5	13	–
Transmission oil check bolt	10	88	–
Transmission oil drain plug (crankcase)	29	–	22

CHAPTER ONE

GENERAL INFORMATION

This detailed and comprehensive manual covers the 1997-2001 Honda CR250R.

The text provides complete information on maintenance, tune-up, repair and overhaul. Hundreds of photos and drawings guide the reader through every job.

A shop manual is a reference tool and as in all Clymer manuals, the chapters are thumb tabbed for easy reference. Important items are indexed at the end of the book. All procedures, tables and figures are designed for the reader who may be working on the machine for the first time. Frequently used specifications and capacities from individual chapters are summarized in the *Quick Reference Data* at the front of the book.

Tables 1-6 are at the end of this chapter.

Table 1 lists general motorcycle dimensions.

Table 2 lists technical abbreviations.

Table 3 lists general torque specifications.

Table 4 lists conversion tables.

Table 5 lists metric tap and drill sizes.

Table 6 lists decimal and metric equivalents.

MANUAL ORGANIZATION

All dimensions and capacities are expressed in metric and U.S. standard units of measurement.

This chapter provides general information on shop safety, tool use, service fundamentals and shop supplies. The tables at the end of the chapter include general vehicle information.

Chapter Two provides methods for quick and accurate diagnosis of problems. Troubleshooting procedures present typical symptoms and logical methods to pinpoint and repair the problem.

Chapter Three explains all routine maintenance and recommended tune-up procedures necessary to keep the motorcycle running well.

Subsequent chapters describe specific systems such as engine, transmission, clutch, drive system, fuel and exhaust systems, suspension and brakes. Each disassembly, repair and assembly procedure is discussed in step-by-step form.

Some of the procedures in this manual specify special tools. In most cases, the tool is illustrated in use. Well-equipped mechanics may be able to substitute similar tools or fabricate a suitable replacement. However, in some cases, the specialized equipment or expertise may make it impractical for the home mechanic to attempt the procedure. When necessary, such operations are identified in the text with the recommendation to have a dealership or specialist perform the task. It may be less expensive to have a professional perform these jobs, especially when considering the cost of the equipment.

WARNINGS, CAUTIONS AND NOTES

The terms WARNING, CAUTION and NOTE have specific meanings in this manual.

A WARNING emphasizes areas where injury or even death could result from negligence. Mechanical damage may also occur. WARNINGS *are to be taken seriously.*

A CAUTION emphasizes areas where equipment damage could result. Disregarding a CAUTION could cause permanent mechanical damage, though injury is unlikely.

A NOTE provides additional information to make a step or procedure easier or clearer. Disregarding a NOTE could cause inconvenience, but would not cause equipment damage or personal injury.

SAFETY

Professional mechanics can work for years and never sustain a serious injury or mishap. Follow these guidelines and practice common sense to safely service the motorcycle.

1. Do not operate the motorcycle in an enclosed area. The exhaust gasses contain carbon monoxide, an odorless, colorless and tasteless poisonous gas. Carbon monoxide levels build quickly in small enclosed areas and can cause unconsciousness and death in a short time. Make sure the work area is properly ventilated or operate the motorcycle outside.

2. *Never* use gasoline or any extremely flammable liquid to clean parts. Refer to *Cleaning Parts* and *Handling Gasoline Safely* in this chapter.

3. *Never* smoke or use a torch in the vicinity of flammable liquids, such as gasoline or cleaning solvent.

4. If welding or brazing on the motorcycle, remove the fuel tank, carburetor and shocks to a safe distance at least 50 ft. (15 m) away.

5. Use the correct type and size of tools to avoid damaging fasteners.

6. Keep tools clean and in good condition. Replace or repair worn or damaged equipment.

7. When loosening a tight fastener, be guided by what would happen if the tool slips.

8. When replacing fasteners, make sure the new fasteners are of the same size and strength as the original ones.

9. Keep the work area clean and organized.

10. Wear eye protection *anytime* eye injury is possible. This includes procedures involving drilling, grinding, hammering, compressed air and chemicals.

11. Wear the correct clothing for the job. Tie up or cover long hair so it cannot get caught in moving equipment.

12. Do not carry sharp tools in clothing pockets.

13. Always have an approved fire extinguisher available. Make sure it is rated for gasoline (Class B) and electrical (Class C) fires.

14. Do not use compressed air to clean clothes, the motorcycle or the work area. Debris may be blown into the eyes or skin. *Never* direct compressed air at anyone. Do not allow children to use or play with any compressed air equipment.

15. When using compressed air to dry rotating parts, hold the part so it cannot rotate. Do not allow the force of the air to spin the part. The air jet is capable of rotating parts at extreme speed. The part may be damaged or disintegrate, causing serious injury.

16. Do not inhale the dust created by brake pad and clutch wear. In most cases these particles contain asbestos. In addition, some types of insulating materials and gaskets may contain asbestos. Inhaling asbestos particles is hazardous to health.

17. Never work on the motorcycle while someone is working under it.

18. When placing the motorcycle on a stand, make sure it is secure before leaving.

Handling Gasoline Safely

Gasoline is a volatile, flammable liquid and is one of the most dangerous items in the shop.

Because gasoline is used so often, it is easy to forget that it is hazardous. Only use gasoline as fuel for gasoline internal combustion engines. Keep in mind, when working on a motorcycle, gasoline is always present in the fuel tank, fuel line and carburetor. To avoid a disastrous accident when working around the fuel system, carefully observe the following precautions:

1. *Never* use gasoline to clean parts. See *Cleaning Parts* in this chapter.

2. When working on the fuel system, work outside or in a well-ventilated area.

3. Do not add fuel to the fuel tank or service the fuel system while the motorcycle is near open flames, sparks or where someone is smoking. Gasoline vapor is heavier than air, it collects in low areas and is more easily ignited than liquid gasoline.

4. Allow the engine to cool completely before working on any fuel system component.

5. When draining the carburetor, catch the fuel in a plastic container and then pour it into an approved gasoline storage device.

6. Do not store gasoline in glass containers. If the glass breaks, a serious explosion or fire may occur.

7. Immediately wipe up spilled gasoline. Store the contaminated shop cloths in a metal container with a lid until they can be properly disposed, or place them outside in a safe place for the fuel to evaporate.

8. Do not pour water onto a gasoline fire. Water spreads the fire and makes it more difficult to put out. Use a class B, BC or ABC fire extinguisher to extinguish the fire.

9. Always turn off the engine before refueling. Do not spill fuel onto the engine or exhaust system. Do not overfill the fuel tank. Leave an air space at the top of the tank to allow room for the fuel to expand due to temperature fluctuations.

Cleaning Parts

Cleaning parts is one of the more tedious and difficult service jobs performed in the home shop. There are many types of chemical cleaners and solvents available for shop use. Most are poisonous and extremely flammable. To prevent chemical exposure, vapor buildup, fire and serious injury, observe each product warning label and note the following:

1. Read and observe the entire product label before using any chemical. Always know what type of chemical is being used and whether it is poisonous and/or flammable.

2. Do not use more than one type of cleaning solvent at a time. If mixing chemicals is called for, measure the proper amounts according to the manufacturer.

3. Work in a well-ventilated area.

4. Wear chemical-resistant gloves.

5. Wear safety glasses.

6. Wear a vapor respirator when necessary.

7. Wash hands and arms thoroughly after cleaning parts.

8. Keep chemical products away from children and pets.

9. Thoroughly clean all oil, grease and cleaner residue from any part that must be heated.

10. Use a nylon brush when cleaning parts. Wire brushes may cause a spark.

11. When using a parts washer, only use the solvent recommended by the manufacturer. Check that the parts washer is equipped with a metal lid that will lower in case of fire.

Warning Labels

Most manufacturers attach information and warning labels to the motorcycle. These labels contain instructions that are important to personal safety when operating, servicing, transporting and storing the motorcycle. Refer to the owner's manual for the description and location of labels. Order replacement labels from the manufacturer if they are missing or damaged.

BASIC SERVICE METHODS

Most of the procedures in this manual are straightforward and can be performed by anyone reasonably competent with tools. However, consider personal capabilities carefully before attempting any operation involving major disassembly of the engine.

1. Front, in this manual, refers to the front of the motorcycle. The front of any component is the end closest to the front of the motorcycle. The left and right sides refer to the position of the parts as

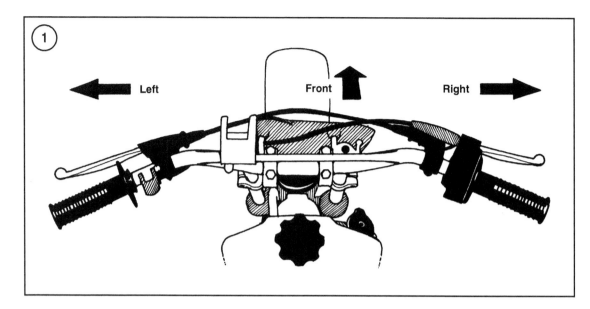

viewed by the rider sitting on the seat facing forward (**Figure 1**).

2. Whenever servicing an engine or suspension component, secure the motorcycle in a safe manner.

3. Tag all similar parts for location and mark all mating parts for position. Record the number and thickness of any shims as they are removed. Identify parts by placing them in sealed and labeled plastic bags.

4. Tag disconnected wires and connectors with masking tape and a marking pen. Do not rely on memory alone.

5. Protect finished surfaces from physical damage or corrosion. Keep gasoline and other chemicals off painted surfaces.

6. Use penetrating oil on frozen or tight bolts. Avoid using heat where possible. Heat can warp, melt or affect the temper of parts. Heat also damages the finish of paint and plastics.

7. When a part is a press-fit or requires a special tool for removal, the information or type of tool is identified in the text. Otherwise, if a part is difficult to remove or install, determine the cause before proceeding.

8. Cover all openings to prevent objects or debris from falling into the engine.

9. Read each procedure thoroughly and compare the illustrations to the actual components before starting the procedure. Perform the procedure in sequence.

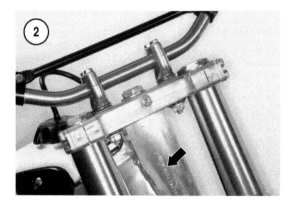

10. Recommendations are occasionally made to refer service to a dealership or specialist. In these cases, the work can be performed more economically by the specialist than by the home mechanic.

11. The term replace means to discard a defective part and replace it with a new part. Overhaul means to remove, disassemble, inspect, measure, repair and/or replace parts as required to recondition an assembly.

12. Some operations require the use of a hydraulic press. If a press is not available, have these operations performed by a shop equipped with the necessary equipment. Do not use makeshift equipment that may damage the motorcycle.

13. Repairs are much faster and easier if the motorcycle is clean before starting work. Degrease the motorcycle with a commercial degreaser; follow the directions on the container for the best results. Clean all parts with cleaning solvent as they are removed.

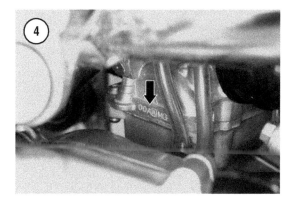

CAUTION
Do not apply a chemical degreaser to an O-ring drive chain. These chemicals will damage the O-rings. Use kerosene to clean O-ring type chains.

CAUTION
Do not direct high-pressure water at steering bearings, carburetor hoses, wheel bearings, suspension and electrical components, or O-ring drive chains. The water will force the grease out of the bearings and possibly damage the seals.

14. If special tools are required, have them available before starting the procedure. When special tools are required, they will be described in the procedure.

15. Make diagrams of similar-appearing parts. For instance, crankcase bolts are often not the same lengths. Do not rely on memory alone. It is possible that carefully laid out parts will become disturbed, making it difficult to reassemble the components correctly without a diagram.

16. Make sure all shims and washers are reinstalled in the same location and position.

17. Whenever rotating parts contact a stationary part, look for a shim or washer.

18. Use new gaskets if there is any doubt about the condition of old ones.

19. If self-locking fasteners are used, replace them with new ones. Do not install standard fasteners in place of self-locking ones.

20. Use grease to hold small parts in place if they tend to fall out during assembly. Do not apply grease to electrical or brake components.

SERIAL NUMBERS

Serial numbers are stamped onto the frame and engine. Record these numbers in the *Quick Reference Data* section at the front of the book. Have these numbers available when ordering parts.

The frame number is stamped on the right side of the steering head (**Figure 2**).

The engine number (**Figure 3**) is stamped on the left crankcase, below the countershaft sprocket.

The carburetor identification number is stamped on the left side of the carburetor (1997-2000 models) (**Figure 4**), or the front of the carburetor (2001 models).

FASTENERS

Proper fastener selection and installation is important to ensure that the motorcycle operates as designed, and can be serviced efficiently. Check that replacement fasteners meet all the same requirements as the originals.

Threaded Fasteners

Threaded fasteners secure most of the components on the motorcycle. Most are tightened by turning them clockwise (right-hand threads). If the normal rotation of the component being tightened would loosen the fastener, it may have left-hand threads. If a left-hand threaded fastener is used, it is noted in the text.

Two dimensions are required to match the threads of the fastener: the number of threads in a given distance and the outside diameter of the threads.

Two systems are currently used to specify threaded fastener dimensions: the U.S. standard system and the metric system (**Figure 5**). Pay particular attention when working with unidentified fasteners; mismatching thread types can damage threads.

> *NOTE*
> *To ensure that fastener threads are not mismatched or do not become cross-threaded, start all fasteners by hand. If a fastener is hard to start or turn, determine the cause before tightening with a wrench.*

The length (L), diameter (D) and distance between thread crests, or pitch (T) (**Figure 6**), classify metric screws and bolts. A typical bolt may be identified by the numbers, 8-1.25 × 130. This indicates the bolt has diameter of 8 mm, the distance between thread crests is 1.25 mm and the length is 130 mm. Always measure bolt length as shown in **Figure 7** to avoid purchasing replacements of the wrong length.

The numbers located on the top of the fastener (**Figure 6**) indicate the strength of metric screws and bolts. The higher the number, the stronger the fastener. Unnumbered fasteners are the weakest.

Many screws, bolts and studs are combined with nuts to secure particular components. To indicate the size of a nut, manufacturers specify the internal diameter and the thread pitch.

The measurement across two flats on a nut or bolt indicates the wrench size.

> *WARNING*
> *Do not install fasteners with a strength classification lower than what was originally installed by the manufacturer. Doing so may cause equipment failure and/or damage.*

Torque Specifications

The materials used in the manufacture of the motorcycle may be subjected to uneven stresses if the fasteners of the various subassemblies are not installed and tightened correctly. Fasteners that are improperly installed or work loose can cause extensive damage. It is essential to use an accurate torque wrench, described in this chapter, with the torque specifications in this manual.

Specifications for torque are provided in Newton-meters (N•m), foot-pounds (ft.-lb.) and inch-pounds (in.-lb.). Refer to **Table 4** for torque

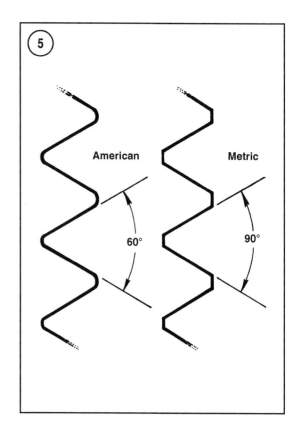

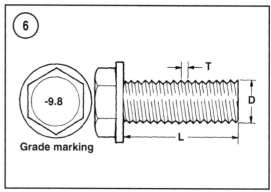

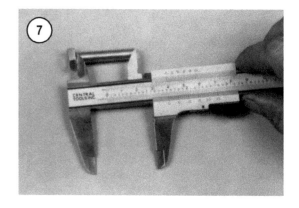

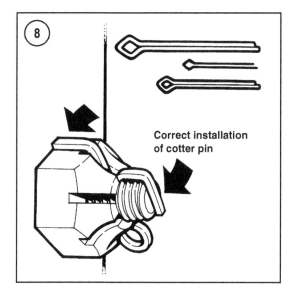

Correct installation
of cotter pin

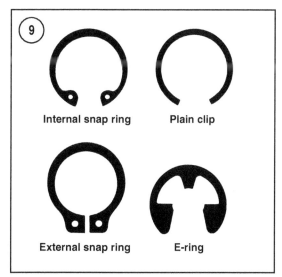

Internal snap ring   Plain clip

External snap ring   E-ring

conversions and **Table 3** for general specifications. To use **Table 3**, first determine the size of the fastener as described in *Fasteners* in this chapter. Torque specifications for specific components are at the end of the appropriate chapters. Torque wrenches are covered in the *Basic Tools* section.

Self-Locking Fasteners

Several types of bolts, screws and nuts incorporate a system that creates interference between the two fasteners. Interference is achieved in various ways. The most common type is the nylon insert nut and a dry adhesive coating on the threads of a bolt.

Self-locking fasteners offer greater holding strength than standard fasteners, which improves their resistance to vibration. Most self-locking fasteners cannot be reused. The materials used to form the lock become distorted after the initial installation and removal. It is a good practice to discard and replace self-locking fasteners after their removal. Do not replace self-locking fasteners with standard fasteners.

Washers

There are two basic types of washers: flat washers and lockwashers. Flat washers are simple discs with a hole to fit a screw or bolt. Lockwashers are used to prevent a fastener from working loose. Washers can be used as spacers and seals, or to help distribute fastener load and to prevent the fastener from damaging the component.

As with fasteners, when replacing washers make sure the replacement washers are of the same design and quality.

Cotter Pins

A cotter pin is a split metal pin inserted into a hole or slot to prevent a fastener from loosening. In certain applications, such as the rear axle on an ATV or motorcycle, the fastener must be secured in this way. For these applications, a cotter pin and castellated (slotted) nut is used.

To use a cotter pin, first make sure the diameter is correct for the hole in the fastener. After correctly tightening the fastener and aligning the holes, insert the cotter pin through the hole and bend the ends over the fastener (**Figure 8**). Unless instructed to do so, never loosen a torqued fastener to align the holes. If the holes do not align, tighten the fastener just enough to achieve alignment.

Cotter pins are available in various diameters and lengths. Measure length from the bottom of the head to the tip of the shortest pin.

Snap Rings and E-clips

Snap rings (**Figure 9**) are circular-shaped metal retaining clips. They are required to secure parts and gears in place on parts such as shafts, pins or rods. External type snap rings are used to retain items on shafts. Internal type snap rings secure parts within housing bores. In some applications, in addition to securing the component(s), snap rings of varying thickness also determine end play. These are usually called selective snap rings.

Two basic types of snap rings are used: machined and stamped snap rings. Machined snap rings can be installed in either direction, since both faces have sharp edges. Stamped snap rings (**Figure 10**) are manufactured with a sharp edge and a round edge. When installing a stamped snap ring in a thrust application, install the sharp edge facing away from the part producing the thrust.

Observe the following when installing snap rings:

1. Remove and install snap rings with snap ring pliers. See *Snap Ring Pliers* in this chapter.

2. In some applications, it may be necessary to replace snap rings after removing them.

3. Compress or expand snap rings only enough to install them. If overly expanded, they lose their retaining ability.

4. After installing a snap ring, make sure it seats completely.

5. Wear eye protection when removing and installing snap rings.

E-clips are used when it is not practical to use a snap ring. Remove E-clips with a flat blade screwdriver by prying between the shaft and E-clip. To install an E-clip, center it over the shaft groove and push or tap it into place.

SHOP SUPPLIES

Lubricants and Fluids

Periodic lubrication helps ensure long service-life for any type of equipment. Using the correct type of lubricant or fluid is as important as performing the service. The following section describes the types of lubricants most often required. Follow the manufacturer's recommendations for lubricant and fluid types.

Engine oil

Engine oil is classified by two standards: the American Petroleum Institute (API) service classification and the Society of Automotive Engineers

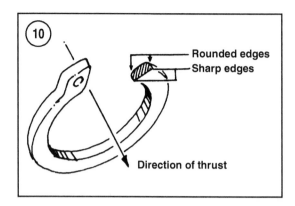

Rounded edges

Sharp edges

Direction of thrust

(SAE) viscosity rating. This information is on the oil container label. Two letters indicate the API service classification. The number or sequence of numbers and letter (10W-40 for example) is the oil's viscosity rating. The API service classification and the SAE viscosity index are not indications of oil quality.

The service classification indicates that the oil meets specific lubrication standards. The first letter in the classification *S* indicates that the oil is for gasoline engines. The second letter indicates the standard the oil satisfies. The classification started with the letter *A* and is currently at the letter *J*.

Always use an oil with a classification recommended by the manufacturer. Using an oil with a classification different than that recommended can cause engine damage.

Viscosity is an indication of the oil's thickness. Thin oils have a lower number while thick oils have a higher number. Engine oils fall into the 5- to 50-weight range for single-grade oils.

Most manufacturers recommend multigrade oil. These oils perform efficiently across a wide range of operating conditions. Multigrade oils are identified by a *W* after the first number, which indicates the low-temperature viscosity.

Engine oils are most commonly mineral (petroleum) based; however, synthetic and semi-synthetic types are used more frequently. When selecting engine oil, follow the manufacturer's recommendation for type, classification and viscosity.

Grease

Grease is lubricating oil with thickening agents. The National Lubricating Grease Institute (NLGI) grades grease. Grades range from No. 000 to No. 6, with No. 6 being the thickest. Typical multipurpose grease is NLGI No. 2. For specific applications, manufacturers may recommend water-resistant type grease or one with an additive such as molybdenum disulfide (MoS_2).

Chain lubricant

There are many types of chain lubricants available. Which type of chain lubricant to use depends on the type of chain.

On O-ring (sealed) chains, the lubricant keeps the O-rings pliable and prevents corrosion. The actual chain lubricant is enclosed in the chain by the O-rings. Recommended types include aerosol sprays specifically designed for O-ring chains, and conventional engine or gear oils. When using a spray lubricant, make sure it is suitable for O-ring chains.

Do not use a high-pressure washer, solvents or gasoline to clean an O-ring chain. Only clean with kerosene.

Foam air filter oil

Filter oil is specifically designed for use in foam air filters. The oil is blended with additives, making it easy to pour and apply evenly to the filter. These additives evaporate quickly, making the filter oil very tacky. This allows the oil to remain suspended within the foam pores, trapping dirt and preventing it from being drawn into the engine.

Do not use engine oil as a substitute for foam filter oil. Engine oils will not remain in the filter. Instead, they will be drawn into the engine, leaving the filter ineffective.

Brake fluid

Brake fluid is the hydraulic fluid used to transmit hydraulic pressure (force) to the wheel brakes. Brake fluid is classified by the Department of Transportation (DOT). Current designations for brake fluid are DOT 3, DOT 4 and DOT 5. This classification appears on the fluid container.

Each type of brake fluid has its own definite characteristics. Do not intermix different types of brake fluid. DOT 5 fluid is silicone-based. DOT 5 is not compatible with other fluids or in systems for which it was not designed. Mixing DOT 5 fluid with other fluids may cause brake system failure. When adding brake fluid, *only* use the fluid recommended by the manufacturer.

Brake fluid will damage any plastic, painted or plated surface it contacts. Use extreme care when working with brake fluid and remove any spills immediately with soap and water.

Hydraulic brake systems require clean and moisture-free brake fluid. Never reuse brake fluid. Keep containers and reservoirs properly sealed.

WARNING
Never put a mineral-based (petroleum) oil into the brake system. Mineral oil will cause rubber parts in the system to swell and break apart, resulting in complete brake failure.

Coolant

Coolant is a mixture of water and antifreeze used to dissipate engine heat. Ethylene glycol is the most common form of antifreeze. Check the manufacturer's recommendations when selecting an antifreeze; most require one specifically designed for use in aluminum engines. These types of antifreezes have additives that inhibit corrosion.

Only mix distilled water with antifreeze. Impurities in tap water may damage internal cooling system passages.

Cleaners, Degreasers and Solvents

Many chemicals are available to remove oil, grease and other residue from the motorcycle.

Before using cleaning solvents, consider how they will be used and disposed of, particularly if they are not water-soluble. Local ordinances may require special procedures for the disposal of many types of cleaning chemicals. Refer to *Safety and Cleaning Parts* in this chapter for more information on their use.

Use brake parts cleaner to clean brake system components when contact with petroleum-based products will damage seals. Brake parts cleaner leaves no residue. Use electrical contact cleaner to clean electrical connections and components without leaving any residue. Carburetor cleaner is a powerful solvent used to remove fuel deposits and varnish from fuel system components. Use this cleaner carefully, as it may damage finishes.

Generally, degreasers are strong cleaners used to remove heavy accumulations of grease from engine and frame components.

Most solvents are designed to be used in a parts washing cabinet for individual component cleaning. For safety, use only nonflammable or high flash-point solvents.

Gasket Sealant

Sealants are used in combination with a gasket or seal and are occasionally alone. Follow the manufacturer's recommendation when using sealants. Use extreme care when choosing a sealant. Choose sealants based on their resistance to heat, various fluids and their sealing capabilities.

One of the most common sealants is RTV, or room temperature vulcanizing sealant. This sealant cures at room temperature over a specific time period. This allows the repositioning of components without damaging gaskets.

Moisture in the air causes the RTV sealant to cure. Always install the tube cap as soon as possible after applying RTV sealant. RTV sealant has a limited shelf life and will not cure properly if the shelf life has expired. Keep partial tubes sealed and discard them if they have surpassed the expiration date.

Applying RTV sealant

Clean all old gasket residue from the mating surfaces. Remove all gasket material from blind threaded holes; it can cause inaccurate bolt torque. Spray the mating surfaces with aerosol parts cleaner and then wipe with a lint-free cloth. The area must be clean for the sealant to adhere.

Apply RTV sealant in a continuous bead 2-3 mm (0.08-0.12 in.) thick. Circle all the fastener holes unless otherwise specified. Do not allow any sealant to enter these holes. Assemble and tighten the fasteners to the specified torque within the time frame recommended by the RTV sealant manufacturer.

Gasket Remover

Aerosol gasket remover can help remove stubborn gaskets. This product can speed up the removal process and prevent damage to the mating

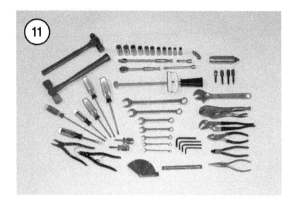

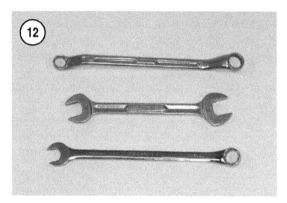

surface that may be caused by using a scraping tool. Most of these types of products are very caustic. Follow the manufacturer's instructions for use.

Threadlocking Compound

Threadlocking compound is a fluid applied to the threads of fasteners. After tightening the fastener, the fluid sets and becomes a solid filler between the threads. This makes it difficult for the fastener to work loose from vibration, or heat expansion and contraction. Some threadlocking compounds also provide a seal against fluid leakage.

Before applying threadlocking compound, remove any old compound from both thread areas and clean them with aerosol parts cleaner. Use the compound sparingly. Excess fluid can run into adjoining parts.

Threadlocking compounds are available in a wide range of compounds for various strength, temperature and repair applications. Follow the particular manufacturer's recommendations regarding compound selection.

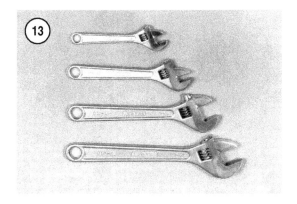

BASIC TOOLS

Most of the procedures in this manual can be carried out with simple hand tools and test equipment familiar to the home mechanic. Always use the correct tools for the job at hand. Keep tools organized and clean. Store them in a tool chest with related tools organized together.

Quality tools are essential. The best are constructed of high-strength alloy steel. These tools are light, easy to use and resistant to wear. Their working surface is devoid of sharp edges and the tool is carefully polished. They have an easy-to-clean finish and are comfortable to use. Quality tools are a good investment.

When purchasing tools to perform the procedures covered in this manual, consider the tools' potential frequency of use. If a tool kit is just now being started, consider purchasing a basic tool set (**Figure 11**) from a large tool supplier. These sets are available in many tool combinations and offer substantial savings when compared to individually purchased tools. As work experience grows and tasks become more complicated, specialized tools can be added.

Screwdrivers

Screwdrivers of various lengths and types are mandatory for the simplest tool kit. The two basic types are the slotted tip (flat blade) and the Phillips tip. These are available in sets that often include an assortment of tip sizes and shaft lengths.

As with all tools, use a screwdriver designed for the job. Make sure the size of the tip conforms to the size and shape of the fastener. Use them only for driving screws. Never use a screwdriver for prying or chiseling metal. Repair or replace worn or damaged screwdrivers. A worn tip may damage the fastener, making it difficult to remove.

Wrenches

Open-end, box-end and combinations wrenches (**Figure 12**) are available in a variety of types and sizes.

The number stamped on the wrench refers to the distance between the work areas. This size must match the size of the fastener head.

The box-end wrench is an excellent tool because it grips the fastener on all sides. This reduces the chance of the tool slipping. The box-end wrench is designed with either a 6- or 12-point opening. For stubborn or damaged fasteners, the 6-point provides superior holding ability by contacting the fastener across a wider area at all six edges. For general use, the 12-point works well. It allows the wrench to be removed and reinstalled without moving the handle over such a wide arc.

An open-end wrench is fast and works best in areas with limited overhead access. It contacts the fastener at only two points, and is subject to slipping under heavy force, or if the tool or fastener is worn. A box-end wrench is preferred in most instances, especially when breaking loose and applying the final tightness to a fastener.

The combination wrench has a box-end on one end, and an open-end on the other. This combination makes it a very convenient tool.

Adjustable Wrenches

An adjustable wrench or Crescent wrench (**Figure 13**) can fit nearly any nut or bolt head that has clear access around its entire perimeter. Adjustable wrenches are best used as a backup wrench to keep a large nut or bolt from turning while the other end is being loosened or tightened with a box-end or socket wrench.

Adjustable wrenches contact the fastener at only two points, which makes them more subject to slipping off the fastener. The fact that one jaw is adjustable and may loosen only aggravates this shortcoming. Make certain the solid jaw is the one transmitting the force.

Socket Wrenches, Ratchets and Handles

Sockets that attach to a ratchet handle (**Figure 14**) are available with 6-point or 12-point openings (**Figure 15**) and different drive sizes. The drive size indicates the size of the square hole that accepts the ratchet handle. The number stamped on the socket is the size of the work area and must match the fastener head.

As with wrenches, a 6-point socket provides superior holding ability, while a 12-point socket needs to be moved only half as far to reposition it on the fastener.

Sockets are designated for either hand or impact use. Impact sockets are made of thicker material for more durability. Compare the size and wall thickness of a 19-mm hand socket and the 19-mm impact socket (**Figure 16**). Use impact sockets when using an impact driver or air tools. Use hand sockets with hand-driven attachments.

> *WARNING*
> *Do not use hand sockets with air or impact tools, as they may shatter and cause injury. Always wear eye protection when using impact or air tools.*

Various handles are available for sockets. The speed handle is used for fast operation. Flexible ratchet heads in varying lengths allow the socket to be turned with varying force, and at odd angles. Extension bars allow the socket setup to reach difficult areas. The ratchet is the most versatile. It allows the user to install or remove the nut without removing the socket.

Sockets combined with any number of drivers make them undoubtedly the fastest, safest and most convenient tool for fastener removal and installation.

Impact Driver

An impact driver provides extra force for removing fasteners, by converting the impact of a hammer into a turning motion. This makes it possible to remove stubborn fasteners without damaging them. Impact drivers and interchangeable bits (**Figure 17**) are available from most tool suppliers. When using a socket with an impact driver make sure the socket is designed for impact use. Refer to *Socket Wrenches, Ratchets and Handles* in this section.

> *WARNING*
> *Do not use hand sockets with air or impact tools as they may shatter and*

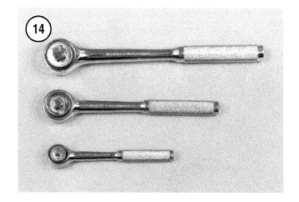

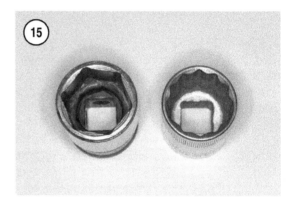

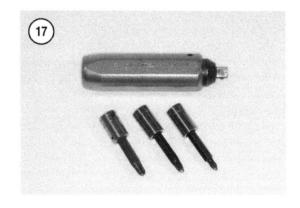

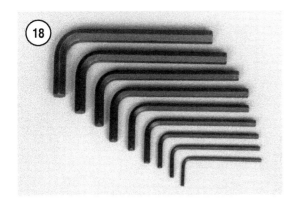

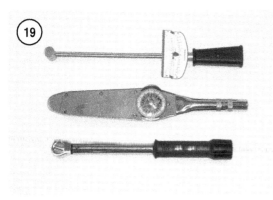

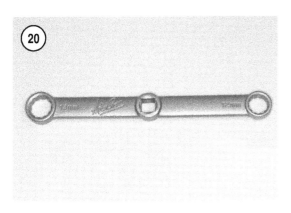

Torque Wrenches

A torque wrench is used with a socket, torque adapter or similar extension to tighten a fastener to a measured torque. Torque wrenches come in several drive sizes (1/4, 3/8, 1/2 and 3/4 in.) and have various methods of reading the torque value. The drive size indicates the size of the square drive that accepts the socket, adapter or extension. Common types of torque wrenches are the deflecting beam, dial indicator and audible click (**Figure 19**).

When choosing a torque wrench, consider the torque range, drive size and accuracy. The torque specifications in this manual provide an indication of the range required.

A torque wrench is a precision tool that must be properly cared for to remain accurate. Store torque wrenches in cases or separate padded drawers within a toolbox. Follow the manufacturer's instructions for their care and calibration.

Torque Adapters

Torque adapters or extensions extend or reduce the reach of a torque wrench. The torque adapter shown in **Figure 20** is used to tighten a fastener that cannot be reached due to the size of the torque wrench head, drive, and socket. If a torque adapter changes the effective lever length (**Figure 21**), the torque reading on the wrench will not equal the actual torque applied to the fastener. It is necessary to recalibrate the torque setting on the wrench to compensate for the change of lever length. When a torque adapter is used at a right angle to the drive head, calibration is not required, since the effective length has not changed.

To recalculate a torque reading when using a torque adapter, use the following formula, and refer to **Figure 21**.

$$TW = \frac{TA \times L}{L + A} = E$$

TW is the torque setting or dial reading on the wrench.

TA is the torque specification and the actual amount of torque that will be applied to the fastener.

cause injury. Always wear eye protection when using impact or air tools.

Allen Wrenches

Allen or set screw wrenches (**Figure 18**) are used on fasteners with hexagonal recesses in the fastener head. These wrenches are available in L-shaped bar, socket and T-handle types. A metric set is required when working on most motorcycles. Allen bolts are sometimes called socket bolts.

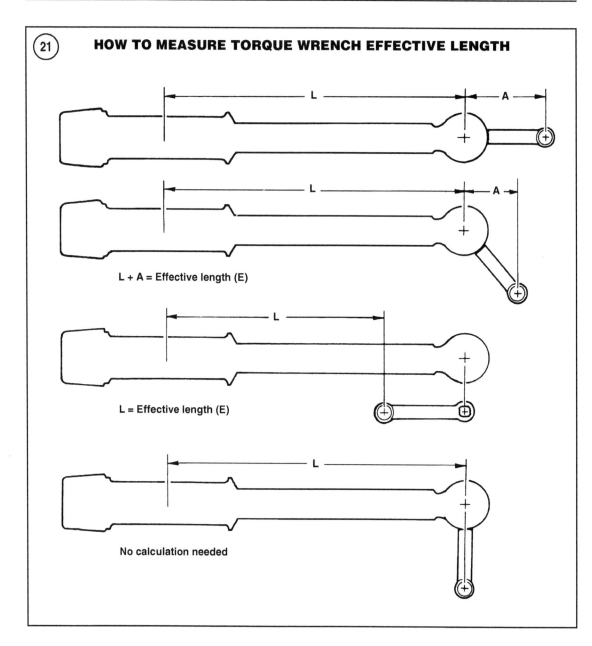

HOW TO MEASURE TORQUE WRENCH EFFECTIVE LENGTH

L + A = Effective length (E)

L = Effective length (E)

No calculation needed

A is the amount that the adapter increases (or in some cases reduces) the effective lever length as measured along the centerline of the torque wrench (**Figure 21**).

L is the lever length of the wrench as measured from the center of the drive to the center of the grip.

E is the effective length of the torque wrench and is the sum of L and A (**Figure 21**).

Example:

TA = 20 ft.-lb.

A = 3 in.

L = 14 in.

$$TW = \frac{20 \times 14}{14 + 3} = \frac{280}{17} = 16.5 \text{ ft. lb.}$$

In this example, the torque wrench would be set to the recalculated torque value (TW = 16.5 ft.-lb.). When using a beam-type wrench, tighten the fastener until the pointer aligns with 16.5 ft.-lb. In this example, although the torque wrench is preset to 16.5 ft.-lb., the actual torque is 20 ft.-lb.

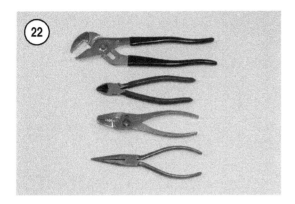

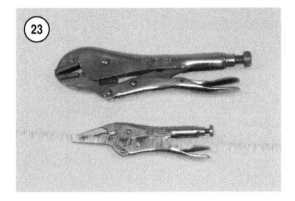

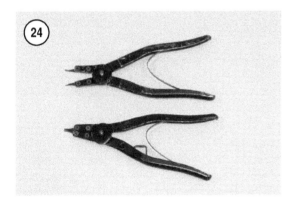

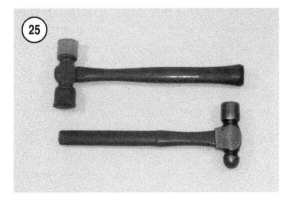

Pliers

Pliers come in a wide range of types and sizes. Pliers are useful for holding, cutting, bending and crimping. Do not use them to turn fasteners. **Figure 22** and **Figure 23** show several types of useful pliers. Each design has a specialized function. Slip-joint pliers are general-purpose pliers used for gripping and bending. Diagonal cutting pliers are needed to cut wire and can be used to remove cotter pins. Needlenose pliers are used to hold or bend small objects. Locking pliers (**Figure 23**), sometimes called Vise Grips, are used to hold objects very tightly. They have many uses, ranging from holding two parts together to gripping the end of a broken stud. Use caution when using locking pliers, as the sharp jaws will damage the objects they hold.

Snap Ring Pliers

Snap ring pliers (**Figure 24**) are specialized pliers with tips that fit into the ends of snap rings to remove and install them.

Snap ring pliers are available with a fixed action (either internal or external) or convertible (one tool works on both internal and external snap rings). They may have fixed tips or interchangeable ones of various sizes and angles. For general use, select a convertible type plier with interchangeable tips.

> *WARNING*
> *Snap rings can slip and fly off when removing and installing them. Also, the snap ring plier tips may break. Always wear eye protection when using snap ring pliers.*

Hammers

Various types of hammers (**Figure 25**) are available to fit a number of applications. A ball-peen hammer is used to strike another tool, such as a punch or chisel. Soft-faced hammers are required when a metal object must be struck without damaging it. *Never* use a metal-faced hammer on engine and suspension components, as damage will occur in most cases.

Always wear eye protection when using hammers. Make sure the hammer face is in good condition and the handle is not cracked. Select the correct hammer for the job and make sure to strike the ob-

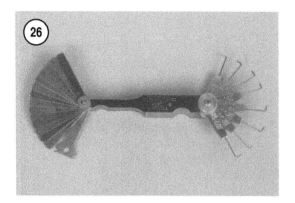

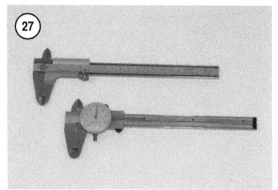

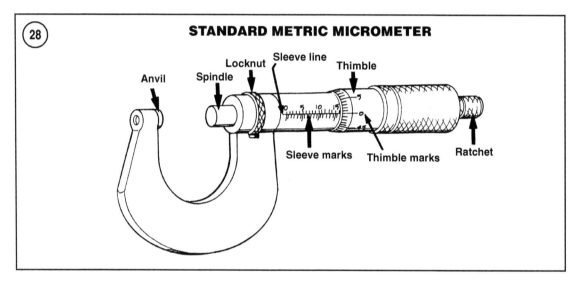

STANDARD METRIC MICROMETER

ject squarely. Do not use the handle or the side of the hammer to strike an object.

PRECISION MEASURING TOOLS

The ability to accurately measure components is essential to successfully inspect and rebuild an engine. Equipment is manufactured to close tolerances, and obtaining consistently accurate measurements is essential to determining which components require replacement or further service.

Each type of measuring instrument is designed to measure a dimension with a certain degree of accuracy and within a certain range. Always use a measuring tool that is designed for the task.

As with all tools, measuring tools provide the best results if cared for properly. Improper use can damage the tool and result in inaccurate results. If any measurement is questionable, verify the measurement using another tool. A standard gauge is usually provided with measuring tools to check accuracy and calibrate the tool if necessary.

Precision measurements can vary according to the experience of the person performing the procedure. Accurate results are only possible if the mechanic possesses a feel for using the tool. Heavy-handed use of measuring tools will produce less accurate results than if the tool is grasped gently by the fingertips so the point at which the tool contacts the object is easily felt. This feel for the equipment will produce more accurate measurements and reduce the risk of damaging the tool or component. Refer to the following sections for specific measuring tools.

Feeler Gauge

The feeler or thickness gauge (**Figure 26**) is used for measuring the distance between two surfaces.

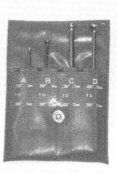

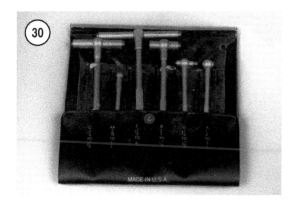

A feeler gauge set consists of an assortment of steel strips of graduated thickness. Each blade is marked with its thickness. Blades can be of various lengths and angles for different procedures.

A common use for a feeler gauge is measuring valve clearance. Wire (round) type gauges are used to measure spark plug gap.

Calipers

Calipers (**Figure 27**) are used to determine outside and depth measurements. Although not as precise as a micrometer, they allow reasonable precision, typically to within 0.05 mm (0.001 in.). Most calipers have a range up to 150 mm (6 in.).

Calipers are available in dial, vernier or digital versions. Dial calipers have a dial readout that provides convenient reading. Vernier calipers have marked scales that must be compared to determine the measurement. The digital caliper uses an LCD to show the measurement.

Properly maintain the measuring surfaces of the caliper. There must not be any dirt or burrs between the tool and the object being measured. Never force

the caliper closed around an object; close the caliper around the highest point so it can be removed with a slight drag. Some calipers require calibration. Always refer to the manufacturer's instructions when using a new or unfamiliar caliper.

Micrometers

A micrometer is an instrument designed for linear measurement using the decimal divisions of the inch or meter (**Figure 28**). While there are many types and styles of micrometers, most of the procedures in this manual call for an outside micrometer. The outside micrometer is used to measure the outside diameter of cylindrical forms and the thickness of materials.

A micrometer's size indicates the minimum and maximum size of a part that it can measure. The usual sizes (**Figure 29**) are 0-1 in. (0-25 mm), 1-2 in. (25-50 mm), 2-3 in. (50-75 mm) and 3-4 in. (75-100 mm).

Micrometers that cover a wider range of measurement are available. These use a large frame with interchangeable anvils of various lengths. This type of micrometer offers a cost savings; however, its overall size may make it less convenient.

Telescoping and Small-Bore Gauges

Use telescoping gauges (**Figure 30**) and small-hole gauges (**Figure 31**) to measure bores. Neither gauge has a scale for direct readings. An outside micrometer must be used to determine the reading.

To use a telescoping gauge, select the correct size gauge for the bore. Compress the movable post and carefully insert the gauge into the bore. Carefully move the gauge in the bore to make sure it is centered. Tighten the knurled end of the gauge to hold the movable post in position. Remove the gauge and measure the length of the posts. Telescoping gauges are typically used to measure cylinder bores.

To use a small-bore gauge, select the correct size gauge for the bore. Carefully insert the gauge into the bore. Tighten the knurled end of the gauge to carefully expand the gauge fingers to the limit within the bore. Do not overtighten the gauge, as there is no built-in release. Excessive tightening can damage the bore surface and damage the tool. Remove the gauge and measure the outside dimension (**Figure 32**). Small-hole gauges are typically used to measure valve guides.

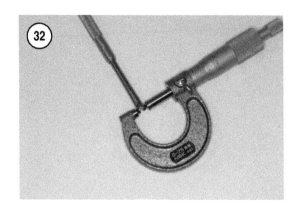

Dial Indicator

A dial indicator (**Figure 33**) is a gauge with a dial face and needle used to measure variations in dimensions and movements. Measuring brake rotor runout is a typical use for a dial indicator.

Dial indicators are available in various ranges and graduations and with three basic types of mounting bases: magnetic, clamp or screw-in stud. When purchasing a dial indicator, select the magnetic stand type, with a continuous dial.

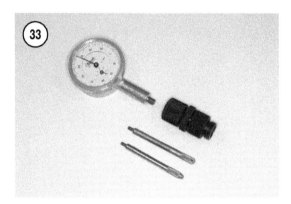

Cylinder Bore Gauge

A cylinder bore gauge is similar to a dial indicator. The gauge set shown in **Figure 34** consists of a dial indicator, handle and different length adapters (anvils) to fit the gauge to various bore sizes. The bore gauge is used to measure bore size, taper and out-of-round. When using a bore gauge, follow the manufacturer's instructions.

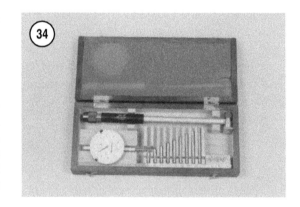

Compression Gauge

A compression gauge (**Figure 35**) measures combustion chamber (cylinder) pressure, usually in psi or kg/cm^2. The gauge adapter is either inserted or screwed into the spark plug hole to obtain the reading. Disable the engine so it will not start and hold the throttle in the wide-open position when performing a compression test. An engine that does not have adequate compression cannot be properly tuned. See Chapter Three.

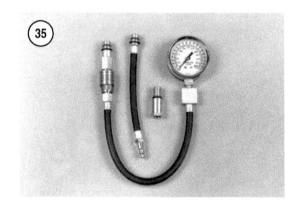

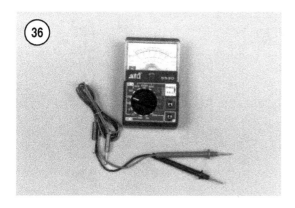

Multimeter

A multimeter (**Figure 36**) is an essential tool for electrical system diagnosis. The voltage function indicates the voltage applied or available to various electrical components. The ohmmeter function tests circuits for continuity, or lack of continuity, and measures the resistance of a circuit.

Some manufacturer's specifications for electrical components are based on results using a specific test meter. Results may vary if using a meter not recommend by the manufacturer. Such requirements are noted when applicable.

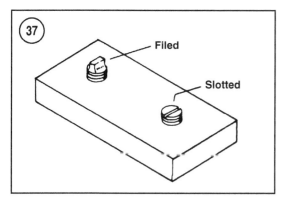

Filed

Slotted

Removing Frozen Fasteners

If a fastener cannot be removed, several methods may be used to loosen it. First, apply penetrating oil, such as Liquid Wrench or WD-40. Apply it liberally and let it penetrate for 10-15 minutes. Strike the fastener several times with a small hammer. Do not hit it hard enough to cause damage. Reapply the penetrating oil if necessary.

For frozen screws, apply penetrating oil as described, then insert a screwdriver in the slot and strike the top of the screwdriver with a hammer. This loosens the rust so the screw can be backed out. If the screw head is too damaged to use this method, grip the head with locking pliers and twist the screw out.

Avoid applying heat unless specifically instructed, as it may melt, warp or remove the temper from parts.

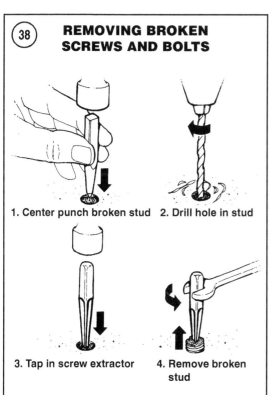

REMOVING BROKEN SCREWS AND BOLTS

1. Center punch broken stud   2. Drill hole in stud

3. Tap in screw extractor   4. Remove broken stud

Removing Broken Fasteners

If the head breaks off a screw or bolt, several methods are available for removing the remaining portion. If a large portion of the remainder projects out, try gripping it with locking pliers. If the projecting portion is too small, file it to fit a wrench or cut a slot in it to fit a screwdriver (**Figure 37**).

If the head breaks off flush, use a screw extractor. To do this, center-punch the exact center of the remaining portion of the screw or bolt. Drill a small hole in the screw and tap the extractor into the hole. Back the screw out with a wrench on the extractor (**Figure 38**).

Repairing Damaged Threads

Occasionally, threads are stripped through carelessness or impact damage. Often the threads can be repaired by running a tap (for internal threads on nuts) or die (for external threads on bolts) through the threads (**Figure 39**). To clean or repair spark plug threads, use a spark plug tap.

If an internal thread is damaged, it may be necessary to install a Helicoil or some other type of thread insert. Follow the manufacturer's instructions when installing their insert.

If it is necessary to drill and tap a hole, refer to **Table 5** for metric tap and drill sizes.

Stud Removal/Installation

A stud removal tool is available from most tool suppliers. This tool makes the removal and installation of studs easier. If one is not available, thread two nuts onto the stud and tighten them against each other. Remove the stud by turning the lower nut (**Figure 40**).

1. Measure the height of the stud above the surface.
2. Thread the stud removal tool onto the stud and tighten it, or thread two nuts onto the stud.
3. Remove the stud by turning the stud remover or the lower nut.
4. Remove any threadlocking compound from the threaded hole. Clean the threads with an aerosol parts cleaner.
5. Install the stud removal tool onto the new stud or thread two nuts onto the stud.
6. Apply threadlocking compound to the threads of the stud.
7. Install the stud and tighten with the stud removal tool or the top nut.
8. Install the stud to the height noted in Step 1 or its torque specification.
9. Remove the stud removal tool or the two nuts.

Removing Hoses

When removing stubborn hoses, do not exert excessive force on the hose or fitting. Remove the hose clamp and carefully insert a small screwdriver or pick tool between the fitting and hose. Apply a spray lubricant under the hose and carefully twist the hose off the fitting. Clean the fitting of any corrosion or rubber hose material with a wire brush.

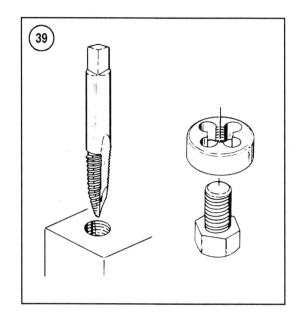

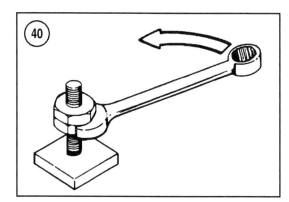

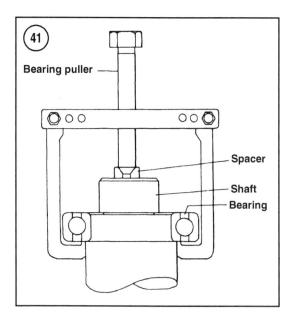

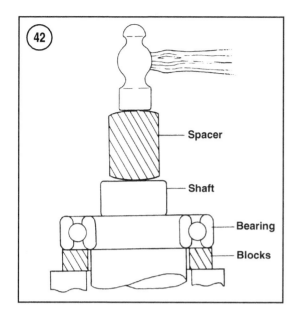

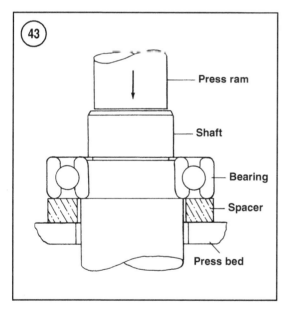

lubrication and maintenance. If a bearing is damaged, replace it immediately. When installing a new bearing, take care to prevent damaging the part. Bearing replacement procedures are included in the individual chapters where applicable; however, use the following sections as a guideline.

NOTE
Unless otherwise specified, install bearings with the manufacturer's mark or number facing outward.

Removal

While bearings are normally removed only when damaged, there may be times when it is necessary to remove a bearing that is in good condition. However, improper bearing removal will damage the bearing and maybe the shaft or case half. Note the following when removing bearings.

1. When using a puller to remove a bearing from a shaft, take care that the shaft is not damaged. Always place a piece of metal between the end of the shaft and the puller screw. In addition, place the puller arms next to the inner bearing race. See **Figure 41**.

2. When using a hammer to remove a bearing from a shaft, do not strike the hammer directly against the shaft. Instead, use a brass or aluminum rod between the hammer and shaft (**Figure 42**) and be sure to support both bearing races with wooden blocks, as shown.

3. The ideal method of bearing removal is with a hydraulic press. Note the following when using a press:

   a. Always support the inner and outer bearing races with a suitable size wooden or aluminum ring (**Figure 43**). If only the outer race is supported, pressure applied against the balls and/or the inner race will damage them.

   b. Always check that the press ram (**Figure 43**) aligns with the center of the shaft. If the ram is not centered, it may damage the bearing and/or shaft.

   c. The moment the shaft is free of the bearing, it will drop to the floor. Secure or hold the shaft to prevent it from falling.

Clean the inside of the hose thoroughly. Do not use any lubricant when installing the hose (new or old). The lubricant may allow the hose to come off the fitting, even with the clamp secure.

Bearings

Bearings are used in the engine and transmission assembly to reduce power loss, heat and noise resulting from friction. Because bearings are precision parts, they must be maintained by proper

Installation

1. When installing a bearing in a housing, apply pressure to the *outer* bearing race (**Figure 44**). When installing a bearing on a shaft, apply pressure to the *inner* bearing race (**Figure 45**).

2. When installing a bearing as described in Step 1, some type of driver is required. Never strike the bearing directly with a hammer or the bearing will be damaged. When installing a bearing, use a piece of pipe or a driver with a diameter that matches the bearing race. **Figure 46** shows the correct way to use a driver and hammer to install a bearing.

3. Step 1 describes how to install a bearing in a case half or over a shaft. However, when installing a bearing over a shaft and into a housing at the same time, a tight fit will be required for both outer and inner bearing races. In this situation, install a spacer underneath the driver tool so that pressure is applied evenly across both races (**Figure 47**). If the outer race is not supported, the balls will push against the outer bearing race and damage it.

Interference fit

1. Follow this procedure when installing a bearing over a shaft. When a tight fit is required, the bearing inside diameter will be smaller than the shaft. In this case, driving the bearing on the shaft using normal methods may cause bearing damage. Instead, heat the bearing before installation. Note the following:

    a. Secure the shaft so it is ready for bearing installation.

    b. Clean all residue from the bearing surface of the shaft. Remove burrs with a file or sandpaper.

    c. Fill a suitable container with clean mineral oil. Place a thermometer rated above 120° C (248° F) in the oil. Support the thermometer so that it does not rest on the bottom or side of the container.

    d. Remove the bearing from its wrapper and secure it with a piece of heavy wire bent to hold it in the container. Hang the bearing so it does not touch the bottom or sides.

    e. Turn the heat on and monitor the thermometer. When the oil temperature rises to approximately 120° C (248° F), remove the bearing and quickly install it. If necessary, place a socket on the inner bearing race and tap the bearing into place. As the bearing chills, it

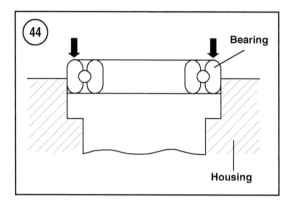

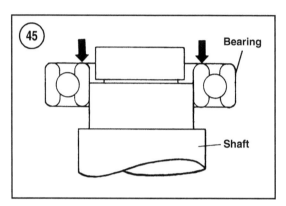

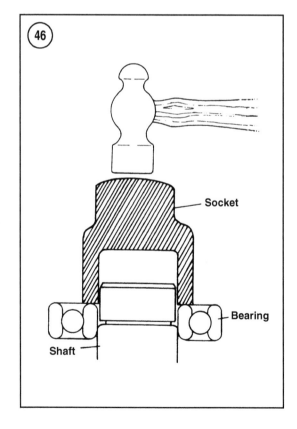

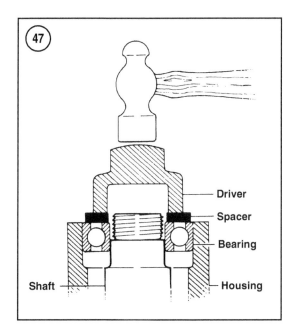

Driver

Spacer

Bearing

Shaft

Housing

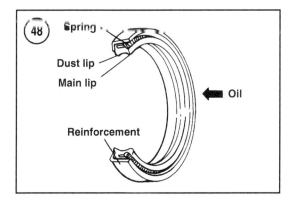

Spring

Dust lip

Main lip

Oil

Reinforcement

will tighten on the shaft, so installation must be done quickly. Make sure the bearing is installed completely.

2. Follow this step when installing a bearing in a housing. Bearings are generally installed in a housing with a slight interference fit. Driving the bearing into the housing using normal methods may damage the housing or cause bearing damage. Instead, heat the housing before the bearing is installed. Note the following:

CAUTION
Before heating the housing in this procedure, wash the housing thoroughly with detergent and water. Rinse and rewash the cases as required to remove all traces of oil and other chemical deposits.

a. Heat the housing to approximately 212° F (100° C) in an oven or on a hot plate. An easy way to check that it is at the proper temperature is to place tiny drops of water on the housing; if they sizzle and evaporate immediately, the temperature is correct. Heat only one housing at a time.

CAUTION
Do not heat the housing with a propane or acetylene torch. Never bring a flame into contact with the bearing or housing. The direct heat will destroy the case hardening of the bearing and will likely warp the housing.

b. Remove the housing from the oven or hot plate. Wear insulated gloves or use kitchen pot holders.

NOTE
Remove and install the bearings with a suitable size socket and extension.

c. Hold the housing with the bearing side down and tap the bearing out. Repeat for all bearings in the housing.

d. Before heating the bearing housing, place the new bearing in a freezer if possible. Chilling a bearing slightly reduces its outside diameter while the heated bearing housing assembly is slightly larger due to heat expansion. This will make bearing installation easier.

NOTE
Always install bearings with the manufacturer's mark or number facing outward.

e. While the housing is still hot, install the new bearing(s) into the housing. Install the bearings by hand, if possible. If necessary, lightly tap the bearing(s) into the housing with a socket placed on the outer bearing race (**Figure 44**). Do not install new bearings by driving on the inner bearing race. Install the bearing(s) until it seats completely.

Seal Replacement

Seals (**Figure 48**) are used to contain oil, water, grease or combustion gasses in a housing or shaft. Improper removal of a seal can damage the housing or shaft. Improper installation of the seal can damage the seal. Note the following:

1. Prying is generally the easiest and most effective method of removing a seal from a housing. However, always place a rag under the pry tool (**Figure 49**) to prevent damage to the housing.

2. Pack waterproof grease in the seal lips before the seal is installed.

3. Install seals so the manufacturer's numbers or marks face out.

4. Install seals with a socket placed on the outside of the seal as shown in **Figure 50**. Drive the seal squarely into the housing. Never install a seal by hitting the top of the seal with a hammer.

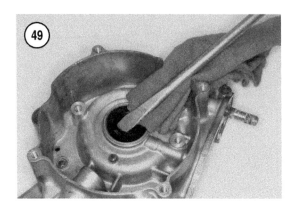

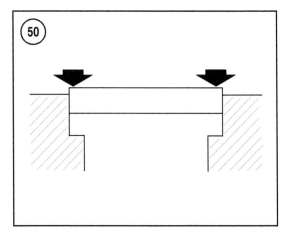

STORAGE

Several months of non-use can cause a general deterioration of the motorcycle. This is especially true in areas of extreme temperature variations. This deterioration can be minimized with careful preparation for storage. A properly stored motorcycle will be much easier to return to service.

Storage Area Selection

When selecting a storage area, consider the following:

1. The storage area must be dry. A heated area is best, but not necessary. It should be insulated to minimize extreme temperature variations.

2. If the building has large window areas, mask them to keep sunlight off the motorcycle.

3. Avoid buildings in industrial areas where corrosive emissions may be present. Avoid areas close to saltwater.

4. Consider the area's risk of fire, theft or vandalism. Check with an insurer regarding motorcycle coverage while in storage.

Preparing the Motorcycle for Storage

The amount of preparation a motorcycle should undergo before storage depends on the expected length of non-use, storage area conditions and personal preference. Consider the following list the minimum requirement:

1. Wash the motorcycle. Remove all dirt, mud and road debris.

2. Start the engine and allow it to reach operating temperature. Drain the engine oil regardless of the riding time since the last service. Fill the engine with the recommended type of oil.

3. Drain all fuel from the fuel tank, run the engine until all the fuel is consumed from the lines and carburetor.

4. Remove the spark plug and pour a teaspoon of engine oil into the cylinder. Place a shop cloth over the opening and slowly turn the engine over to distribute the oil. Reinstall the spark plug.

5. Cover the exhaust and intake openings.

6. Reduce the normal tire pressure by 20%.

7. Apply a protectant to the plastic and rubber components, including the tires. Follow the manufacturer's instructions for each type of product being used.

8. Place the motorcycle on a stand or wooden blocks so the wheels are off the ground. If this is not possible, place a piece of plywood between the tires and the ground. Inflate the tires to the recommended pressure if the motorcycle cannot be elevated.

9. Cover the motorcycle with a drop cloth or similar cover. Do not use plastic covers; these will trap moisture and promote corrosion.

Returning the Motorcycle to Service

The amount of service required to return a motorcycle to operating condition depends on the length of non-use and storage conditions. Follow the above procedure and install/check each area that was prepared at time of storage. Also check that the brakes, clutch, throttle and engine stop switch work properly before operating the motorcycle. Refer to the maintenance and lubrication schedule in Chapter Three and determine which areas require additional service.

Table 1 GENERAL MOTORCYCLE DIMENSIONS

	mm	in.
Overall length	2189	86.3
Overall width	823	32.4
Overall height	1263	49.7
Wheelbase		
1997-1999	1483	58.4
2000-2001	1487	58.5
Ground clearance	331	13.0
Seat height		
1997-1999	942	37.1
2000-2001	933	36.7
Footpeg height	412	16.2
Dry weight	97 kg	214 lb.

Table 2 TECHNICAL ABBREVIATIONS

ABDC	After bottom dead center
ATDC	After top dead center
BBDC	Before bottom dead center
BDC	Bottom dead center
BTDC	Before top dead center
C	Celsius (Centigrade)
cc	Cubic centimeters
cid	Cubic inch displacement
CDI	Capacitor discharge ignition
cu. in.	Cubic inches
F	Fahrenheit
ft.	Feet
ft.-lb.	Foot-pounds
gal.	Gallons
H/A	High altitude
hp	Horsepower
in.	Inches
in.-lb.	Inch-pounds
I.D.	Inside diameter
kg	Kilograms
kgm	Kilogram meters
km	Kilometer
kPa	Kilopascals
L	Liter
m	Meter
(continued)	

Table 2 TECHNICAL ABBREVIATIONS (continued)

MAG	Magneto
ml	Milliliter
mm	Millimeter
N•m	Newton-meters
O.D.	Outside diameter
oz.	Ounces
psi	Pounds per square inch
PTO	Power take off
pt.	Pint
qt.	Quart
rpm	Revolutions per minute

Table 3 GENERAL TORQUE SPECIFICATIONS

	N•m	ft.-lb.
5 mm bolt and nut	5	3.5
6 mm bolt and nut	10	7
8 mm bolt and nut	22	16
10 mm bolt and nut	35	25
12 mm bolt and nut	55	40
5 mm screw	4	3
6 mm screw	9	7
6 mm flange bolt (8 mm head)	9	7
6 mm flange bolt		
(10 mm head) and nut	12	9
8 mm flange bolt and nut	27	20
10 mm flange bolt and nut	40	29

Table 4 CONVERSION TABLES

Multiply:	By:	To get the equivalent of:
Length		
Inches	25.4	Millimeter
Inches	2.54	Centimeter
Miles	1.609	Kilometer
Feet	0.3048	Meter
Millimeter	0.03937	Inches
Centimeter	0.3937	Inches
Kilometer	0.6214	Mile
Meter	0.0006214	Mile
Fluid volume		
U.S. quarts	0.9463	Liters
U.S. gallons	3.785	Liters
U.S. ounces	29.573529	Milliliters
Imperial gallons	4.54609	Liters
Imperial quarts	1.1365	Liters
Liters	0.2641721	U.S. gallons
Liters	1.0566882	U.S. quarts
Liters	33.814023	U.S. ounces
Liters	0.22	Imperial gallons
Liters	0.8799	Imperial quarts

(continued)

Table 4 CONVERSION TABLES (continued)

Fluid volume (continued)

Milliliters	0.033814	U.S. ounces
Milliliters	1.0	Cubic centimeters
Milliliters	0.001	Liters

Torque

Foot-pounds	1.3558	Newton-meters
Foot-pounds	0.138255	Meters-kilograms
Inch-pounds	0.11299	Newton-meters
Newton-meters	0.7375622	Foot-pounds
Newton-meters	8.8507	Inch-pounds
Meters-kilograms	7.2330139	Foot-pounds

Volume

Cubic inches	16.387064	Cubic centimeters
Cubic centimeters	0.0610237	Cubic inches

Temperature

Fahrenheit	$(F - 32°) \times 0.556$	Centigrade
Centigrade	$(C \times 1.8) + 32$	Fahrenheit

Weight

Ounces	28.3495	Grams
Pounds	0.4535924	Kilograms
Grams	0.035274	Ounces
Kilograms	2.2046224	Pounds

Pressure

Pounds per square inch	0.070307	Kilograms per square centimeter
Kilograms per square centimeter	14.223343	Pounds per square inch
Kilopascals	0.1450	Pounds per square inch
Pounds per square inch	6.895	Kilopascals

Speed

Miles per hour	1.609344	Kilometers per hour
Kilometers per hour	0.6213712	Miles per hour

Table 5 METRIC TAP AND DRILL SIZES

Metric size	Drill equivalent	Decimal fraction	Nearest fraction
3 × 0.50	No. 39	0.0995	3/32
3 × 0.60	3/32	0.0937	3/32
4 × 0.70	No. 30	0.1285	1/8
4 × 0.75	1/8	0.125	1/8
5 × 0.80	No. 19	0.166	11/64
5 × 0.90	No. 20	0.161	5/32
6 × 1.00	No. 9	0.196	13/64
7 × 1.00	16/64	0.234	15/64
8 × 1.00	J	0.277	9/32
8 × 1.25	17/64	0.265	17/64
9 × 1.00	5/16	0.3125	5/16
9 × 1.25	5/16	0.3125	5/16
10 × 1.25	11/32	0.3437	11/32
10 × 1.50	R	0.339	11/32
11 × 1.50	3/8	0.375	3/8
12 × 1.50	13/32	0.406	13/32
12 × 1.75	13/32	0.406	13/32

Table 6 DECIMAL AND METRIC EQUIVALENTS

Fractions	Decimal in.	Metric mm	Fractions	Decimal in.	Metric mm
1/64	0.015625	0.39688	33/64	0.515625	13.09687
1/32	0.03125	0.79375	17/32	0.53125	13.49375
3/64	0.046875	1.19062	35/64	0.546875	13.89062
1/16	0.0625	1.58750	9/16	0.5625	14.28750
5/64	0.078125	1.98437	37/64	0.578125	14.68437
3/32	0.09375	2.38125	19/32	0.59375	15.08125
7/64	0.109375	2.77812	39/64	0.609375	15.47812
1/8	0.125	3.1750	5/8	0.625	15.87500
9/64	0.140625	3.57187	41/64	0.640625	16.27187
5/32	0.15625	3.96875	21/32	0.65625	16.66875
11/64	0.171875	4.36562	43/64	0.671875	17.06562
3/16	0.1875	4.76250	11/16	0.6875	17.46250
13/64	0.203125	5.15937	45/64	0.703125	17.85937
7/32	0.21875	5.55625	23/32	0.71875	18.25625
15/64	0.234375	5.95312	47/64	0.734375	18.65312
1/4	0.250	6.35000	3/4	0.750	19.05000
17/64	0.265625	6.74687	49/64	0.765625	19.44687
9/32	0.28125	7.14375	25/32	0.78125	19.84375
19/64	0.296875	7.54062	51/64	0.796875	20.24062
5/16	0.3125	7.93750	13/16	0.8125	20.63750
21/64	0.328125	8.33437	53/64	0.828125	21.03437
11/32	0.34375	8.73125	27/32	0.84375	21.43125
23/64	0.359375	9.12812	55/64	0.859375	22.82812
3/8	0.375	9.52500	7/8	0.875	22.22500
25/64	0.390625	9.92187	57/64	0.890625	22.62187
13/32	0.40625	10.31875	29/32	0.90625	23.01875
27/64	0.421875	10.71562	59/64	0.921875	23.41562
7/16	0.4375	11.11250	15/16	0.9375	23.81250
29/64	0.453125	11.50937	61/64	0.953125	24.20937
15/32	0.46875	11.90625	31/32	0.96875	24.60625
31/64	0.484375	12.30312	63/64	0.984375	25.00312
1/2	0.500	12.70000	1	1.00	25.40000

CHAPTER TWO

TROUBLESHOOTING

Diagnosing problems with the motorcycle, either mechanical or electrical, can be relatively easy if the fundamental operating requirements are kept in mind. By doing so, problems can be approached in a logical and methodical manner. The first step is to:

1. Define the symptoms of the problem.
2. Determine which areas could exhibit those symptoms.
3. Test and analyze the suspect area.
4. Isolate the problem.

Being quick to assume a particular area is at fault can lead to increased problems, lost time and unnecessary parts replacement. The easiest way to keep troubleshooting simple is to perform the lubrication, maintenance and tune-up procedures described in Chapter Three. The rider will gain a better understanding of the condition and functions of the motorcycle.

Always start with the simple and obvious checks when troubleshooting. This would include engine stop switch operation, fuel level, fuel valve position and spark plug cap tightness. If the problem cannot be solved, stop and evaluate all conditions prior to

the problem. If the motorcycle must be taken to a dealership, the mechanic will want to know as many details as possible.

For removal, installation and test procedures for some components, refer to the specific chapter in the manual. When applicable, tables at the end of each chapter also provide specifications and wear limits.

OPERATING REQUIREMENTS

There are three requirements for an engine to run properly. These are a correct air/fuel mixture, compression and a properly timed spark. If one of these requirements is not correct, the engine will not run, or will run poorly. Two-stroke engine operation is shown in **Figure 1**.

STARTING THE ENGINE

Before starting the engine, always perform the *Pre-ride Inspection* described in Chapter Three.

① TWO-STROKE OPERATING PRINCIPLES

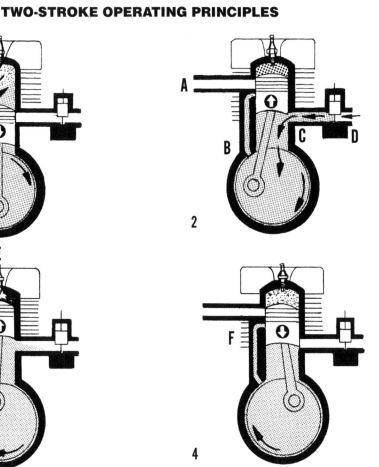

As the piston travels downward, the exhaust port (A) is uncovered, allowing pressurized exhaust gases to escape from the cylinder. A fresh fuel/air charge that has been slightly compressed by the downward movement of the piston travels into the cylinder through the transfer port (B). This charge enters under pressure and helps to push out the exhaust gases.

The crankshaft continues to rotate and the piston moves upward, covering the transfer port (B) and the exhaust port (A).

The piston compresses the new fuel/air mixture and creates a low-pressure area in the crankcase. As the piston continues to move upward, it uncovers the intake port (C). A fresh fuel/air charge from the carburetor (D) is drawn through the intake port because of the low pressure in the crankcase.

As the piston nears the top of the cylinder, the spark plug fires (E), igniting the compressed fuel/air mixture. The piston is then pushed downward (F) by the expanding gases. The cycle repeats.

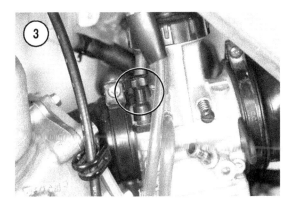

Starting a Cold Engine

1. Shift the transmission into neutral.

2. Turn the fuel valve (**Figure 2**) to the ON position.

3. Fully pull the choke knob (**Figure 3**) out to richen the air/fuel mixture.

4. Slowly stroke the kickstarter five times to charge the cylinder.

5. After five strokes, slowly depress the kickstarter until resistance is felt on the compression stroke.

6. While keeping the throttle *closed*, firmly kick the kickstarter through its entire stroke.

> *WARNING*
> *Opening the throttle during the starting procedure can cause the kickstarter to kick back.*

7. When the engine starts, warm up the engine by operating the throttle in its lower range. Close the choke as soon as the engine will remain running, usually in about 30 seconds.

> *NOTE*
> *Do not race or over-choke the engine during the warm-up period.*

Starting a Warm Engine

1. Shift the transmission into neutral.

2. Turn the fuel valve (**Figure 2**) to the ON position.

3. Slowly depress the kickstarter until resistance is felt on the compression stroke.

4. While keeping the throttle *closed*, firmly kick the kickstarter through its entire stroke.

> *WARNING*
> *Opening the throttle during the starting procedure can cause the kickstarter to kick back.*

Starting a Flooded Engine

If the engine fails to start after several tries (particularly if the choke has been used), it is probably flooded. This occurs when too much fuel is drawn into the engine and the spark plug fails to ignite the mixture. The smell of gasoline is often evident when the engine is flooded. Troubleshoot a flooded engine as follows:

1. Look for gasoline overflowing from the carburetor or overflow hose. If gasoline is evident, the carburetor float is stuck. Remove and repair the float assembly as described in Chapter Eight.

2. Check that the choke knob is fully closed (depressed).

3. Firmly kick the kickstarter through its entire stroke several times to clear the engine.

4. If the engine does not fire, remove and check the spark plug. If the plug is wet, clean the plug, or install a new plug.

ENGINE SPARK TEST

An engine spark test will indicate whether the ignition system is providing power to the spark plug. It is a quick way to determine if a problem is in the electrical system or fuel system.

> *CAUTION*
> *When performing this test, the spark plug lead must be grounded before cranking the engine. If it is not, it is*

*possible to damage the CDI unit. A spark plug can be used for this test, but a spark tester (**Figure 4**) will clearly show if spark is occurring. This tester can be purchased at parts supply stores or suppliers of ignition test equipment.*

1. Remove the spark plug. Inspect the spark plug by comparing its condition to the plugs shown in Chapter Three.
2. Connect the spark plug lead to the spark plug, or to a spark tester.
3. Ground the plug to bare metal on the engine (**Figure 5**). Position the plug so the firing end can be viewed.
4. Kick over the engine and observe the spark. A fat, blue spark should appear at the firing end. The spark should fire consistently as the engine is kicked over.
5. If the spark appears weak, or fires inconsistently, check the following areas for the cause:
   a. Fouled or improperly gapped spark plug.
   b. Faulty or shorted spark plug lead and cap.
   c. Loose connection in ignition system.
   d. Dirty or shorted engine stop switch.
   e. Faulty coil.
   f. Faulty exciter coil.
   g. Faulty ignition control module.

ENGINE PERFORMANCE

If the engine does not operate at peak performance, the following lists of possible causes can help isolate the problem. Always perform the easiest checks throughout the list before proceeding to component disassembly.

Engine Will Not Start or Starts and Dies

1. *Fuel system:*
   a. Fuel tank empty.
   b. Clogged fuel tank cap vent.
   c. Contaminated fuel.
   d. Improper choke knob operation.
   e. Engine flooded.
   f. Clogged air filter.
   g. Clog in fuel valve, fuel line or carburetor.
   h. Low idle speed.
   i. Pilot air screw misadjusted.
   j. Incorrect jetting for altitude.
   k. Carburetor float valve sticking.

   l. Intake manifold air leak.
   m. Air leak in crankcase seals or gaskets.
2. *Ignition:*
   a. Fouled or improperly gapped spark plug.
   b. Faulty or shorted spark plug lead and cap.
   c. Dirty or shorted engine stop switch.
   d. Loose connection in ignition system.
   e. Faulty ignition coil.
   f. Faulty exciter coil.
   g. Faulty ignition pulse generator.
   h. Faulty ignition control module.
3. *Engine:*
   a. Loose spark plug.
   b. Loose cylinder head bolts.
   c. Worn piston and/or cylinder.
   d. Leaking cylinder head gasket.

Poor Idle and Low Speed Performance

1. *Fuel system:*
   a. Improper choke knob operation.
   b. Engine flooded.
   c. Clogged air filter.
   d. Low idle speed.
   e. Clogged fuel tank cap vent.
   f. Pilot air screw not adjusted properly.
   g. Incorrect fuel level.
   h. Incorrect jetting for altitude.
   i. Jet needle misadjusted.
   j. Carburetor float valve sticking.
   k. Clogged carburetor jets.
   l. Loose carburetor mounting bolts.
   m. Intake manifold air leak.
   n. Clogged muffler.
   o. Damaged reed valves.
   p. Air leak in crankcase seals or gaskets.
2. *Ignition:*

a. Fouled or improperly gapped spark plug.
b. Faulty or shorted spark plug lead and cap.
c. Faulty ignition coil.
d. Faulty exciter coil.
e. Faulty ignition pulse generator.
f. Faulty ignition control module.
g. Faulty power jet solenoid (1997-1998 models).
3. *Engine:*
a. Loose spark plug.
b. Loose cylinder head bolts.
c. Worn piston and/or cylinder.
d. Leaking cylinder head gasket.
e. Exhaust valve assembly malfunctioning.

Engine Lacks Power and Acceleration

1. *Fuel system:*
a. Clogged air filter.
b. Choke lever in use.
c. Incorrect carburetor fuel level.
d. Pilot air screw not adjusted properly.
e. Incorrect jetting for altitude.
f. Jet needle misadjusted.
g. Clogged fuel tank cap vent.
h. Restricted fuel flow.
i. Clogged carburetor jets.
j. Clogged muffler.
k. Air leak in crankcase seals or gaskets.
2. *Ignition:*
a. Fouled or improperly gapped spark plug.
b. Faulty or shorted spark plug lead and cap.
c. Faulty ignition coil.
d. Faulty exciter coil.
e. Faulty ignition pulse generator.
f. Faulty ignition control module.
g. Faulty power jet solenoid (1997-1998 models)

3. *Engine:*
a. Loose spark plug.
b. Loose cylinder head bolts.
c. Worn piston and/or cylinder.
d. Leaking cylinder head gasket.
e. Exhaust valve assembly malfunctioning.

Poor High Speed Performance

1. *Fuel system:*
a. Clogged air filter.
b. Choke lever in use.
c. Clogged muffler.
d. Incorrect jetting for altitude.
e. Jet needle misadjusted.
f. Clogged fuel tank cap vent.
g. Restricted fuel flow.
h. Clogged carburetor jet.
i. Air leak in crankcase seals or gaskets.
2. *Ignition:*
a. Fouled or improperly gapped spark plug.
b. Faulty or shorted spark plug lead and cap.
c. Faulty ignition coil.
d. Faulty exciter coil.
e. Faulty ignition pulse generator.
f. Faulty ignition control module.
g. Faulty regulator/rectifier (1997-1998 models).
h. Faulty power jet solenoid (1997-1998 models).
3. *Engine:*
a. Loose spark plug.
b. Loose cylinder head bolts.
c. Worn piston and/or cylinder.
d. Leaking cylinder head gasket.
e. Exhaust valve assembly malfunctioning.

Engine Backfires

1. Fuel mixture too lean.
2. Air leaks into exhaust system.
3. Faulty ignition control module.

Engine Overheating

1. *Cooling system:*
a. Leak at fitting or gasket.
b. Low coolant level.
c. Defective radiator cap.
d. Clogged radiators.
e. Improper coolant mix.
f. Damaged water pump.

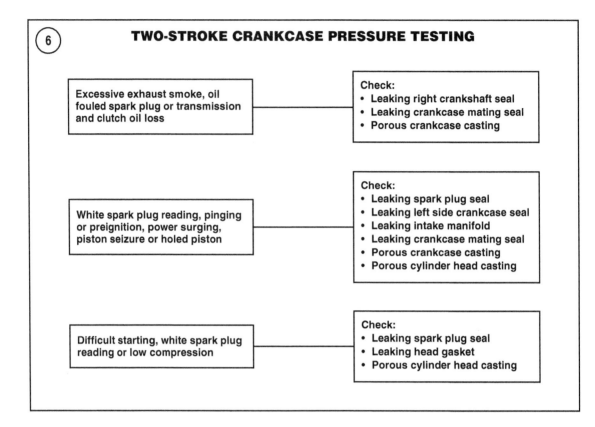

⑥ TWO-STROKE CRANKCASE PRESSURE TESTING

| Excessive exhaust smoke, oil fouled spark plug or transmission and clutch oil loss | Check:
• Leaking right crankshaft seal
• Leaking crankcase mating seal
• Porous crankcase casting |

| White spark plug reading, pinging or preignition, power surging, piston seizure or holed piston | Check:
• Leaking spark plug seal
• Leaking left side crankcase seal
• Leaking intake manifold
• Leaking crankcase mating seal
• Porous crankcase casting
• Porous cylinder head casting |

| Difficult starting, white spark plug reading or low compression | Check:
• Leaking spark plug seal
• Leaking head gasket
• Porous cylinder head casting |

g. Clogged water passages.

h. Collapsed coolant hoses.

2. *Other causes:*

a. Clutch slippage.

b. Improper timing due to faulty ignition control module.

c. Brakes dragging.

d. Incorrect air/fuel mixture.

e. Incorrect jetting for altitude.

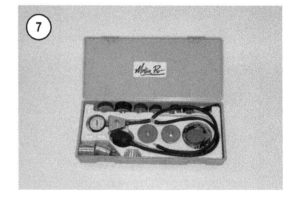

ENGINE NOISE

Noise is often the first indicator that something is not correct with the engine. In many cases, damage can be avoided or minimized if the rider immediately stops the bike and diagnoses the source of the noise. Anytime engine noises are ignored, even when the bike seems to be running correctly, the rider risks causing more damage and personal injury.

Pinging During Acceleration

1. Poor quality or contaminated fuel.

2. Lean fuel mixture.

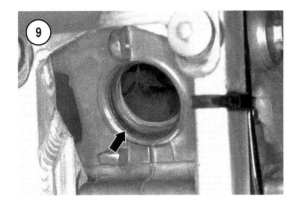

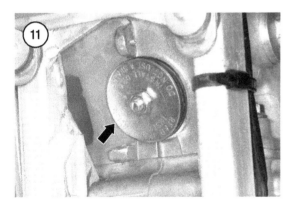

3. Excessive carbon buildup in combustion chamber.
4. Faulty ignition control module.

Knocks, Ticks or Rattles

1. Loose exhaust system.
2. Loose/missing body fasteners.
3. Damaged piston or connecting rod.
4. Worn, stuck or damaged piston ring.
5. Excessive wear between piston and cylinder.

ENGINE LEAKDOWN TEST

For a two-stroke engine to operate properly, the crankcase must alternately be under vacuum and pressure. This vacuum or pressure condition occurs as the piston rises and lowers during one engine revolution. Refer to **Figure 1** for a step-by-step depiction and explanation of two-stroke engine operation. As seen in **Figure 1**, in order for the piston to produce crankcase vacuum or pressure, the crankcase must be sealed. If there is leakage, the engine will run poorly or not at all. Air leakage can create a lean running condition and this can lead to piston and cylinder head damage. **Figure 6** shows the typical effects of leakage at various locations on the engine.

A standard compression test will not reveal any crankcase leaks because it measures pressure above the piston. To pressure test the crankcase, a two-stroke pressure kit is required (**Figure 7**). Components that vent to the crankcase must be removed, then the openings plugged. The pressure test kit is then installed at the intake opening and pressure is applied. If the crankcase does not maintain pressure, leakage is occurring. Leaks are traced with a solution of soapy water, sprayed over the seals and engine joints.

1. Remove the carburetor as described in Chapter Eight. Leave the rubber insulator on the engine (**Figure 8**).
2. Remove the exhaust pipe as described in Chapter Four. Clean any carbon deposits from the exhaust port (**Figure 9**) so a good seal can be achieved.
3. Remove the flywheel and stator assembly (**Figure 10**) as described in Chapter Nine.
4. Plug the exhaust port with an expandable rubber plug (**Figure 11**). Install the plug tightly.
5. Install a suitably-sized pressure adapter into the intake insulator (**Figure 12**). Tighten the insulator clamp tightly around the adapter. Install the pressure hose and bulb onto the adapter.

6. Pressurize the crankcase to 5-6 psi (34-41 kPa) (**Figure 13**).

> *CAUTION*
> *Do not apply more than 8 psi (55 kPa)*
> *to the crankcase or the seals may be*
> *damaged.*

7. Observe the pressure gauge. If pressure is maintained within 1 psi (7 kPa) for 5 minutes, the engine is in good condition. If pressure drops immediately, or drops by 1 psi (7 kPa) within 1 minute, leakage is excessive. Locate the leakage by spraying soapy water around the following areas while there is pressure in the crankcase. Look for bubbles, which indicate leakage.

    a. Left crankshaft seal (**Figure 14**).

    b. Right crankshaft seal (**Figure 15**). If the right crankcase cover is installed, an acceptable way of checking this seal is to submerge the end of the transmission breather hose (**Figure 16**) in a shallow pan of soap solution. If bubbling is evident, remove the right crankcase cover and repeat the check at the right crankshaft seal.

    c. Cylinder base joint.

    d. Crankcase joint.

    e. Reed valve joint.

    f. Cylinder head joint.

    g. Spark plug.

    h. Exhaust valve covers.

CLUTCH

The two main clutch problems are clutch slip (clutch does not fully engage) and clutch drag (clutch does not fully disengage). Both of these problems are usually caused by incorrect clutch adjustment, a worn clutch lever, a worn cable or a worn lifter lever at the engine. Perform the following checks before removing the clutch:

1. Check the clutch cable routing from the handlebar to the engine. Check that the cable is free when the handlebars are turned side to side and that the ends are installed correctly.

2. With the engine off, pull and release the clutch lever. If the lever is hard to pull, or the action is rough, check for the following:

    a. Damaged cable.

    b. Incorrect cable routing.

    c. Cable pivots not lubricated.

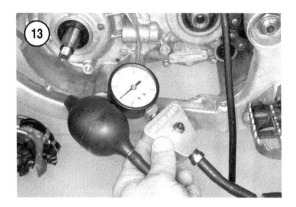

    d. Damaged lever and perch assembly at the handlebar.

    e. Damaged lifter lever at the engine.

3. If the parts in the previous steps are in good condition, and the lever moves without excessive roughness or binding, check the clutch adjustment as described in Chapter Three. Note the following:

    a. If the clutch cannot be adjusted to the specifications in Chapter Three, the clutch cable is stretched or damaged.

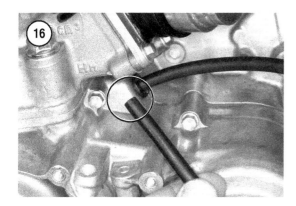

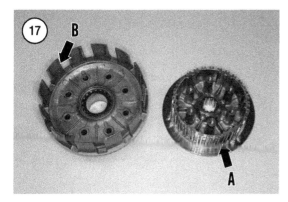

b. If the clutch cable and its adjustment are in good condition, the friction plates may be worn.

Clutch Slipping

When the clutch slips, the engine accelerates faster than what the actual forward speed indicates. Because the clutch plates are spinning against each other, excessive heat is quickly built up in the assembly. This causes plate wear, warp and spring fa-

tigue. One or more of the following can cause the clutch to slip:
1. Clutch wear or damage.
   a. Incorrect clutch adjustment.
   b. Weak or damaged clutch springs.
   c. Loose clutch springs.
   d. Worn friction plates.
   e. Warped steel plates.
   f. Clutch release mechanism wear or damage.
2. Clutch/transmission oil:
   a. Low oil level.
   b. Oil additives.
   c. Low viscosity oil.

Clutch Dragging

When the clutch drags, the plates are not completely separating. This will cause the bike to creep or lurch forward when the transmission is put into gear. Once underway, shifting is difficult. If this condition is not corrected, it can cause transmission gear and shift fork damage, due to the abnormal grinding and actions of the parts. One or more of the following can cause the clutch to drag:
1. Clutch wear or damage.
   a. Clutch release mechanism wear or damage.
   b. Incorrect lifter and lifter rod engagement.
   c. Damaged clutch lifter rod.
   d. Warped steel plates.
   e. Swollen friction plates.
   f. Warped pressure plate.
   g. Incorrect clutch spring tension.
   h. Incorrectly assembled clutch.
   i. Loose clutch nut.
   j. Notched clutch center splines (A, **Figure 17**).
   k. Notched clutch outer grooves (B, **Figure 17**).
2. Clutch and transmission oil:
   a. Oil level too high.
   b. High viscosity oil.

Clutch Noise

Excessive clutch noise is usually caused by worn or damaged parts, and is more noticeable at idle or low engine speeds. Clutch noise can be caused by the following conditions:
1. Wear or play in the clutch needle bearing (**Figure 18**), collar or clutch outer bore. The noise is reduced or eliminated when a load is put on the clutch.
2. Excessive friction plate to clutch outer clearance.

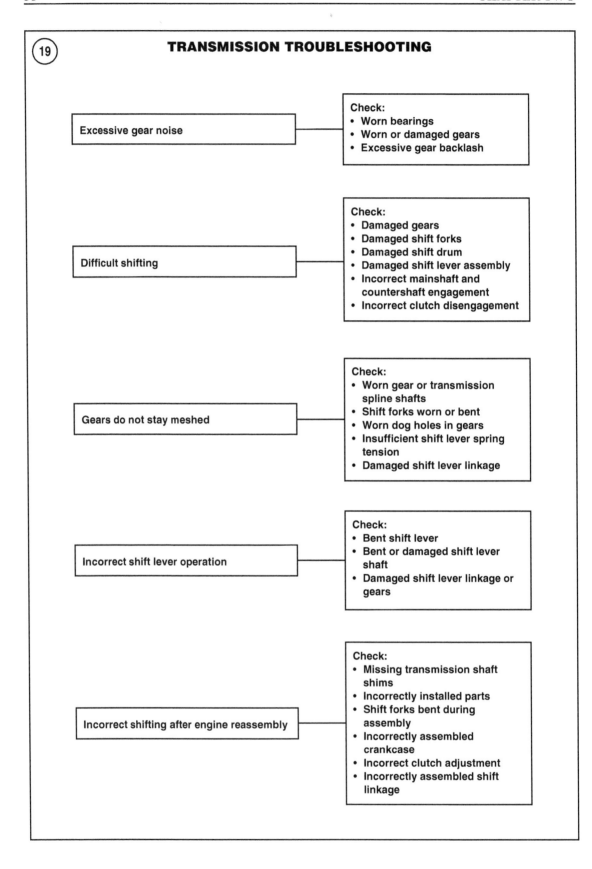

(19) **TRANSMISSION TROUBLESHOOTING**

Excessive gear noise

Check:
• Worn bearings
• Worn or damaged gears
• Excessive gear backlash

Difficult shifting

Check:
• Damaged gears
• Damaged shift forks
• Damaged shift drum
• Damaged shift lever assembly
• Incorrect mainshaft and
  countershaft engagement
• Incorrect clutch disengagement

Gears do not stay meshed

Check:
• Worn gear or transmission
  spline shafts
• Shift forks worn or bent
• Worn dog holes in gears
• Insufficient shift lever spring
  tension
• Damaged shift lever linkage

Incorrect shift lever operation

Check:
• Bent shift lever
• Bent or damaged shift lever
  shaft
• Damaged shift lever linkage or
  gears

Incorrect shifting after engine reassembly

Check:
• Missing transmission shaft
  shims
• Incorrectly installed parts
• Shift forks bent during
  assembly
• Incorrectly assembled
  crankcase
• Incorrect clutch adjustment
• Incorrectly assembled shift
  linkage

3. Excessive clutch outer to primary drive gear backlash.

4. Worn or damaged clutch outer and primary drive-gear teeth.

5. Excessive wear in the clutch lifter assembly.

EXTERNAL SHIFT MECHANISM AND TRANSMISSION

Transmission problems are often difficult to distinguish from problems with the clutch and external shift mechanism. Often, the problem is symptomatic of one area, while the actual problem is in another area. For example, if the gears grind during shifting, the problem may be caused by a dragging clutch, not a damaged transmission. Of course, if the clutch is not repaired, the transmission will eventually become damaged too. Therefore, evaluate all of the variables that exist when the problem occurs, and always start with the easiest checks in the troubleshooting chart (**Figure 19**).

When the transmission exhibits abnormal noise or operation, drain the transmission oil and check it for contamination or metal particles. Examine a small quantity of oil under bright light. If a metallic cast or pieces of metal are seen, excessive wear and/or part failure is occurring. Some transmission noises are caused by the following:

1. Insufficient oil level.
2. Contaminated oil.
3. Oil viscosity too low.
4. Worn or damaged transmission gear(s).
5. Worn or damaged bearings.
6. Worn or damaged kickstarter idle gear.
7. Kickstarter ratchet wheel not disengaging from kickstarter gear.

Besides the shift lever, the external shift mechanism includes all parts related to transmission shifting that are not within the crankcase halves. This includes the shift shaft, torsion spring, guide plate, drum shifter, stopper arm and shift drum center. These parts are located at the rear of the engine, behind the right crankcase cover. Refer to Chapter Six for additional views of the parts and how they are assembled. Troubleshoot as follows:

NOTE
When trying to shift a constant-mesh transmission, one of the transmission shafts must be turning. Have an assistant turn the rear wheel (with chain installed, and spark plug removed and grounded), so the gears can be shifted and the action of the linkage viewed.

1. Check that the clutch is properly adjusted and in good condition. If the clutch is good, continue with the procedure.

2. Support the bike with the rear wheel off the ground.

3. Remove the clutch as described in Chapter Six.

4. Turn the rear wheel and shift the transmission. Note the following:

 a. Check that the torsion spring (A, **Figure 20**) is fitted around the pin and the shift shaft is engaged with the collar on the drum shifter assembly (B).

 b. If the parts are in place, but shifting is not correct, remove and inspect the shift shaft assembly for possible damage or missing parts. Continue with the procedure, if necessary.

5. Remove the guide plate and drum shifter assembly, then shift the transmission while observing the shift drum center and stopper arm (**Figure 21**). Turn

the shift drum center to shift the transmission. While shifting, note the following:

a. The stopper arm is spring-loaded. The roller on the arm should move in and out of the detents on the shift drum center. Each detent represents a different gear selection. The raised detent is the neutral position. If the roller is not seating or staying in contact with the shift drum center, remove the parts and check for damage.

b. If the shift drum center and stopper arm are good, and the shifting problem no longer exists, inspect the guide plate and drum shifter assembly (**Figure 22**) for wear or damage.

c. If the shift drum center and stopper arm are good, and the shifting problem still exists, continue with the procedure.

6. Check the shift drum as follows:

a. Shift the transmission into neutral (if possible) and make a mark on the crankcase that aligns with the neutral detent on the shift drum center.

b. While turning the rear wheel or mainshaft, turn the shift drum center to change gears. Each time the shift drum center moves, and a new detent mark aligns with the crankcase mark, the transmission should be in another gear.

c. The transmission should shift into each gear. If the shift drum cannot be turned, or if it locks into a particular gear position, the transmission is damaged. A locked shift drum indicates a damaged shift fork, seized bearing or gear, or a damaged shift drum.

7. If necessary, disassemble the crankcase and transmission as described in Chapter Five and Chapter Seven.

8. Assemble and install all parts removed as described in the appropriate chapters.

KICKSTARTER

When the kickstarter lever does not operate properly, the cause of failure is often easy to troubleshoot after the right crankcase cover is removed. The kickstarter mechanism consists of the spindle, pinion gear, starter ratchet, washers and torsion spring assembly (A, **Figure 23**), and the kick idle gear (B). The following are common problems and their causes:

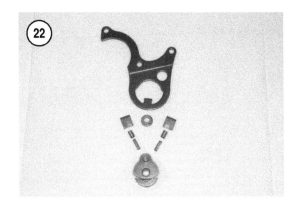

1. *Kickstarter lever or shaft slips.*
   a. Lever pinch bolt loose.
   b. Broken ratchet spring.
   c. Worn splines on spindle.
   d. Worn or damaged pinion gear.
   e. Worn or damaged idle gear.
   f. Worn engagement teeth between ratchet and pinion gear.
   g. Damaged snap ring groove or snap ring.

2. *Kickstarter does not return.*
   a. Kickstarter incorrectly installed in crankcase.
   b. Weak or damaged torsion spring.
   c. Improperly installed torsion spring.
   d. Pinion gear seized on shaft.
   e. Kickstarter ratchet guide loose or damaged.

3. *Kickstarter is hard to kick over.*
   a. Pinion gear seized on spindle.
   b. Kickstarter idle gear seized.
   c. Damaged right crankcase cover.
   d. Seized piston in cylinder.
   e. Seized crankshaft.
   f. Damaged bearings.

BRAKES

The disc brakes are critical to riding performance and safety. Inspect the brakes frequently and replace worn or damaged parts immediately. The brake system requires DOT 4 brake fluid. Always use new fluid, from a sealed and closed container. The troubleshooting checks in **Figure 24** assist in isolating the majority of disc brake problems.

When checking brake pad wear, check that the pads in each caliper squarely contact the disc. Uneven pad wear on one side of the disc can indicate a warped or bent disc, damaged caliper or pad pins.

STEERING

Correct poor steering immediately after it is detected, since loss of control is possible. Check the following areas:

1. Excessive handlebar vibration:
   a. Incorrect tire pressure.
   b. Unbalanced tire and rim.
   c. Loose/broken spokes.
   d. Loose or damaged handlebar clamps.
   e. Loose steering stem nut.
   f. Worn or damaged front wheel bearings.
   g. Bent or loose axle.
   h. Damaged rim.
   i. Cracked frame or steering head.
2. Handlebar is hard to turn:
   a. Low front tire pressure.
   b. Incorrect cable routing.
   c. Tight steering stem adjustment.
   d. Bent steering stem.
   e. Improperly lubricated or damaged steering bearings.

ELECTRICAL TESTING

Refer to Chapter Nine for testing the ignition system and the wiring diagram at the back of the manual.

Before testing a component, check the electrical connections related to that component. Check for corrosion and bent or loose terminals. Most of the connectors have a lock mechanism molded into the connector body. If these are not fully locked, a terminal connection may not be made. If connectors are not locked, pull the connector apart and clean the terminals. Fill the connector with dielectric grease, to prevent future corrosion, and reassemble the connector.

Figure 24 appears on the following page.

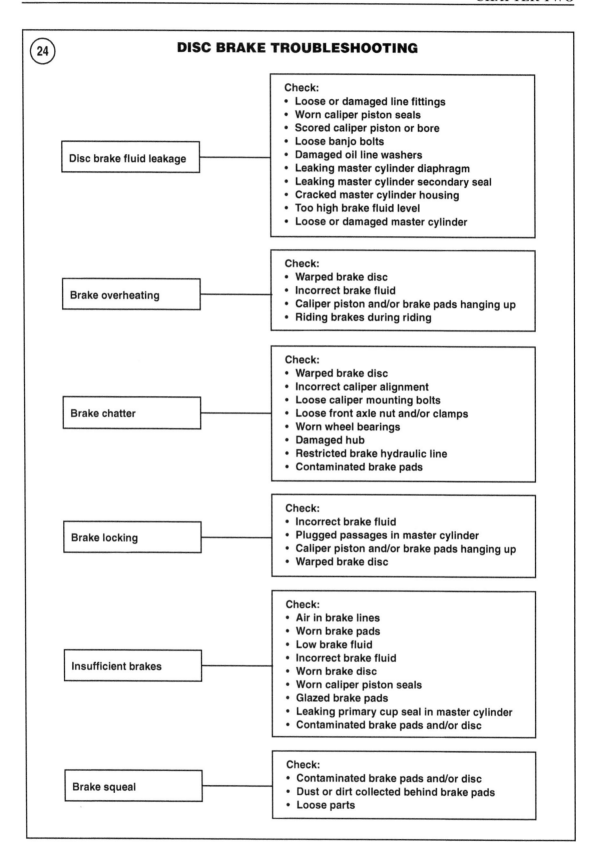

(24)   **DISC BRAKE TROUBLESHOOTING**

Disc brake fluid leakage

Check:
- Loose or damaged line fittings
- Worn caliper piston seals
- Scored caliper piston or bore
- Loose banjo bolts
- Damaged oil line washers
- Leaking master cylinder diaphragm
- Leaking master cylinder secondary seal
- Cracked master cylinder housing
- Too high brake fluid level
- Loose or damaged master cylinder

Brake overheating

Check:
- Warped brake disc
- Incorrect brake fluid
- Caliper piston and/or brake pads hanging up
- Riding brakes during riding

Brake chatter

Check:
- Warped brake disc
- Incorrect caliper alignment
- Loose caliper mounting bolts
- Loose front axle nut and/or clamps
- Worn wheel bearings
- Damaged hub
- Restricted brake hydraulic line
- Contaminated brake pads

Brake locking

Check:
- Incorrect brake fluid
- Plugged passages in master cylinder
- Caliper piston and/or brake pads hanging up
- Warped brake disc

Insufficient brakes

Check:
- Air in brake lines
- Worn brake pads
- Low brake fluid
- Incorrect brake fluid
- Worn brake disc
- Worn caliper piston seals
- Glazed brake pads
- Leaking primary cup seal in master cylinder
- Contaminated brake pads and/or disc

Brake squeal

Check:
- Contaminated brake pads and/or disc
- Dust or dirt collected behind brake pads
- Loose parts

CHAPTER THREE

LUBRICATION, MAINTENANCE AND TUNE-UP

This chapter provides information and procedures for properly lubricating, fueling and adjusting the motorcycle. Refer to **Table 1** for the recommended service intervals and those components that require inspection, lubrication or adjustment.

Refer to the sections in this chapter for performing many of the maintenance procedures described in **Table 1**. For services that require extensive disassembly of a component, refer to the appropriate chapter(s) in the manual for inspection and repair.

When performing maintenance procedures on the bike, observe the shop and safety practices described in Chapter One.

PRE-RIDE INSPECTION

Perform the following checks before the first race or ride of the day. Perform the checks when the engine is *cold*. Refer to the procedures and tables in this chapter for information concerning fuel, lubricants, tire pressure and component adjustments.

Start the bike as described in *Starting the Engine* in Chapter Two.

1. Check fuel lines and fittings for leakage.
2. Check fuel level.
3. Check transmission oil level.
4. Check coolant level.
5. Check brake operation and lever/pedal free play.
6. Check throttle operation and free play.
7. Check clutch operation and free play.
8. Check tightness of CDI and coil connections.
9. Check steering for smooth operation and no cable binding.
10. Check tire condition and air pressure.
11. Check wheel condition and spoke tightness.
12. Check axle nut tightness.
13. Check for loose nuts and bolts.
14. Check exhaust system for tightness.
15. Check drive chain condition and adjustment.
16. Check rear sprocket for tightness.
17. Check air cleaner for debris buildup.
18. Check suspension for leakage and proper settings for riding conditions.

19. Check engine stop switch for proper operation.

ENGINE BREAK-IN

If the engine bearings, crankshaft, piston, piston rings or cylinder have been serviced, perform the following break-in procedure.

1. Make the following checks and observations when breaking in the engine:
   a. Operate the bike on flat ground. Do not run in sand, mud or up hills. This will overload and possibly overheat the engine.
   b. Vary the throttle position. Do not keep the throttle in the same position for more than a few seconds.
   c. Check the spark plug frequently. The electrode should be dry and clean, and the insulator should be light to medium-tan in color. Refer to the spark plug chart in this chapter for identifying the different spark plug conditions.
   d. Check that the air filter is clean.
   e. Check that the engine is filled with the proper amount and grade of transmission oil.
   f. Check that the cooling system is filled.

2. Start the engine and allow it to warm up. During this time, check for proper idle speed and leaks.

3. Operate the motorcycle in the lower gears at no more than 1/2 throttle for the first 10 minutes. During this time, vary the throttle speed and do not lug the engine. Shut off the engine and allow it to cool.

4. Repeat Step 2 and Step 3 a second time.

5. Start the engine and run it at no more than 3/4 throttle for 10 minutes. During this time, vary the throttle speed and do not lug the engine. Shut off the engine and allow it to cool. Repeat this step three times.

SERVICE INTERVALS

The service intervals in **Table 1** are based on typical use of the bike in competition. If the bike is regularly operated in extreme weather conditions, or subjected to water or sand, perform the service procedures more frequently.

Keep track of when each service is performed and record it in the maintenance log at the back of the manual. This will be easier to plan maintenance and have the necessary parts on hand.

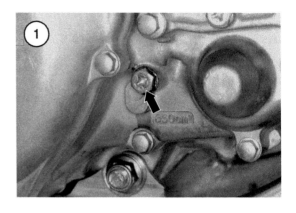

FUEL AND LUBRICANTS

Fuel Requirements

The engine requires unleaded pump-grade gasoline, with an octane rating of 92 or higher. This fuel produces fewer engine emissions and spark plug deposits. Always premix the fuel with two-stroke engine oil, or severe engine damage will occur.

Engine Oil

The engine oil must be premixed with the fuel. Do not pour oil and then fuel directly into the fuel tank. Always premix in a separate container. Use a two-stroke engine oil that can be mixed at a ratio of 32:1. Refer to **Table 2** for the recommended engine oil.

Fork Oil

Refer to **Table 2** for the recommended fork oil.

Transmission Oil

> *CAUTION*
> *Some oils and additives can cause clutch slippage and erratic operation. Do not use oils or oil additives that contain graphite, molybdenum or other friction modifiers.*

Refer to **Table 2** for the recommended transmission oil.

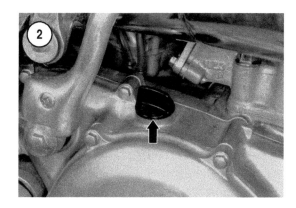

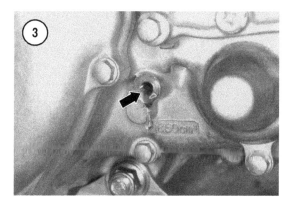

Grease

Use a good quality, lithium-based grease to lubricate components requiring grease. Some components require the extreme-pressure qualities of a grease containing molybdenum disulfide. When this grease is required, it is indicated in the procedures throughout this manual. Grease components frequently, as this will purge water and grit from the component and extend its life.

Chain Lubricant

Use a good quality chain lubricant that is compatible with the type of chain installed on the bike. An O-ring chain was not standard equipment for the years covered by this manual. If an O-ring chain has been installed, use chain lubricant that is specifically for O-ring chains. Since the links of an O-ring chain are permanently lubricated and sealed, O-ring chain lubricant is formulated to prevent exterior corrosion of the chain and to condition the O-rings. It is not tacky and resists the adhesion of dirt. Avoid lubricants that are tacky and for conventional chains. These lubricants will attract dirt and subject

the O-rings to unnecessary abrasion. If O-ring chain lubricant is not readily available, use SAE 10W-30 engine oil as a temporary lubricant.

Control Cable Lubricant

Use lithium grease to lubricate the control cable pivots. Honda recommends lubricating the cable pivot points and levers, but not the cable. If the clutch or throttle cable continues to operate poorly after pivot lubrication, replace the cable.

TRANSMISSION AND COMPONENT LUBRICATION

Fork Oil Replacement

The fork legs must be removed and disassembled to change the fork oil. Refer to Chapter Twelve for removal and servicing procedures.

Transmission Oil Level Check

Check the transmission oil at the oil check bolt (**Figure 1**) and replenish it at the dipstick (**Figure 2**). Perform the oil check after the engine has been warmed up.

1. Support the bike so it is vertical and level. Allow the bike to stand undisturbed for 5 minutes. This will allow the oil to drain to the bottom of the engine and establish an accurate level.

2. Loosen the dipstick.

3. Remove the oil check bolt. A small amount of oil should flow out of the inspection hole (**Figure 3**).

   a. If oil slowly drips from the inspection hole, the level is correct. Install and tighten the oil check bolt and dipstick. Tighten the check bolt to the specification in **Table 5**.

   b. If oil does not flow from the inspection hole, add oil at the dipstick until oil flows from the inspection hole. Allow excess oil to drain from the hole. When the oil slowly drips from the inspection hole, install and tighten the oil check bolt and dipstick. Tighten the check bolt to the specification in **Table 5**.

Transmission Oil Change

Change the transmission oil at the intervals recommended in **Table 1**. Always change the oil when the engine is warm. Contaminants will remain suspended in the oil and it will drain more completely and quickly.

1. Support the bike so it is vertical and level.
2. Loosen the dipstick (**Figure 2**).
3. Loosen the transmission drain plug (**Figure 4**), then place a drain pan below the plug. Remove the drain plug and allow the oil to drain.
4. Install a *new* sealing washer on the drain plug.
5. Install the drain plug. Torque the plug to the specification in **Table 5**.
6. Fill the engine with the required quantity and weight of oil. Refer to **Table 2** for oil type and capacity.
7. Insert the dipstick and screw into place.
8. Perform the *Transmission Oil Level Check* in this chapter to ensure that the level is correct.
9. Dispose the used transmission oil in an environmentally safe manner.
10. Dispose of oily rags and wash hands thoroughly.

> *WARNING*
> *Prolonged contact with used engine oil may cause skin cancer. Minimize contact with motor oil.*

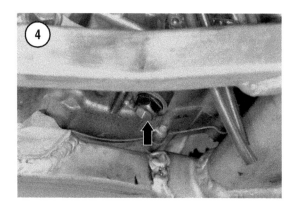

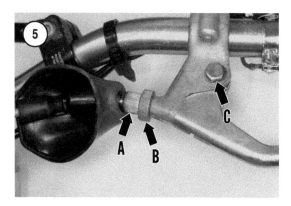

Cable Lubrication

If binding or drag is detected in the throttle or clutch, this can indicate a lack of cable lubrication or worn parts. Use lithium grease to lubricate the control cable pivots. Honda recommends lubricating the cable pivot points and levers, but not the cable. If the clutch or throttle cable continues to operate poorly after pivot lubrication, replace the cable.

Clutch cable

Lubricate the clutch lever, and clutch cable at both ends, with lithium grease.

1. Pull the boot away from the clutch lever and adjuster.
2. Loosen the locknut (A, **Figure 5**) and turn the cable adjuster (B) to create slack in the cable.
3. Remove the clutch lever pivot bolt (C, **Figure 5**), then remove the cable from the loose lever.
4. Clean and lubricate the cable end, lever, mounting hole and pivot bolt.

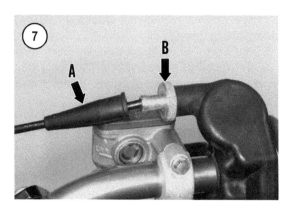

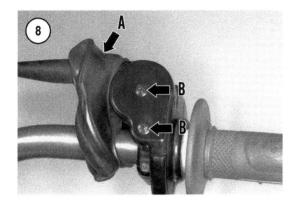

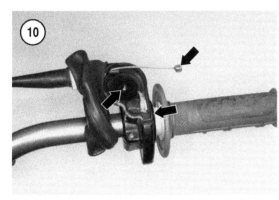

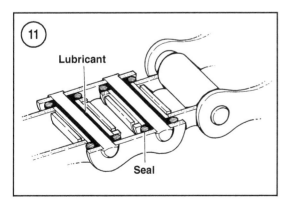

5. Remove the alternator cover to access the other end of the clutch cable.

6. Remove the cable from the lifter lever (**Figure 6**), then clean and lubricate the lifter lever and cable end. Install the cable onto the lever.

7. Assemble and install the cable and lever at the handlebar. Torque the pivot bolt to the specifications in **Table 5**.

8. Check that the cable is still seated in the lifter lever, then install the alternator cover.

9. Adjust the clutch lever as described in this chapter.

Throttle cable

Lubricate the throttle and cable end with lithium grease.

1. Pull back the rubber boot from the throttle cable adjuster (A, **Figure 7**).

2. Loosen the locknut (B, **Figure 7**) and turn the cable adjuster to create slack in the cable.

3. Pull back the rubber boot from the throttle housing (A, **Figure 8**).

4. Remove the screws (B, **Figure 8**) from the throttle housing, then remove the cover.

5. Remove the cable end from the throttle control (**Figure 9**).

6. Remove the cable roller, then lubricate the cable end, cable pivot and roller pivot with lithium grease (**Figure 10**).

> *NOTE*
> *Lubrication of the cable is not recommended. Whenever the cable drags or binds, replace the cable.*

7. Insert the cable end into the throttle control.

8. Wrap the cable around the cable roller, then put the roller on the pivot.

9. Install the housing cover and boot.

10. Adjust the cable as described in this chapter.

Drive Chain Cleaning and Lubrication

The bike comes with a standard chain (no O-rings) that requires routine cleaning and lubrication. If the chain has been replaced with an O-ring-type chain that is internally lubricated and sealed by O-rings (**Figure 11**), it too requires regular cleaning, lubrication and adjustment for long life. Although O-ring chains are internally lubricated and sealed, the O-rings need to be kept clean and lubricated, to prevent them from drying out and disintegrating.

Chains should never be cleaned with high-pressure water sprays or strong solvents. This is particularly true for O-ring chains. If water is forced past the O-rings, water will then be trapped inside the links. Strong solvents can soften the O-rings so they tear or damage easily.

Although chains are often lubricated while they are installed on the bike, periodically remove the chain from the bike and thoroughly clean it. The following procedure describes the preferred method for cleaning and lubricating the chain.

1. Refer to *Drive Chain Removal and Installation* in Chapter Eleven to remove the chain.

2. Immerse the chain in kerosene and work the links so dirt is loosened.

3. Lightly scrub the chain with a soft-bristle brush.

CAUTION
Brushes with coarse or wire bristles can damage O-rings.

4. Rinse the chain with clean kerosene and wipe dry.

NOTE
While the chain is removed, check that it is still within the wear limit as described in **Drive Chain and Sprocket Inspection** *in this chapter.*

5. Lubricate the chain with chain lubricant. Lubricate an O-ring chain with lubricant specifically for O-ring chains. If chain lubricant is not readily available, use SAE 10W-30 engine oil.

CAUTION
Since the links of an O-ring chain are permanently lubricated and sealed, O-ring chain lubricant is formulated to prevent exterior corrosion of the chain and to condition the O-rings. It is not tacky and resists the adhesion of dirt. Avoid lubricants that are tacky and for conventional chains. These lubricants will attract dirt and subject the O-rings to unnecessary abrasion.

6. Install the chain and reassemble the master link as described in Chapter Eleven.

7. Adjust the chain as described in this chapter.

Air Filter Cleaning and Lubrication

The engine is equipped with a reusable, foam air filter. Clean the air filter often. Do not operate the bike without the air filter installed. Performance will not be enhanced and rapid engine wear will occur.

1. Remove the seat as described in Chapter Fifteen.

2. Remove the retaining bolt and washer (**Figure 12**) from the air filter assembly, then remove the assembly from the engine.

3. Remove the air filter (A, **Figure 13**) from the holder (B).

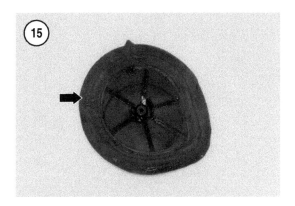

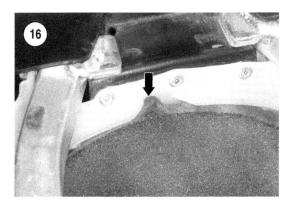

4. Wash all parts in solvent (kerosene), a commercial filter wash, or hot soapy water. *Squeeze* the cleaner from the filter. Do not wring the filter, as tearing may occur. Shake the filter to get rid of any particles that may remain on the filter.

5. Allow the filter to completely dry.

6. Apply filter oil to the filter, squeezing the filter so the oil is distributed evenly. Squeeze out the excess oil. Handle the filter with disposable gloves, or put the filter in a plastic bag to squeeze and distribute the oil. Follow the manufacturer's instructions when oiling the filter.

> *NOTE*
> *Use oil specifically formulated for foam filters. This type of oil stays adhered to the foam and traps dust effectively.*

7. Install the holder into the filter. Align the small hole in the filter with the projection on the holder (**Figure 14**).

8. Apply lithium grease around the perimeter of the filter (**Figure 15**). This will help seal the filter against the housing.

9. Insert the washer and retaining bolt into the filter assembly.

10. Fit the filter assembly into the air filter housing. Align the tab on the filter so it is vertical (**Figure 16**), then seat the projection on the holder into the housing. Check that the filter is completely seated against the housing.

11. Install the seat as described in Chapter Fifteen.

MAINTENANCE AND INSPECTION

Fastener Inspection

Inspect all fasteners on the bike for tightness and condition.

1. Retorque nuts, bolts and screws as recommended in the tables at the end of each chapter.

2. Check that all cotter pins are secure and undamaged.

3. Check that tie straps, used to secure cables and electrical wiring, are not broken or missing.

Muffler Cleaning and Repacking

Refer to *Muffler Repacking* in Chapter Four to clean and repack the muffler.

Coolant Level Inspection

> *WARNING*
> *Inspect the cooling system when the engine and coolant are cold. Severe injury could occur if the system is checked while it is hot. If the radiator cap must be removed while the coolant is still warm, cover the cap with a towel and open it slowly. Do not remove the cap until all pressure is relieved.*

1. Support the bike so it is vertical and level.

2. Remove the radiator cap and inspect the radiator for the following:

   a. The coolant level should be to the bottom of the filler neck on the radiator (**Figure 17**).

   b. If the coolant level is below the filler neck, add coolant mixture to raise the level. Refer to **Table 2** for the recommended coolant and mixing ratio.

   c. Install the radiator cap.

Cooling System Inspection

Annually check the condition of the cooling system, or whenever it is suspected that overheating is occurring. The radiator cap and cooling system are checked individually, using a cooling system tester. This tester applies the required pressure to the cooling system and cap. A pressure gauge attached to the tester is observed and leakage can be detected. A Honda dealership can perform this inspection, or a tester can be purchased from an automotive parts supplier. Connect the tester following the manufacturer's instructions. Test the radiator cap and cooling system as follows:

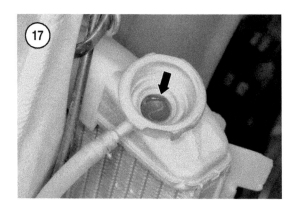

> *WARNING*
> *Test the cooling system when the engine and coolant are cold. Severe injury could occur if the system is checked while it is hot.*

1. Support the bike so it is vertical and level.
2. Remove the radiator cap.
3. Check the rubber seals (A, **Figure 18**) for cracks, compression and pliability. Replace the cap if damage is evident.
4. Check the valve (B, **Figure 18**) for damage. Replace the cap if damage is evident.

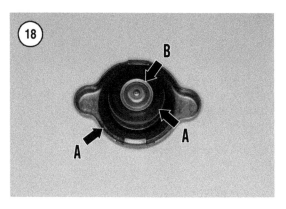

5. Determine the cap relief pressure. Wet the seal on the radiator cap, then attach the cap to the tester (**Figure 19**). Apply pressure to the cap. Relief pressure for the cap is 108-137 kPa (16-20 psi). Observe the pressure gauge and do the following:
   a. If the gauge holds pressure up to the relief pressure range, the cap is good.
   b. If the gauge does not hold pressure, or the relief pressure is too high or low, replace the cap.
6. Check that the radiator is filled to the bottom of the filler neck (**Figure 17**). Attach the tester to the radiator, then pump the tester to 137 kPa (20 psi).

> *CAUTION*
> *Do not exceed 137 kPa (20 psi). Excessive pressure can damage the cooling system components.*

Observe the pressure gauge and note the following:
   a. If the gauge holds the required pressure, the cooling system is in good condition.

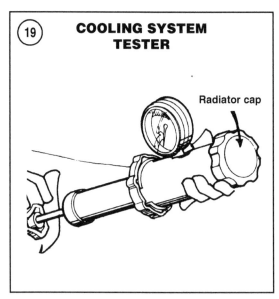

COOLING SYSTEM TESTER

Radiator cap

   b. If the gauge does not hold the required pressure, check for leakage at the radiator and all fittings. If the pressure lowers and then stabilizes, check for swollen radiator hoses. Replace or repair the cooling system components so they maintain the test pressure.

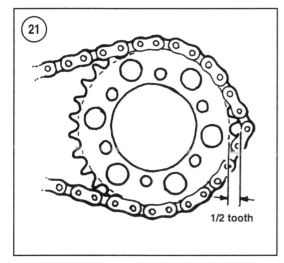

1/2 tooth

Coolant Replacement

WARNING
Replace the coolant in the cooling system when the engine and coolant are cold. Severe injury could occur if the system is drained while it is hot.

CAUTION
Do not allow coolant to contact painted surfaces. If contact does occur, immediately wash the surface with water.

1. Support the bike so it is vertical and level.
2. Place a drain pan under the right side of the engine, below the water pump.
3. Remove the coolant drain bolt (**Figure 20**). Coolant will begin to drain from the engine. Slowly loosen and remove the radiator cap so the flow from the engine increases. Be ready to reposition the drain pan, if necessary.

4. Flush the cooling system with clean tap water directed through the radiator filler neck. Check that all water drains from the system.
5. Install a *new* sealing washer on the coolant drain bolt, then install and torque the drain bolt to the specification in **Table 5**.
6. Refill the radiator with the coolant mixture specified in **Table 2**.
   a. Tip the bike from side to side to allow the coolant to flow through the engine, and to purge air from the water jackets.
   b. Refill the radiator as the coolant level goes down.
   c. When the coolant level no longer goes down, fill the radiator to the bottom of the filler neck (**Figure 17**). Install the radiator cap.
7. Start the engine and allow the coolant to circulate. Shut off the engine and do the following:

WARNING
Cover the cap with a towel and open it slowly. Do not remove the cap until all pressure is relieved.

   a. Remove the radiator cap and check the level. If necessary, add coolant to bring the level to the bottom of the filler neck. Install the radiator cap.
   b. Check the drain bolt and all other connections for leakage.
8. Rinse the frame and engine where coolant was splashed.
9. Dispose the old coolant in an environmentally-safe manner.

Drive Chain and Sprockets Inspection

A worn drive chain and sprockets are both unreliable and potentially dangerous. Inspect the chain and rear sprocket for wear and replace if necessary. If wear is detected, replace both sprockets and the chain. Mixing old and new parts will prematurely wear the new parts.

To determine if the chain should be measured for wear, pull one chain link away from the rear sprocket. If more than 1/2 the height of the sprocket tooth is visible (**Figure 21**), the chain should be accurately measured for wear. Refer to the following procedure to measure chain wear and inspect the rear sprocket.

1. Loosen the axle nut (A, **Figure 22**).

2. Loosen the chain adjuster locknuts (B, **Figure 22**) on both sides of the wheel.

3. Equally turn the chain adjusters (C, **Figure 22**) until the chain is taut.

> *NOTE*
> *If the chain is removed from the sprockets, lay the chain on a flat surface and pull the ends of the chain to remove the slack.*

4. Measure the length of any 16-link (17 pin) span (**Figure 23**). Measure center-to-center from the pins.

   a. The service limit for the chain is 259 mm (10.2 in.). If the measured distance meets or exceeds the service limit, replace the chain.

   b. If the chain is within the service limit, inspect the inside surfaces of the link plates. The plates should be shiny at both ends of the chain roller. If one side of the chain is worn, the chain has been running out of alignment. This also causes premature wear of the rollers and pins. Replace the chain if abnormal wear is detected.

5. Inspect the teeth on the front and rear sprockets. Compare the sprockets to **Figure 24**. The teeth should be symmetrical and uniform. If either sprocket is worn out, replace both sprockets.

6. Adjust the drive chain as described in this section.

Drive Chain Adjustment

The drive chain must have adequate play so it can adjust to the actions of the swing arm when the bike is in use. Too little play can cause the chain to become excessively tight and cause unnecessary wear to the driveline components. Too much play can cause excessive looseness and possibly cause the chain to come off the sprockets.

1. Support the bike so the rear wheel is off the ground.

2. Pull up on the chain, midway between the sprockets (**Figure 25**), and measure the chain slack as follows:

   a. Check several sections of the chain, since chains do not wear evenly, and find the tightest length (least amount of play). The amount of play should be 25-35 mm (1.0-1.4 in.). If

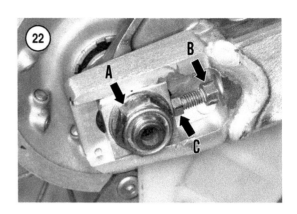

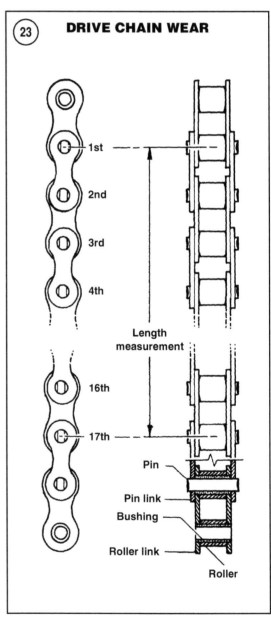

DRIVE CHAIN WEAR

1st

2nd

3rd

4th

Length measurement

16th

17th

Pin

Pin link

Bushing

Roller link

Roller

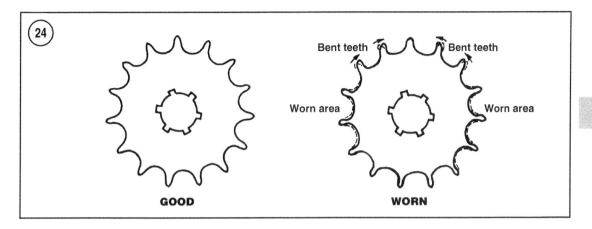

GOOD   WORN

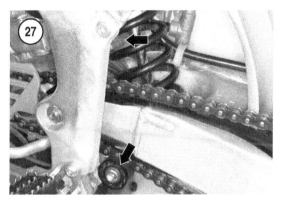

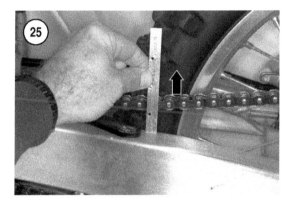

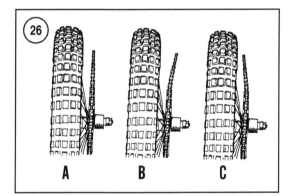

the tightest measurement is less, loosen the chain to add play. If the tightest measurement is greater, tighten the chain to reduce play.

3. Adjust chain play as follows:

a. Loosen the axle nut (A, **Figure 22**).

b. Loosen the chain adjuster locknuts (B, **Figure 22**) on both sides of the wheel.

c. Equally turn the chain adjuster nuts (C, **Figure 22**) until the chain play is correct. Use the adjustment gauges to equally adjust the chain.

Push the wheel forward against the adjusters to remove play.

> *NOTE*
> *If free play cannot be adjusted within the limits of the adjusters, replace the excessively worn chain.*

d. When free play is correct, check that the wheel is aligned (**Figure 26**). If the chain curves in or out, readjust the chain so the wheel is aligned with the rest of the bike.

e. Apply pressure to the top of the chain and tighten the axle nut to lock the setting. Torque the nut to the specifications in **Table 5**.

f. Tighten the adjuster locknuts.

Drive Chain Rollers and Sliders Inspection

Inspect the following parts for wear or damage.

1. Chain rollers (**Figure 27**).

a. Inspect the upper and lower chain rollers for wear or binding.

b. Measure the outside diameter of the rollers (**Figure 28**). Refer to **Table 4** for the required diameter.

2. Chain sliders (**Figure 29**).

a. Inspect the upper and lower surface of the slider for wear or damage.

b. Measure the depth of wear in the upper surface of the slider. Replace the slider when it reaches a worn depth of 5 mm (0.2 in.).

3. Chain guide slider (A, **Figure 30**).

a. Inspect the surface of the slider for wear or damage.

b. Replace the slider when the bottom edge of the chain is level with the bottom edge of the inspection window (B, **Figure 30**).

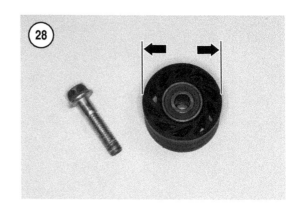

Throttle Cable Adjustment

Refer to Chapter Eight for throttle cable replacement procedures. Before adjusting the throttle cable, check that it is in good condition. To achieve accurate cable adjustment, the cable must not bind or drag. Make sure the engine idle speed is correct before adjusting the cable.

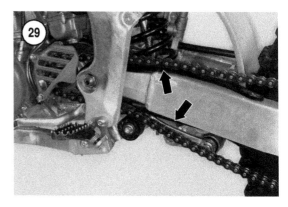

1. Measure the amount of throttle grip free play at the flange on the grip (**Figure 31**). Correct free play is 3-5 mm (1/8-1/4 in.). If free play is incorrect, adjust the cable as described in the following steps.

2. Pull back the rubber boot from the throttle cable adjuster (A, **Figure 32**).

3. Loosen the locknut (B, **Figure 32**), then turn the cable adjuster to increase or decrease play in the cable and throttle.

NOTE
For 1997, 1998 and 2001 models, if adjustment cannot be achieved at the handlebar, major adjustment can be made at the carburetor. Before using this adjuster, reset the throttle adjuster to a neutral position, so it can be used to fine-adjust the cable. At the carburetor, loosen the locknut and turn the cable adjuster in or out to closely set play in the cable and throttle. Tighten the locknut, then make fine adjustments at the throttle.

4. Tighten the locknut.

5. Install the rubber boot.

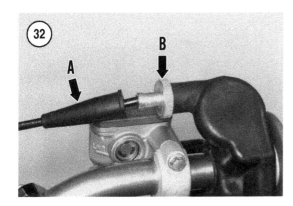

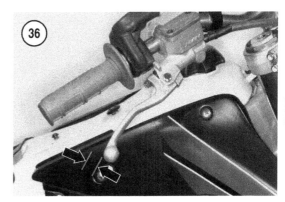

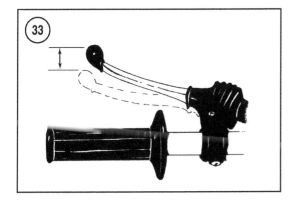

Clutch Cable Adjustment

The clutch cable must be adjusted properly to ensure smooth shifting, full clutch engagement and minimal wear on the clutch plates.

1. Measure the amount of free play at the end of the clutch lever (**Figure 33**). Correct free play is 10-20 mm (3/8-3/4 in.). If free play is incorrect, adjust the cable as described in the following steps.

2. Pull back the rubber boot from the clutch cable adjuster.

3. Loosen the locknut (A, **Figure 34**) and turn the cable adjuster (B) to increase or decrease play in the cable and lever.

> *NOTE*
> *If adjustment cannot be achieved at the lever, major adjustment can be made at the in-line adjuster in the cable (**Figure 35**). Before using this adjuster, reset the lever adjuster to a neutral position, so it can be used to fine-adjust the cable. Loosen the locknut (A, **Figure 35**) and turn the cable adjuster (B) in or out to closely set play in the cable and lever. Tighten the locknut, then make fine adjustments at the clutch lever.*

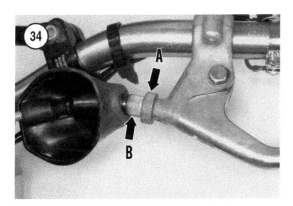

4. Tighten the locknut.
5. Install the rubber boot.

Front Brake Lever Adjustment

The front brake lever must be adjusted so the brake is fully actuated within the normal range of lever travel. However, there must be enough play in the lever to prevent brake drag when the lever is not being used.

1. Measure the amount of brake lever travel (**Figure 36**). Measure the travel between the end of the

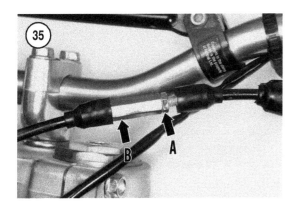

lever and the throttle grip. Correct travel is 10-20 mm (3/8-3/4 in.). If travel is more or less than this, adjust the lever as described in the following steps.

2. Remove the rubber boot from the lever adjuster.

3. Loosen the locknut (A, **Figure 37**) and turn the adjuster (B) to increase or decrease play in the lever.

4. Tighten the locknut.

5. Install the rubber boot.

Rear Brake Pedal Adjustment

The rear brake pedal can be adjusted to rider preference. When adjusting the pedal, ensure the brake can be fully actuated. However, there must be enough play in the pedal to prevent brake drag when the pedal is not being used.

1. Loosen the locknut (A, **Figure 38**) on the brake pushrod (B).

2. Turn the pushrod in or out to increase or decrease the pedal height. The pushrod adjuster is under the rubber boot.

3. Tighten the locknut.

4. Check the brake pedal adjustment from the riding position.

Brake Fluid Level Inspection

1. Support the bike so the brake fluid reservoir being checked is level.

2. Inspect the reservoirs as follows:

   a. On the front reservoir, the fluid level should be above the low mark (**Figure 39**). On the rear reservoir the fluid level should be between the lower and upper marks (**Figure 40**).

   b. If the fluid level is below the low mark on the front reservoir, remove the cover and diaphragm, then add DOT 4 brake fluid to the upper mark (on inner wall of reservoir). Replace the diaphragm and cap. Check for leaks and worn brake pads.

   c. If the fluid level is below the low mark on the rear reservoir, remove the cover, plate and diaphragm, then add DOT 4 brake fluid to the upper mark. Replace the diaphragm, plate and cap. Check for leaks and worn brake pads.

NOTE
If the brake fluid is not clear to slightly yellow, the fluid is contami-

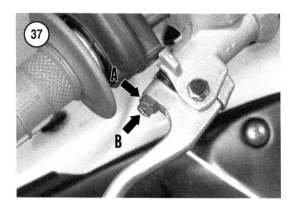

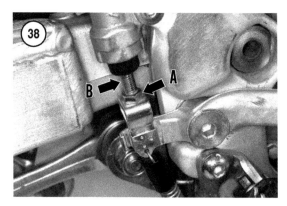

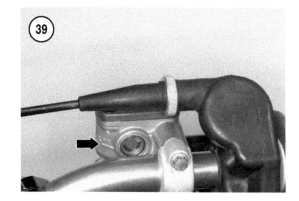

nated and should be replaced. Drain and bleed the brake system (Chapter Fourteen).

Brake Pad and Disc Inspection

Check the brake discs and pads regularly to ensure they are in good condition. Under racing conditions, the scoring of a disc can occur rapidly if the brake pads are damaged or have debris lodged in the pad material. If damage is evident for any of the following inspections, refer to Chapter Fourteen for

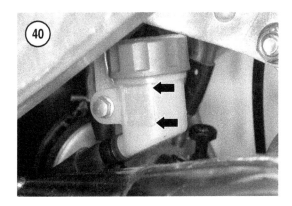

c. Disc thickness. If the disc shows wear in the friction area, measure the thickness of both discs.

3. Inspect the brake pads. If the front or rear pads are worn to their wear indicator grooves (**Figure 41** and **Figure 42**), replace the pad set for that wheel.

Steering Head Bearing Inspection

Inspect the steering head tapered roller bearings after every race, or whenever the steering feels loose or uncontrollable. The bearings must be greased and torqued in order to prevent wear and to maintain proper handling characteristics.

1. Support the bike so the front wheel is off the ground.

2. Inspect the steering head as follows:
   a. Turn the handlebar in both directions and feel for roughness or binding.
   b. Grasp the fork legs near the axle and check for front-to-back play.

3. If roughness, binding or play is detected in the steering head, refer to *Steering Play Check and Adjustment* in Chapter Twelve to adjust the steering head.

Swing Arm Bearing Inspection

The following procedure is a general lateral inspection of the swing arm bearings. To perform a more thorough inspection, refer to *Swing Arm Bearing Inspection* in Chapter Thirteen.

1. Support the bike so the rear wheel is off the ground.

2. Have an assistant steady the bike, then grasp the ends of the swing arm and move it from side to side. There should be no detectable play. If play is evident, refer to Chapter Thirteen for servicing the swing arm.

Front and Rear Suspension Adjustment

The front fork and rear shock absorber are adjustable to meet various riding conditions. Refer to *Fork Adjustment* in Chapter Twelve to adjust the front fork. Refer to *Rear Suspension Adjustment* in Chapter Thirteen to adjust the shock absorber.

brake pad replacement, disc specifications and service limits.

1. Support the bike so the wheels are off the ground.

2. Visually inspect the front and rear discs for the following:
   a. Scoring. The disc should be smooth in the friction area.
   b. Runout. Spin the wheel and visually check for lateral movement of the disc. Runout should not be evident.

Fork Air Release Screw

The fork is designed to operate with a cushion of air in the spring chamber of the fork cap. When riding, the air warms and expands, increasing the pressure in the chamber. This increase in pressure will affect the action of the suspension. Release the pressure often, usually between race and practice heats. Release the pressure as follows:

1. Support the bike with the front wheel off the ground.

2. Remove the air screw (**Figure 43**) from the fork cap to relieve the air pressure.

3. Install and tighten the air release screw. Repeat for the other fork leg.

Tire Pressure

The tires must be inflated to meet the demands of the riding conditions. Standard air pressure is 100 kPa (15 psi). Slight over- or under-inflation is permissible if the riding conditions justify the change. However, *do not exceed the inflation range embossed on the tire sidewall*. Since inner tubes are used in the tires, air pressure that is too low for the riding conditions can cause the tire to slip on the rim. This can bend the valve stem, as shown in **Figure 44**. Running with the valve stem bent can sever the valve stem and deflate the tire. Correct the condition by adjusting the tire and inner tube positions as described in this section.

Tube Alignment

When the tube valve stem is bent, as shown in **Figure 44**, the tube must be realigned to prevent valve stem damage. A bent valve stem can sever and deflate the tire. Align the tube as follows:

1. Wash the tire and rim.

2. Remove the valve stem core and deflate the tire.

3. Loosen the locknut on the rim lock.

4. With an assistant steadying the bike, break the tire-to-rim seal completely around both sides of the tire.

5. Support the bike so the wheel is off the ground.

6. Check that the valve stem is loose.

7. Lubricate both tire beads by spraying with soapy water.

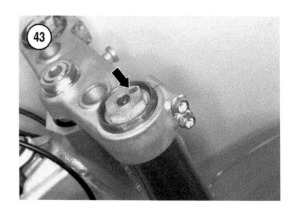

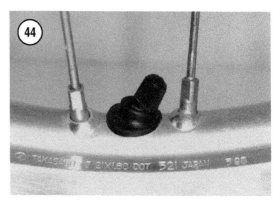

8. Have an assistant apply the brake for the wheel being aligned.

9. Grasp the tire, then turn it and the tube until the valve stem is straight.

10. When the tube is correctly positioned, install the valve stem and inflate the tire. If necessary, reapply the soap solution to the beads to help seat the tire on the rim. Check that the beads uniformly seat around the rim.

> *WARNING*
> *Do not over-inflate the tire to seat the beads. If the beads will not seat, deflate the tire and relubricate the beads.*

Spoke Tension

Check spoke tension during the break-in period and whenever the wheel has been respoked. During the break-in period, check spoke tension often. After break-in, check spoke tension regularly. Refer to *Rim and Spoke Service* in Chapter Eleven for inspecting and properly tightening the spokes.

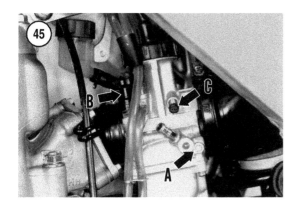

ENGINE TUNE-UP

Carburetor Idle Speed and Mixture Adjustment

The carburetor must be adjusted so the idle speed keeps the engine running, but is also low enough to provide compression braking. Additionally, the pilot air screw must be adjusted so throttle response is good from an idle to 1/8 throttle. Use the following procedure for adjusting the idle speed and pilot air screw for the *standard* jets and needle. Refer to Chapter Eight for procedures to adjust or change the jets and needle.

1. Check the throttle cable for proper adjustment.
2. Check the air filter for cleanliness.
3. Set the pilot air screw (A, **Figure 45**) to the number of turns listed in **Table 3**. This is a starting point for adjustment. Lightly seat the screw before turning it out the required number of turns. Do not overtighten the screw.
4. Start the engine and allow it to warm up.
5A. For 1997-1998 models, adjust the idle speed by turning the choke knob (B, **Figure 45**). Set the engine idle speed to a smooth, low speed. There is no specified idle speed. Raise and lower the engine speed a few times to ensure that it returns to the idle speed and that the engine remains running.
5B. For 1999-2001 models, adjust the idle speed by turning the throttle stop (C, **Figure 45**). Set the engine idle speed to a smooth, low speed. There is no specified idle speed. Raise and lower the engine speed a few times to ensure that it returns to the idle speed and that the engine remains running.
6. Note or mark the position of the pilot air screw. From its initial setting, turn the pilot air screw in and out in small increments to find the points where the engine speed begins to decrease. Set the pilot screw

between the two points. Note the amount of adjustment from the initial setting.
7. Reset the idle speed to bring it within its original setting.
8. Test ride the bike and check throttle response. If throttle response is poor from an idle, adjust the pilot screw out (leaner) or in (enrichen) by 1/8 turn increments until the engine accelerates smoothly.

NOTE
The minimum to maximum adjustment range of the pilot air screw is one to three turns out from the seated position. If the pilot air screw is over three turns out, install the next smaller size slow jet. If the pilot air screw is under one turn out, install the next larger size slow jet.

Engine Timing Check

The ignition timing is electronically controlled by the ignition control module. No routine adjustment of the timing necessary. Check the timing when ignition system problems are suspected, or whenever the ignition control module, stator, ignition pulse generator or flywheel are replaced. Refer to *Ignition Timing* in Chapter Nine to check timing.

Compression Check

A cylinder compression check can quickly verify the condition of the piston, rings and cylinder head gasket without disassembling the engine. By recording the compression reading in the maintenance log in the back of the manual at each tune-up, readings can be compared to determine if normal wear is occurring.

Honda does not give a required compression range for this engine; however, an engine of this design typically has 180 psi (1195 kPa) or more compression when broken in properly. It is recommended that the owner perform regular compression checks and record the readings. If a current reading is extremely different from the previous reading, troubleshooting can begin to correct the problem. Operating the engine when compression readings are abnormal can lead to severe engine damage.

1. Warm the engine to operating temperature.

2. Remove the spark plug. Insert the spark plug into the cap, then ground the plug to the cylinder.

3. Thread a compression gauge into the spark plug hole. The gauge must be fitted airtight in the hole for an accurate reading.

4. Hold or secure the throttle fully open.

5. Kick the engine over several times until the highest gauge reading is achieved.

6. Record the reading. Compare the reading with previous readings, if available. Under normal operating conditions, compression will slowly lower from the original specification, due to wear of the piston rings.

    a. A higher than normal reading can be caused by carbon buildup in the combustion chamber. This can cause high combustion chamber temperatures and potential engine damage.

    b. A lower than normal reading can be caused by worn piston rings, damaged piston, leaking head gasket or a combination of these. To help pinpoint the source of leakage, pour 15 cc (1/2 oz.) of two-stroke engine oil through the spark plug hole and into the cylinder. Turn the engine over to distribute the oil. Recheck compression. If compression increases, the piston rings are worn or damaged. If compression is the same, the piston or head gasket is worn or damaged.

Spark Plug Caps

The spark plug cap should fit tight to the spark plug and be in good condition. A cap that does not seal and insulate the spark plug terminal can lead to flashover (shorting down the side of the plug), particularly when the bike is operated in wet conditions. To help prevent water from migrating under the cap, wipe a small amount of dielectric grease around the interior of the cap before installing it on the plug.

Spark Plug Removal

Careful removal of the spark plug is important in preventing grit from entering the combustion chamber. It is also important to know how to remove a plug that is seized, or is resistant to removal. Forcing a seized plug can destroy the threads in the cylinder head.

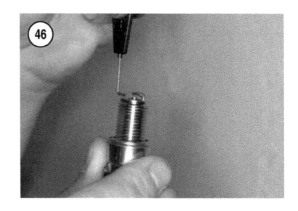

1. Grasp the spark plug cap and twist it to loosen it from the spark plug. There may be a slight suction and resistance as the cap is removed.

2. Fit a spark plug wrench and extension over the spark plug, then remove it by turning the wrench counterclockwise. If the plug is seized or drags excessively during removal, stop and try the following techniques:

    a. Apply a penetrating lubricant such as Liquid Wrench or WD-40 and allow it to stand for 15 minutes.

    b. If the plug is completely seized, apply moderate pressure in both directions with the wrench. Only attempt to break the seal so lubricant can penetrate under the spark plug and into the threads. If this does not work, and the bike is still operable, replace the spark plug cap and start the engine. Allow it to completely warm up. The heat of the engine may be enough to expand the parts and allow the plug to be removed.

    c. When a spark plug has been loosened, but drags excessively during its removal, apply penetrating lubricant around the spark plug threads. Turn the plug *in* (clockwise) to help distribute the lubricant onto the threads. Slowly remove the plug, working it in and out of the cylinder head as lubricant is added. Do not reuse the spark plug.

    d. Inspect the threads in the cylinder head for damage. Clean and true the threads with a spark plug thread-chaser.

3. After the plug is removed, inspect the plug condition to determine if the engine is operating properly.

4. Clean spark plugs that will be reused after inspection with electrical contact cleaner and a shop

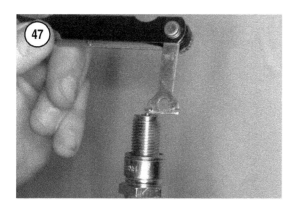

cloth. Do not use abrasives or wire brushes to clean the plugs.

Spark Plug Gapping and Installation

Proper adjustment of the electrode gap is important for reliable and consistent spark. Also, the proper preparation of the spark plug threads will ensure that the plug can be removed easily in the future, without damage to the cylinder head threads.

1. Refer to **Table 3** for the required spark plug gap.
2. Insert a wire feeler gauge (the size of the required gap) between the center electrode and the ground electrode (**Figure 46**).
3. Pull the gauge through the gap. If there is slight drag, the setting is correct. If the gap is too large or small, adjust the gap by bending the ground electrode (**Figure 47**) with the adjusting tool to achieve the required gap. Do not pry the electrode with a screwdriver or other tool. Damage to the center electrode and insulator is possible.
4. Inspect the spark plug to ensure it is fitted with a crush washer.
5. Wipe a small amount of antiseize compound onto the spark plug threads. Do not allow the compound to get on the electrodes.
6. Insert the plug into the socket and extension, then finger-tighten the spark plug into the cylinder head. This will ensure the plug is not cross-threading.
7. Torque the spark plug to the specification in **Table 5**. If a torque wrench is not available, tighten a new spark plug 1/4-1/2 turn from the seated position; a used spark plug 1/8-1/4 turn from the seated position.
8. Press and twist the cap onto the spark plug.

Reading Spark Plugs

The spark plug is an excellent indicator of how the engine is operating. By correctly evaluating the condition of the plug, it is possible to diagnose and pinpoint problems or potential problems. Whenever the spark plug is removed, compare the firing tip with the ones shown in **Figure 48**. The following paragraphs provide a description, as well as common causes for each of the conditions.

Refer to *Spark Plug Selection* if a change in spark plug heat range is being considered.

> *CAUTION*
> *In all cases, when the spark plug does not read normal, find the cause of the problem before continuing engine operation. Severe engine damage is possible when abnormal plug readings are ignored.*

Normal

The plug has light tan or gray deposits on the tip. No erosion of the electrodes or abnormal gap is evident. This indicates an engine that has properly adjusted carburetion, ignition timing, and proper fuel. This heat range of plug is appropriate for the conditions in which the engine has been operated. The plug can be cleaned and reused.

Oil fouled

The plug is wet with black, oily deposits on the electrodes and insulator. The electrodes do not show wear.

1. Incorrect fuel/oil mixture.
2. Incorrect carburetor jetting.
3. Prolonged idling or low idle speed.
4. Spark plug range too cold.
5. Ignition component failure.
6. Worn piston rings.

Carbon fouled

The plug is black with a dry, sooty deposit on the entire plug surface. This dry sooty deposit is conductive and can create electrical paths that bypass the electrode gap. This often results in misfiring of the plug.

1. Fuel mixture too rich.
2. Spark plug range too cold.

SPARK PLUG CONDITIONS

(48)

NORMAL

GAP BRIDGED

CARBON FOULED

OVERHEATED

OIL FOULED

SUSTAINED PREIGNITION

3. Faulty ignition component.

4. Prolonged idling.

5. Clogged air filter.

6. Poor compression.

Overheated

The plug is dry and the insulator has a white or light gray cast. The insulator may also appear blistered. The electrodes may have a bluish-burnt appearance.

1. Fuel mixture too lean or incorrect jetting.

2. Spark plug range too hot.

3. Air leak into intake system.

4. No crush washer on plug.

5. Plug improperly tightened.

6. Faulty ignition component.

Gap bridged

The plug is clogged with deposits between the electrodes. The electrodes do not show wear.

1. Wrong oil type being used.

2. Incorrect fuel or fuel contamination.

3. Incorrect fuel/oil mixture.

4. Carbon deposits in combustion chamber.

5. High-speed operation after excessive idling.

Preignition

The plug electrodes are severely eroded or melted. This condition can lead to severe engine damage.

1. Faulty ignition component.

2. Spark plug range too hot.

3. Air leak into intake system.

4. Carbon deposits in combustion chamber.

Worn out

The plug electrodes are rounded from normal combustion. There is no indication of abnormal combustion or engine conditions. Replace the plug.

Spark Plug Selection

CAUTION
The following section provides general information and operation fundamentals that apply to all spark plugs. Before using a plug other than the recommended type, make sure that the spark plug manufacturer specifically recommends it for this motorcycle. Poor performance or engine damage can occur by installing a spark plug that is not compatible with this engine.

Refer to **Table 3** for the recommended resistor-type spark plugs and gap. Depending on the manufacturer, the plugs may have a U- or V-shaped electrode, and utilize nickel-chrome, copper or platinum in their construction. These plugs are specifically designed for high performance two-stroke motorcycles.

Heat range

Plugs with heat ranges that are either hotter or colder than the original plugs are available. However, in most cases the heat range of the spark plugs originally installed by the manufacturer (**Table 3**) will perform adequately under most conditions. Do not change the spark plug heat range to compensate for adverse engine or carburetion conditions. This will only compound the problem.

In general, use a hot plug for low speeds and low temperatures. Use a cold plug for high speeds and high temperatures. The plugs should operate hot enough to burn off unwanted deposits, but not so hot that it becomes damaged or causes preignition. Determine if plug heat range is correct by examining the insulator as described in *Spark Plug Reading*.

When replacing plugs with another type, make sure the reach (thread length) is correct. The thread length of any replacement spark plug must be the same as the original, which matches the length of the threads in the cylinder head. A longer than standard plug could interfere with the piston, causing engine damage. A short plug will provide poor ignition.

Tables 1-5 are on the following pages.

Table 1 MAINTENANCE AND LUBRICATION SCHEDULE

Every race (2.5 hours[1])
 Inspect/replace spark plug
 Adjust drive chain
 Inspect/lubricate drive chain
 Inspect front and rear sprockets
 Inspect drive chain sliders and rollers
 Inspect coolant level and hoses[3]
 Inspect/clean air filter[2]
 Inspect/adjust throttle
 Inspect/adjust clutch
 Inspect/lubricate cables
 Inspect brake fluid level[3]
 Inspect brake pads
 Inspect wheels, tires and axle nut
 Inspect spokes and tire pressure
 Inspect fork and steering system
 Equalize air pressure in fork legs
 Inspect fasteners
Every 3 races (7.5 hours[1])
 Inspect/lubricate rear suspension pivots
 Inspect/lubricate swing arm
 Clean cylinder head
 Clean exhaust valve and linkage
 Replace piston and rings
 Replace reed valve
 Replace transmission oil
 Replace drive chain
 Replace fork tube/slider oil[4]
Every 9 races (22.5 hours[1])
 Replace fork damper oil
 Replace piston pin
 Replace connecting rod small end bearing
 Replace drive chain
 Inspect steering head bearings

1. Perform the procedures at either the hours or races indicated, whichever occurs first.
2. Clean the air filter after every race in dusty conditions.
3. Replace every 2 years.
4. Replace after initial break-in.

Table 2 FUEL, LUBRICANTS AND FLUIDS

Fuel type	Unleaded gasoline; 92 octane minimum
Fuel tank capacity	7.5 liters (2 U.S. gal.)
Engine oil	Pro Honda HP-2, 2-Stroke Oil or equivalent
Engine oil mixing ratio	32:1
Transmission oil type	Pro Honda HP transmission oil or Pro Honda GN4 4-stroke 10W-40 SF/SG engine oil or equivalent
Transmission oil capacity	
Overhaul capacity	0.85 L (0.9 U.S. qt.)
Change capacity	0.75 L (0.8 U.S. qt.)
Coolant type	Ethylene glycol containing silicate-free corrosion inhibitors for aluminum engines
Coolant mixture	50/50 (antifreeze/distilled water)
Cooling system capacity	
1997-1999	
At change	1.26 liters (1.32 U.S. qt.)

(continued)

Table 2 FUEL, LUBRICANTS AND FLUIDS (continued)

Cooling system capacity (continued)	
1997-1999 (continued)	
At disassembly	1.28 liters (1.35 U.S. qt.)
2000-2001	
At change	1.22 liters (1.29 U.S. qt.)
At disassembly	1.35 liters (1.43 U.S. qt.)
Fork oil grade	Pro-Honda HP fork oil 5W or equivalent
Fork oil capacity (standard)	Refer to Chapter 12 for minimum/maximum capacities
1997	369 cc (12.5 U.S. oz.)
1998	375 cc (12.7 U.S. oz.)
1999	373 cc (12.6 U.S. oz.)
2000	386 cc (13.6 U.S. oz.)
2001	383 cc (13.0 U.S. oz.)
Air filter	Foam air filter oil
Brake fluid type	DOT 4
Control cable pivots	Cable lube
Drive chain	Pro Honda chain lubricant or equivalent

Table 3 TUNE-UP SPECIFICATIONS

Pilot air screw turns out	
1997-1999	2
2000	1 1/2
2001	1 3/4
Spark plug	
Standard	NGK BR8EG
	Denso W24ESR-V
	Champion QN-86
Optional	NGK BR8EV
	Denso W24ESR-G
	Champion QN-2G
Spark plug gap	0.5-0.6 mm (0.020-0.024 in.)
Ignition timing	
1997	18° at 3000 rpm
1998-2001	18° ± 2° at 3000 rpm

Table 4 ROUTINE CHECK AND ADJUSTMENT SPECIFICATIONS

Drive chain	
Slack	25-35 mm (1.0-1.4 in.)
Length wear limit (16 pitch/17 pins)	259 mm (10.2 in.)
Slider thickness wear limit	5.0 mm (0.2 in.)
Tensioner roller diameter wear limit	
1997	25 mm (1.0 in.)
1998	
Upper	25 mm (1.0 in.)
Lower	35 mm (1.4 in.)
1999	
Upper	25 mm (1.0 in.)
Lower	39 mm (1.54 in.)
2000-2001	
Upper and lower	25 mm (1.0 in.)
Wheels	
Axle runout (front/rear)	0.20 mm (0.008 in.)

(continued)

Table 4 ROUTINE CHECK AND ADJUSTMENT SPECIFICATIONS (continued)

Wheels (continued)	
Rim runout (radial and lateral)	2.0 mm (0.08 in.)
Tire pressure (front/rear)	100 kPa (15 psi)
Radiator cap relief pressure	108-137 kPa (16-20 psi)
Throttle grip free play	3-5 mm (1/8-1/4 in.)
Clutch lever free play	10-20 mm (3/8-3/4 in.)

Table 5 MAINTENANCE TORQUE SPECIFICATIONS

	N•m	in.-lb.	ft.-lb.
Axle nut (front)	88	–	65
Axle nut (rear)			
1997	93	–	69
1998-1999	108	–	80
2000-2001	127	–	94
Coolant drain bolt	10	88	–
Clutch lever pivot bolt	2	18	–
Clutch lever pivot nut	10	88	–
Drive chain adjusting nut	27	–	20
Drive chain guide			
mounting nut	12	106	–
Drive chain roller bolt			
1997-2000	22	–	16
2001	12	106	—
Drive sprocket bolt	26	–	20
Driven sprocket nuts	32	–	24
Rim lock	13	115	–
Shift lever bolt	12	88	–
Spark plug	18	–	13
Spokes	3.8	33	–
Throttle housing bolts	9	80	–
Throttle housing			
cover screw	1.5	13	–
Transmission oil			
check bolt	10	88	–
Transmission oil drain			
plug (crankcase)	29	–	22

CHAPTER FOUR

ENGINE TOP END

This chapter provides information for the removal, inspection and replacement of the assemblies that make up the engine top end. This includes the exhaust system, cylinder head, cylinder, piston, exhaust valves and reed valves. All the parts can be removed with the engine mounted in the frame. Refer to the tables at the end of this chapter for specifications.

Read this chapter before attempting any repair to the engine top end. Become familiar with the procedures and illustrations to understand the skill and equipment required. Refer to Chapter One for tool usage and techniques.

SHOP CLEANLINESS

Always clean the engine before starting repairs. If the engine will remain in the frame, clean the surrounding framework and under the fuel tank. Avoid letting dirt enter the engine.

Keep the work environment as clean as possible. Store parts and assemblies in well-marked plastic bags and containers. Keep reconditioned parts lubricated and wrapped until they will be installed.

EXHAUST SYSTEM

Removal and Installation

Do not attempt to remove the exhaust pipe or muffler when the engine is hot.

1. Support the bike so it is stable and secure.

2. Remove the seat and right side cover as described in Chapter Fifteen.

3. Remove the muffler as follows:

    a. Remove the bolts securing the muffler to the frame (**Figure 1**).

    b. Remove the muffler from the exhaust pipe. Do not hammer on the muffler if it is stuck to the exhaust pipe. Twist the muffler off the pipe.

c. Remove the sealing rubber.

d. If necessary, repack the muffler as described in this section.

e. Reverse this procedure to install the muffler.

4. Remove the exhaust pipe as follows:

a. Loosen the bolts that secure the exhaust pipe to the frame (**Figure 2**).

b. Remove the exhaust pipe springs at the cylinder head (**Figure 3**).

c. Remove the bolts securing the exhaust pipe to the frame.

d. Remove the sealing gasket from the exhaust port.

5. Reverse these steps to install the exhaust pipe. Note the following:

a. Install a *new* sealing gasket.

b. Torque the front retainer bolt to the specification in **Table 3**.

Muffler Repacking

The following procedure describes the repacking procedure for the muffler that is originally installed on the bike. The engine is designed to operate with a correctly packed muffler. Do not expect an increase in power by removing or not replacing the packing material. Whenever the exhaust becomes noticeably louder, it is likely that the packing material has disintegrated. Refer to **Figure 4**.

1. Remove the muffler as described in this section.

2. Remove the bolts that secure the inner pipe to the muffler case.

3. Remove the inner pipe from the case.

4. Remove all packing material from the inner pipe and case.

5. Clean the inner pipe with a wire brush. Remove all carbon and rust accumulation.

6. Measure and cut the new packing material so it will fit snugly between the inner pipe and case.

7. Wrap the packing material around the inner pipe and partially insert the pipe into the case.

8. Apply a bead of high-temperature sealant to the perimeter of the inner pipe where it seals against the muffler case.

9. Seat the inner pipe into the case.

10. Install and tighten the case bolts.

11. Install the muffler as described in this section.

CYLINDER HEAD

This section describes removal, inspection and installation of the cylinder head (**Figure 5**). The cylinder head can be removed with the engine in the frame. Before removing the cylinder head, perform a leakdown test as described in Chapter Two to identify any air leaks that may be causing poor engine performance.

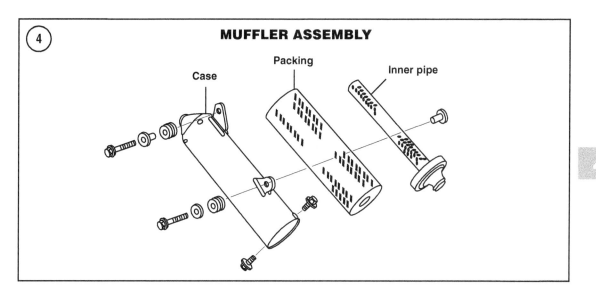

MUFFLER ASSEMBLY

Case

Packing

Inner pipe

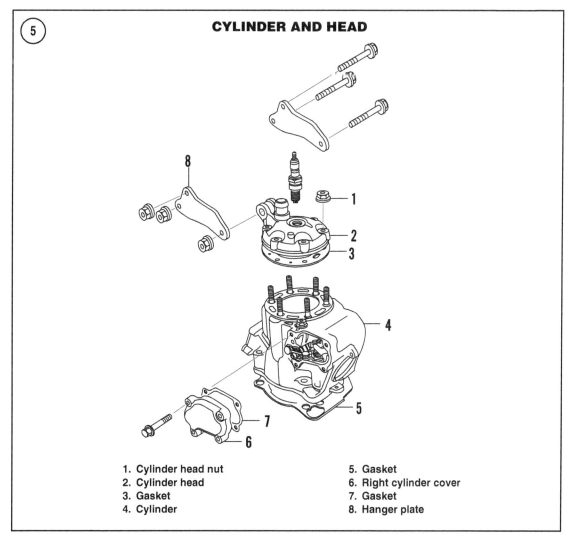

CYLINDER AND HEAD

8

1. Cylinder head nut
2. Cylinder head
3. Gasket
4. Cylinder
5. Gasket
6. Right cylinder cover
7. Gasket
8. Hanger plate

4

Removal

1. Remove the seat (Chapter Fifteen) and fuel tank (Chapter Eight).
2. Drain the cooling system as described in Chapter Three.
3. Remove the spark plug cap and hose clamp (**Figure 6**). Note the position and direction of the clamp so it can be reinstalled in the same position.
4. Remove the coolant hose from the head fitting.
5. Remove the spark plug from the head.
6. Remove the bolts securing the engine hanger plates (**Figure 7**). Note the direction of the bolts, then remove the plates from the engine and frame.
7. Loosen the cylinder head nuts (**Figure 8**). Loosen the nuts equally in three passes and in a crossing pattern. Do not loosen the nuts more than 1/4 turn on each pass.

> *CAUTION*
> *Failure to loosen the nuts equally can warp the cylinder head.*

8. Remove the cylinder head and gasket.
9. Inspect and install the cylinder head and hanger plates as described in this section.

Inspection

1. Wash the cylinder head in solvent and dry with compressed air.
2. Check all passageways for blockage.
3. Check that all gasket residue is removed from the cylinder head mating surface. If necessary, use a soft scraper to remove residue. Do not use sharp-edged tools that can scratch or gouge the surface.
4. Remove all carbon deposits from the combustion chamber (**Figure 9**). Use solvent and a fine wire brush, mounted in a drill or drill press. If necessary, use a soft scraper to remove buildup. Do not use sharp-edged tools that can scratch or gouge the surface.

> *CAUTION*
> *Scratches in the cylinder head can become extremely hot during combustion and cause preignition and heat erosion.*

5. Inspect the spark plug hole threads. If the threads are dirty or mildly damaged, use a spark plug thread

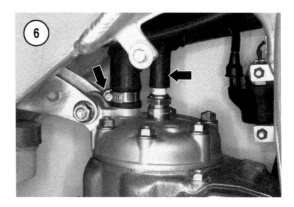

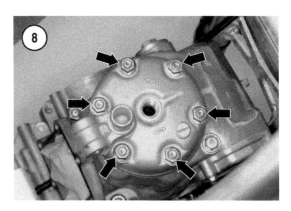

tap to clean and straighten the threads. Lubricate the tap with kerosene or aluminum tap-cutting fluid.

> *NOTE*
> *If the threads are galled, stripped or cross-threaded, fit the cylinder head with a steel thread insert, such as a HeliCoil.*

> *NOTE*
> *Thread damage can be minimized by applying antiseize compound to the*

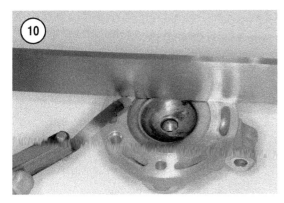

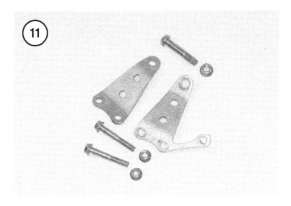

*spark plug threads before installation.
Do not overtighten the spark plug.*

6. Inspect the cylinder head for cracks in the combustion chamber, water jackets and bolt holes. Replace the head if damaged.

7. Inspect the cylinder head for warp as follows:

   a. Lay a machinist's straightedge across the cylinder head as shown in **Figure 10**. The straightedge should bridge two adjacent cylinder stud holes.

   b. Try to insert a flat feeler gauge between the straightedge and the machined surface of the head. If clearance exists, record the measurement.

   c. Repeat the inspection, working around the perimeter of the cylinder head. Always lay the straightedge across adjacent cylinder stud holes.

8. Compare any measurements in Step 7 to the warp service limit listed in **Table 2**. If the clearance is not within the service limit, take the cylinder head to a dealership or machine shop for further inspection and possible resurfacing. If the head is mildly warped, true the head as follows:

   a. Tape a sheet of 400-600 grit wet emery paper to a thick sheet of glass or a surface plate.

   b. Place the head on the wet emery paper and move the head in a figure-eight pattern.

   c. Rotate the head at regular intervals so material is equally removed.

   d. Check the progress often, measuring the clearance with the straightedge and feeler gauge. If clearance is excessive, or increases, stop the procedure and take the head to a dealership or machine shop to see if it can be reconditioned.

9. After service work has been performed, wash the cylinder head in hot, soapy water. Rinse thoroughly with clean, cool water.

10. Install the cylinder head as described in this section.

Engine Hanger Plate Inspection

1. Wash the hanger plates, nuts and bolts (**Figure 11**) in solvent.

2. Inspect the hanger plates for cracks and/or elongated mounting holes. Replace the plates and hardware if either condition exists.

3. Inspect the nuts and bolts for damage. The threads must be in good condition so they can be torqued properly.

4. Install the hanger plates as described in this section.

Installation

1. Check that all gasket residue is removed from all mating surfaces. All cylinder and cylinder head surfaces should be clean and dry.

2. Install a *new* cylinder head gasket. Install the gasket so the UP mark is visible and centered at the rear of the cylinder (**Figure 12**).

CAUTION
Failure to install the gasket correctly can cause engine overheating and possibly severe engine damage.

3. Install the cylinder head, checking that the mounting boss is centered at the rear of the engine.
4. Lubricate the cylinder studs and finger-tighten the head nuts.
5. Torque the nuts (**Figure 8**) equally in three passes and in a crossing pattern. Refer to **Table 3** for the required torque.
6. Install the the engine hanger plates (**Figure 7**). Do not tighten any nuts until both plates and all bolts have been installed. Note the correct direction of the bolts when installing. Torque the hanger plate nuts to the specifications in **Table 3**.

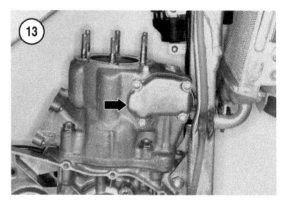

7. Install the spark plug. Torque the plug to the specifications in **Table 3**.
8. Install the coolant hose onto the head fitting. Align and tighten the hose clamp in its original position.
9. Install the spark plug cap onto the spark plug
10. Fill the cooling system as described in Chapter Three.
11. Install the seat (Chapter Fifteen) and fuel tank (Chapter Eight).
12. Start the engine and check for coolant leaks.
13. Perform the *Exhaust Valve Operation Check* as described in this chapter.
14. If new parts were installed (piston, rings or cylinder), perform the *Engine Break-in* procedure in Chapter Three.

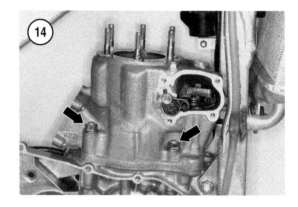

CYLINDER

The cylinder can be removed with the engine mounted in the frame. Read all procedures completely before attempting a repair. The cylinder inspection procedure also includes steps for replacing cylinder head studs.

Removal

1. Remove the exhaust pipe, cylinder head and reed valve assembly as described in this chapter.

2. Remove the carburetor as described in Chapter Eight.
3. Remove the right cylinder cover and gasket (**Figure 13**).
4. Loosen the cylinder base nuts (**Figure 14**) on both sides of the cylinder. Loosen the nuts equally in three passes and in a crossing pattern. Do not loosen the nuts more than 1/4 turn on each pass.

CAUTION
Failure to loosen the nuts equally can cause cylinder damage.

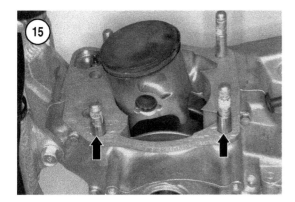

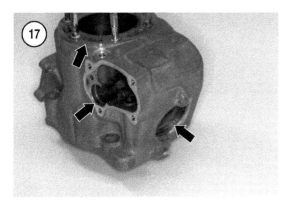

5. Loosen the cylinder by tapping around the base with a soft mallet.

6. Rotate the crankshaft so the piston is at BDC.

CAUTION
In the following step, do not twist the cylinder from the piston. The piston rings could snag in the intake port, causing damage to the ring and piston.

NOTE
If the cylinder is difficult to raise, the dowels on the left cylinder studs are

probably seized to the cylinder. Apply penetrating oil to the left studs/dowels and carefully tap the cylinder until it is loose.

7. *Slowly* raise the cylinder from the crankcase and piston. When the cylinder base is near the top of the studs, perform the following:
   a. Stuff a clean shop cloth around the piston. This will protect the piston and prevent debris from falling into the engine.
   b. Account for the two dowels that are fitted around the left crankcase studs (**Figure 15**). If the crankcase opening is not properly covered, the dowels could drop into the engine if they are lifted from the studs.

8. Remove the cylinder from the engine.

9. Remove the two dowels from the studs.

10. Remove the base gasket.

11. Remove and inspect the exhaust valve assembly as described in this chapter.

12. Inspect the cylinder as described in this chapter.

Inspection

This inspection procedure assumes all assemblies have been removed from the cylinder so it can be measured and reconditioned.

1. Remove all gasket residue from the top and bottom cylinder block surfaces. If necessary, use solvent and a soft scraper to remove residue. Do not use sharp-edged tools that can scratch or gouge the surfaces. A fine-wire brush in a hand drill can aid in removing residue from the surfaces and dowel bores (**Figure 16**).

2. Clean all deposits from the water jackets, exhaust port and exhaust valve subchamber (**Figure 17**).

3. Wash the cylinder in solvent and dry with compressed air.

4. Inspect the overall condition of the cylinder. Check for cracks around studs and in the water jackets.

5. Inspect the cylinder bore for obvious scoring or gouges. If damage is evident, replace or resleeve the cylinder.

6. Inspect the top cylinder surface for warp as follows:
   a. Lay a machinist's straightedge across the cylinder as shown in **Figure 18**. The straightedge should be against two adjacent cylinder studs.

b. Try to insert a flat feeler gauge between the straightedge and the machined surface of the cylinder. If clearance exists, record the measurement.

c. Repeat the inspection, working around the perimeter of the cylinder. Always lay the straightedge against adjacent cylinder studs.

7. Compare any measurements in Step 6 to the warp service limit in **Table 2**. If the clearance is not within the service limit, take the cylinder to a dealership or machine shop for further inspection and possible resurfacing.

8. Measure and check the cylinder for wear, taper and out-of-round. Measure the inside diameter of the cylinder with a bore gauge or inside micrometer (**Figure 19**) as follows:

a. Measure the cylinder at the five specific points along the bore axis (**Figure 20**). Note the required X and/or Y measurement(s) at each point. Measure in line (Y measurement) with the piston pin, and 90° to the pin (X measurement). Record and identify the seven measurements so the cylinder checks can be made.

CAUTION
*Before determining the cylinder wear, the cylinder size must be identified. Cylinders and pistons are matched according to their dimensions at time of manufacture. The cylinder code, A or B, is indicated on the left side of the cylinder (**Figure 21**). When referring to **Table 2**, use the dimensions that are specific to the cylinder size.*

b. For *cylinder wear*, use the largest measurement recorded (X or Y) to compare to the specifications and service limit in **Table 2**. If the cylinder bore is not within the service limit, replace or resleeve the cylinder.

c. For *cylinder out-of-round*, determine the difference between the X and Y measurements at both points near the top of the bore. Compare the largest difference to the service limit in **Table 2**. If the cylinder bore is not within the service limit, replace or resleeve the cylinder.

d. For *cylinder taper*, find the difference between the largest X measurement near the top of the cylinder and the X measurement at the bottom of the cylinder. Compare the difference to the service limit in **Table 2**. If the cyl-

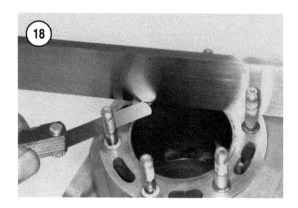

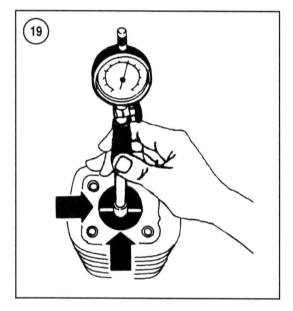

inder bore is not within the service limit, replace or resleeve the cylinder.

CAUTION
If the cylinder must be replaced, it must be the correct size (A or B) to match the current piston. If both the cylinder and piston will be replaced, check that both parts are identically sized before assembling the engine.

9. Check the tightness and condition of the cylinder studs.

a. If a stud is loose, but in good condition, torque the stud to the specifications in **Table 3**. Use the torquing technique described in Step 10.

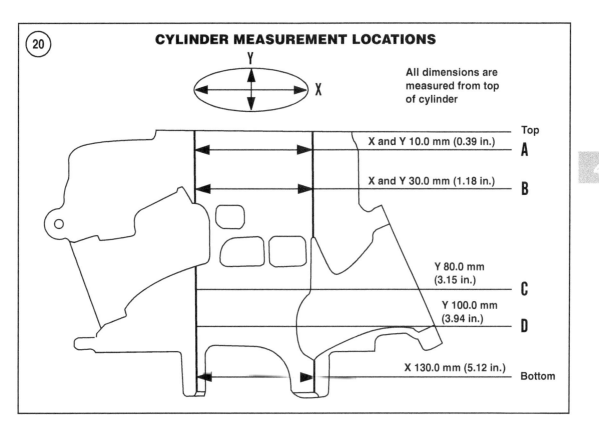

(20)

CYLINDER MEASUREMENT LOCATIONS

All dimensions are measured from top of cylinder

Top

X and Y 10.0 mm (0.39 in.) **A**

X and Y 30.0 mm (1.18 in.) **B**

Y 80.0 mm (3.15 in.) **C**

Y 100.0 mm (3.94 in.) **D**

X 130.0 mm (5.12 in.) Bottom

4

(21)

(22)

b. If the threads are only lightly damaged, use the appropriate-size metric thread die to true the threads.

c. If the stud is broken in the case, remove the stud as described in Chapter One. When the broken stud has been removed, install the new stud as described in Step 10.

10. Replace damaged cylinder studs as follows:

NOTE
If a stud removal tool is available, use the tool to remove or install the studs, when appropriate, throughout the procedure.

a. Thread two nuts onto the stud, as shown in **Figure 22**. Fit a wrench onto the lower nut (**Figure 23**) and snug the nut against the top nut. Turn the wrench counterclockwise to remove the stud. If necessary, apply penetrating oil to the stud threads in the case. Work the stud back and forth, easing it from the case.

b. Clean the case threads and check for damage. If the threads are only lightly damaged, use the appropriate-size metric thread tap to true the threads.

c. Check that the length of the new stud (below the shoulder) is identical to the length of the removed stud.

d. Remove the nuts from the damaged stud and place them on the new stud (**Figure 24**).

e. Seat the new stud into the case.

f. Torque the stud (**Figure 25**) to the specifications in **Table 3**.

> *NOTE*
> *The shoulders on the two studs on the exhaust side of the cylinder rest above the cylinder surface (**Figure 26**). Do not overtorque the studs when attempting to seat them into the cylinder.*

g. Use two wrenches to separate and remove the nuts. Hold the lower nut and turn the upper nut counterclockwise.

11. Wash the cylinder in hot, soapy water, then rinse with clean, cool water. Dry with compressed air. Lubricate the cylinder bore with two-stroke engine oil to prevent corrosion.

12. Install the exhaust valve assembly as described in this chapter.

13. Perform any service to the piston assembly before installing the cylinder.

14. Keep the reconditioned cylinder wrapped in plastic until engine reassembly.

Installation

> *NOTE*
> *The exhaust valve assembly must be installed in the cylinder before installing the cylinder.*

1. Check that all gasket residue is removed from all mating surfaces.

2. Install the dowels on the two left cylinder studs (**Figure 15**).

3. Install a *new* base gasket onto the crankcase.

4. Support the piston so it is stabilized (**Figure 27**).

> *NOTE*
> *A piston holding fixture can be made as shown in **Figure 28**. The holding tool will limit piston movement and will prevent the piston from contact-*

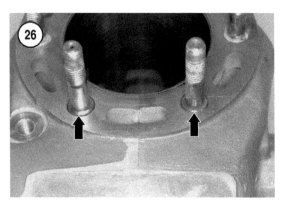

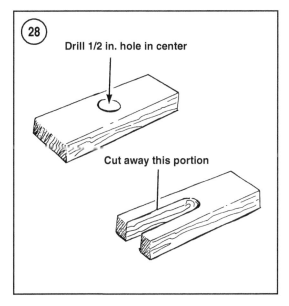

Drill 1/2 in. hole in center

Cut away this portion

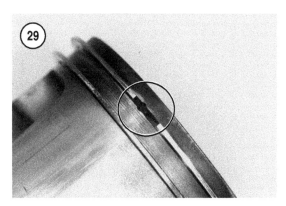

ing the crankcase when the cylinder is lowered into place. Place the holding tool under the piston so it is straddling the connecting rod. Turn the crankshaft to seat the piston against the fixture.

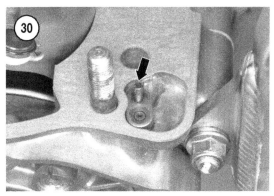

5. Lubricate the piston, rings and cylinder bore with two-stroke engine oil.

6. Check that each ring end gap is properly located around its respective locating pin (**Figure 29**).

7. At the top of the crankcase, apply lithium-base grease to the pinion joint cavity and position the pinion shaft as shown in **Figure 30**.

CAUTION
In the following step, do not twist the cylinder when installing it over the piston. The piston rings could snag in the intake port, causing damage to the ring and piston.

8. Install the cylinder as follows:

   a. Align the cylinder over the piston.

   b. Compress each ring by hand and guide the piston straight into cylinder. Rest the cylinder on the piston holding fixture.

   c. Turn the valve link counterclockwise and check that the flap valve and subexhaust valves are fully closed.

NOTE
In the next substep, the slot in the valve drive shaft (Figure 31) must engage with the pin on the pinion shaft (Figure 30) as the cylinder is lowered into place. When lowering the cylinder, turn the valve link, as needed, to align the slot with the pin. If the parts do not engage, the exhaust valve system will not operate.

   d. Remove the piston holding fixture, then guide the cylinder and exhaust valve linkage into place. Check that the cylinder is fully seated on the crankcase.

9. Lubricate the crankcase studs and finger-tighten the cylinder base nuts.

10. Torque the nuts (**Figure 32**) equally in three passes and in a crossing pattern. Refer to **Table 3** for the required torque.

> *NOTE*
> *A torque wrench adapter is required to torque the cylinder base nuts. When the adapter is attached to the torque wrench as shown in **Figure 33**, the torque specification does not have to be recalculated. The adapter shown is made by Motion Pro. Refer to Chapter One for additional information about torque wrenches and recalculating torque specifications.*

11. If the exhaust valves and linkage have been serviced, perform the *Exhaust Valve Linkage Adjustment* as described in this chapter.

12. Install a *new* gasket and the right cylinder cover (**Figure 13**).

13. Install the cylinder head and reed valve assembly as described in this chapter.

> *NOTE*
> *At this point of assembly, it is recommended to perform a leakdown test as described in Chapter Two to ensure the engine is air-tight.*

14. Install the carburetor as described in Chapter Eight.

15. Install the exhaust pipe as described in this chapter.

PISTON AND PISTON RINGS

Refer to Chapter Three for the recommended replacement intervals for the individual piston components. Keep accurate records as to when parts have been replaced. This will help in troubleshooting and determining the parts to have on hand when rebuilding the top end.

As each component of the piston assembly is cleaned and measured, record and identify all measurements. The measurements will be referred to when calculating clearances and checking wear limits.

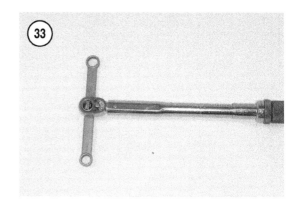

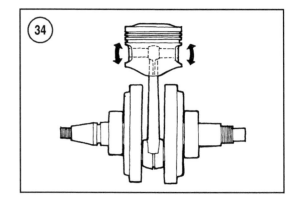

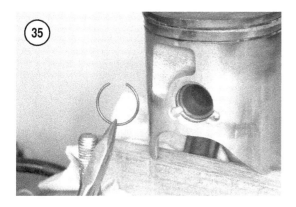

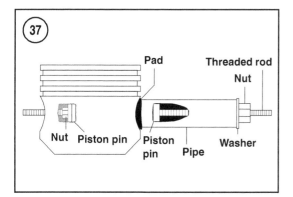

Pad   Threaded rod

Nut

Nut   Piston pin   Piston   Washer
                     pin   Pipe

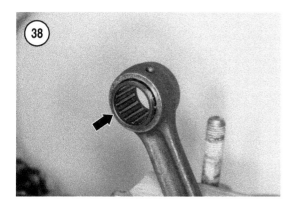

Piston Removal

1. Remove the cylinder as described in this chapter.
2. Before removing the piston, hold the rod and try to rock the piston side to side (**Figure 34**). If rocking (not sliding) motion is detected, this indicates wear on either the piston pin, pin bore or needle bearing. Wear could be on any combination of the three parts. Careful inspection will be required to determine which parts should be replaced.
3. Wrap clean shop cloths around the connecting rod to prevent debris and small parts from falling into the crankcase (**Figure 27**).
4. Remove the circlips from the piston pin bore (**Figure 35**). Discard the circlips.

CAUTION
New circlips must be installed during assembly.

5. Press the piston pin out of the piston (**Figure 36**). If the pin is tight, a simple removal tool can be made as shown in **Figure 37**. The end of the padded pipe rests against the piston, not the piston pin. The hole in the pipe must be larger than the diameter of the piston pin. As the nut on the end of the rod is tightened, the nut and washer at the opposite end pull the piston pin into the pipe.

CAUTION
Do not attempt to drive the pin out with a hammer and drift. The piston and connecting rod assembly will likely be damaged.

6. Lift the piston off the connecting rod.
7. Remove the needle bearing from the connecting rod (**Figure 38**).
8. Wrap and protect the connecting rod with a shop cloth.
9. Inspect the piston and piston pin as described in this section.

Piston Inspection

1. Remove the piston rings as described in this section.
2. Clean the carbon from the piston crown using a soft scraper and solvent. Do not use tools that can gouge or scratch the surface. This type of damage can cause hot spots on the piston when the engine is running.

3. Clean the piston pin bore, ring grooves and piston skirt. Clean the ring grooves with a soft brush (such as a toothbrush), or use a broken piston ring (**Figure 39**) to remove carbon and oil residue. Replace the piston if there is evidence of galling or discoloration of the piston skirt.

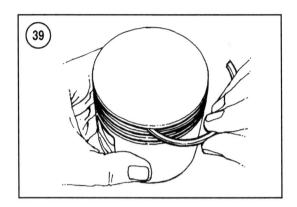

> *CAUTION*
> *Do not use a wire brush to clean the piston.*

4. Inspect the piston crown for signs of wear or damage. If the piston is pitted, overheating is likely occurring. This can be caused by a lean fuel mixture and/or preignition. If damage is evident, troubleshoot the problem as described in Chapter Two.

5. Inspect the ring grooves for dents, nicks, cracks or other damage. The grooves should be uniform for the circumference of the piston. The locating pin in each ring groove should be tight and not missing. Replace the piston if any type of damage is detected.

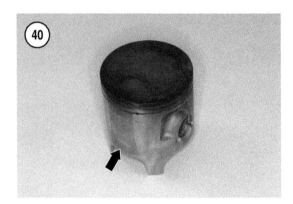

6. Inspect the piston skirt (**Figure 40**). If the skirt shows signs of severe galling or partial seizure (bits of metal imbedded in the skirt), replace the piston.

7. Inspect the interior of the piston (**Figure 41**). Check the crown, skirt, piston pin bores and bosses for cracks or other damage. Check the circlip grooves for cleanliness and damage. Replace the piston if necessary.

8. Measure the piston pin bores with a small hole gauge and micrometer (**Figure 42**). Measure each bore horizontally and vertically. Record the measurements. Compare the largest measurement to the specifications in **Table 2**. Keep this measurement for determining the piston pin-to-piston clearance, as described in *Piston Pin and Connecting Rod Inspection*.

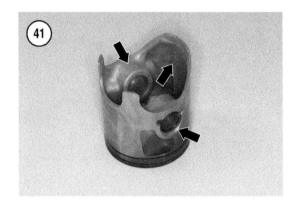

9. Inspect the piston ring to ring groove clearance as described in *Piston Ring Inspection and Removal* in this chapter.

Piston-to-Cylinder Clearance Check

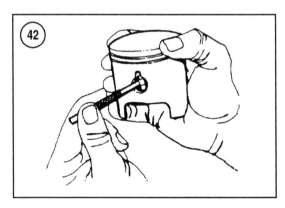

> *CAUTION*
> *Before determining the piston wear, the piston size must be identified. Cylinders and pistons are matched according to their dimensions at time of manufacture. The piston code, A or B, is indicated on the top of the piston. When referring to **Table 2**, use the dimensions that are specific to the piston size.*

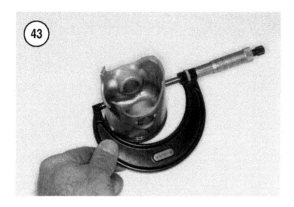

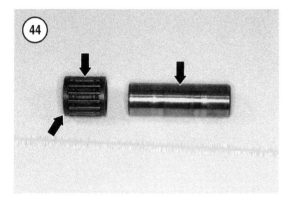

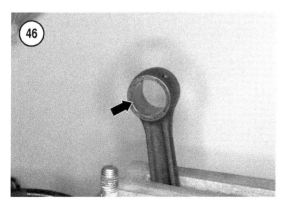

1. Measure the outside diameter of the piston. Measure 15-25 mm (0.59-0.98 in.) up from the bottom edge of the piston skirt and 90° to the direction of the piston pin (**Figure 43**). Record the measurement. Compare the measurement to the specifications in **Table 2**. If the piston is in good condition, proceed to Step 2.

2. Determine clearance by subtracting the piston measurement from the largest cylinder measurement. If cylinder measurements are not yet known, the procedure is described under *Cylinder Inspection* in this chapter. Replace or resleeve the cylinder if the clearance exceeds the specification in **Table 2**. The cylinder cannot be overbored.

Piston Pin, Needle Bearing and Connecting Rod Inspection

1. Clean the piston pin and needle bearing in solvent, then wipe dry.

2. Inspect the pin and bearing rollers (**Figure 44**) for flaking, wear or discoloration. Check the bearing cage for cracks or fatigue.

3. Measure the outside diameter of the pin at the three contact points (**Figure 45**). Compare the measurements to the specifications in **Table 2**.

4. Determine the piston pin-to-piston clearance. Subtract the smallest piston pin end measurement from the largest piston pin bore measurement. The bore measurement is described in *Piston Inspection* in this section. Compare the measurement to the specifications in **Table 2**.

5. Inspect the bore in the small end of the connecting rod (**Figure 46**) as follows:

    a. Check for scoring, uneven wear and discoloration.

    b. Measure the inside diameter of the bore and compare the measurement to the specifications in **Table 2**. If the rod is worn, the rod and crankshaft must be replaced as a single part.

    c. Insert the needle bearing and piston pin into the connecting rod (**Figure 47**). Check for perceptible play in the pin and bearing. If the rod bore is within specification, and play is detected, replace the piston pin and bearing.

Piston Ring Removal and Inspection

1. Remove the top ring with a ring expander or by hand (**Figure 48**). Spread the ring only enough to clear

the piston. Label the ring so it may be reinstalled in the correct groove. Repeat this step for the second ring.

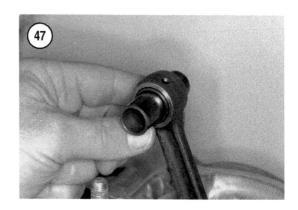

> *WARNING*
> *Piston ring edges are sharp. Be care-*
> *ful when handling.*

> *CAUTION*
> *Piston rings are brittle. Do not over-*
> *spread rings when removing.*

2. Clean and inspect the piston as described under *Piston Inspection* in this section.
3. Inspect the end gap of each ring as follows:
   a. Insert the ring into the bottom of the cylinder. Use the piston to push the ring squarely into the cylinder. Push the ring far enough into the cylinder so it fully contacts the cylinder wall. This area of the cylinder should have minimal wear.

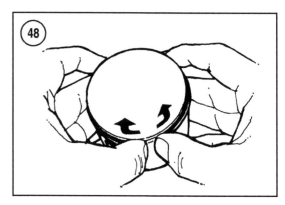

   b. Measure the end gap with a feeler gauge (**Figure 49**). Replace both rings if any gap measurement exceeds the service limit in **Table 2**. Always replace rings as a set. If new rings are to be installed, gap the new rings after the cylinder has been serviced. If the new ring gap is too narrow, carefully widen the gap using a fine-cut file as shown in **Figure 50**. Work slowly and measure often.
4. Roll each ring around its piston groove and check for binding or snags (**Figure 51**). Repair minor damage with a fine-cut file.

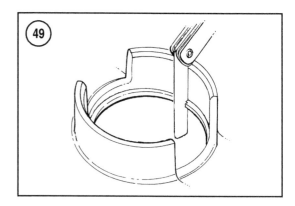

5. Install the rings on the piston as described in *Piston Ring Installation* in this section, then measure the piston ring-to-ring groove clearance as follows:
   a. Press the top ring into the groove, so the ring is nearly flush with the piston.
   b. Insert a flat feeler gauge between the ring and groove (**Figure 52**). Record the measurement. Repeat this step at other points around the piston. Replace the rings if any measurement exceeds the service limit in **Table 2**. If excessive clearance remains after new rings are installed, replace the piston.
   c. Repeat Step 5 for the second ring.

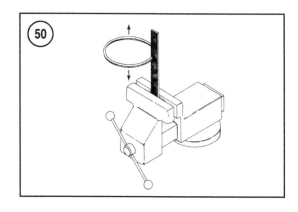

Piston Ring Installation

1. Check that the piston and rings are clean and dry.

> *CAUTION*
> *When installing rings, check that the IT*
> *mark (stamped near the end gap) on*

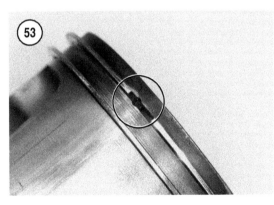

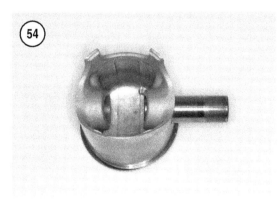

*each ring faces up. Piston rings are brittle. Do not overspread rings when installing. Install rings with a ring expander or by hand (**Figure 48**). Spread rings only enough to clear the piston.*

2. Lubricate the rings and ring grooves with two-stroke engine oil.

3. Install the rings into their respective ring grooves as follows:

    a. Check that the IT mark on the bottom ring is facing up.

    b. Position the ring over the piston so the ring end gap is aligned with the groove locating pin.

    c. Spread the ring and slide it over the piston and into the groove.

    d. Check that the ring is free in the groove. The ends of the ring must seat to both sides of the locating pin (**Figure 53**).

4. Repeat Step 3 to install the top ring.

Piston Installation

1. Install the piston rings onto the piston as described in this chapter.

2. Check that parts are clean and ready to be installed.

> *CAUTION*
> *Never install used circlips. Severe engine damage could occur. Circlips fatigue and distort when they are removed, even though they appear reusable.*

3. Install a *new* circlip into one end of the pin boss. Rotate the circlip in the groove until the end gap is facing away from the piston cutouts.

4. Lubricate the following components with two-stroke engine oil.

    a. Piston pin.

    b. Piston bores.

    c. Connecting rod bore.

    d. Needle bearing.

5. Insert the needle bearing into the connecting rod bore (**Figure 38**).

6. Start the piston pin into the open pin bore (**Figure 54**).

7. Place the piston over the connecting rod so the IN mark stamped on the piston crown faces the rear (intake side) of the engine. Align the piston with the rod, then slide the pin through the rod and opposite piston bore.

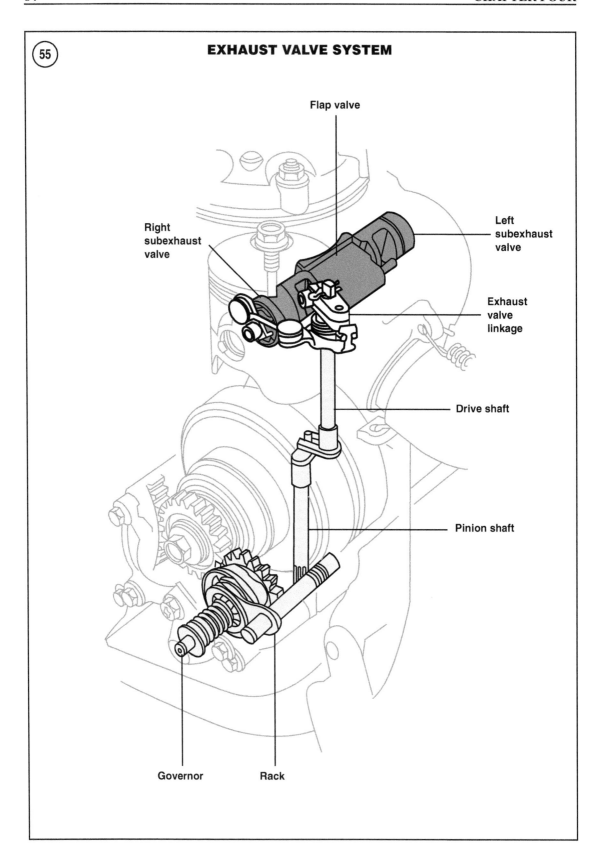

EXHAUST VALVE SYSTEM

⑤⑤

Flap valve

Right subexhaust valve

Left subexhaust valve

Exhaust valve linkage

Drive shaft

Pinion shaft

Governor

Rack

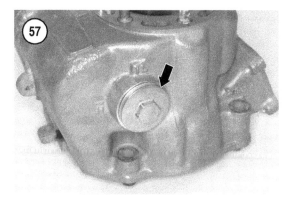

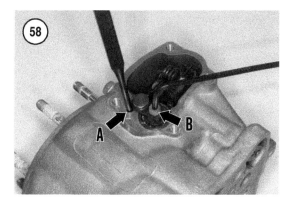

8. Install the other new circlip into the end of the pin boss. Rotate the circlip in the groove until the end gap is facing away from the piston cutouts.

9. Install the cylinder as described in this chapter.

EXHAUST VALVE SYSTEM

The exhaust valve system (Honda Composite Racing Valve) is designed to broaden the powerband from low to high engine speeds. This is achieved by varying the exhaust port timing, and

the amount of exhaust pulse to the expansion chamber. The exhaust valve system consists of three major assemblies, as shown in **Figure 55**. These assemblies are:

1. Subexhaust valves and flap valve. This also includes the shafts, bearings and flap valve. These parts are located in the cylinder.

2. Exhaust valve linkage. This includes the valve link assembly and drive shaft. These parts are located in the cylinder.

3. Exhaust valve governor and linkage. This includes the governor assembly, rack and pinion shaft. These parts are located in the crankcase.

At low engine speeds, the flap valve closes the *timed* exhaust port, and the exhaust valves route a portion of the exhaust to a subexhaust chamber, cast into the cylinder. This alters the exhaust pulse to the expansion chamber and enhances low-end power. As engine speed increases, the flap valve opens and the exhaust valves close, routing the complete exhaust pulse to the expansion chamber and realizing the full power potential.

The flap valve and exhaust valves are linked and controlled by a centrifugal governor, driven by the primary drive gear. The recommended time interval for disassembling and cleaning the exhaust valve system is the same as that for replacing the piston and rings. Always clean and inspect the exhaust valve system whenever the cylinder is removed. Always replace parts that are worn or damaged.

The following procedures detail the removal and servicing of the three major assemblies shown in **Figure 55**.

SUBEXHAUST VALVES
AND FLAP VALVE

Removal

1. Remove the cylinder as described in this chapter.

2. Remove the right cylinder cover (**Figure 56**) and the left exhaust valve cap (**Figure 57**).

3. Disconnect the valve link from the right subexhaust valve as follows:

    a. Insert a drift or punch into the hole to the left of the link (A, **Figure 58**). This will prevent binding of the linkage when the socket bolt is removed.

    b. Remove the Allen bolt (B, **Figure 58**).

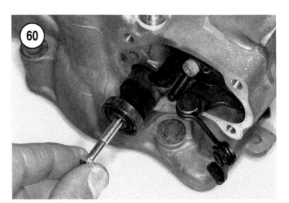

4. Loosen the stopper bolt (**Figure 59**) and back it out at least 7 mm (0.3 in.). Remove the bolt if the cylinder will be reconditioned.

5. Remove the bearing, right subexhaust valve and shaft from the cylinder (**Figure 60**).

> *NOTE*
> *The shaft can be difficult to remove from the subexhaust valve if there is buildup on the shaft. Work slowly and avoid bending the shaft. If the shaft is bent, it must be replaced. A bent shaft will not allow the subexhaust valve to operate properly.*

6. Remove the snap ring and collar (**Figure 61**) from the left subexhaust valve.

7. Remove the bearing and left subexhaust valve (**Figure 62**).

8. Remove the flap valve shaft (**Figure 63**), then remove the flap valve as follows:

   a. On 1997-1998 models, remove the flap valve through the exhaust port.

   b. On 1999-2001 models, remove the flap valve through the cylinder (**Figure 64**).

9. Clean and inspect the parts as described in this section.

10. Remove the exhaust valve linkage as described in this section.

11. Clean and inspect the cylinder as described in this chapter.

Inspection

1. Soak the parts in solvent and allow the carbon and oil buildup to soften. Use a wire brush to scrub heavy buildup. Avoid scratching the parts. Flush all parts with clean solvent.

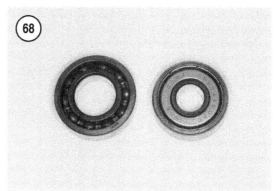

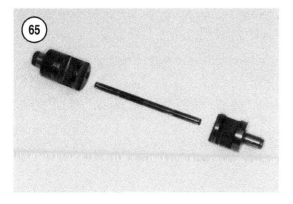

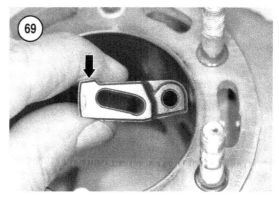

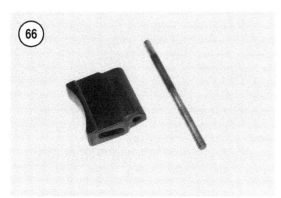

2. Inspect the subexhaust valves and shaft for wear or damage (**Figure 65**).

3. Inspect the flap valve and shaft for wear or damage (**Figure 66**).

4. Measure the outside diameter of both shafts at all contact areas along the shafts (**Figure 67**). Refer to **Table 2** for the service limit.

5. Inspect the bearings (**Figure 68**). Check that they operate smoothly and have no play in the bearing races.

6. Install the parts as described in this section.

Installation

1. Install the flap valve and shaft as follows:

    a. Apply molybdenum paste to the flap valve shaft.

    b. Insert the flap valve into the cylinder, checking that the projection on the flap valve faces up (**Figure 69**).

> *NOTE*
> *On 1997-1998 models, install the flap valve through the exhaust port. On 1999-2001 models, install the flap valve through the cylinder.*

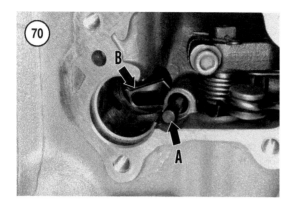

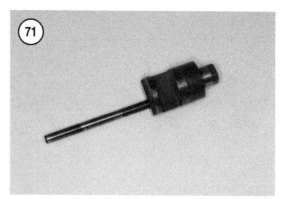

c. Align the hole in the flap valve, then insert the shaft through the valve (A, **Figure 70**).

2. Install the right subexhaust valve and shaft as follows:

a. Apply molybdenum paste to the shaft.

b. Apply two-stroke engine oil to the valve.

c. Insert the shaft into the valve (**Figure 71**).

d. Position the flap valve so the slot in the valve is visible (B, **Figure 70**).

e. Insert the valve and shaft assembly into the cylinder, guiding the shaft through the slot in the flap valve (**Figure 72**).

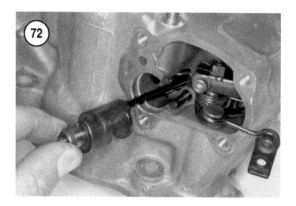

3. Install the stopper bolt and washer as follows:

a. Turn the exhaust valve so the cutaway on the end of the valve is facing up.

b. Thread the stopper bolt down so the end of the bolt is in the cutaway area (**Figure 73**).

c. Torque the stopper bolt to the specification in **Table 3**.

4. Install the bearing (**Figure 74**) with the manufacturer's marks facing out.

5. Install the left subexhaust valve assembly (**Figure 75**) as follows:

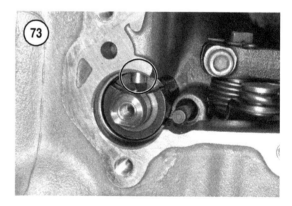

a. Apply two-stroke engine oil to the valve and collar.

b. Align the hole in the valve with the shaft (**Figure 76**), then install the valve onto the shaft.

c. Install the bearing with the manufacturer's marks facing out.

d. Install the collar with the stepped side (**Figure 77**) facing in.

e. Install the snap ring.

f. Install a *new*, lubricated O-ring on the left exhaust valve cap. Apply molybdenum paste to the cap threads, then torque the cap to the specifications in **Table 3**.

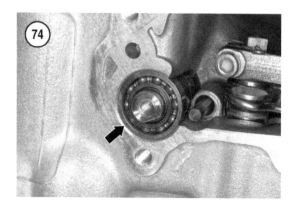

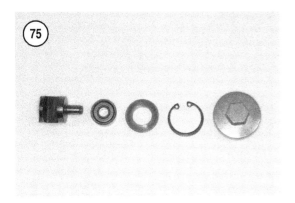

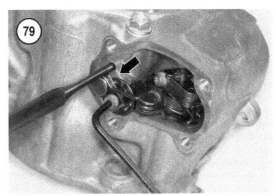

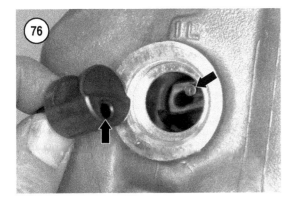

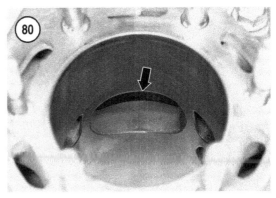

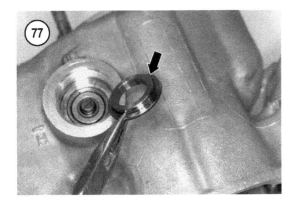

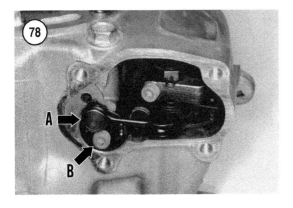

NOTE
If necessary, install the exhaust valve
linkage into the cylinder at this time.
Return to Step 6 to complete the in-
stallation.

6. Connect the valve link to the right subexhaust valve as follows:

   a. Seat the link (A, **Figure 78**) against the end of the valve. The tab on the link plate should fit under the end of the valve. Finger-tighten the socket bolt (B) to temporarily hold the assembly in place.

   b. Rotate the valve link counterclockwise, then insert a drift or punch into the hole to the right of the link (**Figure 79**). This will prevent binding of the linkage when the socket bolt is tightened.

   c. Tighten the socket bolt.

7. Operate the valve link and verify that the flap valve opens and closes (**Figure 80**). The flap valve must fully close when the valve link is turned counterclockwise. If the flap valve does not fully close, refer to the *Exhaust Valve Linkage Adjustment* pro-

cedure in this chapter. The adjustment is made after the cylinder is installed on the crankcase.

8. Install the cylinder as described in this chapter.

> *NOTE*
> *Do not install the right cylinder cover until the cylinder has been bolted to the crankcase. Access to the exhaust valve linkage is necessary to properly align the cylinder linkage with the crankcase linkage.*

> *NOTE*
> *Perform the **Exhaust Valve Operation Check** after the engine is assembled and will start.*

EXHAUST VALVE LINKAGE

The exhaust valve linkage in the cylinder includes the valve link assembly and the drive shaft (**Figure 55**). The linkage opens and closes the exhaust valves and flap valve. Whenever the linkage is disassembled, it must be readjusted to synchronize the governor with the exhaust valves and flap valve.

Removal

1. Disconnect the valve link from the subexhaust valve (A, **Figure 81**), as described in *Subexhaust Valves and Flap Valve Removal* in this chapter.
2. Loosen the Allen bolt (B, **Figure 81**).
3. Remove the clip from the drive shaft (**Figure 82**).
4. Remove the valve link assembly from the drive shaft, while pulling the drive shaft and bushing (**Figure 83**) out the bottom of the cylinder.
5. Separate the parts of the linkage: valve link (A, **Figure 84**), bushing (B), spring (C) and drive pinion (D).
6. Inspect the parts as described in this section.

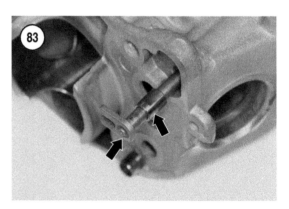

Inspection

1. Soak the parts in solvent and allow the carbon and oil buildup to soften. If necessary, use a wire brush to scrub heavy buildup. Flush all parts with clean solvent.
2. Inspect all parts for wear, fatigue or damage.
3. Check the fit of:

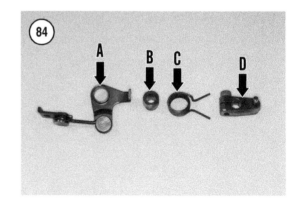

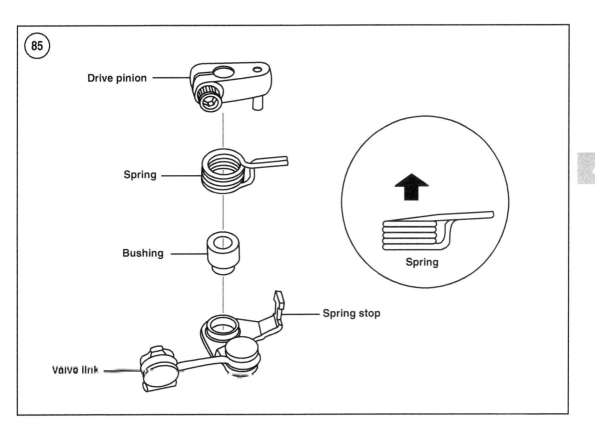

Drive pinion

Spring

Bushing

Spring

Spring stop

Valve link

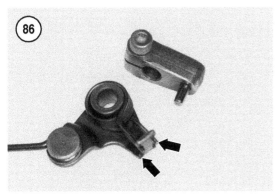

a. The drive shaft in the drive pinion. The drive pinion should not be excessively loose and the shaft should not be worn where the pinion attaches.

b. The bushing on the drive shaft. The bushing should be not be excessively loose, or tight on the shaft.

4. Install the valve linkage as described in this section.

Installation

1. Assemble the valve linkage (**Figure 85**) before installing it into the cylinder. Assemble as follows:

   a. Lay the valve link on a flat surface.

   b. Insert the narrow end of the bushing into the valve link.

   c. Orient the spring so the ends are at the top. Compress the ends together so the spring is preloaded, then fit the spring around the bushing and spring stop (**Figure 86**).

   d. Place the drive pinion on top of the linkage assembly. Fit the pin in the drive pinion between the spring (**Figure 87**).

2. Apply grease to the drive shaft and bushing.

3. Fit the bushing onto the drive shaft, then guide the shaft through the bottom of the cylinder (**Figure 83**).

4. Align the valve linkage assembly with the drive shaft, then slide the shaft through the assembly.

5. Insert the clip into the drive shaft (**Figure 82**).

> *NOTE*
> *If necessary, install the subexhaust valves and flap valve into the cylinder at this time. Return to Step 6 to complete the installation.*

6. Connect the valve link to the subexhaust valve (A, **Figure 81**), as described in *Subexhaust Valves and Flap Valve Installation* in this chapter. Operate the valve link and check for smooth operation.

> *NOTE*
> *Do not tighten the drive pinion socket bolt at this time. The socket bolt will be tightened when the linkage is adjusted, after cylinder installation.*

7. Apply molydisulfide oil to the valve link joints.

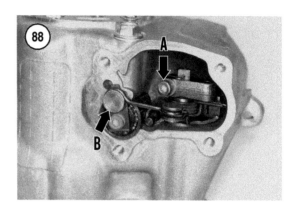

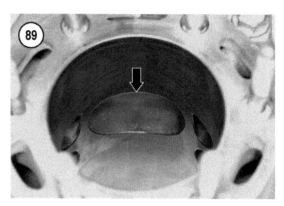

Adjustment

Whenever the Allen bolt (B, **Figure 81**) is loosened from the drive pinion, the linkage must be adjusted to synchronize the governor with the exhaust valves and flap valve. Adjust the linkage after the cylinder has been installed on the crankcase. All parts of the exhaust valve system, including those in the crankcase, must be installed.

1. Check that the Allen bolt (A, **Figure 88**) is loose and the drive pinion is free on the drive shaft.

2. Rotate the valve link (B, **Figure 88**) counterclockwise and verify that the flap valve is fully closed (**Figure 89**). Hold the valve link in this position.

3. Tighten the Allen bolt so the drive pinion grips the drive shaft. Torque the bolt to the specifications in **Table 3**.

4. Check the ends of the spring against the spring stop. There should be 0-0.5 mm (0-0.02 in) clearance between the spring and stop (**Figure 90**). If clearance is not correct, loosen the Allen bolt and readjust the linkage.

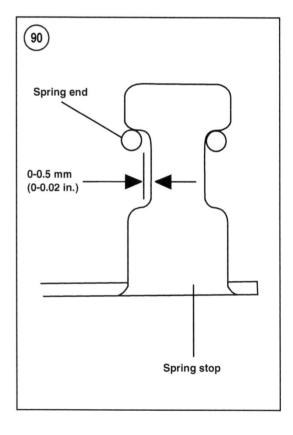

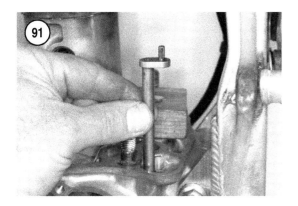

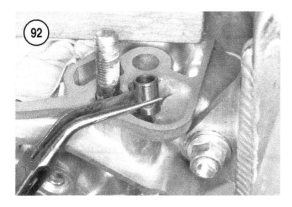

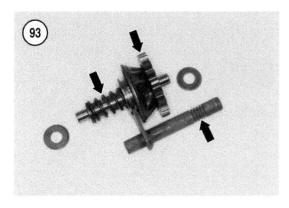

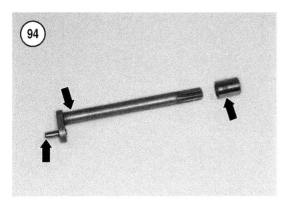

EXHAUST VALVE GOVERNOR AND LINKAGE

The exhaust valve governor and linkage is located in the crankcase. Refer to **Figure 55** to see how it is linked to the exhaust valve components in the cylinder.

Removal

1. Remove the cylinder as described in this chapter.
2. Remove the right crankcase cover as described in Chapter Six.
3. Remove the pinion shaft from the crankcase (**Figure 91**).
4. Remove the pinion shaft bushing from the crankcase (**Figure 92**).
5. Remove the governor, rack and washers. A washer is at each end of the governor.
6. Inspect the parts as described in this section.

Inspection

The governor cannot be disassembled. If damage is evident, the governor assembly must be replaced.
1. Wash the parts in solvent and dry with compressed air.
2. Inspect the governor and rack (**Figure 93**) for:
    a. Broken or worn gear teeth.
    b. Broken spring.
    c. Worn or damaged rack teeth.
3. Inspect the pinion shaft and bushing (**Figure 94**) for:
    a. Shaft and bushing wear. The bushing should be not be excessively loose, or tight on the shaft.
    b. Shaft pin wear.

Installation

1. Apply transmission oil to the governor bearing and sliding surface of the rack.
2. Apply molybdenum paste to the pinion shaft and bushing.
3. Seat the bushing into the crankcase (**Figure 95**).
4. Assemble the governor as follows:
    a. Place a washer (A, **Figure 96**) on each end of the governor shaft.

b. Engage the rack (B, **Figure 96**) with the groove in the governor.

5. Insert the governor assembly into the crankcase, aligning the rack teeth (A, **Figure 97**) with the pinion shaft guide (B). Hold the governor in this position.

6. Insert the pinion shaft into the crankcase (**Figure 91**) and engage it with the rack (**Figure 98**).

7. Install the right crankcase cover as described in Chapter Six.

8. Install the cylinder as described in this chapter.

EXHAUST VALVE OPERATION CHECK

Check the exhaust valve operation after the engine is assembled and capable of running.

1. Warm the engine to operating temperature, then shut off the engine.

2. Remove the left exhaust valve cap so the end of the left exhaust valve is visible.

3. Check that the groove in the exhaust valve (A, **Figure 99**) is aligned with the L index mark on the cylinder (B, **Figure 99**).

4. Start the engine.

5. While viewing the slot in the exhaust valve, raise the engine speed and check that the slot rotates counterclockwise and aligns with the H index mark on the cylinder (C, **Figure 99**).

6. Stop the engine. If the marks aligned correctly, lubricate the cap O-ring (replace if necessary) and threads with molybdenum paste. Then torque the cap to the specification in **Table 3**. If the marks did not align, check the following areas of the exhaust valve system for the cause:

   a. Carbon buildup on exhaust valves and linkage.

   b. Loose Allen bolt on drive pinion.

   c. Valve drive shaft and pinion shaft not engaged.

REED VALVES

Removal

> *NOTE*
> *If the engine is equipped with an aftermarket reed valve assembly, refer to the manufacturer's instructions for removal, inspection and installation.*

1. Remove the carburetor as described in Chapter Eight.

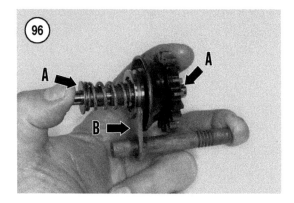

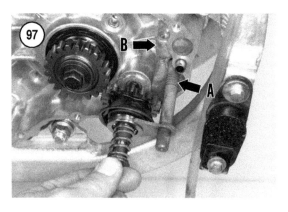

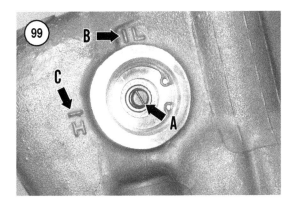

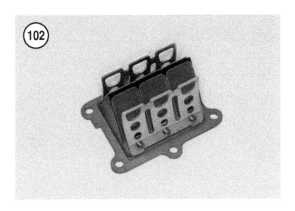

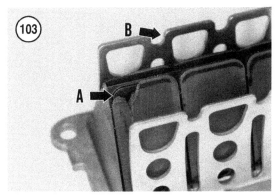

2. Remove the bolts securing the clutch cable clamp and insulator to the engine (**Figure 100**).

3. Remove the insulator (**Figure 101**).

4. Remove the reed valve assembly and gasket (**Figure 102**).

5. Disassemble and inspect the reed valves as described in this section.

Inspection and Disassembly

Record the reed valve replacement intervals in the maintenance log at the back of the manual. Refer to Chapter Three for recommended replacement intervals.

1. Inspect the reed valve assembly for:
   a. Broken, cracked or fatigued reed valves (A, **Figure 103**).
   b. Broken, cracked or damaged reed valve stoppers (B, **Figure 103**).
   c. Loose or missing stopper screws.

2. Disassemble and assemble the reed valve assembly as follows:
   a. Remove the screws at the base of each reed valve stopper and disassemble the parts.
   b. Install the reed valves and stopper by aligning the trimmed corners of both parts (**Figure 104**), then screwing the parts to the reed holder.

> *NOTE*
> *Use a small amount of threadlocking compound on the screw threads. Do not allow the compound to get on the reed valves.*

3. Use a flat feeler gauge and check reed valve clearance at the ends of the reeds (**Figure 105**). Clearance should be 0.2 mm (0.01 in.).

4. Install the reed valve assembly as described in this section.

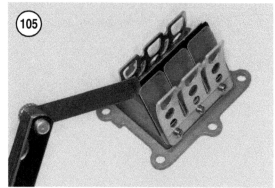

Installation

1. Place a *new* gasket on the crankcase.
2. Install the reed valve assembly with the tabbed edge (**Figure 106**) facing up.
3. Install the insulator (**Figure 101**).
4. Install the clutch cable clamp, then finger-tighten the bolts (**Figure 100**). Tighten the bolts evenly after the assembly is seated.
5. Install the carburetor as described in Chapter Eight.

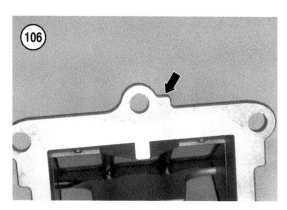

Table 1 ENGINE SPECIFICATIONS

Engine type	2-stroke, single cylinder, liquid cooled
Engine intake system	Crankcase reed valve
Engine displacement	249.3 cc (15.2 cu. in.)
Engine dry weight	23.3 kg (51.4 lb.)
Bore and stroke	66.4 × 72.0 mm (2.61 × 2.83 in.)
Lubrication	32:1 fuel/oil premixture
Compression ratio	8.7:1
Crankshaft	Assembly type
Ignition timing	
1997	18° at 3000 rpm
1998-2001	18° ± 2° at 3000 rpm

Table 2 ENGINE SERVICE SPECIFICATIONS

	New mm (in.)	Service limit mm (in.)
Cylinder bore diameter		
Measurement point	See text	
Inside diameter		
Size A cylinder	66.398-66.405	66.430
	(2.6141-2.6144)	(2.615)
Size B cylinder	66.390-66.398	66.428
	(2.6138-2.6141)	(2.615)
	(continued)	

Table 2 ENGINE SERVICE SPECIFICATIONS (continued)

	New mm (in.)	Service limit mm (in.)
Cylinder warp limit	–	0.05 (0.002)
Cylinder taper limit	–	0.05 (0.002)
Cylinder out of round limit	–	0.05 (0.002)
Cylinder head warp limit	–	0.05 (0.002)
Piston		
Outside diameter		
measurement point	15-25 (0.59-0.98) from skirt bottom	
Outside diameter		
Size A piston	66.330-66.338 (2.6114-2.6117)	66.28 (2.609)
Size B piston	66.323-66.330 (2.6111-2.6114)	66.273 (2.609)
Piston-to-cylinder clearance	0.060-0.075 (0.0024-0.0029)	0.09 (0.004)
Piston pin bore ID	18.007-18.013 (0.7089-0.7092)	18.02 (0.709)
Piston pin OD	17.994-18.000 (0.7084-0.7087)	17.98 (0.707)
Piston pin-to-piston clearance	0.007-0.019 (0.0003-0.0007)	0.04 (0.0016)
Piston ring-to-ring groove clearance		
Top ring	0.045 0.075 (0.002-0.003)	0.095 (0.0037)
Second ring	0.025-0.055 (0.001-0.002)	0.075 (0.026)
Piston ring end gap	0.40-0.55 (0.016-0.022)	0.65 (0.13)
Piston mark direction	IN facing intake side	
Connecting rod small end ID	21.997-22.009 (0.8660-0.8665)	22.02 (0.867)
Exhaust valve shaft OD	4.988-5.000 (0.1964-0.1969)	4.968 (0.196)

Table 3 ENGINE TORQUE SPECIFICATIONS

	N•m	in.-lb.	ft.-lb.
Cylinder mounting nuts	39	–	29
Cylinder head nuts	27	–	20
Cylinder stud bolts	12	106	–
Cylinder cover bolts (right)	10	88	–
Engine upper mounting nut			
1997-1999	39	–	29
2000-2001	54	–	40
Engine lower mounting nuts			
1997-1998	39	–	29
1999	64	–	47
2000-2001	54	–	40
Engine hanger plate nuts	26	–	20
Engine stop button screw	1.5	13	–
	(continued)		

Table 3 ENGINE TORQUE SPECIFICATIONS (continued)

	N•m	in.-lb.	ft.-lb.
Exhaust front chamber bolt			
1998-1999	10	88	–
2000	12	106	–
2001	14	–	10
Exhaust valve cap (left)	13	115	–
Exhaust valve stopper bolt	16	–	–
Exhaust valve			
linkage Allen bolt	5.4	48	–
Exhaust valve pinion holder			
Allen bolt	5.4	48	–
Spark plug	18	–	13

CHAPTER FIVE

ENGINE LOWER END

This chapter provides procedures for servicing or removing the following lower end components:

1. Crankcase, bearings and seals.
2. Crankshaft and connecting rod.
3. Transmission.

To access and service these components, the engine must be removed from the frame to separate the crankcase.

Read this chapter before attempting repairs to the engine lower end. Become familiar with the procedures and illustrations to understand the skill and equipment required. Refer to Chapter One for tool usage and techniques.

SHOP CLEANLINESS

Prior to removing and disassembling the engine, clean the engine and frame with degreaser. The disassembly job will go easier and there will be less chance of dirt entering the assemblies. Keep the work environment as clean as possible. Store parts and assemblies in well-marked plastic bags and containers. Keep reconditioned parts wrapped and lubricated until they will be installed.

ENGINE

The following removal and installation procedure outlines the basic steps necessary to remove the engine from the frame. Depending on the planned level of disassembly, it may be easier to remove top end components, and those located in the crankcase covers, while the engine remains in the frame. Since the frame keeps the engine stabilized, tight nuts and bolts are easier to remove if the engine is held steady. Also, the actual engine problem may be discovered in an assembly other than the crankcase.

Refer to the appropriate chapters for removal, inspection and installation procedures for the components in the engine top end and crankcase covers.

Removal and Installation

1. Support the bike so it is stable and level.

2. If possible, perform a compression test as described in Chapter Three and leakdown test as described in Chapter Two before dismantling the engine.

3. Remove the seat, fuel tank, side covers and radiator shrouds as described in the appropriate chapters.

4. Drain the engine coolant and transmission oil as described in Chapter Three.

5. Remove the exhaust pipe as described in Chapter Four.

6. Remove the brake pedal and rear brake master cylinder reservoir as described in Chapter Fourteen.

7. Remove the drive chain, guard and drive sprocket as described in Chapter Eleven.

8. Disconnect the clutch cable at the engine as described in Chapter Six.

9. Remove the carburetor as described in Chapter Eight.

10. Disconnect the ignition system.

   a. On 1997-1999 models, the connectors are located between the frame members (**Figure 1**).

   b. On 2000-2001 models, the connectors are located at the steering head.

11. Remove the spark plug cap and coolant hose on the cylinder head (**Figure 2**).

12. Remove the coolant hose from the water pump (**Figure 3**).

13. Remove the bolts and hanger plates at the top of the engine (**Figure 4**). Note the direction of the bolts when removing.

14. Remove the lower mounting nuts (**Figure 5**). Do not remove the bolts at this time.

15. Remove the swing arm pivot nut (**Figure 6**). Do not remove the pivot shaft at this time.

16. Check that all hoses, cables and wires are disconnected from the engine.

> *WARNING*
> *Check that the frame is properly supported and stable before removing the lower mounting bolts and pivot bolt. Get assistance when removing the engine from the frame.*

17. Note the direction of the lower mounting bolts, then remove the bolts.

18. Note the direction of the swing arm pivot shaft, then remove the shaft.

19. Remove the engine from the frame.

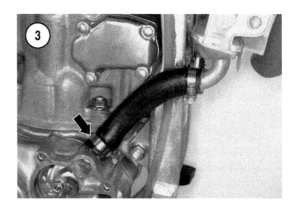

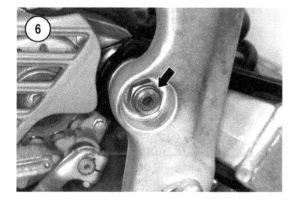

NOTE
If the engine is difficult to remove, raise the frame with a jack. This will separate the swing arm from the rear engine boss.

20. Clean and inspect the engine mounting area of the frame. Check for cracks and damage, particularly at welded joints.

21. Refer to the procedures in this chapter for servicing the crankcase assembly.

22. Reverse this procedure to install the engine. Note the following:

    a. Before installing the engine into the frame, remove the pivot shaft and raise the frame with a jack (**Figure 7**). Adjust the jack as necessary to allow the engine to fit into place. Install the lower mounting bolts, noting their original direction. Finger-tighten the nuts at this time.

    b. Lower the jack so the frame and swing arm align. Lubricate the pivot shaft, then insert it through the engine and swing arm, noting the original direction of the shaft. Finger-tighten the nut at this time.

NOTE
*If the chain is endless (no master link) and was not separated at the time of engine removal, route the chain over the swing arm pivot (**Figure 8**) before aligning the swing arm to the frame.*

    c. Install the engine hanger plates, bolts and nuts. Finger-tighten the nuts at this time. Note the original direction of the bolts during installation.

NOTE
If the engine top end is not installed when the engine is mounted in the frame, do not tighten any mounting nuts until the hanger plates have been installed and aligned with their mounting points.

    d. Torque the mounting nuts and swing arm pivot nut to the specification in **Table 2**.

    e. Carefully route electrical wires so they are not pinched or in contact with surfaces that get hot.

    f. Apply dielectric grease to electrical connections before reconnecting.

g. If assemblies have been removed from the top end or crankcase covers, install those components. Refer to the appropriate chapters for inspection and installation procedures.

h. Fill the engine with transmission oil as described in Chapter Three.

i. Fill the cooling system with coolant as described in Chapter Three.

j. Adjust the clutch free play as described in Chapter Three.

k. Check throttle cable adjustment as described in Chapter Three.

l. Check rear brake pedal height as described in Chapter Three.

m. Check chain adjustment as described in Chapter Three.

n. Start the engine and check for leaks.

o. If the crankcase was separated, inspect for leakage at the inspection hole on the bottom of the crankcase (**Figure 9**).

p. Check throttle and clutch operation.

q. If the engine top-end was rebuilt, perform a compression check. Record the results and compare them to future checks.

r. Refer to the *Engine Break-In* procedure in Chapter Three.

CRANKCASE

The following procedures detail the disassembly and reassembly of the crankcase. When the two halves of the crankcase are disassembled or split, the crankshaft and transmission assemblies can be removed for inspection and repair. Before starting this procedure, remove the engine from the frame as described in this chapter.

The crankcase halves are made of cast aluminum alloy. Do not hammer or excessively pry on the cases. The cases will fracture or break. The cases are aligned and sealed at the joint by dowels and a gasket.

The crankshaft (**Figure 10**) consists of two full-circle flywheels that are a press-fit on the crankpin. The assembly is supported at each end by a ball bearing. The connecting rod and crankshaft are only available from Honda as a single part. If the connecting rod is damaged, it may be possible for a machine shop to disassemble the crankshaft, so an aftermarket connecting rod can be installed. Have

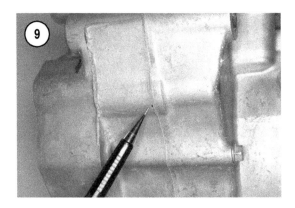

the machine shop evaluate the crankshaft to determine the possibility of repair.

Disassembly

Any reference to the *left* or *right* side of the engine, refers to the side of the engine as it is mounted in the frame, not on the workbench. As components are removed, keep each part separated from the other components. Keep seals and O-rings oriented with their respective parts.

1. Place the engine on wooden blocks with the left side facing up (**Figure 11**).

2. Loosen the 11 crankcase bolts (**Figure 11**). Loosen each bolt 1/4 turn, working in a crisscross pattern. Loosen the bolts until they can be removed by hand.

> *NOTE*
> *Anytime the bolt lengths vary, make a drawing of the crankcase shape on a piece of cardboard. Punch holes in the cardboard at the same locations as the bolts. As each bolt is removed from the crankcase, put the bolt in its respective hole in the template (**Figure 12**). This will ensure that the bolts are correctly located during assembly.*

3. Separate the crankcase halves as follows:

a. Attach a crankcase puller to the left case and the end of the crankshaft (**Figure 13**). Apply grease to the end of the crankshaft before threading the pressure bolt against the shaft.

> *CAUTION*
> *The puller must be mounted and remain parallel to the case when the*

CRANKCASE ASSEMBLY

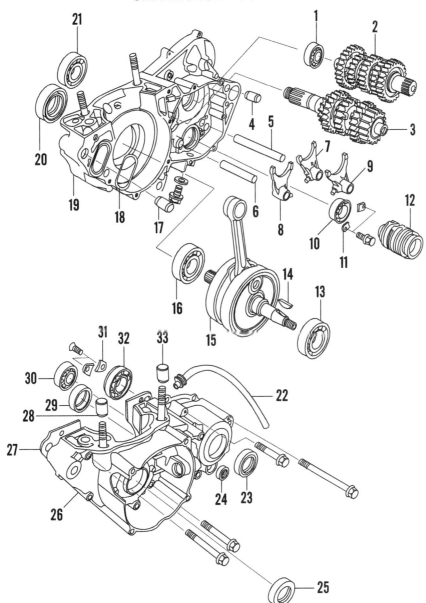

1. Countershaft bearing	12. Shift drum	23. Countershaft seal
2. Countershaft	13. Crankshaft bearing	24. Shift shaft seal
3. Mainshaft	14. Woodruff key	25. Crankshaft bearing seal
4. Dowel	15. Crankshaft	26. Left crankcase
5. Shift fork shaft	16. Crankshaft bearing	27. Gasket
6. Shift fork shaft	17. Dowel	28. Dowel
7. Right shift fork	18. O-ring	29. Shift drum bearing
8. Center shift fork	19. Right crankcase	30. Mainshaft bearing
9. Left shift fork	20. Crankshaft bearing seal	31. Bearing retainer
10. Shift drum bearing	21. Mainshaft bearing	32. Countershaft bearing
11. Bearing retainer	22. Breather tube	33. Dowel

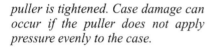

puller is tightened. Case damage can occur if the puller does not apply pressure evenly to the case.

NOTE
The crankcase puller (part No. 07937-4300000 or part No. 07937-4300001) and 6 mm bolt (part No. 07PMC-KZ40100) are available from a Honda dealership.

   b. Tighten the puller while occasionally tapping the case joint with a soft mallet. If necessary, tap on the end of the countershaft to loosen it from the left case. Work slowly and separate the cases equally. Do not allow the case to bind. If binding occurs, reseat the case halves and start again. When the cases separate, remove the puller.

CAUTION
Do not hammer or pry on the engine cases. Do not pry on gasket surfaces.

   c. Slowly raise and remove the left crankcase.
   d. Remove the two dowels (if loose) and O-ring from the case (**Figure 14**).
   e. Remove the gasket and residue from the case halves.

4. Remove the transmission assembly (**Figure 15**) from the case as follows:

CAUTION
Take extreme care when removing, handling and storing the transmission. Wrap and store the assembly until it will be inspected. Do not expose the assembly to dirt or place it in an area where it could roll and fall to the floor.

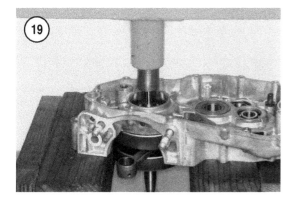

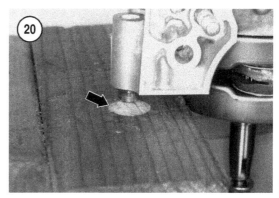

a. Remove the two shift fork shafts (**Figure 16**).

b. Remove the shift drum (**Figure 17**), disengaging it from the shift forks.

c. Remove the shift forks (**Figure 18**).

d. Remove the mainshaft and countershaft assemblies as a unit, keeping the gears meshed.

e. Disassemble and inspect the transmission as described in Chapter Seven.

5. Remove the crankshaft assembly from the case, using a press. Remove as follows:

> *CAUTION*
> *Take extreme care when removing, handling and storing the crankshaft. When pressing the crankshaft out of the crankcase, the crankshaft will fall from the case. Have adequate padding and assistance when performing this procedure. Wrap and store the crankshaft until it will be inspected. Do not expose the assembly to dirt or place it in an area where it could roll and fall to the floor. If the crankshaft is dropped, the crankpin will likely be knocked out of alignment.*

a. Support the right crankcase in a press, as shown in **Figure 19**. The case must rest flat on all support areas.

> *NOTE*
> *Ensure that the gasket surface cannot become scratched or gouged. If the dowels are still in the case, provide holes for the dowels (**Figure 20**), so pressure is not applied to the dowels. Check that the connecting rod is positioned at bottom dead center so it cannot jam against the supports or press bed.*

b. Center the crankshaft under the press ram and drive the crankshaft out of the case.

6. If the right crankshaft bearing comes out of the case, remove it from the crankshaft by one of the following methods:

a. If a press is available, fit a bearing splitter under the bearing, then support it in the press so the crankshaft can be driven from the bearing.

b. If a press is not available, fit a bearing splitter under the bearing, then attach a puller to the splitter, as shown in **Figure 21**. Pull the bearing from the crankshaft.

> *CAUTION*
> *Protect the crankshaft when removing the bearing. The bearing must be replaced whenever the crankshaft is removed from the engine. Replace the bearing as described in this chapter.*

7. Inspect the crankshaft and cases as described in this chapter.

Assembly

Refer to **Figure 10**.

1. Follow these practices when assembling the engine:

a. Check that all mating surfaces are clean and smooth. Minor irregularities can be repaired with an oil stone.

b. Install *new* gaskets and O-rings. Do not reuse gaskets and O-rings. Lubricate the O-rings as they are installed.

c. Lightly oil the lip of each seal so the shafts can pass through smoothly. Wrap the splines on shafts with tape to prevent the splines from snagging the seals.

d. Lubricate all surfaces of the transmission assembly and the crankshaft assembly with two-stroke engine oil. Apply two-stroke engine oil to all bearings.

2. To install the crankshaft, the assembly tool shaft (part No. 07965-1660200), assembly collar (part No. 07965-166030A) and threaded adapter (part No. 07965-KA30000) are required (**Figure 22**). The parts can be ordered from a Honda dealership. Install the crankshaft as follows:

a. Insert the splined end of the crankshaft into the right crankcase (A, **Figure 23**).

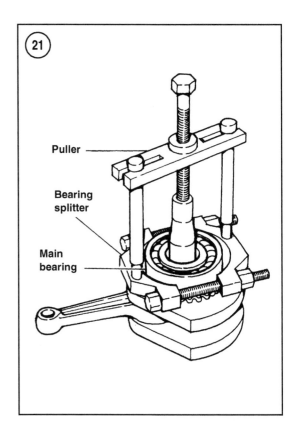

Puller

Bearing splitter

Main bearing

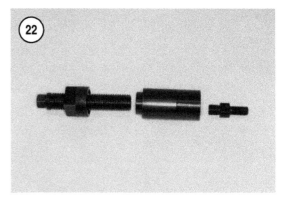

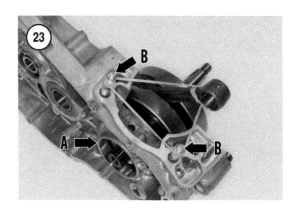

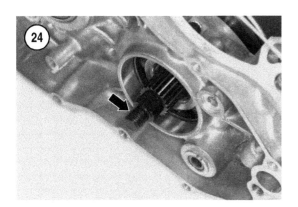

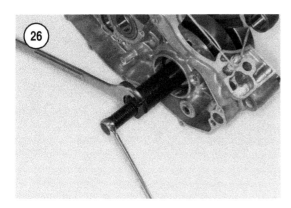

b. The crankshaft will turn when it is being pulled into the bearing. To prevent damage to the connecting rod and the engine cases, temporarily thread two cylinder bolts into the crankcase (B, **Figure 23**). Wrap a strong rubber band around the connecting rod and the bolts, forming a triangle. As the crankshaft is turned, the connecting rod will stay centered and away from the crankcase.

c. Install the threaded adapter onto the end of the crankshaft (**Figure 24**).

d. Install the assembly collar (A, **Figure 25**) over the end of the crankshaft, then pass the assembly shaft (B) through the collar and to the adapter. Thread the shaft into the collar and hand-tighten the shaft.

e. Hold the assembly collar with a wrench and tighten the assembly shaft with a second wrench (**Figure 26**). Tighten the shaft until the crankshaft is seated in the bearing.

NOTE
If possible, have an assistant keep the case steady.

f. Remove the installation tools from the crankshaft. Make sure the crankshaft is seated in the case as shown in **Figure 27**.

g. If desired, leave the connecting rod supported by the rubber band until it must be removed.

3. Install the transmission as follows:

a. Support the right case so the transmission shafts can pass through the case.

b. Mesh the two shafts together (**Figure 28**). Check that all thrust washers are properly located on the ends of the shafts, as required.

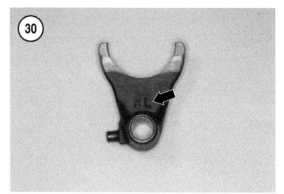

c. Hold the assembly in one hand, with the countershaft positioned as shown in **Figure 28**. Use the other hand to guide the transmission into the case (**Figure 29**).

d. Identify the shift forks. Each fork is marked (**Figure 30**) to indicate its position: left, center, or right (**Figure 31**).

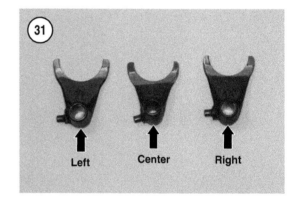

e. Install the shift forks in the positions shown in **Figure 32**. The left and right fork markings should face up when installed. The center fork marking should face down when installed. As each fork is installed, engage it with the appropriate shaft groove. The left and right forks engage with the countershaft. The center fork engages with the mainshaft.

f. Install the the shift drum (**Figure 33**).

g. Rotate the shift drum and engage the pin on the center shift fork with its matching groove in the drum (A, **Figure 34**).

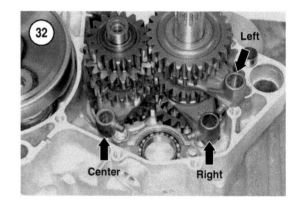

h. Align the bore in the shift fork, then insert the shift fork shaft (B, **Figure 34**) through the bore and into the case. Check that the shaft is fully seated in the case.

i. Repeat substeps g and h to install the left and right forks and the shift fork shaft (**Figure 35**).

4. Check transmission operation. While turning the countershaft and shift drum, observe the action of the shift drum and forks. Make sure the shift drum moves through its complete rotation and the forks operate smoothly.

5. Install the left crankcase onto the right crankcase as follows:

a. Check that all mating surfaces are clean and dry.

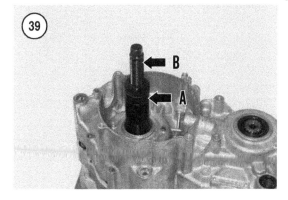

b. Install the breather tube, seating it in the left case (**Figure 36**).

c. Check that the rubber block is in the right case (**Figure 37**).

d. Insert the dowels (if removed) and a *new* lubricated O-ring on the right crankcase (**Figure 38**).

e. Place a *new* gasket on the right crankcase.

f. Align and rest the left case squarely onto the right case.

NOTE
To assemble the cases, the assembly tool shaft (part No. 07965-1660200) and assembly collar (part No. 07965-166030A) are required. The parts can be ordered from a Honda dealership.

g. Install the assembly collar (A, **Figure 39**) over the end of the crankshaft, then pass the assembly shaft (B) through the collar and to the crankshaft. Thread the shaft into the crankshaft and hand-tighten.

h. Hold the assembly collar with a wrench and slowly tighten the assembly shaft with a sec-

ond wrench (**Figure 40**). While tightening, use a soft mallet to seat the case over the dowels (**Figure 41**). The cases must come together evenly (**Figure 42**). Tighten the shaft until the crankshaft is seated in the bearing.

NOTE
If possible, have an assistant keep the case steady and observe the progress.

   i. Remove the installation tools from the crankshaft.

6. Install the left and right main bearing seals as described in this chapter.

7. Remove each crankcase bolt from the template and insert the bolts into the appropriate holes. Finger-tighten the bolts.

8. Tighten the bolts equally in three passes and in a crossing pattern.

9. Rotate the crankshaft and transmission shafts and check for smooth operation. If binding is evident, separate the cases and correct the problem.

10. Trim the excess gasket material from the cylinder base gasket surface (**Figure 43**).

11. The crankcase assembly (**Figure 44**) is ready for installation into the frame. If desired, top end components and those located in the side covers can be installed at this time. Refer to the appropriate chapters for inspection and installation procedures for the components in the engine top end and crankcase covers.

Inspection

1. Remove the oil seals as described in this chapter and Chapter One.

2. Remove all residue from the gasket surfaces.

3. Clean the crankcase halves with solvent. Flush all bearings last, using clean solvent.

4. Dry the cases with compressed air.

WARNING
When drying a bearing with compressed air, do not spin the inner bearing race. Since the bearing is not lubricated, damage or destruction could quickly occur.

5. Flush all passages with compressed air.

6. Lightly oil the engine bearings before inspecting their condition.

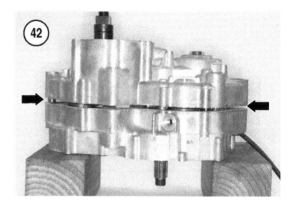

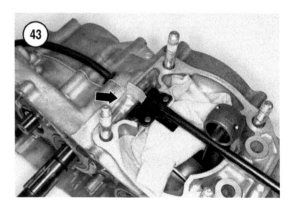

7. Inspect the bearings for roughness, pitting, galling and play. Replace any bearing that is not in good condition or is a loose fit in the crankcase bore. Always replace the opposing bearing at the same time.

8. Inspect the cases for fractures around all mounting and bearing bosses, stiffening ribs and threaded holes. If repair is required, take the case to a dealership or machine shop that repairs precision aluminum castings.

9. Check all threaded holes for damage or buildup. Clean threads with the correct size metric tap. Lubricate the tap with kerosene or aluminum tap fluid.

CRANKCASE SEAL AND BEARING REPLACEMENT

When performing a complete engine rebuild, replace the following crankcase oil seals:

1. Left and right main bearings.
2. Left countershaft bearing.
3. Shift shaft.
4. Clutch lifter lever.

NOTE
Refer to Chapter Six for inspection of the bearing and seal for the clutch lifter lever. The bearing and seal are located on the outside of the left crankcase (Figure 45).

Refer to Chapter One for additional removal and installation techniques for bearings and seals. Also refer to *Interference Fit* if heat will be used for the removal and installation of the bearings in the housings.

Countershaft and Shift Shaft Oil Seal Replacement

Refer to **Figure 10**.

1. Pry out the old seal (**Figure 46**). Always protect the case from damage.

CAUTION
When prying, do not allow the end of the tool to touch the seal bore or snag an oil hole in the bore. Scratches in the bore will cause leakage and heavy-handed prying can break the casting.

2. If a new bearing will be installed, replace the bearing before installing the new seal.
3. Clean the oil seal bore.
4. Pack grease into the lip of the new seal.
5. Place the seal in the bore, with the closed side of the seal facing out. The seal must be square to the bore.

CAUTION
The left countershaft seal must be installed to a depth of 1.0 mm (0.40 in) below the top edge of the bore. Installing the seal deeper than this can block lubrication passages, causing bearing failure.

6. Depending on the type of oil seal, seals are either installed by hand or by a driver tool. Observe the following when installing seals by either method:

a. Hand installation. For this engine, the left countershaft seal and shift shaft seal can be installed by hand (**Figure 47**). Install the countershaft seal uniformly and to a depth of 1.0 mm (0.40 in) below the edge of the bore. Measure the seal depth to ensure that it is not too deep.

b. Driver installation. When driving seals with a seal driver or socket, the driver must fit at the perimeter of the seal (**Figure 48**). If the driver presses toward the center of the seal, the seal can distort and the internal garter spring can become dislodged, causing the seal to leak.

Crankshaft Oil Seal Replacement

Refer to **Figure 10**.

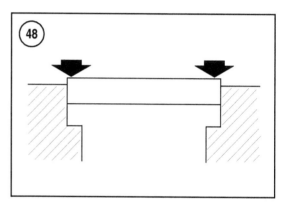

> *NOTE*
> *These seals are replaced after the crankcase halves are assembled. Refer to the* **Crankshaft Seal and Bearing Replacement** *procedure in this section for replacing main bearing seals.*

To install the crankshaft seals, the assembly tool shaft (part No. 07965-1660200), assembly collar and washer (part No. 07965-166030A), and threaded adapter (part No. 07965-KA30000) are required (**Figure 49**). The parts can be ordered from a Honda dealership. The procedure shows the right seal being installed. The left seal is installed identically, except the threaded adapter tool will not be required. Install the seals as follows:

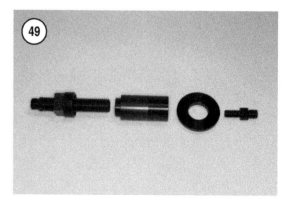

1. Clean the oil seal bore.

2. Pack grease into the lip of the new seal.

3. Place the seal in the bore, with the closed side of the seal facing out. The seal must be square to the bore (**Figure 50**).

> *CAUTION*
> *The right crankhaft seal must be installed to a depth of 1.0 mm (0.40 in) below the top edge of the bore. The left crankshaft seal must be installed to a depth of 2.0 mm (0.80 in) below the top edge of the bore. Installing the seals deeper than this can block lubri-*

*cation passages (**Figure 51**), causing bearing failure.*

4. Place the washer over the seal and install the threaded adapter onto the end of the crankshaft (**Figure 52**).

5. Install the assembly collar over the end of the crankshaft, then pass the assembly shaft through the collar and to the adapter. Thread the shaft into the collar and hand-tighten the shaft.

6. Hold the assembly collar with a wrench and tighten the assembly shaft with a second wrench (**Figure 53**). Slowly tighten the shaft until the seal enters the bore. Remove the tool and measure the seal depth. Continue driving the seal and measuring the depth until the seal is properly located (**Figure 54**).

Crankcase Bearing Drivers

If bearing drivers will be used to replace the bearings, use the following Honda tools, or an equivalent. All tools can be ordered from a dealership.

1. Driver (part No. 07749-0010000).

2. A 32 × 35 mm attachment (part No. 07746-0010100) is required for the following model/component:

    a. 1997 left mainshaft bearing.

    b. 1997 right countershaft bearing.

3. A 37 × 40 mm attachment (part No. 07746-0010200) is required for the following model/component:

    a. Left shift drum bearing.

    b. 1998-2001 right countershaft bearing.

4. A 42 × 47 mm attachment (part No. 07746-0010300) is required for the following model/component:

    a. 1998-2001 left mainshaft bearing.

    b. 1997-1999 left countershaft bearing.

    c. 1997 right mainshaft bearing.

    d. Right shift drum bearing.

5. A 52 × 55 mm attachment (part No. 07746-0010400) is required for the following model/component:

    a. 1998-2001 right mainshaft bearing.

    b. 2000-2001 left countershaft bearing.

6. A 17 mm pilot (part No. 07746-0040400) is required for the following model/component:

    a. Left mainshaft bearing.

    b. Right countershaft bearing.

7. A 20 mm pilot (part No. 07746-0040500) is required for the 1997 right mainshaft bearing.

8. A 25 mm pilot (part No. 07746-0040600) is required for the following model/component:

    a. Right shift drum bearing.

    b. 1998-2001 right mainshaft bearing.

Crankcase Bearings

Refer to Chapter Six for inspection of the bearing and seal for the clutch lifter lever. The bearing and seal are located on the outside of the left crankcase (**Figure 45**).

Refer to **Figure 10**.

1. When replacing crankcase bearings, note the following:

    a. Where used, remove bearing retainers (**Figure 55**) before attempting bearing removal. When installing retainers, clean the screw threads and install the screws using threadlocking compound. Torque the retainer screws to the specifications in **Table 2**.

    b. Identify and record the size code of each bearing before it is removed from the case. This will eliminate confusion when installing the bearings in their correct bores.

    c. Record the orientation of each bearing in its bore. Note if the size code faces toward the inside or outside of the case. Unless otherwise noted, the mark should *face up* when installing the bearing.

    d. Use a hydraulic press or a set of bearing drivers to remove and install bearings. All bearings in the crankcases are an interference-fit. Removal and installation of the bearings is eased by using heat, as described in *Interference Fit* in Chapter One.

    e. Bearings that are only accessible from one side of the case are removed with a blind bearing puller (**Figure 56**). The puller is fitted through the bearing, then expanded to grip the back side of the bearing. A sliding weight on the tool is quickly pulled backward to dislodge the bearing.

2. The following list identifies the *left* crankcase bearings. Unless otherwise noted, remove and install the bearings with a press or hand-driver set. Refer to **Figure 57** for the lettered identifications:

    a. Crankshaft bearing (A).

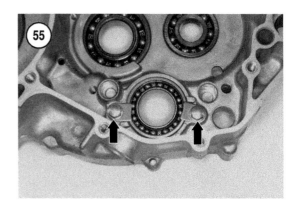

    b. Mainshaft bearing (B). Remove this bearing, using a blind bearing puller.

    c. Countershaft bearing (C).

    d. Shift drum bearing (D). Remove this bearing, using a blind bearing puller.

3. The following list identifies the *right* crankcase bearings. Unless otherwise noted, remove and install the bearings with a press or hand-driver set. Refer to **Figure 58** for the lettered identifications:

    a. Crankshaft bearing (A). If the bearing is removed from the crankcase when the crankshaft is removed, the bearing must be replaced.

    b. Mainshaft bearing (B). Remove this bearing, using a blind bearing puller.

    c. Countershaft bearing (C).

    d. Shift drum bearing (D). Remove this bearing, using a blind bearing puller.

Bearing replacement

All of the bearings, except those removed with a blind bearing puller, can be removed using the steps described in this procedure. All of the bearings can be installed using this procedure. Read the entire procedure before replacing any bearing.

CAUTION
If the right crankcase bearing is removed from the crankcase when the crankshaft is removed, the bearing must be replaced.

CAUTION
*Before performing this procedure, refer to **Crankcase Bearings** in this chapter to determine if there is spe-*

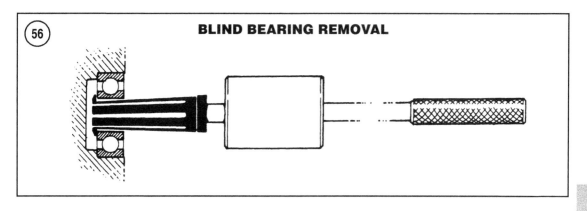

BLIND BEARING REMOVAL

56

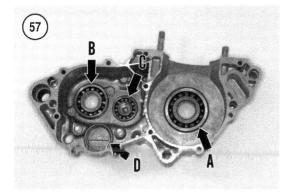

57

5

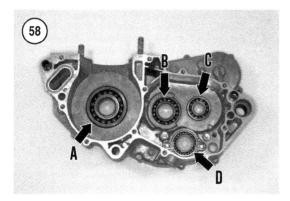

58

59

cific information related to the bearing being installed. Do not install a
bearing until any specific information
is known.

1. Heat the crankcase as described in *Interference
Fit* in Chapter One. Observe all safety and handling
procedures when the case is heated.

2. Support the heated crankcase on wooden
blocks, allowing space for the bearing to fall from
the bore.

3. Remove the damaged bearing from the bore, using a press or hand-driver set.

4. Clean and inspect the bore.

5. Place the new bearing in a freezer for at least one
hour.

6. When the bearing is chilled, reheat the crankcase.

7. Position the heated crankcase on the wooden
blocks, then lubricate the bore and bearing. Place
the bearing squarely over the bore and check that it
is properly oriented.

> *CAUTION*
> *For bearings that are not sealed on ei-*
> *ther side, place the manufacturer's*
> *marks (stamped on the side of the*
> *bearing) facing up. Bearings with one*
> *side sealed should have the sealed*
> *side facing down.*

8. Press the bearing into place, using a driver that
fits on the outer bearing race.

> *NOTE*
> *If a press is not available, the bearing*
> *can be seated by hand, using a driver*
> *and hammer. Place the driver*
> *squarely over the bearing (**Figure**
> **59**), then drive the bearing into the*

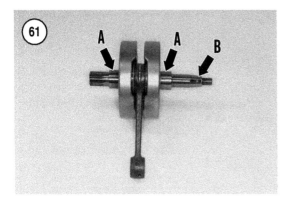

*case (**Figure 60**). Do not use exces-sive force when driving the bearing. Bearing and case damage could oc-cur.*

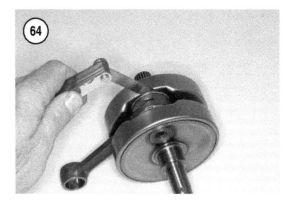

CRANKSHAFT

Inspection

Carefully handle the crankshaft assembly during inspection. Do not place the crankshaft where it could accidentally roll off the workbench. The crankshaft is an assembly-type, with its two halves joined by a crankpin. The crankpin is hydraulically pressed into the flywheels and aligned, both verti-cally and horizontally, with calibrated equipment.

The connecting rod and crankshaft are only avail-able from Honda as a single part. If the connecting rod is damaged, it may be possible for a machine shop to disassemble the crankshaft so an aftermar-ket connecting rod can be installed. Have the ma-chine shop evaluate the crankshaft to determine the possibility of repair.

1. Clean the crankshaft with solvent and dry with compressed air.

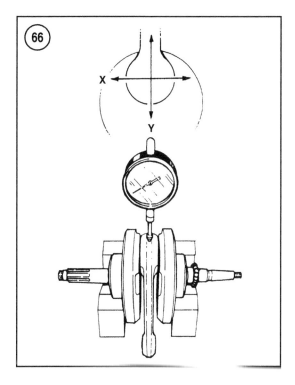

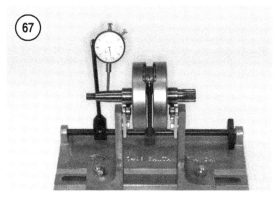

2. Inspect the crankshaft bearing surfaces (A, **Figure 61**) for scoring, heat discoloration or other damage. Minor damage can be repaired with 320-grit carborundum cloth.

3. Inspect the splines, sprocket and shaft taper for signs of wear or damage (B, **Figure 61**).

4. Inspect the connecting rod small end (**Figure 62**) as follows:

    a. Inspect the rod end for scoring, galling or heat damage.

    b. Inspect and measure the bore. Refer to Chapter Four for the inspection procedures and specifications for the bore, bearing, piston pin and piston.

5. Measure the crank wheel width at 90° intervals (**Figure 63**). If the measurement is not identical at each point, have a dealership evaluate the part to see if it can be retrued.

6. Inspect the big end of the connecting rod as follows:

    a. Slide the connecting rod to one side and check the connecting rod side clearance with a flat feeler gauge (**Figure 64**). Refer to **Table 1** for service limits.

    b. Place the crankshaft on V-blocks and measure the connecting rod radial clearance with a dial indicator (**Figure 65**). Measure in both the X and Y axis (**Figure 66**). Refer to **Table 1** for the service limit.

7. Place the crankshaft on a set of V-blocks and measure crankshaft runout with a dial indicator (**Figure 67**). Support the crankshaft at the bearing surfaces and measure at the main journal. If the runout exceeds the service limit in **Table 1**, have a dealership evaluate the part to see if it can be retrued.

Table 1 ENGINE SERVICE SPECIFICATIONS

	New mm (in.)	Service limit mm (in.)
Connecting rod small end ID	21.997-22.009 (0.8660-0.8665)	22.02 (0.867)
Crankshaft		
Side clearance	0.4-0.8 (0.016-0.032)	0.9 (0.035)
Radial clearance	0.010-0.022 (0.0004-0.0009)	0.03 (0.001)
Runout	–	0.05 (0.002)

Table 2 ENGINE TORQUE SPECIFICATIONS

	N•m	in.-lb.	ft.-lb.
Bearing retainer screws	10	88	–
Engine upper mounting nut			
1997-1999	39	–	29
2000-2001	54	–	40
Engine lower mounting nuts			
1997-1998	39	–	29
1999	64	–	47
2000-2001	54	–	40
Engine hanger plate nuts	26	–	20
Swing arm pivot nut	88	–	65

CHAPTER SIX

CLUTCH AND GEARSHIFT LINKAGE

This chapter describes service procedures for the following right side crankcase components:

1. Clutch cover.
2. Right crankcase cover.
3. Clutch.
4. External gearshift linkage.
5. Kickstarter.
6. Primary drive gear.

Read this chapter before attempting repairs to the clutch and linkage. Become familiar with the procedures and illustrations to understand the skill and equipment required. Refer to Chapter One for tool usage and techniques.

CLUTCH COVER

Removal and Installation

The clutch cover can be removed to disassemble and inspect the clutch components. If the entire clutch assembly is to be removed from the engine, remove the right crankcase cover so the clutch outer can be removed. Refer to **Figure 1**.

1. Drain the transmission oil as described in Chapter Three.
2. Remove the rear brake pedal as described in Chapter Fourteen.
3. Remove the six bolts (**Figure 2**) securing the cover to the case.
4. Remove the cover and O-ring.
5. To install the cover, reverse this procedure. Note the following:
   a. Inspect the O-ring condition. Replace if necessary. Lubricate the O-ring before installing the cover.
   b. Check that the transmission oil and coolant levels are correct as described in Chapter Three.
   c. Start the engine and inspect for leaks.

RIGHT CRANKCASE COVER

Removal/Inspection/Installation

Refer to **Figure 1**.

1. Drain the engine coolant and transmission oil as described in Chapter Three.
2. Remove the exhaust pipe (Chapter Four).

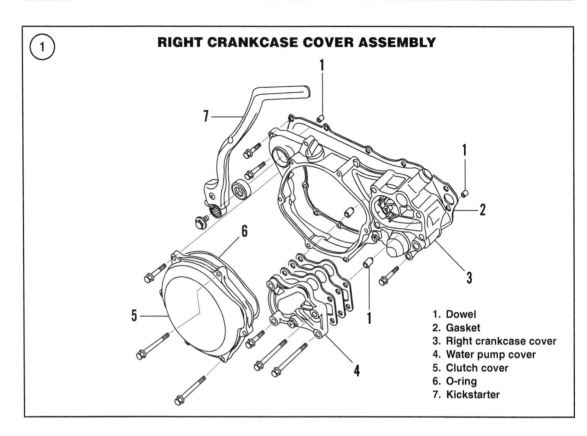

RIGHT CRANKCASE COVER ASSEMBLY

1. Dowel
2. Gasket
3. Right crankcase cover
4. Water pump cover
5. Clutch cover
6. O-ring
7. Kickstarter

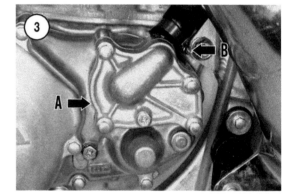

3. Remove the water pump cover (A, **Figure 3**) as described in Chapter Ten.

4. Remove the coolant hose (B, **Figure 3**) from the crankcase cover.

5. Remove the kickstarter retaining bolt (**Figure 4**) and kickstarter.

6. Remove the clutch cover as described in this chapter.

7. Remove the remaining seven bolts from the perimeter of the crankcase cover (**Figure 5**).

8. Remove the crankcase cover as follows:

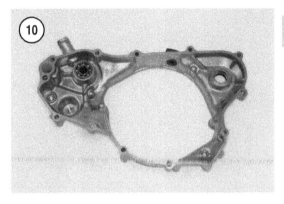

NOTE
*Due to the tab (**Figure 6**) in the lower left corner, the cover cannot be removed by pulling it straight off the engine.*

a. Lightly tap the crankcase cover to loosen it from the engine.

b. Pull the cover away from the engine until the tab is near the frame.

c. Pivot the right side of the cover away from the engine, then lift the left side free.

9. Remove the washer from the end of the exhaust valve governor (**Figure 7**).

10. Remove the washer from the water pump impeller shaft (**Figure 8**).

11. Remove the two dowels that fit between the crankcase and cover (**Figure 9**).

12. Remove the cover gasket.

13. Refer to the procedures in this chapter to service the clutch, gearshift linkage, kickstarter and primary drive gear. Refer to Chapter Four for servicing the exhaust valve governor assembly. Refer to Chapter Ten for servicing the water pump.

14. Inspect the right crankcase cover (**Figure 10**) as follows:

a. Wipe the cover clean.

CAUTION
Do not submerge the cover in solvent
if the kickstarter seal and water pump
assembly are not removed.

b. Inspect the cover for cracks around bosses and reinforcement ribs.
c. Inspect the kickstarter seal (**Figure 11**). If necessary, replace the seal.

15. Reverse these steps to install the right crankcase cover assembly. Note the following:

a. Check that the washers are installed on the water pump impeller (**Figure 8**) and exhaust valve governor (**Figure 7**).
b. Check that both dowels are installed in the case (**Figure 9**).
c. Install a *new* cover gasket on the crankcase dowels.
d. When installing the crankcase cover, first install the tabbed corner behind the frame and start the kickstarter shaft into the cover. Then, pivot the right side of the cover toward the engine. Turn the water pump impeller shaft and engage it with the primary drive gear while seating the cover into place.
e. Adjust the brake pedal height as described in Chapter Three.

CLUTCH

The clutch assembly (**Figure 12**) consists of an outer housing and a clutch center. A set of clutch discs and friction plates are alternately locked to the two parts. The gear-driven clutch outer is mounted on the transmission mainshaft and can rotate freely. The outer receives power from the primary drive gear mounted on the crankshaft. As the clutch is engaged, the clutch outer and friction plates transfer the power to the clutch discs, locked to the clutch center. The clutch center is splined to the mainshaft and powers the transmission. The plate assembly is engaged by springs and disengaged by a cable-actuated lifter lever assembly.

The clutch operates immersed in the transmission oil supply. The use of the incorrect transmission oil can cause creeping, while oil additives can cause slippage. When troubleshooting these problems, always check the quality and quantity of oil in the engine before disassembling the clutch.

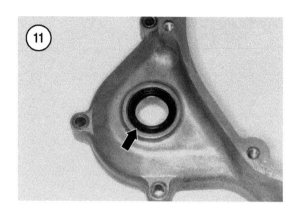

The clutch cover can be removed to disassemble and inspect the clutch components. If the entire clutch assembly is to be removed from the engine, remove the right crankcase cover so the clutch outer can be removed. The following procedure details the complete removal of the clutch assembly from the engine. The procedure also includes steps for removing the lifter lever from the left side of the engine.

If necessary, refer to *Clutch Cable Replacement* in this chapter.

Removal

1. Remove the right crankcase cover as described in this chapter.
2. Slowly remove the six bolts compressing the clutch springs (**Figure 13**). Make several passes to equally relieve the pressure on the bolts. Remove the bolts, springs and pressure plate from the clutch.
3. Remove the clutch lifter (A, **Figure 14**) and rod (B).
4. Remove the plates from the clutch outer and clutch center (**Figure 15**).
5. Bend the tabs on the lockwasher (A, **Figure 16**) away from the locknut (B).
6. Remove the clutch locknut as follows:

a. Attach a clutch center holder (**Figure 17**) tool to the clutch center.

CAUTION
Do not hold the gears with screwdrivers or other tools. This could result in gear breakage. Instead, use the Honda clutch center holder tool (part No. 07724-0050002).

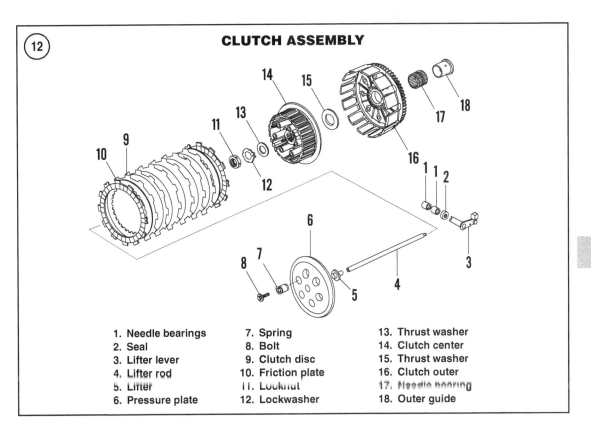

CLUTCH ASSEMBLY

1. Needle bearings	7. Spring	13. Thrust washer
2. Seal	8. Bolt	14. Clutch center
3. Lifter lever	9. Clutch disc	15. Thrust washer
4. Lifter rod	10. Friction plate	16. Clutch outer
5. Lifter	11. Locknut	17. Needle bearing
6. Pressure plate	12. Lockwasher	18. Outer guide

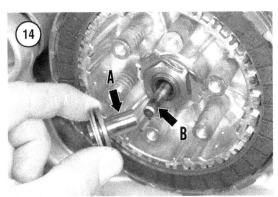

b. While grasping the holder tool, loosen the locknut with a socket.

c. Remove the clutch locknut (A, **Figure 18**), lockwasher (B) and thrust washer (C).

7. Remove the clutch center from the transmission mainshaft.

8. Remove the thrust washer and clutch outer from the shaft (**Figure 19**).

9. Remove the needle bearing and clutch outer guide from the shaft (**Figure 20**).

10. Remove the lifter lever from the left side of the engine as follows:

a. Remove the alternator cover, flywheel and stator as described in Chapter Nine.

b. Remove the clutch cable from the lifter lever (**Figure 21**). If necessary, loosen the cable adjuster at the handlebar.

c. Remove the lifter lever.

11. Inspect the clutch assembly as described in this chapter.

Installation

1. Lubricate all parts with transmission oil, except where noted.

2. Install the lifter lever as follows:

a. Lubricate the lifter lever with molybdenum grease, then insert the lever into the left case (**Figure 21**).

b. Attach the clutch cable to the lever. Do not adjust the cable until all assembly is completed.

c. Install the stator, flywheel and alternator cover as described in Chapter Nine.

NOTE
If desired, install the stator and flywheel after all other clutch assembly is completed. If there are any problems that are related to the lifter lever, it can be easily removed.

3. Install the outer guide and needle bearing onto the mainshaft (**Figure 20**).

4. Install the clutch outer and thrust washer onto the shaft (**Figure 19**).

5. Install a *new* lockwasher onto the shaft (**Figure 22**). Install the lockwasher so the tabs (**Figure 23**) are engaged with a rib on the clutch center.

6. Install the clutch locknut as follows:

a. Attach a clutch center holder tool to the clutch center (**Figure 17**).

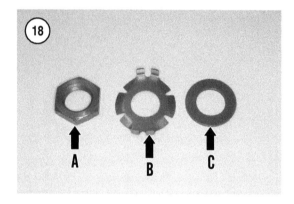

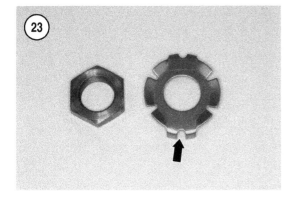

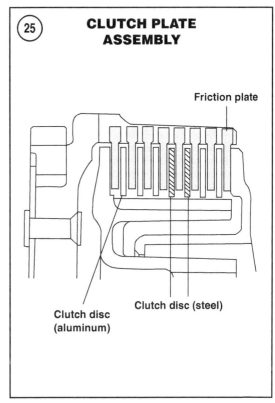

CLUTCH PLATE ASSEMBLY

Friction plate

Clutch disc (steel)

Clutch disc (aluminum)

CAUTION
Do not hold the gears with screwdrivers or other tools. This could result in gear breakage. Instead, use the Honda clutch center holder tool (part No. 07724-0050002).

b. While grasping the holder tool, tighten the locknut with a socket. Torque the nut to the specifications in **Table 2**.

c. Bend the tabs on the lockwasher so they are tight against the flats on the nut (**Figure 24**).

7. Install the clutch plates as follows:

a. Separate the clutch plates. There are eight friction plates, five aluminum discs and two steel discs.

b. Lubricate the plates with transmission oil.

c. Refer to **Figure 25** for plate order. Beginning with a friction plate, alternately install friction plates and clutch discs into the clutch outer and clutch center (**Figure 26**).

8. Install the lifter rod into the mainshaft (B, **Figure 14**). Make sure the correct end of the rod is inserted first.

9. Install the clutch lifter (A, **Figure 14**) onto the lifter rod.

10. Install and lock the pressure plate to the clutch center (**Figure 13**) as follows:

    a. Position the pressure plate on the clutch center.

    b. Install the clutch springs on the center bosses.

    c. Finger-tighten the six bolts.

    d. Tighten the bolts, working in a crisscross pattern. Make several passes so all bolts are tightened evenly and equally. Torque the bolts to the specifications in **Table 2**.

11. Install the right crankcase cover and clutch cover as described in this chapter.

12. After assembly is complete, check the clutch adjustment as described in Chapter Three.

CAUTION
If the stator and flywheel were removed during the procedure, the ignition timing must be checked, as described in Chapter Nine.

Inspection

Always replace clutch discs, friction plates or springs (**Figure 12**) as a set if they do not meet specifications. If parts show other signs of wear or damage, replace them, regardless of their specifications.

Refer to the specifications listed in **Table 1** for service limits of the components being inspected.

1. Clean the components in solvent and dry with compressed air.

2. Inspect the friction plates (plates bonded with friction material) as follows:

    a. Inspect the plates for scoring or discoloration.

    b. Measure the thickness of each friction plate (**Figure 27**). Measure at several locations around the perimeter.

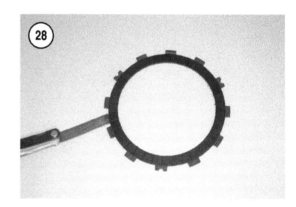

    c. Measure each friction plate for warp (**Figure 28**). Lay each plate on a surface plate, or thick piece of glass, and measure any gap around the perimeter of the plate. Although Honda does not provide a warp specification for the friction plates, check the plates to ensure that they are reasonably uniform. Normally, friction plates will have less warp than clutch discs.

    d. Inspect the tabs on the friction plates (**Figure 29**). The tabs must not be damaged and should slide smoothly in the clutch outer.

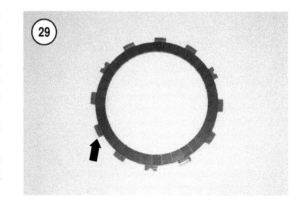

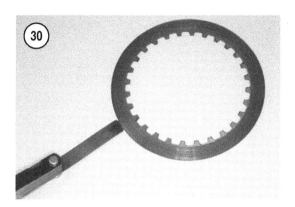

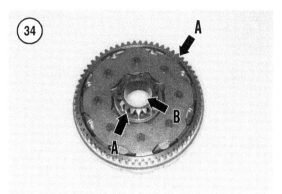

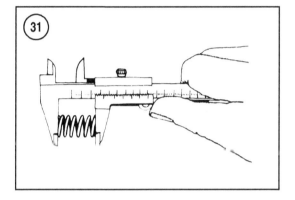

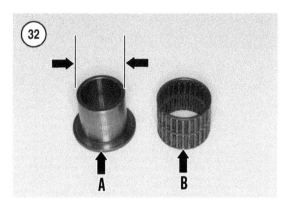

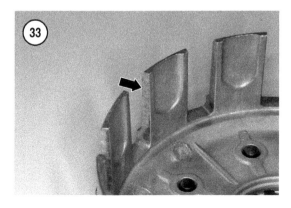

3. Inspect the clutch discs (metal plates) as follows:
   a. Inspect the plates for scoring or discoloration.
   b. Measure each clutch disc for warp (**Figure 30**). Lay each plate on a surface plate, or thick piece of glass, and measure any gap around the perimeter of the plate.
   c. Inspect the inner teeth on the plates. The teeth must not be damaged and should slide smoothly on the clutch center.

4. Measure the free length of each clutch spring (**Figure 31**).

5. Inspect the clutch outer guide (A, **Figure 32**) for wear and damage. Measure the outside diameter of the guide. If the guide is damaged, also inspect the mainshaft for damage.

6. Inspect the needle bearing (B, **Figure 32**) for wear and damage. Check the bearing cage for cracks. Inspect the rollers for flat spots and scoring.

7. Inspect the clutch outer as follows:
   a. Inspect the slots for nicks, wear and damage (**Figure 33**). Light damage can be repaired using a fine-cut file or oilstone. The slots must be smooth and free of defects so the friction plates will move smoothly in the slots.
   b. Inspect the gear teeth for wear or damage (A, **Figure 34**).
   c. Inspect the bore for scoring or damage (B, **Figure 34**).

8. Inspect the clutch center as follows:
   a. Inspect the shaft splines (A, **Figure 35**).
   b. Inspect the outer splines (B, **Figure 35**) for nicks, wear and damage. The splines must be smooth and free of defects so the clutch discs will move smoothly on the splines.

9. Inspect the pressure plate for cracked bosses (**Figure 36**) or other damage.

10. Inspect the lifter and lifter rod (**Figure 37**) as follows:

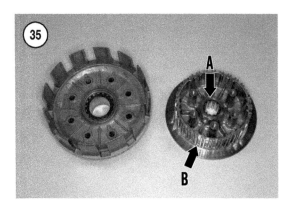

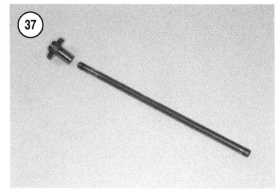

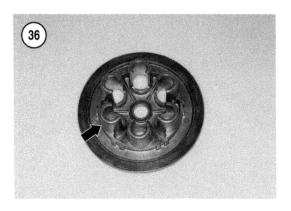

a. Rotate the lifter on the rod and check for smooth operation. If roughness is detected, the bearing in the lifter is worn.

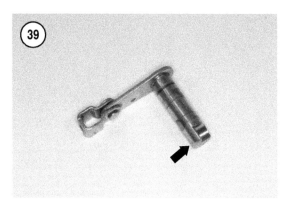

b. Inspect the end of the lifter (**Figure 38**). It must be smooth and flat.

c. Roll the lifter rod on a flat surface. The rod must be straight.

d. Inspect the lifter rod for wear, particularly at the end where it makes contact with the lifter lever.

11. Inspect the lifter lever (**Figure 39**) and bearings (**Figure 40**) as follows:

a. Inspect the end of the lever where it contacts the lifter rod. The contact point should not be worn or rounded.

b. Inspect the shaft of the lever. It should be smooth and show no signs of wear.

c. Insert the lever into the bearing. The lever should turn smoothly and have minimal play. If looseness or damage is detected, replace the bearings and seal as described in Step 12.

12. If necessary, replace the lifter lever bearings and oil seal (**Figure 40**) as follows:

a. Pry the seal out of the bore, taking care not to scratch the bore.

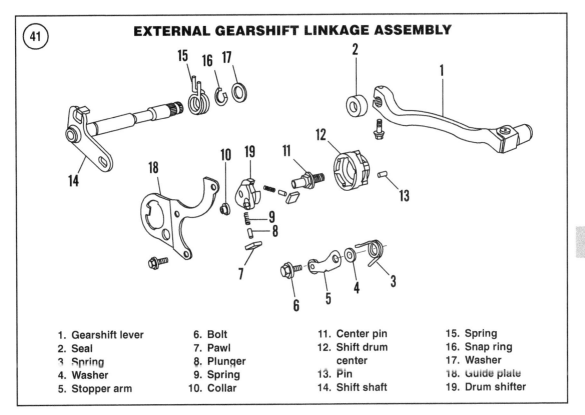

EXTERNAL GEARSHIFT LINKAGE ASSEMBLY

1. Gearshift lever
2. Seal
3. Spring
4. Washer
5. Stopper arm
6. Bolt
7. Pawl
8. Plunger
9. Spring
10. Collar
11. Center pin
12. Shift drum center
13. Pin
14. Shift shaft
15. Spring
16. Snap ring
17. Washer
18. Guide plate
19. Drum shifter

b. Pull the bearings out of the bore. If necessary, use a hooked, stiff wire to snag the bearings.

c. Wipe the bore clean.

d. Lubricate the new bearings with molybdenum grease.

e. Insert the bearings into the bore. If necessary, push the bearings in with a socket or similar driver that fits at the outside edge of the bearings.

f. Lubricate the new seal with molybdenum grease.

g. Press the seal into place. Drive the seal squarely into place with a socket or similar driver that fits at the outside edge of the seal.

GEARSHIFT LINKAGE

Removal

Refer to **Figure 41**.

1. Remove the right crankcase cover as described in this chapter.

2. Remove the clutch assembly as described in this chapter.

3. Remove the gearshift lever. The bolt (**Figure 42**) must be completely removed for the lever to come off the shaft.

4. Remove the shift shaft assembly and washer (**Figure 43**) from the crankcase.

5. Remove the collar (**Figure 44**).

NOTE
In the following step use care in removing the assembly from the shift drum center. The drum shifter contains springs, plungers and pawls. To prevent lost parts, place the assembly in a plastic bag.

6. Remove the three bolts (**Figure 45**) securing the guide plate. Carefully remove the guide plate and

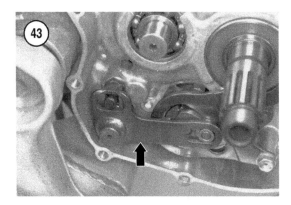

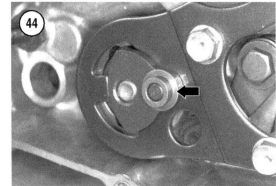

drum shifter as an assembly. Place the parts in the plastic bag, then disassemble the parts.

7. Pry the stopper arm (A, **Figure 46**) away from the shift drum center (B), then remove the center pin (C) and drum center.

8. Remove the bolt (**Figure 47**) from the stopper arm, then remove the stopper arm, washer and spring.

9. Remove the pin from the shift drum (**Figure 48**).

10. Inspect the parts as described in this section.

Inspection

Inspect the components of the gearshift linkage and replace parts that are worn, damaged or fatigued.

1. Inspect the shift shaft, torsion spring and washer assembly as follows:

   a. Inspect the shaft splines (A, **Figure 49**) for damage.

   b. Inspect the shaft for straightness.

   c. Inspect the engagement hole (B, **Figure 49**) for wear. The hole should be symmetrical and not excessively worn.

   d. Inspect the washer (C, **Figure 49**) for wear.

   e. Inspect the torsion spring (A, **Figure 50**) for wear and fatigue cracks.

   f. Inspect the snap ring (B, **Figure 50**). Check that it is seated and that the groove is not rounded.

2. Inspect the guide plate and drum shifter assembly as follows:

   a. Inspect the guide plate (A, **Figure 51**) for wear.

   b. Inspect the drum shifter (B, **Figure 51**) for wear.

   c. Inspect the springs, plungers and pawls (C, **Figure 51**) for wear. The pawls are rounded at the end that seats in the drum shifter. The opposite end must be square in order to stay engaged in the shift drum center.

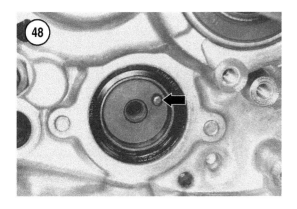

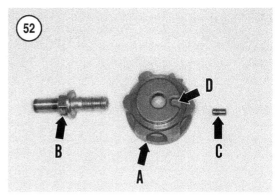

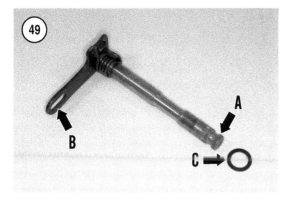

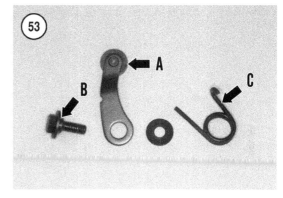

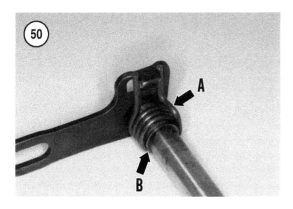

d. Inspect the collar (D, **Figure 51**) for wear. Fit the collar into the shift shaft and check for excessive play.

3. Inspect the shift drum center, center pin and drum pin as follows:

   a. Inspect the detents on the back of the drum center (A, **Figure 52**). The detents must not be worn or shifting will be incorrect.

   b. Inspect the depressions in the front side of the drum center. If the depressions are rounded at their shoulders, the pawls in the drum shifter assembly can slip.

   c. Inspect the center pin (B, **Figure 52**) for wear. Fit the drum center on the pin. The drum center should fit firmly, but turn freely.

   d. Inspect the drum pin (C, **Figure 52**) and the mating notch (D) in the back of the drum center. The pin and notch must be symmetrical with no signs of wear.

4. Inspect the stopper arm assembly as follows:

   a. Inspect the roller (A, **Figure 53**) on the lever. It must be symmetrical, turn freely, but be firmly attached to the lever.

   b. Inspect the fit of the shouldered bolt in the lever hole (B, **Figure 53**). The bolt must fit in

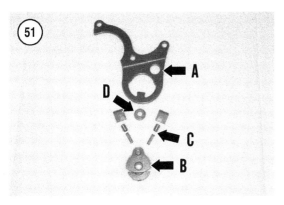

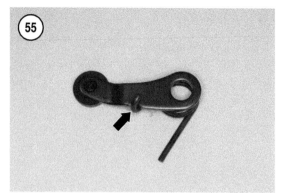

the hole firmly, but not bind or drag when the lever is pivoted.

c. Inspect the spring (C, **Figure 53**) for wear or fatigue.

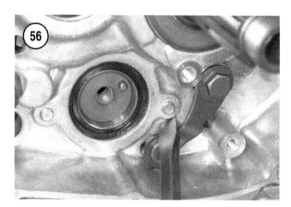

Installation

Refer to **Figure 41**.

1. Install the drum pin (**Figure 48**) into the shift drum.

2. Assemble the stopper arm as shown in **Figure 54**. Install the spring so the hooked end seats in the notch in the stopper arm (**Figure 55**). Check that the spring is oriented properly to the arm.

3. Install the stopper arm and finger-tighten the stopper bolt (**Figure 47**). Check that the spring is seated against the crankcase. Torque the bolt to the specifications in **Table 2**. Check that the arm pivots.

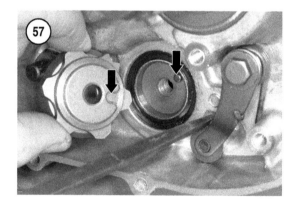

4. Install the shift drum center as follows:

   a. Apply threadlocking compound to the threads of the center pin.

   b. Pivot and hold the stopper arm away from the end of the shift drum (**Figure 56**).

   c. Install the shift drum center. Check that the notch in the back of the drum center aligns with the drum pin (**Figure 57**).

   d. Thread the center pin through the drum center and into the shift drum. Finger-tighten the pin and release the stopper arm. Torque the center pin to the specifications in **Table 2**.

5. Rotate the drum center to put the transmission in any gear, *but not neutral*. The neutral position is indicated when the roller on the stopper arm aligns with the mark on the shift drum center (**Figure 58**). Avoid this position.

6. Assemble the drum shifter and guide plate as follows:

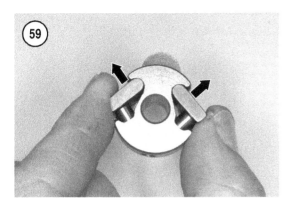

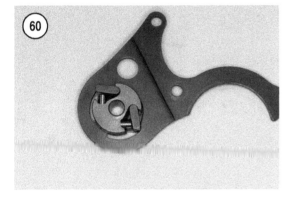

a. Insert the springs, plungers and pawls into the drum shifter. When installed, the pawls should have a spring-action (**Figure 59**).

NOTE
The rounded end of the pawls seat into the drum shifter.

b. Keep the pawls compressed and insert the assembly into the guide plate (**Figure 60**). Note the orientation of the assembly in the guide plate.

7. Install and seat the guide plate and drum shifter assembly into the drum center. Hold in place and tighten the bolts (**Figure 45**).

8. Install the collar onto the drum shifter. The shouldered side of the collar faces out (**Figure 61**).

9. Install the shift shaft as follows:

a. Place the washer on the shaft.

b. Insert the shaft through the crankcase.

c. Align and seat the shaft. The return spring must fit around the stud and the lever around the collar (**Figure 62**).

10. Install the gearshift lever. Position the lever on the shaft before inserting the bolt (**Figure 42**).

11. Check the shift action of the linkage. The linkage can be temporarily held in place with a piece of bar stock bolted to the crankcase (**Figure 63**). The stock lightly contacts the end of the shift shaft. If necessary, turn the mainshaft to aid in shifting the gears. After proper operation is verified, lubricate the parts with transmission oil.

12. Install the clutch assembly as described in this chapter.

13. Install the right crankcase cover as described in this chapter.

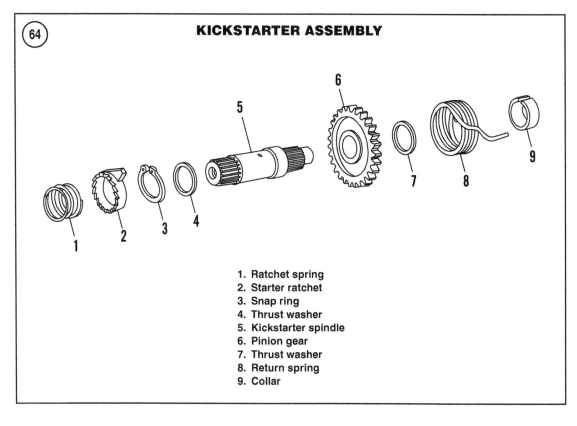

KICKSTARTER ASSEMBLY

1. Ratchet spring
2. Starter ratchet
3. Snap ring
4. Thrust washer
5. Kickstarter spindle
6. Pinion gear
7. Thrust washer
8. Return spring
9. Collar

KICKSTARTER AND IDLE GEAR

Removal

Refer to **Figure 64**.
1. Remove the right crankcase cover as described in this chapter.
2. Remove the clutch as described in this chapter.
3. Remove the the idle gear and bushing from the countershaft (**Figure 65**).
4. While grasping the spindle and torsion spring (**Figure 66**), pull the assembly from the crankcase (**Figure 67**).
5. Disassemble and clean the kickstarter assembly (**Figure 68**).
6. Inspect the parts as described in this section.

Inspection

Inspect the components of the kickstarter assembly and replace parts that are worn, damaged or fatigued.
1. Inspect the springs (**Figure 69**) for wear or fatigue. Check the return spring at all bends in the spring.

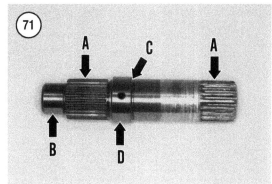

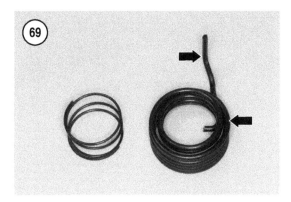

2. Inspect the pinion gear and starter ratchet as follows:
    a. Inspect the ratchet teeth (A, **Figure 70**) on the gear and ratchet. When the two parts are mated, the ratchet teeth must smoothly slip in one direction and positively lock in the other direction.
    b. Inspect the splines/bore (B, **Figure 70**) in the parts. The splines must be straight and the bore must not be scored or damaged.
    c. Inspect the gear teeth (C, **Figure 70**) for breakage or scoring.
    d. Measure the inside diameter of the pinion gear bore. Record the measurement. Compare the measurement to the specifications in **Table 1**.
3. Inspect the spindle as follows:
    a. Inspect the splines (A, **Figure 71**) for breakage or wear.
    b. Inspect the end of the spindle (B, **Figure 71**) for scoring or wear.
    c. Inspect the return spring hole for cleanliness.
    d. Inspect the snap ring groove (C, **Figure 71**) for wear or rounding of the groove at the upper edges.
    e. Measure the outside diameter of the shaft, where the pinion gear is mounted (D, **Figure 71**). Record the measurement. Compare the measurement to the specifications in **Table 1**.
4. Inspect the spindle bore in the case (A, **Figure 72**) for scoring or wear.
5. Inspect the ratchet retainer (B, **Figure 72**) for damage and tightness.
6. Inspect the idle gear and bushing as follows:
    a. Inspect the gear teeth for wear or damage.
    b. Inspect the gear bore and bushing for scoring.
    c. Measure the inside diameter of the gear (**Figure 73**). Record the measurement. Compare

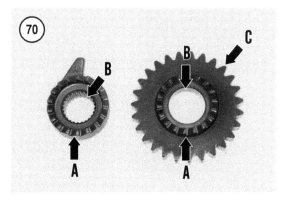

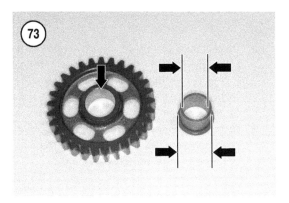

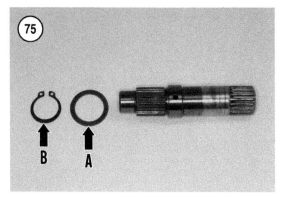

the measurement to the specifications in **Table 1**.

   d. Measure the inside and outside diameter of the bushing (**Figure 73**). Record the measurements. Compare the measurements to the specifications in **Table 1**.

7. Measure the outside diameter of the countershaft (**Figure 74**). Record the measurement. Compare the measurement to the specifications in **Table 1**.

8. Inspect the collar and thrust washers for wear or damage.

Installation

1. Assemble the kickstarter assembly (**Figure 64**) as follows:

   a. Install the thrust washer (A, **Figure 75**) and a *new* snap ring (B) onto the spindle. Install the snap ring so the flat side faces toward the splines (**Figure 76**).

   b. Install the pinion gear (A, **Figure 77**) and thrust washer (B). Install the gear so the ratchet teeth face toward the snap ring (**Figure 78**).

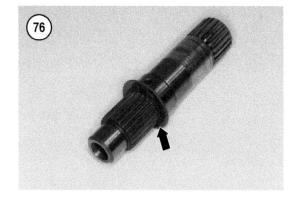

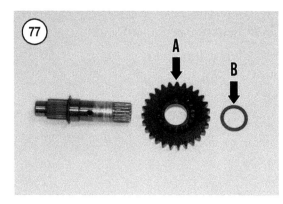

c. Install the return spring and collar (**Figure 79**). Insert the end of the spring into the spindle hole, checking that the opposite end of the spring fits around the pinion gear. Slide the collar onto the spindle and fit the collar around the spring (**Figure 80**).

d. Align the punch marks on the ratchet and spindle, then slide the ratchet onto the spindle (**Figure 81**). Install the ratchet so the ratchet teeth engage with the teeth on the kick gear.

e. Install the ratchet spring next to the ratchet. Refer to **Figure 67**.

f. Lubricate all parts with transmission oil.

2. Install the bushing and idle gear onto the countershaft (**Figure 82**). Install the idle gear with its smooth side facing out.

3. Check that the bore in the engine case is clean and lubricated (**Figure 72**).

4. Insert the kickstarter assembly into the engine case. While guiding the assembly into the case, check that the stopper on the ratchet fits behind the ratchet retainer (A, **Figure 83**) and the return spring fits into the case (B).

5. Install the clutch as described in this chapter.

6. Install the right crankcase cover as described in this chapter.

PRIMARY DRIVE GEAR

Removal and Inspection

1. Remove the right crankcase cover as described in this chapter.
2. Remove the exhaust valve governor as described in Chapter Four.
3. Disassemble the clutch as described in this chapter. Disassemble the clutch down to the clutch outer. The clutch outer will be removed after the primary gear bolt is loosened.
4. To remove the primary drive gear bolt (**Figure 84**), lock the primary drive and driven gears together with the Honda gear holder (part No. 07724-0010100). Alternatively, lock the gears together using a discarded drive gear as shown in **Figure 85**. Place the gear above the primary drive and driven gears. The gear must mesh with both sets of gear teeth.

> *CAUTION*
> *Do not jam the gears with screwdrivers or other tools. This can result in gear tooth breakage.*

5. Loosen the primary drive gear bolt by turning it counterclockwise.
6. Remove the clutch outer, needle bearing and outer guide.
7. Remove the primary drive gear bolt, washer and primary drive gear.
8. Remove the collar (**Figure 86**).
9. Inspect the primary drive gear for:
    a. Worn or broken teeth.
    b. Damaged splines.

Installation

1. Lubricate the parts with transmission oil.
2. Install the collar onto the crankshaft. Insert the smooth edge first (**Figure 87**). Seat the collar into the seal so that the stepped edge faces out (**Figure 86**).
3. Install the primary drive gear onto the crankshaft. Install the shouldered side first (**Figure 88**). The gear should be flush with the end of the crankshaft (**Figure 89**).
4. Install the washer and finger-tighten the primary drive gear bolt (**Figure 90**).

5. Install the clutch outer guide, needle bearing and clutch outer onto the mainshaft as described in this chapter.

6. Lock the primary drive and driven gears together with the Honda gear holder (part No. 07724-0010100). Alternatively, lock the gears together using a discarded drive gear as shown in **Figure 91**. Place the gear below the primary drive and driven gears. The gear must mesh with both sets of gear teeth.

CAUTION
Do not jam the gears with screwdrivers or other tools. This can result in gear tooth breakage.

7. Tighten the primary drive gear bolt by turning it clockwise. Torque the nut to the specifications in **Table 2**. Remove the special tool or gear from the engine.

8. Install the remainder of the clutch as described in this chapter.

9. Install the exhaust valve governor as described in Chapter Four.

10. Install the right crankcase cover as described in this chapter.

CLUTCH CABLE REPLACEMENT

1. Remove the fuel tank as described in Chapter Eight.

2. Loosen the clutch cable at the handlebar and disconnect it from the lever as described in Chapter Three.

3. Remove the alternator cover as described in Chapter Nine.

4. Disconnect the cable from the lifter lever (**Figure 92**).

NOTE
Before removing the cable, make a drawing or photograph of the cable

routing and the location of all cable retainers. The cable must be installed correctly or binding can occur. Always install a replacement cable in the same location as the original cable.

5. Remove the cable from the cable retainers.

6. Lubricate the cable ends.

7. Attach the cable to the lifter lever and to the handlebar lever.

8. Secure the cable with the cable retainers.

9. Adjust the cable as described in Chapter Three.

10. Install the alternator cover as described in Chapter Nine.

11. Install the fuel tank as described in Chapter Eight.

Table 1 CLUTCH SERVICE SPECIFICATIONS

	New mm (in.)	Service limit mm (in.)
Clutch friction plate thickness	2.92-3.08 (0.114-0.121)	2.85 (0.112)
Clutch dics warp	–	0.20 (0.008)
Clutch spring free length	45.7 (1.80)	44.7 (1.76)
Clutch outer guide outer diameter	27.987-28.000 (1.1018-1.1024)	27.97 (1.101)
Kickstarter pinion gear inner diameter	22.007-22.028 (0.8664-0.8672)	22.05 (0.868)
Kickstarter spindle outer diameter	21.959-21.980 (0.8645-0.8654)	21.95 (0.864)
Kickstarter idle gear inner diameter	20.020-20.041 (0.7882-0.7890)	20.07 (0.790)
Kickstarter idle gear bushing		
Inside diameter	17.000-17.018 (0.6693-0.6700)	17.04 (0.671)
Outside diameter	19.979-20.000 (0.7866-0.7874)	19.96 (0.786)
Countershaft outer diameter at kickstarter idle gear	16.966-16.984 (0.6680-0.6687)	16.95 (0.667)

Table 2 CLUTCH TORQUE SPECIFICATIONS

	N•m	in.-lb.	ft.-lb.
Clutch center locknut	80	–	59
Clutch lever pivot bolt	2	18	–
Clutch lever pivot nut	10	88	–
Clutch lever holder bolts	9	80	–
Clutch spring bolts	10	88	–
Kickstarter bolt			
1997-2000	26	–	20
2001	38	–	28
Primary drive gear bolt	64	–	47
Shift drum bearing			
retainer plate screw	10	88	–
Shift drum stopper bolt	12	106	–
Shift drum center pin	22	–	16
Shift lever bolt	12	106	–

CHAPTER SEVEN

TRANSMISSION AND
INTERNAL SHIFT MECHANISM

This chapter covers all transmission and internal shift mechanism service. Refer to Chapter Five for procedures to separate the crankcase for access to the transmission/shift assemblies.

SERVICE NOTES

Review the entire chapter before considering repairs to the transmission and shift mechanism (**Figure 1**). Make sure that the necessary skill required is understood and that all equipment required is avail-

able. Refer to Chapter One for tool usage and techniques.

Careful inspection of the parts is required, as well as keeping the parts oriented so they are reinstalled in the correct direction on the shafts. The gears, washers and snap rings *must* be installed in the same direction as they were before disassembly. If necessary, thread a piece of wire through the parts as they are removed, or, make an identification mark on each part to indicate orientation.

Always install new snap rings. The snap rings will fatigue and distort when they are removed. Do not reuse them, although they appear to be in good condition. To install a *new* snap ring without distorting it, hold the closed side of the snap ring with a pair of pliers while the open side is spread with snap ring pliers. While holding the snap ring with both tools, slide it over the shaft and to its position.

TRANSMISSION OPERATION

The motorcycle is equipped with a five-speed constant-mesh transmission. The gears on the

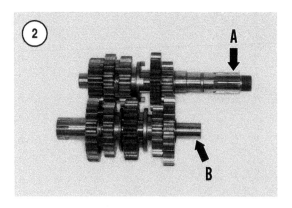

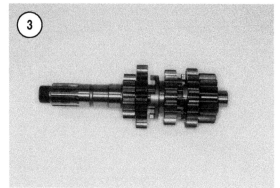

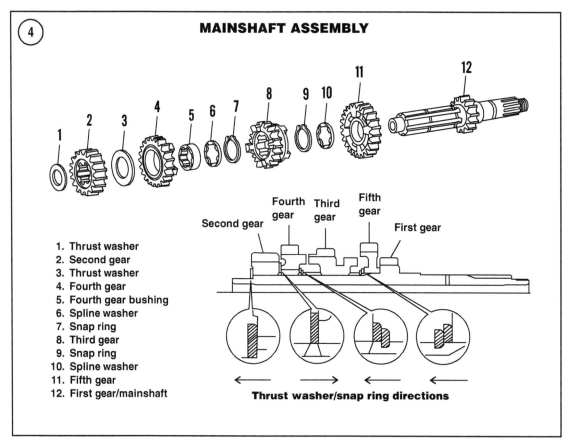

MAINSHAFT ASSEMBLY

1. Thrust washer
2. Second gear
3. Thrust washer
4. Fourth gear
5. Fourth gear bushing
6. Spline washer
7. Snap ring
8. Third gear
9. Snap ring
10. Spline washer
11. Fifth gear
12. First gear/mainshaft

Second gear
Fourth gear
Third gear
Fifth gear
First gear

Thrust washer/snap ring directions

mainshaft (A, **Figure 2**) are meshed with the gears on the countershaft (B). Each pair of meshed gears represents one gear ratio. For each pair of gears, one of the gears is splined to its shaft, while the other gear freewheels on its shaft.

Next to each freewheeling gear is a gear that is splined to the shaft. This locked gear can slide on the shaft and lock into the freewheeling gear, making that gear ratio active. Anytime the transmission is *in gear* one pair of meshed gears are locked to their shafts, and that gear ratio is selected. All other meshed gears have one freewheeling gear, making those ratios inoperative.

To engage and disengage the various gear ratios, the shift forks move the splined gears. The shift forks are guided by the shift drum, which is operated by the shift lever. As the bike is upshifted and downshifted, the shift drum rotates and guides the forks to engage and disengage pairs of gears on the transmission shafts.

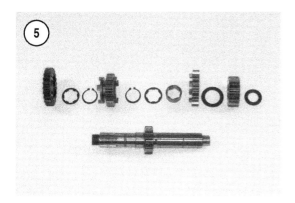

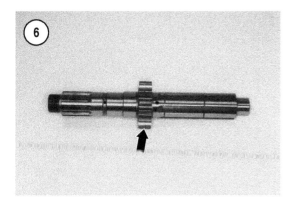

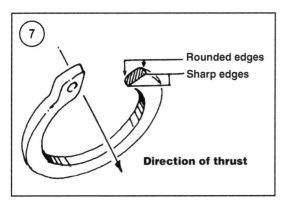

MAINSHAFT

Disassembly

Remove the parts from the mainshaft (**Figure 3**) in the order below. Refer to **Figure 4**.

> *CAUTION*
> *Keep parts oriented so their direction and order of assembly is known. Clean and organize the parts as they are removed, as shown in **Figure 5**.*

1. Disassemble the mainshaft in the following order:
   a. Thrust washer.
   b. Second gear.
   c. Thrust washer.
   d. Fourth gear.
   e. Fourth gear bushing.
   f. Spline washer.
   g. Snap ring.
   h. Third gear.
   i. Snap ring.
   j. Spline washer
   k. Fifth gear.

2. Inspect each part as described in this chapter, then return it to its place until assembly.

Assembly

Before beginning assembly, have two new snap rings on hand. Throughout the procedure, the orientation of many parts is made in relationship to first gear (**Figure 6**), which is part of the mainshaft.

> *CAUTION*
> *Although snap rings and washers appear identical on both sides, one side has rounded edges while the other side has sharp edges (**Figure 7**). This is caused by the manufacturer's stamping die. It is critical that the side with sharp edges be oriented as described in the procedure. This side of the part is called the **flat side** throughout the procedure. When oriented properly, the flat side of the snap ring always points in the direction of thrust. The sharp edge prevents the snap ring from **rolling** out of its groove when thrust is applied.*

Refer to the close-up views in **Figure 4** for the orientation of the snap rings and thrust washers. Also, look at the gear profiles to ensure installation is correct.

1. Clean and dry all parts before assembly. Lubricate all parts with transmission oil.

2. Install fifth gear. The gear dogs (**Figure 8**) must face *out*, or away from first gear.

3. Install the spline washer (A, **Figure 9**) and a *new* snap ring (B). The flat side of both parts must face

away from first gear. The snap ring must seat in the groove in the shaft.

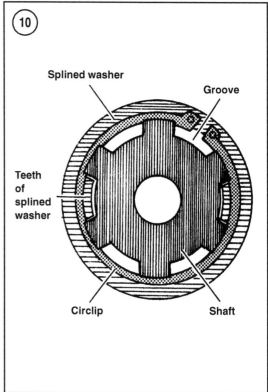

> CAUTION
> Install the snap ring so its ends align with a groove in the splines (**Figure 10**).

4. Install third gear (A, **Figure 11**) so the shift groove (B) faces first gear.

5. Install a *new* snap ring (A, **Figure 12**) and the spline washer (B). The flat side of both parts must face away from first gear. The snap ring must seat in the groove in the shaft.

> CAUTION
> Install the snap ring so its ends align with a groove in the splines (**Figure 10**).

6. Install the splined fourth gear bushing (A, **Figure 13**). If necessary, install the bushing so any oil holes in the bushing are aligned with any matching holes in the shaft. If the hole in the collar is offset, align it as close to the shaft hole as possible.

7. Install fourth gear (B, **Figure 13**) onto the fourth gear bushing. The gear dogs (**Figure 14**) must face toward first gear.

8. Install the thrust washer (**Figure 15**). The flat side must face toward first gear.

9. Install second gear (A, **Figure 16**), so the recessed side of the gear faces away from first gear.

10. Install the thrust washer (B, **Figure 16**), seating it in the gear recess. The flat side of the washer must face away from first gear.

11. Check the direction of the gears on the shaft (**Figure 17**).

12. Wrap a heavy rubber band around the end of the shaft to prevent parts from sliding off the shaft.

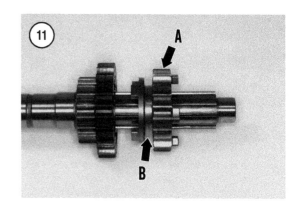

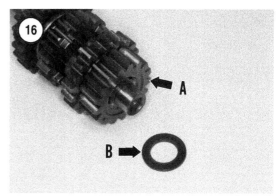

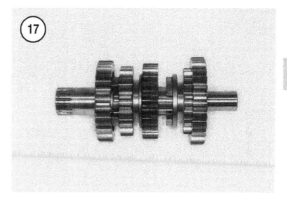

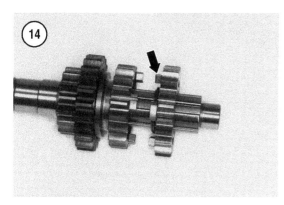

Wrap and store the assembly until it is ready for installation into the crankcase. Install the complete transmission assembly as described in *Crankcase Assembly* in Chapter Five.

COUNTERSHAFT

Disassembly

Refer to **Figure 18**.

> *CAUTION*
> *Completely disassemble one end of the countershaft before disassembling the other end of the shaft. Keep parts oriented so their direction and order of assembly is known. Clean and organize the parts as they are removed, as shown in **Figure 19**.*

1. Beginning at second gear, disassemble the countershaft in the following order:
   a. Thrust washer.
   b. Second gear.
   c. Second gear bushing.
   d. Thrust washer.

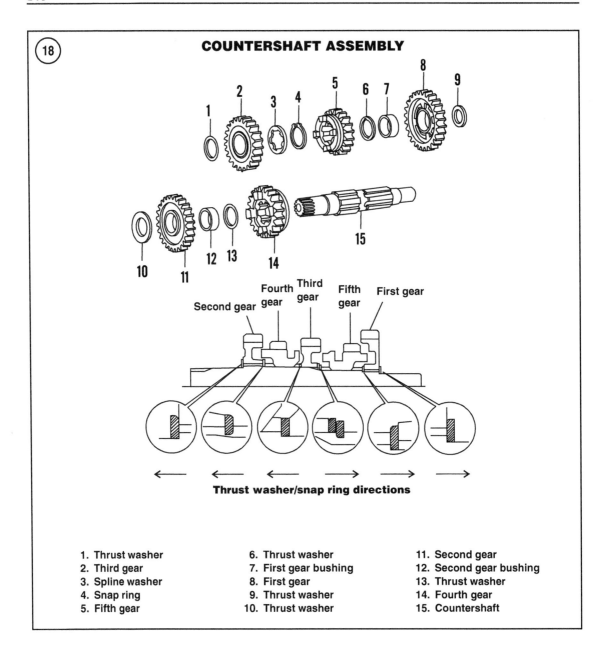

COUNTERSHAFT ASSEMBLY

Second gear   Fourth gear   Third gear   Fifth gear   First gear

Thrust washer/snap ring directions

1. Thrust washer	6. Thrust washer	11. Second gear
2. Third gear	7. First gear bushing	12. Second gear bushing
3. Spline washer	8. First gear	13. Thrust washer
4. Snap ring	9. Thrust washer	14. Fourth gear
5. Fifth gear	10. Thrust washer	15. Countershaft

e. Fourth gear.

NOTE
Continue disassembly from the oppo-site end of the countershaft.

f. Thrust washer.
g. First gear.
h. First gear bushing.
i. Thrust washer.
j. Fifth gear.
k. Snap ring.

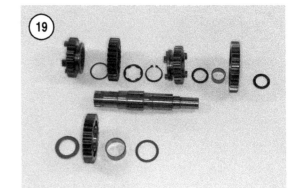

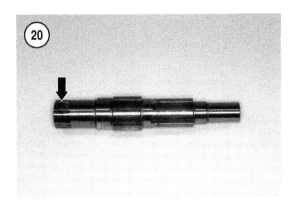

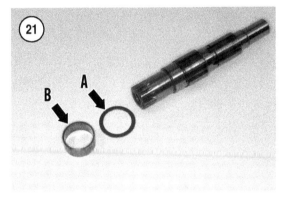

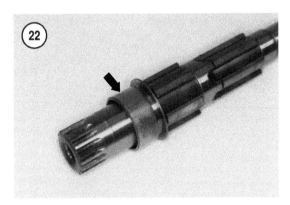

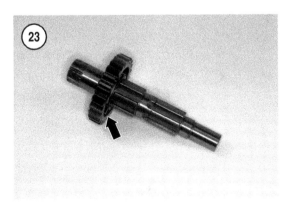

l. Spline washer.

m. Third gear.

n. Thrust washer.

2. Inspect each part as described in this chapter, then return it to its place until assembly.

Assembly

Before beginning assembly, have a new snap ring on hand. Throughout the procedure, the orientation of many parts is made in relationship to the splined end of the countershaft (**Figure 20**).

> *CAUTION*
> *Although snap rings and washers appear identical on both sides, one side has rounded edges while the other side has sharp edges (**Figure 7**). This is caused by the manufacturer's stamping die. It is critical that the side with sharp edges be oriented as described in the procedure. This side of the part is called the **flat side** throughout the procedure. When oriented properly, the flat side of the snap ring always points in the direction of thrust. The sharp edge prevents the snap ring from **rolling** out of its groove when thrust is applied.*

Refer to the close-up views in **Figure 18** for the orientation of the snap rings and thrust washers. Also, look at the gear profiles to ensure installation is correct.

1. Clean and dry all parts before assembly. Lubricate all parts with transmission oil.

> *NOTE*
> *Assembly will begin at the splined end of the countershaft.*

2. Install the thrust washer (A, **Figure 21**). The flat side of the washer must face toward the splined end.

3. Install the second gear bushing (B, **Figure 21**). Slide the bushing against the washer (A, **Figure 22**).

4. Install second gear onto the second gear bushing (**Figure 23**). The gear dogs must face away from the splined end.

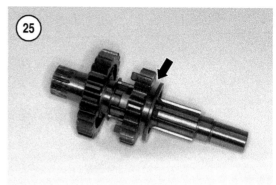

5. Install the thrust washer (**Figure 24**). The flat side of the washer must face toward the splined end.

NOTE
*Continue assembly from the opposite
end of the countershaft.*

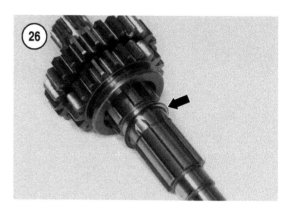

6. Install fourth gear so the shift groove (**Figure 25**) faces away from the splined end.
7. Install the thrust washer (**Figure 26**). The flat side of the washer must face toward the splined end.
8. Install third gear. The gear dogs (**Figure 27**) must face away from the splined end.
9. Install the spline washer (A, **Figure 28**). The flat side of the washer must face away from the splined end.
10. Install a *new* snap ring (B, **Figure 28**). The flat side of the snap ring must face away from the splined end. The snap ring must seat in the groove in the shaft.

*CAUTION
Install the snap ring so its ends align
with a groove in the splines (**Figure
10**).*

11. Install fifth gear (**Figure 29**) so the shift groove faces toward the splined end.
12. Install the thrust washer (A, **Figure 30**). The flat side of the washer must face away from the splined end.
13. Install the first gear bushing (B, **Figure 30**) onto the countershaft.
14. Install first gear (A, **Figure 31**) onto the first gear bushing. The gear dogs must face toward the splined end.
15. Install the thrust washer onto the countershaft (B, **Figure 31**). The flat side of the washer must face away from the splined end.

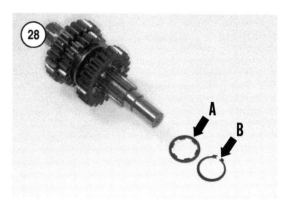

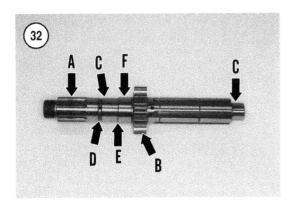

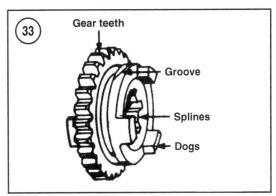

16. Wrap heavy rubber bands around the ends of the shaft to prevent parts from sliding off the shaft.
17. Wrap and store the assembly until it is ready for installation into the crankcase. Install the complete transmission assembly as described in *Crankcase Assembly* in Chapter Five.

TRANSMISSION INSPECTION

Mainshaft Inspection

When measuring the mainshaft parts, refer to **Table 2** for specifications. Record the measurements of each part and keep all parts oriented in their order of assembly. Replace parts that are worn or damaged.

Refer to **Figure 4**.
1. Inspect the mainshaft. Check for:
   a. Worn or damaged splines (A, **Figure 32**).
   b. Broken or damaged gear teeth (B, **Figure 32**).
   c. Wear, galling or other damage on the bearing/bushing surfaces (C, **Figure 32**). A blue discoloration indicates excessive heat.
   d. Oil hole cleanliness (D, **Figure 32**). Flush with solvent and blow clean with compressed air.
   e. Rounded or damaged snap ring grooves (E, **Figure 32**).
   f. Mainshaft wear. Measure the outside diameter of the shaft at the fifth gear position (F, **Figure 32**). Record the measurement. Refer to **Table 2** for the service limit.
2. Check each mainshaft gear for the following. Refer to **Figure 33**.
   a. Broken or damaged teeth.
   b. Worn or damaged splines.
   c. Scored, galled or fractured bore. A blue discoloration indicates excessive heat.

d. Worn or damaged shift fork groove. Check the gear groove with its mating shift fork. Third gear is mated with shift fork *C*.

e. Worn, damaged or rounded gear dogs. Any wear on the dogs and mating recesses should be uniform. If the dogs are not worn evenly, the remaining dogs will be overstressed and possibly fail. Check the engagement of the dogs by placing the gears at their appropriate positions on the mainshaft, then twisting the gears together. Check for positive engagement in both directions. If damage is evident, also check the condition of the shift forks, as described in this chapter.

NOTE
The side of the gear dogs that carries the engine load will wear and eventually become rounded. The unloaded side of the dogs will remain unworn. Rounded dogs will cause the transmission to jump out of gear.

f. Smooth gear operation on the mainshaft. Bored gears should fit firmly on their bushings, yet spin smoothly and freely. For fourth gear, check the fit of the bushing in the gear, and the fit of the bushing on the shaft. Splined gears should fit snugly at their position on the shaft, yet slide smoothly and freely from side to side. If a gear is worn or damaged, also replace the gear it mates to on the countershaft.

g. Measure the inside diameter of bored gears (**Figure 34**) and the inside and outside diameter of the plain bushing (**Figure 35**). Compare the measurements to the specifications in **Table 2**. Compare the fifth gear inside diameter with the shaft measurement made in Step 1.

3. Inspect the spline washers. The teeth in the washer should be uniform, and the washers should have a positive fit on the mainshaft.

4. Inspect the thrust washers. The washers should be smooth and show no signs of wear.

Countershaft Inspection

When measuring the countershaft parts, refer to **Table 2** for specifications. Record the measurements of each part and keep all parts oriented in their order of assembly. Replace parts that are worn or damaged.

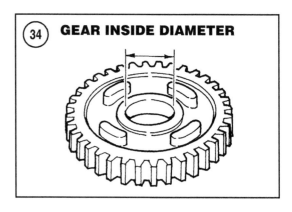

34 **GEAR INSIDE DIAMETER**

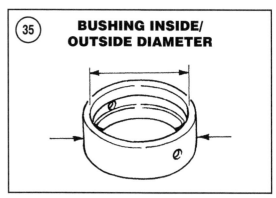

35 **BUSHING INSIDE/ OUTSIDE DIAMETER**

Refer to **Figure 18**.

1. Inspect the countershaft. Check for:
   a. Worn or damaged splines (A, **Figure 36**).
   b. Wear, galling or other damage on the bearing surfaces (B, **Figure 36**). A blue discoloration indicates excessive heat.
   c. Rounded or damaged snap ring groove (C, **Figure 36**).
   d. Countershaft wear. Measure the outside diameter of the shaft at the first, second and third gear positions. Record the measurements. Refer to **Table 2** for the service limit.

2. Check each countershaft gear for the following. Refer to **Figure 33**.
   a. Broken or damaged teeth.
   b. Worn or damaged splines.
   c. Scored, galled or fractured bore. A blue discoloration indicates excessive heat.
   d. Worn or damaged shift fork groove. Check the gear groove with its mating shift fork. Fourth gear is mated with the shift fork *L*. Fifth gear is mated with the shift fork *R*.
   e. Worn, damaged or rounded gear dogs. Any wear on the dogs and mating recesses should be uniform. If the dogs are not worn evenly,

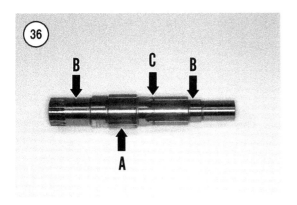

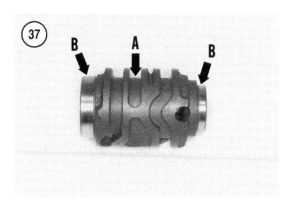

the remaining dogs will be overstressed and possibly fail. Check the engagement of the dogs by placing the gears at their appropriate positions on the countershaft, then twisting the gears together. Check for positive engagement in both directions. If damage is evident, also check the condition of the shift forks, as described in this chapter.

NOTE
The side of the gear dogs that carries the engine load will wear and eventually become rounded. The unloaded side of the dogs will remain unworn. Rounded dogs will cause the transmission to jump out of gear.

f. Smooth gear operation on the countershaft. Bored gears should fit firmly on their bushings, yet spin smoothly and freely. For first and second gears, check the fit of each bushing in its gear, and the fit of the bushing on the shaft. Splined gears should fit snugly at their position on the shaft, yet slide smoothly and freely from side to side. If a gear is worn or

damaged, also replace the gear it mates to on the mainshaft.

g. Measure the inside diameter of bored gears (**Figure 34**) and the inside and outside diameter of the plain bushings (**Figure 35**). Compare the measurements to the specifications in **Table 2**. Compare the third gear inside diameter with the shaft measurement made in Step 1.

3. Inspect the spline washer. The teeth in the washer should be uniform, and the washer should have a positive fit on the mainshaft.

4. Inspect the thrust washers. The washers should be smooth and show no signs of wear.

SHIFT DRUM AND FORKS

As the transmission is upshifted and downshifted, the shift drum and fork assembly engages and disengages pairs of gears on the transmission shafts. Gear shifting is done by the shift forks, which are guided by cam grooves in the shift drum.

It is important that the shift drum grooves, shift forks and mating gear grooves be in good condition. Too much wear between the parts will cause unreliable and poor engagement of the gears. This can lead to premature wear of the gear dogs and other parts.

Inspection

When measuring the shift forks, refer to **Table 2** for specifications and service limits. Record the measurements of each part.

1. Clean all parts in solvent and dry with compressed air.

2. Inspect the shift drum for wear and damage. Check the:
   a. Shift drum grooves (A, **Figure 37**), particularly at the *cam points*. The grooves should be a uniform width. Worn grooves can prevent complete gear engagement, which can cause rough shifting and allow the transmission to disengage.
   b. Bearing surfaces (B, **Figure 37**). Besides wear, look for signs of overheating discoloration and lack of lubrication.

3. Inspect each shift fork for wear and damage. Refer to **Figure 38**. Check the:
   a. Claw thickness. Measure both claws at the end.

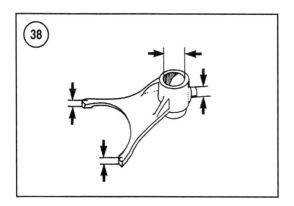

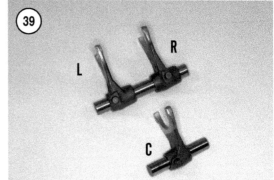

b. Shift fork inside diameter.
c. Guide pin. The pin should be symmetrical and not flat on the sides.
d. Fit of each fork guide pin with the appropriate groove in the shift drum. The pin should fit with slight lateral play.
e. Fit of each fork into the matching gear groove. The forks should fit with slight lateral play.

NOTE
*Fifth gear is mated with the right shift fork (**R**, **Figure 39**), third gear with the center shift fork (**C**), and fourth gear is mated with the left shift fork (**L**).*

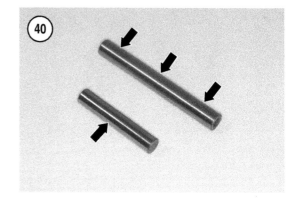

4. Inspect the shift fork shafts for wear and damage. Measure the shafts at the three locations noted in **Figure 40**.

Table 1 TRANSMISSION GENERAL SPECIFICATIONS

	Service limit mm (in.)
Transmission	5-speed constant mesh
Primary reduction	
Type	Gear
Ratio	3.00 (63/21)
Final reduction ratio	
1997	3.769 (49/13)
1998-2001	3.846 (50/13)
Gear ratios	
First gear	1.800 (27/15)
Second gear	1.470 (25/17)
Third gear	1.210 (23/19)
Fourth gear	1.000 (21/21)
Fifth gear	0.869 (20/23)

Table 2 TRANSMISSION SERVICE SPECIFICATIONS

	New mm (in.)	Service limit mm (in.)
Mainshaft assembly		
Mainshaft outer diameter		
at fifth gear	24.959-24.980	24.94
	(0.9826-0.9835)	(0.982)
Fourth gear inner diameter	28.007-28.028	28.05
	(1.1026-1.035)	(1.104)
Fourth gear bushing		
outer diameter	27.959-27.980	27.94
	(1.1007-1.1015)	(1.100)
Fourth gear to bushing		
clearance	0.027-0.069	0.11
	(0.0011-0.0027)	(0.004)
Fifth gear inner diameter	25.020-25.041	25.07
	(0.9850-0.9859)	(0.987)
Fifth gear to shaft clearance	0.040-0.082	0.13
	(0.0016-0.0032)	(0.005)
Countershaft assembly		
Countershaft outer diameter		
at first gear bushing	18.959-18.980	18.94
	(0.7464-0.7472)	(0.746)
Countershaft outer diameter		
at second gear bushing	24.959-24.979	24.96
	(0.9826-0.9834)	(0.983)
Countershaft outer		
diameter at third gear	24.959-24.980	24.94
	(0.9826-0.9835)	(0.982)
First gear inner diameter	22.020-22.041	22.07
	(0.8669-0.8678)	(0.869)
First gear bushing		
outer diameter	21.979-22.000	21.95
	(0.8653-0.8661)	(0.864)
First gear bushing		
inner diameter	19.000-19.021	19.04
	(0.7480-0.7489)	(0.750)
First gear to bushing		
clearance	0.020-0.062	0.12
	(0.0008-0.0024)	(0.005)
First gear bushing to		
shaft clearance	0.020-0.062	0.12
	(0.0008-0.0024)	(0.005)
Second gear inner diameter	30.020-30.041	30.07
	(1.1819-1.1827)	(1.184)
Second gear bushing		
outer diameter	29.979-30.000	29.95
	(1.1802-1.1811)	(1.179)
Second gear bushing		
inner diameter	27.000-27.021	27.04
	(1.0630-1.0638)	(1.064)
Second gear to bushing		
clearance	0.020-0.062	0.12
	(0.0008-0.0024)	(0.005)
Second gear bushing to		
shaft clearance	0.020-0.062	0.12
	(0.0008-0.0024)	(0.005)
Third gear inner diameter	25.020-25.041	25.07
	(0.9850-0.9859)	(0.987)

(continued)

7

Table 2 TRANSMISSION SERVICE SPECIFICATIONS (continued)

	New mm (in.)	Service limit mm (in.)
Countershaft assembly (continued)		
Third gear to shaft clearance	0.041-0.082	0.11
	(0.0016-0.0032)	(0.004)
Shift fork shaft outer diameter		
C fork	10.983-10.994	10.97
	(0.4324-0.4328)	(0.432)
R and L forks	11.966-11.984	11.95
	(0.4711-0.4718)	(0.470)
Shift fork inner diameter		
C fork	11.003-11.024	11.04
	(0.4332-0.4340)	(0.435)
R and L forks	12.035-12.056	12.07
	(0.4738-0.4746)	(0.475)
Shift fork claw thickness	4.93-5.0	4.8
	(0.194-0.197)	(0.19)

CHAPTER EIGHT

FUEL SYSTEM

This chapter provides procedures for removing, disassembling, inspecting and repairing the carburetor. Also included is information on how the different jetting systems affect engine performance. Tables listing the standard carburetor specifications for each model and year of motorcycle are at the end of the chapter.

Refer to this chapter for throttle cable replacement and air filter housing removal. Refer to Chapter Three for throttle cable adjustment and air filter service.

When working on the fuel system, observe the shop and safety practices described in Chapter One.

KEIHIN CARBURETOR (1997-2000 MODELS)

Use the following procedures for all models of Keihin carburetors. When necessary, differences in the carburetors are noted. The main difference between the carburetors is the power jet solenoid, used on 1997-1998 models.

Power Jet Solenoid (1997-1998 Models)

The power jet solenoid is electrically actuated by the ignition control module when engine speed reaches 8100 rpm. At that speed, the solenoid is turned on and fuel is delivered only through the main jet system. When engine speed falls below 8100 rpm, the solenoid shuts off and fuel is delivered through the main jet and power jet. As engine speed continues to decrease, the slow jet also becomes active. This system provides an increase in low and midrange torque, which allows the use of a high-speed main jet. Test procedures for the power jet solenoid are in Chapter Nine.

Removal and Installation

Refer to **Figure 1** and **Figure 2**.
1. Support the bike so it is stable and secure.
2. Shut off the fuel valve, then disconnect the fuel hose (**Figure 3**). If desired, remove the fuel tank as described in this chapter. It is not imperative that the fuel tank be removed.
3. On 1997-1998 models, disconnect the 2-pin connector leading from the power jet solenoid.

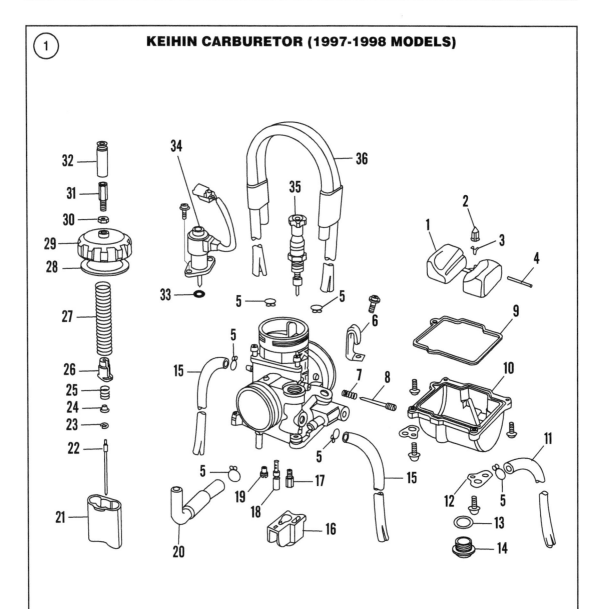

KEIHIN CARBURETOR (1997-1998 MODELS)

1. Float
2. Float valve
3. Clip
4. Float pin
5. Clamp
6. Hose clamp
7. Spring
8. Pilot air screw
9. O-ring
10. Float bowl
11. Overflow hose
12. Hose guide
13. O-ring
14. Drain plug
15. Air vent hose
16. Baffle plate
17. Main jet
18. Slow jet
19. Power jet
20. Fuel hose
21. Throttle valve
22. Jet needle
23. Clip
24. Collar
25. Spring
26. Cable holder
27. Spring
28. Seal
29. Carburetor top
30. Locknut
31. Adjuster
32. Cover
33. O-ring
34. Power jet solenoid
35. Choke/idle speed knob
36. Air vent hoses

KEIHIN CARBURETOR (1999-2000 MODELS)

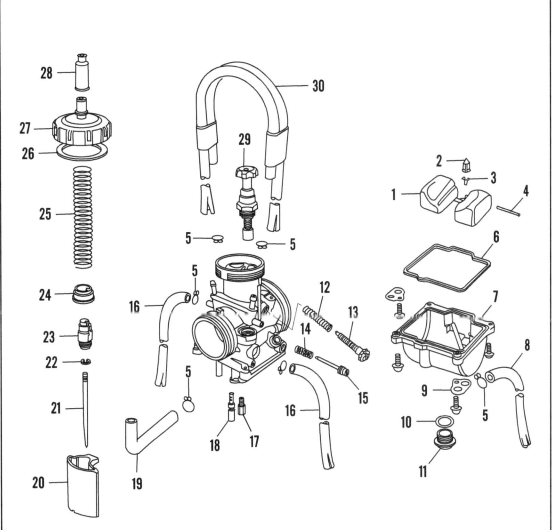

1. Float	11. Drain plug	21. Jet needle
2. Float valve	12. Spring	22. Clip
3. Clip	13. Throttle stop screw	23. Cable holder
4. Float pin	14. Spring	24. Collar
5. Clamp	15. Pilot air screw	25. Spring
6. O-ring	16. Air vent hose	26. Seal
7. Float bowl	17. Main jet	27. Carburetor top
8. Overflow hose	18. Slow jet	28. Cover
9. Hose guide	19. Fuel hose	29. Choke/idle speed knob
10. O-ring	20. Throttle valve	30. Air vent hoses

4. Loosen the band screws (**Figure 4**) clamping the carburetor to the air filter tube and insulator.

5. Check that the throttle cable is free, and then tilt the carburetor to the left side of the engine (**Figure 5**).

6. Unscrew the carburetor top (**Figure 6**), then *carefully* pull the throttle valve assembly from the carburetor (**Figure 7**).

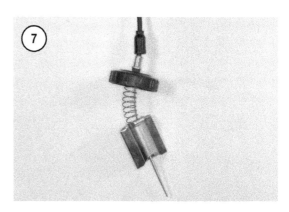

> *CAUTION*
> *When handling the throttle valve and jet needle, protect the jet needle from damage or bending.*

7A. On 1997-1998 models, remove the throttle cable from the cable holder as follows:

  a. Pull up on the spring so the cable holder is visible (**Figure 8**).

  b. Push down on the cable holder and turn it 90° counterclockwise (**Figure 9**).

  c. Remove the cable, holder, collar and spring. If desired, remove the jet needle.

7B. On 1999-2000 models, pull up on the spring and collar (**Figure 10**), then guide the cable out of

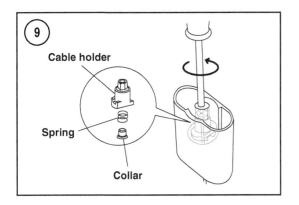

Cable holder

Spring

Collar

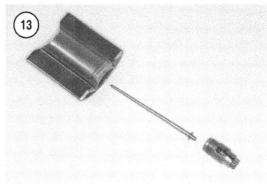

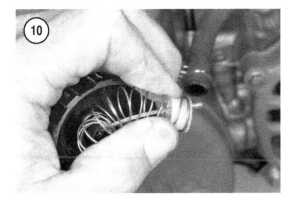

the cable holder slot. If desired, unscrew the cable holder and remove the jet needle.

8. Remove the carburetor from the engine.

9. Drain any remaining fuel from the carburetor.

10. Plug the air filter tube and insulator openings to prevent the entry of dirt.

11. Clean, inspect and repair the carburetor as described in this chapter.

12. Reverse this procedure to install the carburetor and throttle valve assembly. Note the following:

    a. Loosely install the carburetor (**Figure 11**) before installing the throttle valve and cable assembly.

    b. On 1999-2000 models, the tab on the collar must engage with the slot on the cable holder. The collar must completely seat on the cable holder in order to secure the cable.

    c. Align the lug on the carburetor with the groove in the insulator.

    d. Route the air vent and overflow hoses.

    e. Adjust the throttle cable as described in Chapter Three.

    f. Check the throttle for proper operation. The throttle valve should seat in the carburetor body and travel the full height of the opening (**Figure 12**).

    g. Check the carburetor and fuel tank for leaks.

Disassembly and Assembly

Refer to **Figure 1** and **Figure 2**.

1. Remove the jet needle from the throttle valve. On 1999-2000 models, unscrew the cable holder and\ remove the jet needle (**Figure 13**). Make note of where the clip is set on the jet needle (**Figure 14**). Count the grooves from the top of the needle.

2. Disconnect and label the hoses (**Figure 15**).

3. On 1997-1998 models, remove the power jet solenoid and O-ring.

4. Remove the choke/idle speed knob (A, **Figure 16**).

5. On 1999-2000 models, remove the throttle stop screw and spring (B, **Figure 16**).

6. Remove the pilot air screw (C, **Figure 16**) as follows:

    a. Turn the pilot air screw clockwise, while counting the number of turns, until it *lightly* seats.

    b. Record the number of turns.

    c. Turn the pilot air screw counterclockwise and remove it and the spring.

    d. On 1997-1998 models, also remove the O-ring and washer.

7. Remove the screws and hose guides from the float bowl (**Figure 17**), then remove the bowl and O-ring.

8. Remove the drain plug and O-ring from the bowl.

9. Remove the pin (**Figure 18**) from the float assembly, then lift out the float and float valve assembly (**Figure 19**).

10. On 1997-1998 models, remove the baffle plate.

11. Remove the slow jet (A, **Figure 20**).

12. Remove the main jet (B, **Figure 20**).

13. On 1997-1998 models, remove the power jet.

14. Clean and inspect the parts as described in this chapter.

15. Refer to *Carburetor Jetting* in this chapter for the function of the jets and their affect on performance.

16. Reverse this procedure to assemble the carburetor. Note the following:

    a. Install *new*, lubricated O-rings.

    b. Attach the float valve and clip to the float (**Figure 21**) before installing the parts.

    c. Check and adjust the float height. Refer to *Float Adjustment* in this chapter.

    d. Check that the jet needle clip (**Figure 14**) is firmly in place. If necessary, refer to **Table 1** for the recommended setting. Count the grooves from the top of the needle.

    e. When installing the pilot air screw (C, **Figure 16**), *lightly* seat the screw, then turn it out the number of turns recorded during disassembly. If the number of turns is not known, refer to **Table 1** for the basic setting.

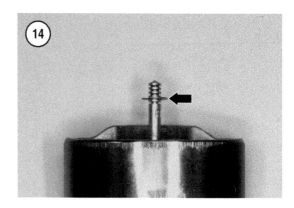

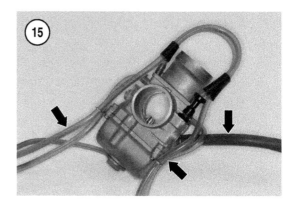

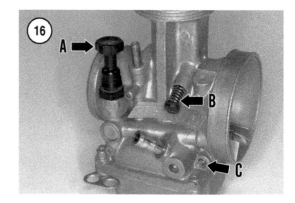

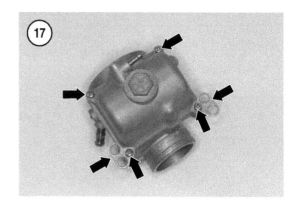

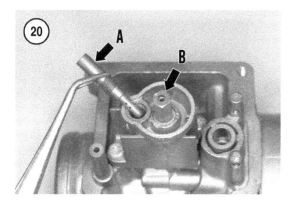

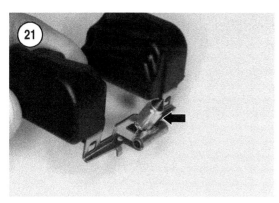

f. Install the carburetor as described in this chapter.

MIKUNI CARBURETOR
(2001 MODELS)

Removal and Installation

Refer to **Figure 22**.

1. Support the bike so it is stable and secure.
2. Shut off the fuel valve, then disconnect the fuel hose. If desired, remove the fuel tank as described in this chapter. It is not imperative that the fuel tank be removed.
3. Turn the handlebar fully to the left.
4. Loosen the band screws, clamping the carburetor to the air filter tube and insulator.
5. Check that the throttle cable is free, then tilt the carburetor to the left side of the engine.
6. Remove the screws (A, **Figure 23**) and the carburetor top (B), then *carefully* pull the throttle valve assembly from the carburetor.

CAUTION
When handling the throttle valve and jet needle, protect the jet needle from damage or bending.

7. Remove the throttle cable from the cable holder as follows:
    a. Pull up on the spring and slide the collar off the cable holder (**Figure 24**).
    b. While keeping the spring compressed, guide the cable out of the cable holder slot (A, **Figure 24**). If desired, unscrew the cable holder and remove the jet needle.
8. Remove the carburetor from the engine.
9. Drain any remaining fuel from the carburetor.
10. Plug the air filter tube and insulator openings to prevent the entry of dirt.
11. Clean, inspect and repair the carburetor as described in this chapter.
12. Reverse this procedure to install the carburetor and throttle valve assembly. Note the following:
    a. Loosely install the carburetor (**Figure 11**) before installing the throttle valve and cable assembly.
    b. The tab on the collar must engage with the slot on the cable holder (B, **Figure 24**). The collar must completely seat on the cable holder in order to secure the cable.

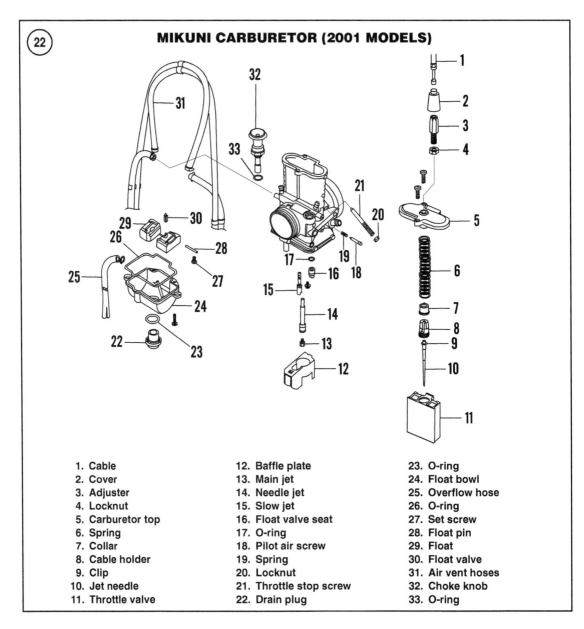

MIKUNI CARBURETOR (2001 MODELS)

1. Cable	12. Baffle plate	23. O-ring
2. Cover	13. Main jet	24. Float bowl
3. Adjuster	14. Needle jet	25. Overflow hose
4. Locknut	15. Slow jet	26. O-ring
5. Carburetor top	16. Float valve seat	27. Set screw
6. Spring	17. O-ring	28. Float pin
7. Collar	18. Pilot air screw	29. Float
8. Cable holder	19. Spring	30. Float valve
9. Clip	20. Locknut	31. Air vent hoses
10. Jet needle	21. Throttle stop screw	32. Choke knob
11. Throttle valve	22. Drain plug	33. O-ring

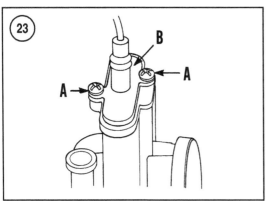

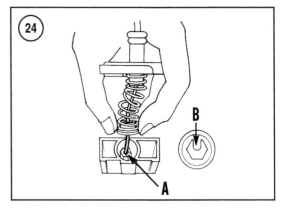

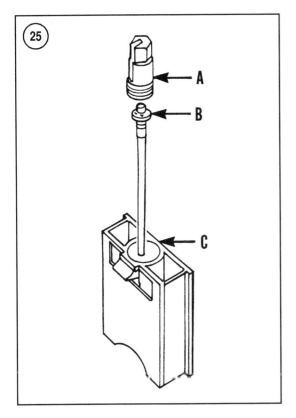

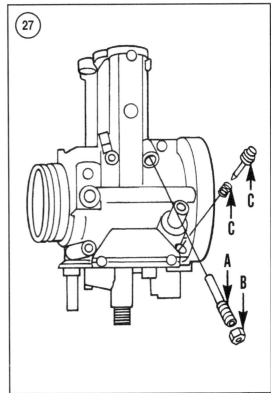

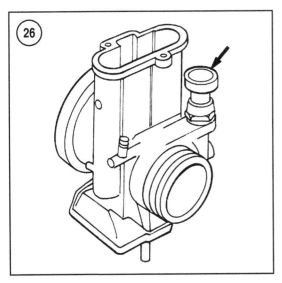

c. Align the lug on the carburetor with the groove in the insulator.

d. Route the air vent and overflow hoses.

e. Adjust the throttle cable as described in Chapter Three.

f. Check the throttle for proper operation. The throttle valve should seat in the carburetor body and travel the full height of the opening (**Figure 12**).

g. Check the carburetor and fuel tank for leaks.

Disassembly and Assembly

Refer to **Figure 22**.

1. Unscrew the cable holder (A, **Figure 25**) and remove the jet needle (B) from the throttle valve (C). Make note of where the clip is set on the jet needle. Count the grooves from the top of the needle.

2. Disconnect and label the hoses.

3. Remove the choke knob (**Figure 26**).

4. Remove the throttle stop screw (A, **Figure 27**) and locknut (B).

5. Remove the pilot air screw (C, **Figure 27**) as follows:

    a. Turn the pilot air screw clockwise, while counting the number of turns, until it *lightly* seats.

    b. Record the number of turns.

c. Remove the pilot air screw (C, **Figure 27**) and spring (D). Turn the screw counterclockwise to remove.

6. Remove the screw (A, **Figure 28**) from the float bowl (B), then remove the bowl and O-ring.

7. Remove the drain plug and O-ring from the bowl.

8. Remove the float assembly as follows:

   a. Remove the float pin set screw (A, **Figure 29**).

   b. Remove the float pin (B, **Figure 29**).

   c. Remove the float (C, **Figure 29**) and float valve (D) as an assembly.

9. Remove the baffle plate (A, **Figure 30**).

10. Remove the main jet (B, **Figure 30**).

11. Remove the needle jet (C, **Figure 30**).

12. Remove the slow jet (D, **Figure 30**).

13. Remove the set screw securing the float valve seat (E, **Figure 30**).

14. Remove the float valve seat and O-ring (F, **Figure 30**).

15. Clean and inspect the parts as described in this chapter.

16. Refer to *Carburetor Jetting* in this chapter for jet function and performance.

17. Reverse this procedure to assemble the carburetor. Note the following:

   a. Install *new*, lubricated O-rings.

   b. Attach the float valve and clip to the float before installing the parts.

   c. Check and adjust the float height. Refer to *Float Adjustment* in this chapter.

   d. Check that the jet needle clip (B, **Figure 25**) is firmly in place. If necessary, refer to **Table 1** for the recommended setting. Count the grooves from the top of the needle.

   e. When installing the pilot air screw (C, **Figure 27**), *lightly* seat the screw, then turn it out the number of turns recorded during disassembly. If the number of turns is not known, refer to **Table 1** for the basic setting.

   f. Install the carburetor as described in this chapter.

CARBURETOR CLEANING AND INSPECTION (ALL MODELS)

Use the following procedure to clean and inspect all makes and models of carburetors used from 1997-2001. If necessary, refer to **Figure 1**, **Figure 2** or **Figure 22** to determine if some parts shown are fitted to the carburetor being inspected. Although parts be-

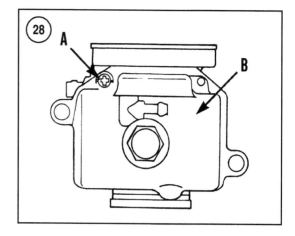

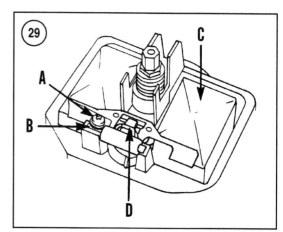

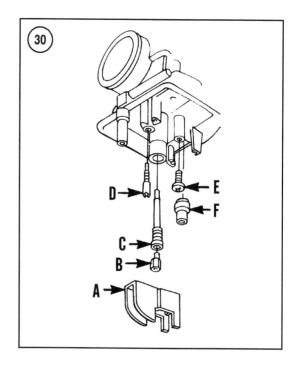

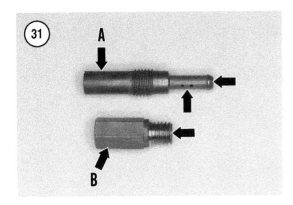

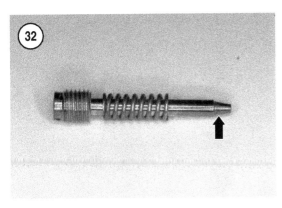

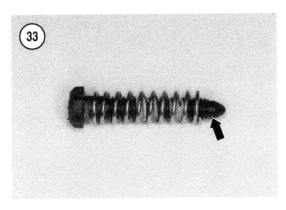

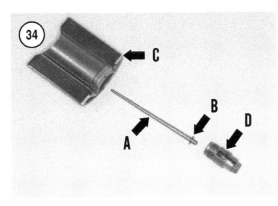

ing inspected may appear different than those in the procedure, the inspection standards are the same.

It is recommended to use a commercial cleaner specifically for carburetors, since the cleaner contains agents for removing fuel residue and buildup. Use a cleaner that is harmless to rubber and plastic parts. Follow the manufacturer's instructions when using the cleaner.

CAUTION
Do not attempt to clean the jet orifices or seats with wire or drill bits. These items can scratch the surfaces and alter flow rates or cause leaking.

NOTE
Because of heat and age, O-rings and gaskets eventually lose there flexibility and do not seal properly. Replace all O-rings and gaskets when rebuilding a carburetor.

1. Clean all the parts in carburetor cleaner. Remove all sediment from the float chamber surfaces, and clean all carburetor passages and hoses with compressed air.

CAUTION
Do not submerge the throttle position sensor or wiring harness in solvent. Only wipe the outside of the unit and wiring harness with a shop cloth.

2. Inspect the jets, including the main jet (A, **Figure 31**) and slow jet (B), the power jet and the needle jet. Check that all holes, in the ends and sides, are clean and undamaged.

3. Inspect the pilot air screw and spring. Inspect the tip for dents (**Figure 32**). The spring coils should be resilient and not crushed.

4. Inspect the throttle stop screw. Inspect the tip for dents (**Figure 33**). The spring coils should be resilient and not crushed.

5. Inspect the throttle valve assembly as follows:
   a. The needle (A, **Figure 34**) must be smooth and evenly tapered. If it is stepped, dented, worn or bent, replace the needle.
   b. The clip (B, **Figure 34**) must fit tight in the needle groove. Replace the clip if loose or damaged.
   c. Check the throttle valve (C, **Figure 34**) for damage. Inspect the fit of the throttle valve in the carburetor body. The valve should fit snugly, but easily slide through the bore. If

drag or binding is felt, replace the throttle valve.

   d. Inspect the cable holder (D, **Figure 34**) for damage.

6. Inspect the float and float valve assembly.

   a. Inspect the tip of the float valve (A, **Figure 35**). If it is stepped or dented (**Figure 36**), replace the float valve and seat.

   b. Lightly press on the spring-loaded pin (B, **Figure 35**) in the float valve. The pin should easily move in and out of the valve. If it is varnished with fuel residue, replace the float valve and seat.

   c. Inspect the float valve seat (C, **Figure 35**). The seat should be clean and scratch-free. If it is not, the float valve will not seat properly and the carburetor will overflow. Replace the seat and float valve.

   d. Inspect the float and pin (**Figure 37**). Submerge the float in water and check for leakage. Replace the float if water or fuel is detected inside the float. Check that the float pin is straight and smooth. It must be a slip-fit in the float.

7. Inspect the float bowl (**Figure 38**). Clean the overflow tube and replace the O-rings on the bowl and drain plug.

8. Inspect the choke knob (**Figure 39**) for cleanliness and stepped wear. 1997-1998 model chokes have a needle on the end. Inspect the needle for straightness and stepped wear.

9. Inspect the carburetor body (**Figure 40** and **Figure 41**). Clean all passages, orifices and vents with compressed air.

10. For carburetors fitted with a power jet solenoid, refer to Chapter Nine for electrically testing the solenoid.

FLOAT ADJUSTMENT

Height Adjustment

The float and float valve maintain a constant fuel level in the float bowl. As fuel is used, the float lowers and allows more fuel past the valve. As the fuel level rises, the float closes the valve when the required fuel level is reached. If the float is out of adjustment, the fuel level will be too high or low, and this can cause fuel overflow and poor engine performance.

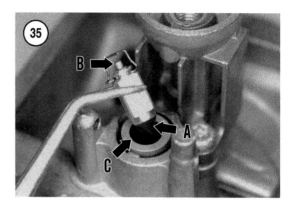

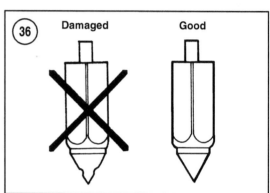

Damaged   Good

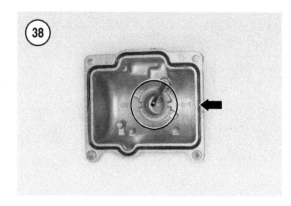

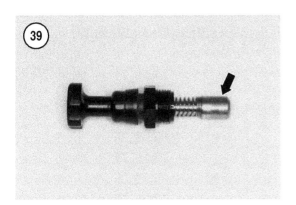

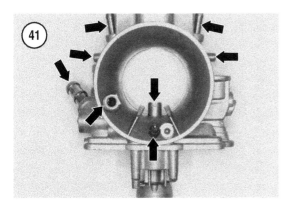

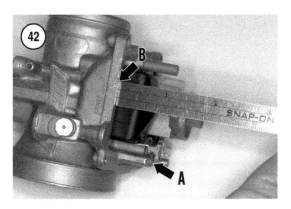

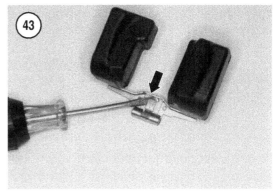

1. Remove the carburetor as described in this chapter.

2. Remove the float bowl.

3. Lightly touch the float to ensure the float valve is seated.

4. Hold the carburetor so the float valve remains seated, but the spring-loaded pin in the valve is not being compressed by the tab on the float (A, **Figure 42**). The tab should only *touch* the pin.

5. Measure the distance from the carburetor gasket surface (**B, Figure 42**) to the highest point on the float. Refer to **Table 1** for the required float height.

NOTE
A float level gauge (part No.07401-010000) is available from a Honda dealership.

6. If the float height is incorrect, remove the float from the carburetor and bend the float tab (**Figure 43**) in the appropriate direction to raise or lower the float. Recheck the height after adjusting the float.

7. Install the float bowl.

8. Install the carburetor as described in this chapter.

CARBURETOR JETTING

The performance of the carburetor is affected by altitude, temperature, humidity and riding conditions.

Before disassembling the carburetor, understand the function of the slow, needle and main jet systems. On 1997-1998 models, the power jet and power jet solenoid are also factors. When evaluating or troubleshooting these systems, keep in mind that their operating ranges overlap one another during the transition from closed to fully open throttle.

If the engine is not running or performing up to expectations, check the following before adjusting or changing the components in the carburetor:

1. Throttle cables. Check that the cables are not dragging and are correctly adjusted.
2. Air filter. Check that the filter is clean.
3. Fuel flow. Check that fuel is adequately flowing from the fuel tank to the carburetor. Inspect in-line filter screens for plugging.
4. Ignition timing. Check that timing is correct.
5. On 1997-1998 models, check that the power jet solenoid is operating properly.
6. Choke. Check that the choke is fully open.
7. Muffler. Check that the muffler is not restricting flow.
8. Brakes. Check that the brake pads are not dragging on the discs.

Slow (Pilot) Jet System

The slow system consists of the slow jet and pilot air screw. The slow system controls the air/fuel ratio from closed throttle to 1/4 throttle. The slow jet draws fuel from the float chamber and mixes it with air from the pilot air jet passage. The atomized air/fuel mixture is then discharged into the throat of the carburetor. Turning the pilot air screw in will richen the air/fuel mixture, while turning the screw out will lean the mixture.

The slow jet is interchangeable with jets that will provide a leaner or richer air/fuel mixture. Replacing the standard slow jet with a larger numbered jet will make the mixture *richer*. Slow jets with a smaller number will make the mixture *leaner*.

Jet Needle

The jet needle is connected to the throttle valve and controls the mixture from approximately 1/4 to 3/4 throttle. The jet needle seats into the needle jet, and regulates the air/fuel mixture from the jet to the carburetor throat. The jet needle used in Keihin carburetors regulates fuel by its taper, diameter and clip position (**Figure 44**). In the closed throttle position, the tapered needle shuts off flow from the needle jet. As the throttle is opened, the needle allows fuel to pass by the taper, and between the straight portion of the needle and jet wall.

The position of the needle in the jet can be adjusted by removing the needle clip and positioning

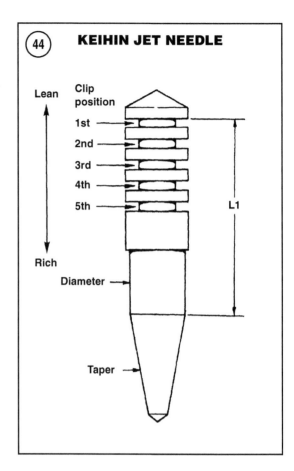

it on a higher or lower groove in the needle. Raising the clip will lower the needle into the jet, creating a *lean* condition. Lowering the clip will raise the needle, creating a *rich* condition.

Adjust the needle if it is determined the engine will perform better for the loads or climate in which it is operated. Do not adjust or resize the needle in an attempt to correct other problems that may exist with the carburetor or engine. Engine damage can

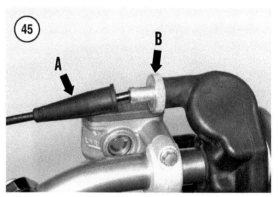

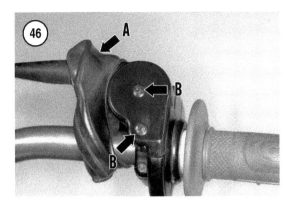

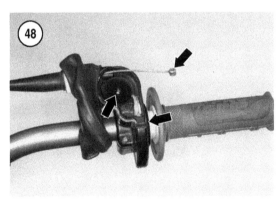

occur if riding conditions do not warrant an overly rich or lean fuel mixture.

Main Jet

The main jet is screwed to the bottom of the needle jet and controls the mixture from approximately 3/4 to full throttle. The main jet is numbered and is interchangeable with jets that will provide a leaner or richer air/fuel mixture. Replacing the standard jet with a larger numbered jet will make the mixture

richer. Jets with a smaller number will make the mixture *leaner.*

The main jet can be accessed by removing the cap on the bottom of the float bowl. The carburetor does not have to be removed.

Changing the Needle or Jets

When changing the needle or jets, note the following practices:
1. Record all settings, including the size number and clip position.
2. Check that the slow system is adjusted correctly before changing the needle or main jet.
3. To check a main jet, run the bike at full throttle in an open area. Shut off the engine while it is running at full throttle, then pull in the clutch and coast to a stop. Remove the spark plug and check it for a lean or rich condition as described in Chapter Three.

THROTTLE CABLE REPLACEMENT

1. Remove the fuel tank as described in this chapter.
2. Pull back the rubber boot from the throttle cable adjuster (A, **Figure 45**).
3. Loosen the locknut (B, **Figure 45**) and turn the cable adjuster in to create slack in the cable.
4. Pull back the rubber boot from the throttle housing (A, **Figure 46**).
5. Remove the screws (B, **Figure 46**) from the throttle housing, then remove the cover.
6. Remove the cable end from the throttle control (**Figure 47**).
7. Disconnect the cable from the carburetor throttle valve as described in the carburetor removal procedure in this chapter.
8. Remove the cable from the bike. Make note of how the cable is routed so the new cable can be routed identically.
9. Identify the cable ends, then route the cable.
10. Remove the cable roller, then lubricate the cable end, cable pivot and roller pivot with lithium grease (**Figure 48**).

NOTE
Lubrication of the cable is not recommended. Whenever the cable drags or binds, replace the cable.

11. Insert the cable end into the throttle control.

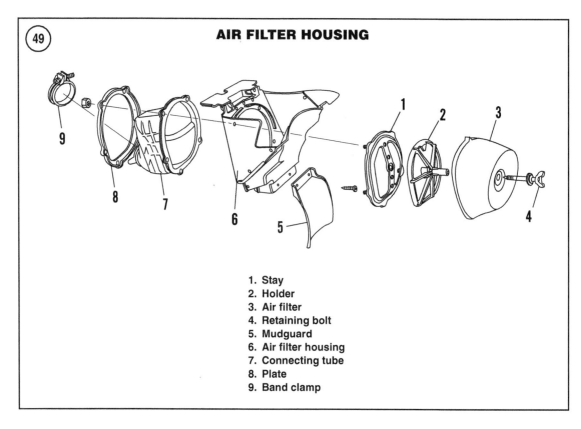

AIR FILTER HOUSING

1. Stay
2. Holder
3. Air filter
4. Retaining bolt
5. Mudguard
6. Air filter housing
7. Connecting tube
8. Plate
9. Band clamp

12. Wrap the cable around the cable roller, then put the roller on the pivot.

13. Install the housing cover and boot.

14. Adjust the cable as described in Chapter Three.

15. Install the fuel tank as described in this chapter.

AIR FILTER HOUSING

The air filter housing assembly (**Figure 49**) is bolted to the subframe (**Figure 50**). It is not necessary to remove the housing in order to service the air filter. Service the air filter as described in Chapter Three. If the air filter housing must be removed, remove the subframe from the motorcycle as described in Chapter Fifteen. Remove the four bolts securing the housing to the subframe.

FUEL TANK

Removal and Installation

1. Remove the seat as described in Chapter Fifteen.

2. Remove the side covers as described in Chapter Fifteen.

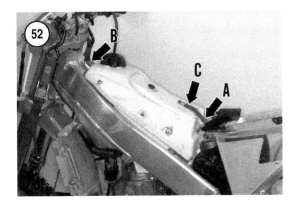

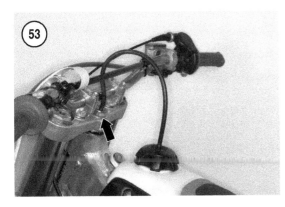

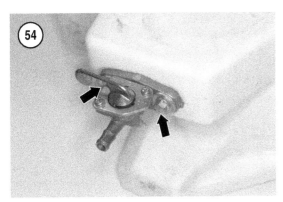

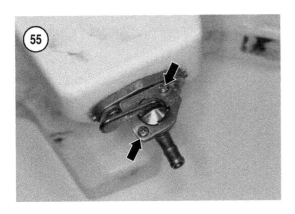

3. Remove the radiator shrouds as described in this chapter.

4. Turn off the fuel valve, then disconnect the fuel line from the valve (**Figure 51**).

5. On 1997-1999 models, remove the upper subframe mounting bolt (A, **Figure 52**).

6. Remove the front mounting bolt (B, **Figure 52**).

7. Remove the band from the fuel tank (C, **Figure 52**).

8. Route the breather hose (**Figure 53**) out of the steering stem.

9. Lift the tank from the frame.

10. To install the fuel tank, reverse this procedure. Note the following:

    a. On 1997-1999 models, torque the upper subframe mounting bolt to 30 N•m (22 in.-lb.).

    b. Check that the hose clamp is in position on the fuel line (**Figure 51**).

    c. Turn on the fuel valve and check for leaks.

FUEL VALVE AND FILTER

Removal, Inspection and Installation

The fuel valve can be removed with the fuel tank mounted on the bike, or with the fuel tank removed. In either case, the fuel must be drained from the fuel tank before removing the valve.

> *WARNING*
> *Drain the fuel into an approved container. Perform the draining procedure a safe distance away from the work area.*

1. Turn off the fuel valve, then disconnect the fuel line from the valve (**Figure 51**).

2. Connect a length of fuel line to the valve so the line can be directed into an approved container or hold an approved container below the fuel valve. Turn on the fuel valve and drain the fuel.

3. Remove the two bolts and collars securing the fuel valve to the fuel tank (**Figure 54**).

4. Remove the two screws (**Figure 55**) securing the valve handle and cover plate.

5. Remove the O-ring from the filter.

6. Inspect the fuel valve (**Figure 56**) as follows:

    a. Wash the valve and fuel filter in solvent.

b. Hold the fuel valve near a light and check for buildup inside the screen.

c. Inspect the valve passages for buildup.

7. Reassemble the valve.

8. Install a *new*, lubricated O-ring over the filter.

9. Install the fuel valve into the fuel tank.

10. Install the collars and bolts.

11. If the fuel tank was not removed, connect the fuel line. Check that the hose clamp is in position on the fuel line (**Figure 51**).

12. If the fuel tank was removed, install the fuel tank as described in this chapter.

13. When filling the tank, start with a small amount of fuel and check for leaks.

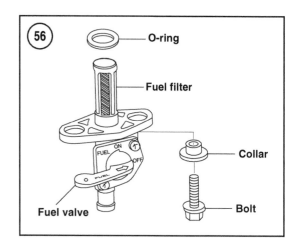

Table 1 CARBURETOR SPECIFICATIONS

Carburetor make and identification number	
1997-1998	Keihin PJ28L
1999	Keihin PWK00A
2000	Keihin PWK00B
2001	Mikuni TMX 11A
Carburetor type and bore diameter	Piston valve; 38 mm
Main jet	
1997-1998	175
1999	190
2000	180
2001	420
Slow jet	
1997-1998	55
1999	42
2000	48
2001	35
Power jet (1997-1998 only)	42
Jet needle	
1997-1998	R1369MS
1999	R1370DKA
2000	A715/289R/A327/A487
2001	6BEH1-73
Jet needle clip position	3rd groove
Pilot air screw turns out	
1997-1999	2
2000	1 1/2
2001	1 3/4
Float height*	
1999-2000	16.0 mm (0.63 in.)
2001	15.0 mm (0.59 in.)

* Float measurement is above gasket surface for float bowl. Float should touch, but not compress needle valve.

CHAPTER NINE

IGNITION SYSTEM

This chapter describes service procedures for the ignition components and carburetor power jet system (1997-1998 models only).

The ignition system consists of the following:

1. A permanent magnet alternator (flywheel and stator), mounted on the left side of the crankshaft.

2. Exciter coil.

3. Ignition pulse generator.

4. Ignition control module.

5. Ignition coil.

Ignition is achieved with a capacitor discharge ignition (CDI) type system. The CDI system operates on a different principle than a conventional ignition coil type system. In a conventional system, power is supplied to the primary side of the ignition coil and stopping the current to the primary windings generates the secondary current required to fire the spark plug. However, in a CDI system the ignition coil is actually a transformer. Current is stored in a capacitor within the ignition control module and released to the ignition coil when the ignition pulse generator indicates the piston is reaching the ignition point. The voltage is then stepped up by the ignition coil to the high voltage required to jump the spark plug gap and fire the plug.

A permanent magnet alternator (stator and flywheel), on the left side of the crankshaft, generates current. The voltage regulator rectifier converts this alternating current to direct current.

The only maintenance required is periodic replacement of the spark plug. Timing does not require adjustment; however, it can be checked when troubleshooting. Refer to Chapter Three for maintenance and Chapter Two for troubleshooting.

ALTERNATOR COVER

Removal/Installation

Refer to **Figure 1**.

1. Remove the four screws from the cover (**Figure 2**).

2. Remove the cover and gasket.

3. Inspect the cover and gasket for damage. Replace the rubber gasket if it is cracked or damaged. The alternator must remain dry at all times.

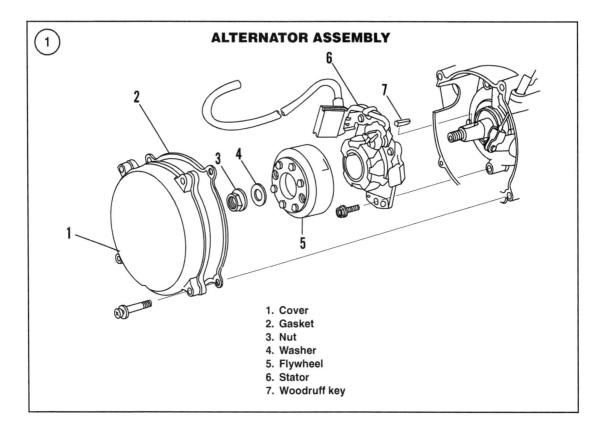

ALTERNATOR ASSEMBLY

1. Cover
2. Gasket
3. Nut
4. Washer
5. Flywheel
6. Stator
7. Woodruff key

4. Reverse this procedure to install the gasket and cover. Tighten the cover screws to the specifications in **Table 2**.

FLYWHEEL

Removal and Installation

In order to remove the flywheel, the nut (**Figure 3**) must be removed. This is achieved by holding the flywheel with a flywheel holder tool, then removing the nut with a socket. A flywheel puller is then used to remove the flywheel from the shaft taper. A universal flywheel holder (part No. 07725-0030000) and flywheel puller (part No. 07733-0010000 or part No. 07933-0010000) are available from Honda.

Refer to **Figure 1**.

1. Remove the alternator cover as described in this chapter.

2. Attach a holding tool (**Figure 4**) to the flywheel and secure the flywheel.

3. Loosen and remove the flywheel nut and washer (**Figure 5**).

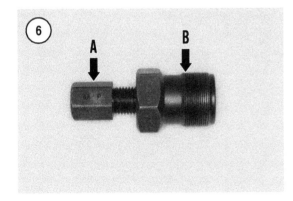

CAUTION
Do not attempt to remove the flywheel without a puller. Damage to the flywheel and crankshaft will likely occur.

4. Install the flywheel puller and remove the flywheel as follows:

    a. Loosen the pressure bolt (A, **Figure 6**). Apply a small amount of grease on the end of the bolt, where it contacts the crankshaft.

    b. Screw the outer part (B, **Figure 6**) of the flywheel puller into the flywheel. The outer part is a left-hand thread.

    c. Hold the outer part of the puller with a wrench, then finger-tighten the pressure bolt against the crankshaft (**Figure 7**).

    d. Turn the pressure bolt with a wrench until the flywheel releases itself from the crankshaft taper.

5. Remove the Woodruff key from the crankshaft (**Figure 8**).

6. Inspect the parts as described in this section.

7. If necessary, remove the stator as described in this chapter.

8. Install the flywheel as follows:

    a. Position the crankshaft so the keyway for the Woodruff key is at the top (**Figure 8**).

    b. Align and install the flywheel over the Woodruff key

    c. Apply oil to the threads and seating surface of the flywheel washer and nut (**Figure 5**). Install the washer and finger-tighten the nut.

    d. Hold the flywheel stable with the flywheel holding tool (**Figure 4**), then tighten the nut to the specification in **Table 2**.

e. Check the air gap between the ignition pulse generator and the flywheel (**Figure 9**). The gap should be 0.46 mm (0.018 in.) If necessary, loosen the ignition pulse generator and adjust the gap.

f. Check the ignition timing as described in this chapter.

g. Install the alternator cover as described in this chapter.

Inspection

The flywheel is permanently magnetized and cannot be tested. Install a known good flywheel to determine if the flywheel is the cause of performance problems. In the following procedure, replace parts that are worn or damaged.

1. Clean the flywheel components so they can be carefully inspected.

2. Inspect the flywheel (**Figure 10**) as follows:

a. Inspect the flywheel for cracks and damage. If damage is evident anywhere on the inside or outside of the flywheel, replace the flywheel. The flywheel will not function properly if damaged.

> *WARNING*
> *The flywheel must be replaced if it is damaged. The flywheel can fly apart at high crankshaft speeds, causing severe personal injury and engine damage.*

b. Inspect the taper in the bore of the flywheel for damage.

3. Inspect the crankshaft and Woodruff key (**Figure 11**) as follows:

a. Inspect the taper on the crankshaft for damage.

b. Inspect the Woodruff key and slot for damage. If the Woodruff key is deformed or damaged, this can cause the ignition system to operate improperly.

4. Inspect the bolt and washer. Replace the parts if worn or damaged.

STATOR

The stator can be tested while it is mounted in the engine. This includes testing the exciter coil and ignition pulse generator. On 1997-1998 models, the

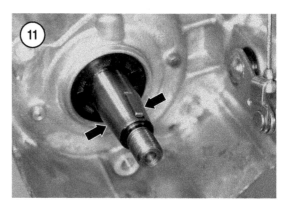

charging coil can also be tested. All tests are described in this chapter.

Removal and Installation

Refer to **Figure 1**.

1. If the stator is to be completely removed from the engine, remove the fuel tank so the wires leading from the stator can be disconnected. Remove the fuel tank as described in Chapter Eight.

2. Disconnect the stator and ignition pulse generator wire leads.

3. Remove the wires from the retaining bands.

4. Remove the alternator cover as described in this chapter.

5. Remove the flywheel as described in this chapter.

6. Remove the two bolts securing the stator (**Figure 12**).

7. Remove the wire grommet (**Figure 12**) while pulling the stator assembly from the case.

8. Inspect both sides of the stator (**Figure 13** and **Figure 14**) for obvious damage.

9. Test the stator as described in this chapter.

10. Reverse this procedure to install the stator. Note the following:

   a. To prevent the entry of moisture, apply dielectric grease to electrical connections before assembly.

   b. Check that all wires are routed and secured properly.

   c. Install the flywheel as described in this chapter.

   d. Check the ignition timing as described in this chapter.

IGNITION SYSTEM TESTING

Read the *Special Tool Requirement* and *Ignition System Precautions and Inspections* before checking the ignition system. Refer to the wiring diagram at the back of the manual. Refer to **Table 1** for specifications. Whenever the ignition control module, stator, ignition pulse generator or flywheel are replaced, check the ignition timing as described in this chapter.

Before testing a component, check the electrical connections related to that component. Check for corrosion and bent or loose terminals. Most of the connectors have a lock mechanism molded into the connector body. If these are not fully locked, a terminal connection may not be made. If connectors are not locked, pull the connector apart and clean the terminals. Fill the connector with dielectric grease, to prevent future corrosion, and reassemble the connector.

Special Tool Requirements

In order to check the peak voltage of the ignition coil, ignition pulse generator and exciter coil, a peak voltage tester is required, If this is not available, a peak voltage adapter is required. The adapter (part No. 07HGJ-0020100) is available from a Honda dealership. The adapter is connected to a digital multimeter as shown in **Figure 15**, and the meter readings are measured in DC volts. A multimeter with an internal impedance of 10M ohms/DCV minimum is required. Meters with differing impedance will not display accurate measurements.

These special tools and voltage tests are necessary to accurately determine the condition of the ignition control module.

Ignition System Precautions and Inspections

The ignition control module and other components of the ignition system can be damaged if the following precautions are not taken:

1. Make sure the engine stop switch and spark plug are in good condition.

2. Work slowly, methodically, and use test equipment that is in good condition. Record all measurements.

3. Never touch the metal tips of the test probes when they are in contact with terminals or connectors.

4. Never disconnect electrical connections while the engine is running or cranking.

5. Always turn off the engine before disconnecting/connecting electrical components.

6. Handle the ignition control module with care. Do not subject the module to unnecessary vibration or impact.

7. Always check wiring for poor connections, corrosion and shorts before replacing components connected to the wiring.

IGNITION CONTROL MODULE

On 1997-1999 models, the ignition control module is located under the fuel tank and between the frame members (**Figure 16**). On 2000-2001 models, the ignition control module is located at the steering head, behind the number plate. The module is not serviceable and must be replaced if it is faulty. To determine if the module is faulty, use a process of elimination and test the other ignition system components. Compare the results to the specifications and figures.

IGNITION COIL

The ignition coil is located at the left side of the engine, near the cylinder head (**Figure 17**).

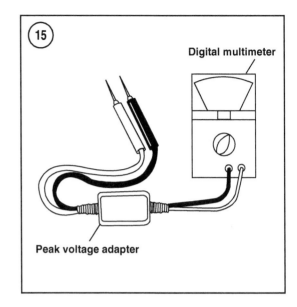

Digital multimeter

Peak voltage adapter

Ignition Coil Primary Peak Voltage Test

This test requires a peak voltage tester or the peak voltage adapter and digital multimeter described in *Special Tool Requirements* in this chapter. Refer to **Figure 18** for test results.

IGNITION COIL PRIMARY PEAK VOLTAGE TROUBLESHOOTING

Low peak voltage

Check in the following order:
- Incorrect peak voltage adapter connections
- Meter impedance is too low
- Cranking speed is too low
- The test sampling and measured pulse were not synchronizing. If measured voltage is over the minimum voltage at least once, the system is normal
- Poorly connected connectors or an open circuit in ignition system
- Faulty exciter coil
- Faulty ignition coil
- Faulty ignition control module (when all of the above are normal)

No peak voltage

Check:
- Incorrect peak voltage adapter connections
- Short circuit in engine stop switch (black and black/white wires)
- Faulty ignition switch or engine stop switch
- Poorly connected ignition control module connectors
- Open circuit or poor connection in ground wire (green) of ignition control module
- Faulty peak voltage adapter
- Faulty exciter coil (measure peak voltage)
- Faulty ignition pulse generator (measure peak voltage)
- Faulty ignition control module (when all of the above are normal)

Peak voltage is normal, but no spark at spark plug

Check:
- Faulty spark plug
- Leaking ignition coil secondary current
- Faulty ignition coil)

1. Remove the spark plug, then attach the cap to the plug. Ground the plug to the cylinder head (**Figure 19**).

NOTE
Make sure the spark plug is in good condition.

2. Locate the primary wire connector (black/yellow wire) at the coil (A, **Figure 17**).

3. Partially pull apart the black/yellow wire connection. The connector must be in contact with the

coil when making the reading. Separate the connector only far enough to insert the positive probe from the meter (**Figure 20**).

4. Ground the negative meter probe to the coil ground (B, **Figure 17**) or frame.

5. Set the meter to DC volts.

WARNING
In the following step, do not touch the meter probes or spark plug. Electrical shock will occur.

6. Have an assistant turn the engine over with the kickstarter. While the engine is turning, observe the meter reading. The meter reading should indicate a minimum of 100 volts DC. If the reading is less than this, refer to **Figure 18**.

7. Remove the test equipment and press the connector together.

8. Install the spark plug and left side cover.

Primary and Secondary Coil Resistance Test

Perform this test with a standard multimeter.

1. Remove the primary wire connector (black/yellow wire) (A, **Figure 17**) from the coil.

2. Remove the spark plug cap from the plug.

3. Check primary coil resistance as follows:
   a. Connect the positive meter probe to the primary wire terminal on the coil (A, **Figure 17**) and the negative meter probe to the coil ground (B, **Figure 17**) or frame.
   b. Measure the resistance. Refer to **Table 1** for the specification. Replace the coil if it is not within specification.

4. Check secondary coil resistance as follows:
   a. Connect the positive meter probe to the primary wire terminal on the coil (A, **Figure 17**) and the negative meter probe to the inside of the the spark plug cap.
   b. Measure the resistance. Refer to **Table 1** for the specification. If the measurement is not within specification, remove the spark plug cap from the lead (**Figure 21**) and repeat the test, touching the negative probe to the end of the lead. Refer to **Table 1** for the specification. Replace the coil if it is out of specification.

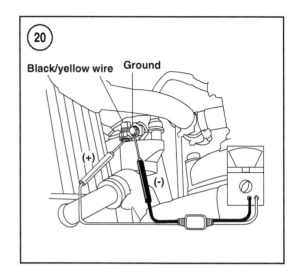

Black/yellow wire   Ground

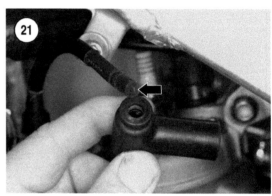

EXCITER COIL

The exciter coil is part of the stator.

Exciter Coil Peak Voltage Test

This test requires a peak voltage tester or the peak voltage adapter and digital multimeter described in *Special Tool Requirements* in this chapter. Refer to **Figure 22** for test results.

NOTE
The following test is made in the wiring harness connector, not at the ignition control module terminals.

1. Check that the spark plug is installed and connected to the ignition coil.

2. Remove the connector from the ignition control module that contains the blue and white wires.

㉒ **EXCITER COIL PEAK VOLTAGE TROUBLESHOOTING**

Low peak voltage —————————

> Check in the following order:
> • Meter impedance is too low
> • Cranking speed is too low
> • The test sampling and measured pulse were
>   not synchronizing. If measured voltage is
>   over the minimum voltage at least once, the
>   system is normal
> • Faulty ignition control module (when all of
>   the above are normal)

No peak voltage —————————

> Check:
> • Faulty peak voltage adapter
> • Faulty exciter coil

---

3. Connect the positive meter probe to the blue wire and the negative meter probe to the white wire.

4. Set the meter to DC volts.

WARNING
In the following step, do not touch the meter probes. Electrical shock will occur.

5. Have an assistant turn the engine over with the kickstarter. While the engine is turning, observe the meter reading. The meter reading should indicate a minimum of 100 volts DC. If the reading is less than this, refer to **Figure 22**.

6. Remove the test equipment and press the connector onto the ignition control module.

Exciter Coil Resistance Test

Perform this test with a standard multimeter.

1. At the ignition control module, remove the connector that contains the blue and white wires.

2. Connect the positive meter probe to the blue wire and the negative meter probe to the white wire.

3. Measure the resistance. Refer to **Table 1** for the specification. Replace the stator if it is out of specification.

IGNITION PULSE GENERATOR

The ignition pulse generator is part of the stator.

**Ignition Pulse Generator
Peak Voltage Test**

This test requires a peak voltage tester, or, the peak voltage adapter and digital multimeter described in *Special Tool Requirements* in this chapter. Refer to **Figure 23** for test results.

NOTE
The following test is made in the wiring harness connector, not at the ignition control module terminals.

1. Check that the spark plug is installed and connected to the ignition coil.

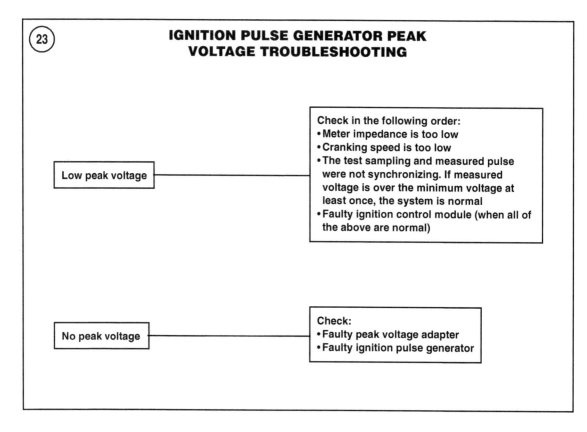

(23)

IGNITION PULSE GENERATOR PEAK VOLTAGE TROUBLESHOOTING

Low peak voltage

Check in the following order:
- Meter impedance is too low
- Cranking speed is too low
- The test sampling and measured pulse were not synchronizing. If measured voltage is over the minimum voltage at least once, the system is normal
- Faulty ignition control module (when all of the above are normal)

No peak voltage

Check:
- Faulty peak voltage adapter
- Faulty ignition pulse generator

2. Remove the connector from the ignition control module that contains the blue/yellow and green/white wires.

3. Connect the positive meter probe to the blue/yellow wire and the negative meter probe to the green/white wire.

4. Set the meter to DC volts.

WARNING
In the following step, do not touch the meter probes. Electrical shock will occur.

5. Have an assistant turn the engine over with the kickstarter. While the engine is turning, observe the meter reading. The meter reading should indicate a minimum of 0.7 volts DC. If the reading is abnormal, refer to **Figure 23**.

6. Remove the test equipment and press the connector onto the ignition control module.

Ignition Pulse Generator Resistance Test

Perform this test with a standard multimeter.

1. At the ignition control module, remove the connector that contains the blue/yellow and green/white wires.

2. Connect the positive meter probe to the blue/yellow wire and the negative meter probe to the green/white wire.

3. Measure the resistance. Refer to **Table 1** for the specification. Replace the stator if it is out of specification.

POWER JET SYSTEM (1997-1998 MODELS ONLY)

1997-1998 models are equipped with a power jet carburetion system that provides an increase in low and midrange engine torque.

The system consists of a power jet solenoid, ignition control module, regulator/rectifier, condenser and alternator charge coil. When the engine is running, the alternating charge coil current is converted to direct current by the regulator/rectifier. The ignition control module then electrically activates the power jet solenoid when the engine speed is above 8100 rpm. When the solenoid is activated, fuel is

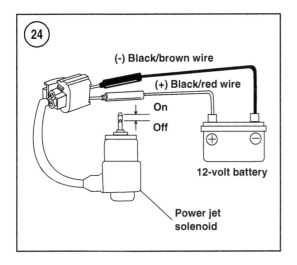

(-) Black/brown wire

(+) Black/red wire

On

Off

12-volt battery

Power jet
solenoid

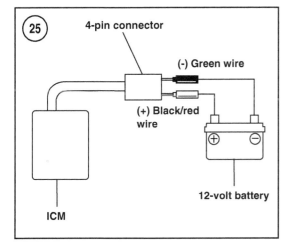

4-pin connector

(-) Green wire

(+) Black/red
wire

12-volt battery

ICM

4. If the solenoid shaft does not extend, the solenoid is faulty.

5. If the solenoid shaft extends, the solenoid is in working condition. Check the following areas for possible causes of solenoid malfunction:

    a. Loose or faulty connectors.

    b. Open or short circuit in wiring harness.

    c. Charging coil.

    d. Regulator/rectifier and condenser.

    e. Ignition control module.

Charging Coil Test
(1997-1998 Models Only)

Perform this test with a standard multimeter after verifying the condition of the power jet solenoid.

1. At the ignition control module, remove the connector that contains the yellow and yellow/white wires.

2. Connect the positive meter probe to the yellow wire and the negative meter probe to the yellow/white wires leading to the alternator.

3. Measure the resistance. Refer to **Table 1** for the specification. Replace the stator if it is out of specification.

4. Check for continuity between each wire and ground. If continuity exists, the stator is shorted and must be replaced.

Regulator/Rectifier and Condenser Test
(1997-1998 Models Only)

Refer to **Figure 25**. Perform this test after verifying the condition of the power jet solenoid and charging coil.

1. Remove the solenoid from the carburetor as described in Chapter Eight. Do not unplug the solenoid.

2. Connect test probes to a fully charged 12-volt battery.

3. Disconnect the 4-pin connector leading from the regulator/rectifier (located by the ignition control module).

NOTE
The following connections are made in the ignition control module side of the wiring harness connector, not in the regulator/rectifier side.

4. Connect the positive battery probe to the black/red wire and the negative battery probe to the green wire.

delivered only through the main jet system. When engine speed drops below 8100 rpm, the solenoid shuts off and fuel is delivered through the main jet and power jet.

Power Jet Solenoid Test
(1997-1998 Models Only)

Refer to **Figure 24**. Perform this test before testing other components of the power jet system.

1. Remove the solenoid from the carburetor as described in Chapter Eight.

2. Connect test probes to a fully charged 12-volt battery.

3. Connect the positive battery probe to the black/red wire. While observing the solenoid, touch the negative battery probe to the black/brown wire.

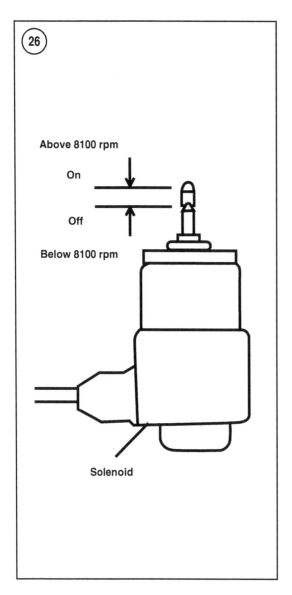

Above 8100 rpm

On

Off

Below 8100 rpm

Solenoid

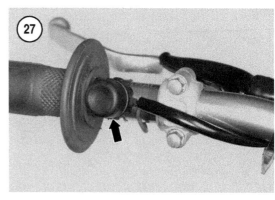

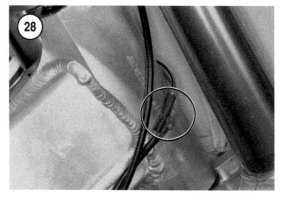

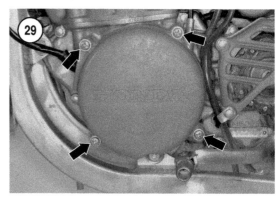

5. Start the engine. While observing the solenoid, raise and lower the engine speed.

   a. If the solenoid shaft extends (**Figure 26**) when the engine speed is above 8100 rpm, and retracts when the engine speed is less than 8100 rpm, the regulator/rectifier and condenser are faulty.

   b. If the solenoid shaft does not extend or retract as the speed is changed, the ignition control module is faulty.

ENGINE STOP SWITCH

Perform this test with a standard multimeter.

F marks

Stator index mark

Crankcase index mark

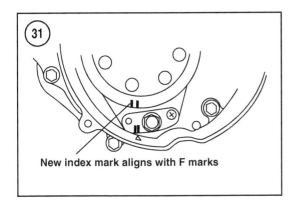

New index mark aligns with F marks

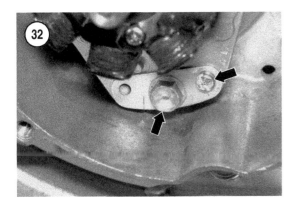

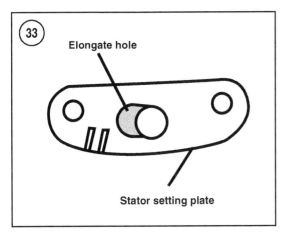

Elongate hole

Stator setting plate

1. Disconnect the black and black/white wires leading from the switch (**Figure 27**). The connectors are at the steering head (**Figure 28**).

2. Connect the positive meter probe to the black wire and the negative meter probe to the black/white wire.

3. Test the switch as follows:

    a. Press and hold the stop switch. Observe the meter. There should continuity. If there is no continuity, the switch is faulty.

    b. Release the stop switch. Observe the meter. There should be no continuity. If there is continuity, the switch is faulty.

IGNITION TIMING

The ignition timing is electronically controlled by the ignition control module. No routine adjustment of the timing is necessary. Check the timing when ignition system problems are suspected, or whenever the ignition control module, stator, ignition pulse generator or flywheel are replaced.

1. Warm up the engine to operating temperature.

2. Remove the alternator cover (**Figure 29**) as described in this chapter.

3. Check that the stator index mark is aligned with the index mark on the crankcase cover (**Figure 30**). If the marks are not aligned, loosen the two bolts securing the stator (**Figure 12**) and realign the marks.

4. Connect a timing light and tachometer following the manufacturer's instructions.

5. Start the engine and hold the speed at 3000 rpm.

6. Direct the timing light at the index marks on the flywheel and stator. The stator index mark should align between the F marks on the flywheel (**Figure 30**).

7. If the timing is correct, shut off the engine and proceed to Step 8. If the timing is not correct, perform the following:

> *NOTE*
> *If timing is erratic and does not stabilize in the vicinity of the index marks, check the condition of the ignition control module, ignition pulse generator and stator before modifying the stator setting plate in the following steps.*

    a. While the engine is running at 3000 rpm, mark a new index mark on the stator setting plate that aligns between the F marks on the flywheel (**Figure 31**).

    b. Shut off the engine.

    c. Remove the screw and bolt securing the setting plate and stator (**Figure 32**).

    d. File and elongate the center hole of the setting plate (**Figure 33**) so stator adjustment can be made. Elongate the hole to the difference between the old and new timing marks.

e. Install the setting plate onto the stator and secure it with the screw.

f. Align the new timing mark on the setting
plate with the crankcase index mark (**Figure
34**), then tighten the stator bolt.

g. Recheck the timing as described in Steps 4-6.
If necessary, repeat Step 7.

h. When the timing is correct, scribe the new
stator index mark into the setting plate and so it
can be differentiated from the old index mark.

8. Disconnect the test equipment and install the alternator cover.

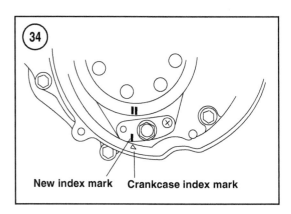

New index mark   Crankcase index mark

Table 1 IGNITION SYSTEM SPECIFICATIONS

Ignition timing	
1997	18° at 3000 rpm
1998-2001	18° ± 2° at 3000 rpm
Spark plug	
Standard	Denso W24ESR-V
	NGK BR8EG
	Champion QN-86
Optional	Denso W24ESR-G
	NGK BR8EV
	Champion QN-2G
Spark plug gap	0.5-0.6 mm (0.020-0.024 in.)
Ignition coil resistance @ 20° C (68° F)	
Primary coil	
1997-1999	0.2-0.4 ohm
2000-2001	0.1-0.3 ohm
Secondary coil with spark plug cap	9-16 ohms
Secondary coil without spark plug cap	4-8 ohms
Ignition coil peak voltage	100 V minimum
Ignition pulse generator	
resistance @ 20° C (68° F)	180-280 ohms
Ignition pulse generator peak voltage	0.7 V minimum
Air gap (Ignition pulse generator	
and flywheel pickups)	0.46 mm (0.018 in.)
Alternator exciter coil resistance @ 20° C (68° F)	
1997-1998	2-20 ohms
1999-2001	9-25 ohms
Alternator exciter coil peak voltage	100 V minimum
Alternator charging coil resistance @ 20° C (68° F)	
1997-1998 only	1-5 ohms

Table 2 IGNITION TORQUE SPECIFICATIONS

	N•m	in.lb.	ft.-lb.
Alternator cover screws	2	18	–
Flywheel nut	54	–	40

CHAPTER TEN

COOLING SYSTEM

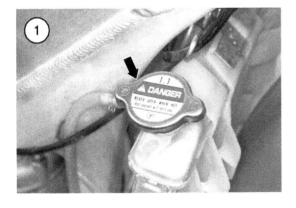

This chapter describes service procedures for the radiator and water pump. Read this chapter before attempting repairs to the cooling system. Become familiar with the procedures, photos and illustrations to understand the skill and equipment required. Refer to Chapter One for tool usage and techniques.

SAFETY PRECAUTIONS

WARNING
Do not remove the radiator cap (Figure 1) immediately after or during engine operation. When the engine has been operated, the liquid in the cooling system is scalding hot and under pressure. Attempting to remove the cap while the engine is hot can cause the coolant to spray violently from the radiator opening, possibly causing personal injury.

Wait for the engine to cool, then place a shop cloth over the cap. *Slowly* turn the cap to relieve any pressure. Turn the cap to the safety stop and check that all pressure is relieved. To remove the cap from the radiator, press down on the cap, then twist it free.

To prevent potential damage to the engine, change the coolant regularly, as described in Chapter Three. Always use an antifreeze solution. Antifreeze contains lubricants and rust inhibitors that protect the components of the cooling system. Always dispose of coolant in an environmentally-safe manner.

RADIATOR

On 1997-1999 models, the bike is equipped with one radiator. On 2000-2001 models, the bike has

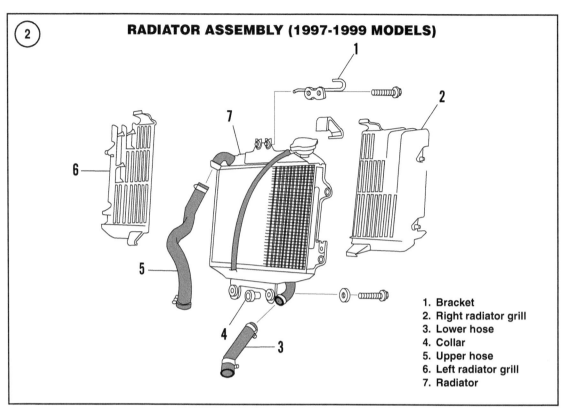

RADIATOR ASSEMBLY (1997-1999 MODELS)

1. Bracket
2. Right radiator grill
3. Lower hose
4. Collar
5. Upper hose
6. Left radiator grill
7. Radiator

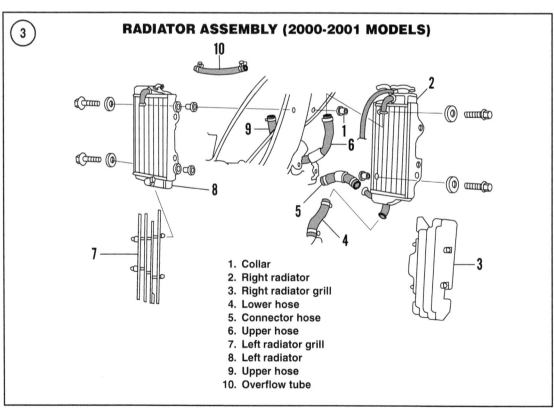

RADIATOR ASSEMBLY (2000-2001 MODELS)

1. Collar
2. Right radiator
3. Right radiator grill
4. Lower hose
5. Connector hose
6. Upper hose
7. Left radiator grill
8. Left radiator
9. Upper hose
10. Overflow tube

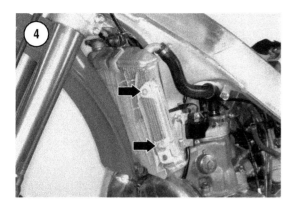

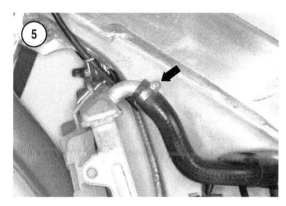

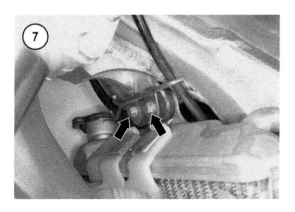

two radiators. Both configurations operate the same. Heated water from the engine enters the radiator by the upper hose. The water is cooled as it circulates to the bottom of the radiator, and enters the engine by the lower hose.

Removal and Installation

Refer to **Figure 2** or **Figure 3**.

1. Drain the cooling system as described in Chapter Three.

2. Remove the fuel tank as described in Chapter Eight.

3. Remove the exhaust pipe as described in Chapter Four.

4. Remove the bolts from the left and right radiator grills (**Figure 4**), and then remove the grills.

5. Remove the upper radiator hose as follows:

   a. Loosen the clamp on the upper radiator hose (**Figure 5**). Note the direction of the clamp so it can be reinstalled in the same position.

   b. Twist the hose from its fitting. If the hose is seized to the fitting, carefully insert a small screwdriver or pick tool between the hose and fitting. Work the tool around the fitting and remove the hose.

6. Repeat Step 5 to remove the lower hose (**Figure 6**).

7. On 2000-2001 models, remove the connector hose and overflow tube.

8A. On 1997-1999 models, remove the upper mounting bolts and bracket (**Figure 7**), then loosen the two lower mounting bolts. If necessary, have assistance in handling the radiator when the mounting bolts are removed. After the bolts are removed, account for the collars that are fitted in the lower radiator mounts.

8B. On 2000-2001 models, remove the upper and lower mounting bolts and collars on each radiator. If necessary, have assistance in handling the radiators when the mounting bolts are removed.

9. Inspect the radiator as described in this chapter.

10. Reverse this procedure to install the radiator(s). Observe the following:

   a. Replace hoses that are hard, cracked or show signs of deterioration, both internally and externally. Hold each hose and flex it in several directions to check for damage. If a hose is difficult to install on a fitting, dip the hose end in hot water until the rubber has softened, then install the hose.

   b. Install clamps in their original positions.

10

c. Fill and bleed the cooling system as described in Chapter Three.

d. Start the engine and allow it to warm up. Check for leaks.

Inspection

1. Clean the exterior of the radiator with a low-pressure water spray. Allow the radiator to dry.

2. Check for damaged cooling fins. Straighten bent fins with a screwdriver. If more than 20% of the cooling area is damaged, replace the radiator.

3. Check the seams and other soldered connections for corrosion (green residue). If corrosion is evident, there could be a leak in that spot. Perform a cooling system pressure check as described in *Cooling System Inspection* in Chapter Three. If the equipment is not available, take the radiator to a radiator repair shop to have it flushed and pressure checked.

4. Fill the radiator with water and check the flow rate out of the radiator. If the flow rate is slow, or if corrosion or other buildup is seen, take the radiator to a radiator repair shop to have it flushed and pressure checked.

WATER PUMP

Inspection

The water pump is located in the right crankcase cover (**Figure 8**). To inspect the condition of the impeller or water passages (**Figure 9**), the water pump cover can be removed without removing the right crankcase cover.

The right crankcase cover is drilled with an inspection hole (**Figure 10**) for the water pump. If leakage is detected at this hole, the seal in the pump is allowing water to leak to the back side of the pump. Removal of the right crankcase cover is necessary to remove the pump assembly and service the bearing and seal.

Removal and Installation

Remove and install the water pump cover and right crankcase cover assembly as follows. Inspect and repair the water pump as described in this chapter.

Refer to **Figure 11**.

1. Drain the cooling system as described in Chapter Three.

2. Remove the water pump cover as follows:

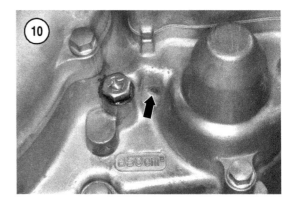

a. Remove the four bolts (**Figure 12**) securing the water pump cover, then remove the cover, outer gasket, plate and inner gasket.

b. Remove the two dowels that are between the cover and housing (**Figure 13**).

3. Remove the right crankcase cover as described in Chapter Six.

NOTE
When the right crankcase cover is removed, account for the copper washer on the end of the impeller shaft.

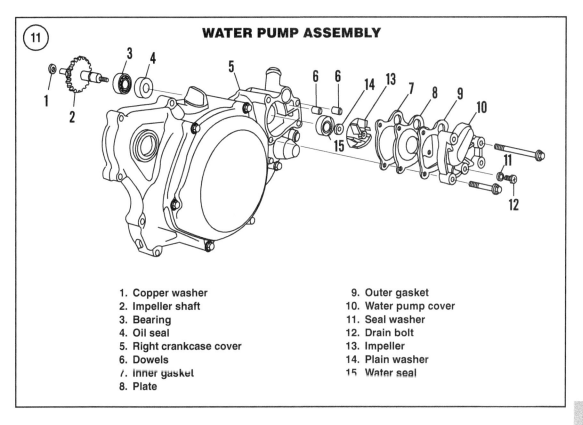

WATER PUMP ASSEMBLY

1. Copper washer
2. Impeller shaft
3. Bearing
4. Oil seal
5. Right crankcase cover
6. Dowels
7. Inner gasket
8. Plate
9. Outer gasket
10. Water pump cover
11. Seal washer
12. Drain bolt
13. Impeller
14. Plain washer
15. Water seal

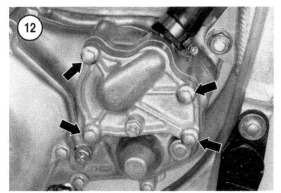

4. Disassemble and inspect the pump as described in this chapter.

5. Reverse these steps to install the water pump cover and right crankcase cover assembly. Note the following:

    a. Make sure the copper washer is on the end of the impeller shaft (**Figure 14**) before installing the right crankcase cover.

    b. Install the right crankcase cover as described in Chapter Six.

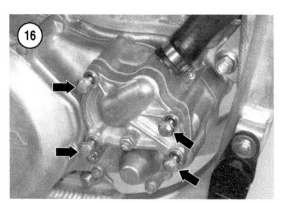

c. Check that both water pump dowels are installed (**Figure 13**).

d. Install *new* inner and outer gaskets (**Figure 15**). The plate goes between the gaskets.

e. Insert all bolts into the cover and check that all exposed lengths are equal before tightening (**Figure 16**). Finger-tighten the bolts.

f. Tighten the cover bolts to the specification in **Table 2**.

g. Fill and bleed the cooling system as described in Chapter Three.

h. Start the engine and allow it to warm up. Check for leaks.

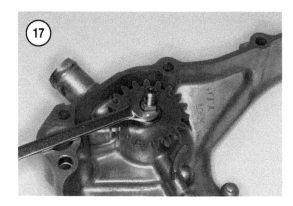

Disassembly, Inspection and Assembly

Refer to **Figure 11**.

1. Hold the impeller shaft with a wrench (**Figure 17**) so the impeller (**Figure 18**) can be removed.

2. Remove the impeller.

3. Remove the washer from the shaft (**Figure 19**).

4. Remove the impeller shaft from back side of the housing (**Figure 20**).

5. Inspect the impeller and shaft.

a. Inspect the impeller (A, **Figure 21**) for damage and deposits.

b. Inspect the impeller shaft (B, **Figure 21**) for deposits and wear at the bearing and seal surfaces.

c. Inspect the gear teeth for wear or damage.

d. Check that the shaft is straight.

6. Inspect the shaft bore in the crankcase for damage (**Figure 22**). Insert the shaft into the bore and check for play and roughness.

7. Inspect the bearing (**Figure 23**) for roughness and play. Check for radial and axial play (**Figure 24**). Check that the bearing fits tightly in the crank-

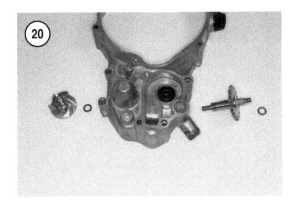

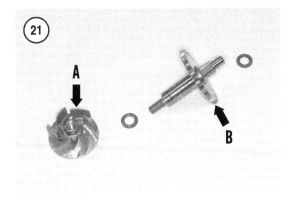

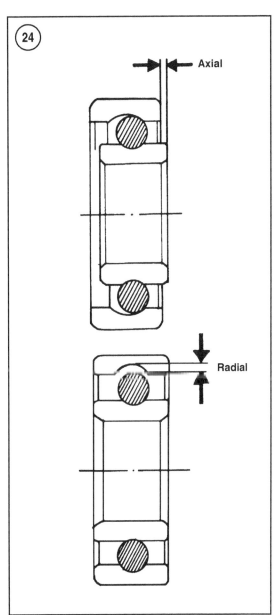

10

case cover. If necessary, replace the bearing as described in this section.

8. Inspect the water seal for damage or deterioration. If necessary, replace the seal as described in this chapter.

9. Lubricate the impeller shaft with grease, then insert the shaft through the back side of the crankcase cover. Lightly twist the shaft through the seals.

10. Install the plain washer onto the shaft (**Figure 19**).

11. Install and finger-tighten the impeller (**Figure 18**).

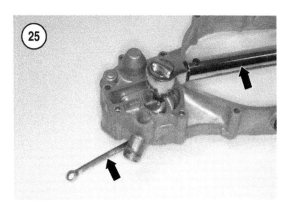

12. Hold the impeller shaft with a wrench, then tighten the impeller (**Figure 25**) to the specification in **Table 2**.

13. Install the copper washer (**Figure 14**) on the impeller shaft.

14. Install the right crankcase cover as described in this chapter.

15. Install the water pump cover assembly (**Figure 26**) as described in this chapter.

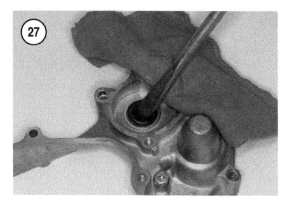

Bearing and Seal Replacement

The water pump has two seals, each with a different purpose. The water seal is inside the pump, next to the impeller. The oil seal is behind the bearing, on the back side of the crankcase housing. The seals must be installed correctly or leakage will occur. Avoid any damage to the inside or outside edges of the seals. Also avoid damage to the seal bores.

Refer to **Figure 11**.

1. Remove the water seal as follows:

   a. Place a folded shop cloth over the housing so it will not get damaged.

   b. Pry the seal out of the housing (**Figure 27**).

> *CAUTION*
> *Do not scratch the seal bore with the pry tool.*

2. Remove the oil seal and bearing together. Remove as follows:

   a. From the back side of the housing, insert a bearing puller through the bearing and seal. Place a large washer on the puller, next to the seal, to ensure good contact with the seal.

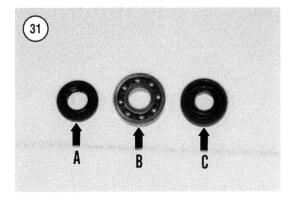

A   B   C

NOTE
The 12 mm bearing remover set (part No. 07936-1660001) is available from a Honda dealership.

   b. Pull the bearing and seal from the housing (**Figure 28**).

3. Clean both bores in the housing (**Figure 29** and **Figure 30**). Inspect both bores for scratches, buildup or other damage that could cause leakage around the seals.

4. Install the oil seal (A, **Figure 31**) and bearing (B) as follows:

   a. Pack lithium grease into the lip of the oil seal.

   b. Drive the seal into the housing, with the open side of the seal facing up. To seat the seal, use a driver that is slightly smaller than the outside diameter of the seal.

   c. Position the bearing over the housing. The manufacturer's marks on the bearing should face up. Drive the bearing into the housing (**Figure 32**) until its outer race is even with the edge of the bore (**Figure 23**).

CAUTION
Do not apply pressure to the inner bearing race or the bearing will be damaged. Apply pressure to the outer race only.

5. Install the water seal (C, **Figure 31**) as follows:

   a. Pack lithium grease into the lip of the water seal.

   b. Position the seal with its open side facing up.

   c. Drive the seal into the housing (**Figure 33**), using a driver that is slightly smaller than the outside diameter of the seal.

CAUTION
Do not apply pressure to the inner inner area of the seal or it will be damaged. Apply pressure to the outer area only.

6. Install the impeller and impeller shaft as described in this section.

10

Table 1 COOLING SYSTEM SPECIFICATIONS

Coolant type	Ethylene glycol containing silicate-free corrosion inhibitors for aluminum engines
Coolant mixture	50/50 (antifreeze/distilled water)
Cooling system capacity	
1997-1999	
At change	1.26 liters (1.32 U.S. qt.)
At disassembly	1.28 liters (1.35 U.S. qt.)
2000-2001	
At change	1.22 liters (1.29 U.S. qt.)
At disassembly	1.35 liters (1.43 U.S. qt.)
Radiator cap relief pressure	108-137 kPa (16-20 psi)

Table 2 TORQUE SPECIFICATIONS

	N•m	in.-lb.	ft.-lb.
Coolant drain bolt	10	88	–
Water pump cover bolts	12	106	–
Water pump impeller	12	106	–

CHAPTER ELEVEN

WHEELS, TIRES AND DRIVE CHAIN

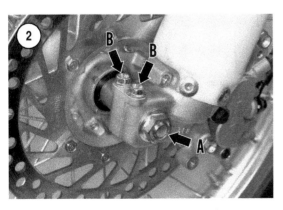

This chapter describes repair procedures for the wheels, drive chain, sprockets and tires. Routine maintenance procedures for these components are in Chapter Three. Refer to the tables at the end of this chapter for specifications.

FRONT WHEEL

Removal and Installation

1. Support the motorcycle so it is stable and the front wheel is off the ground.
2. Remove the brake disc cover (**Figure 1**).
3. Remove the axle nut (A, **Figure 2**).
4. Loosen the pinch bolts at both ends of the axle (B, **Figure 2** and **Figure 3**).
5. Pull up on the wheel to take the weight off the axle, then remove the axle from the right side of the wheel. Roll the wheel forward and out of the fork.
6. Remove the collars from the hub (**Figure 4** and **Figure 5**).
7. Inspect and/or repair the wheel and axle assembly as described in this chapter.
8. Reverse this procedure to install the wheel. Note the following:

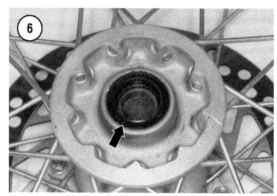

a. Apply grease to the axle and seal lips to prevent damaging the seals as the axle is passed
   through the wheel.

b. Torque the axle nut, then the pinch bolts on
   the *left* side of the wheel. Compress and release the front suspension a few times to seat
   the axle in the holder, then torque the pinch
   bolts on the *right* side of the wheel.

c. Check that the wheel spins freely and the
   brake operates properly.

Inspection

1. Inspect the seal (**Figure 6**) on both sides of the
wheel. Check seals for:

   a. Hard or damaged rubber.

   b. Nicked or missing rubber at the seal lip.

   c. Grease or water seepage from the seal.

2. Inspect the bearing on both sides of the wheel.
Check bearings for:

   a. Roughness. Turn each bearing by hand and
      check for smooth, quiet operation.

   b. Radial and axial play (**Figure 7**). Try to push
      the bearing in and out to check for axial play.

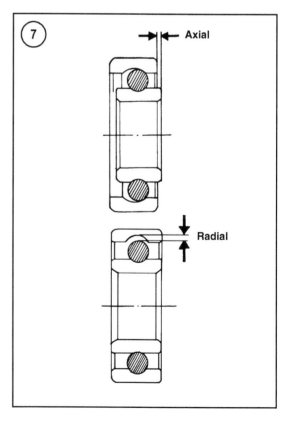

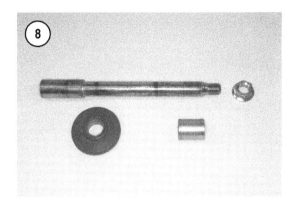

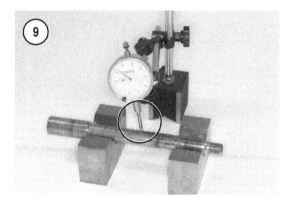

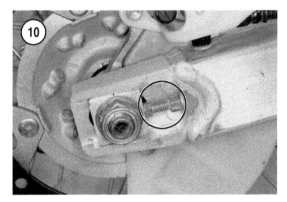

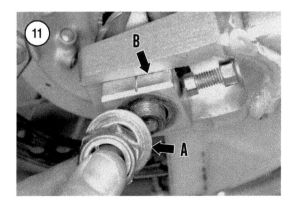

Try to push the bearing up and down to check for radial play. Any play should be difficult to feel. If play is easily felt, the bearing is worn out. Always replace bearings as a pair.

3. If damage is evident in the seals or bearings, refer to *Front and Rear Hubs* in this chapter for seal and bearing replacement procedures.

4. Clean the axle, nut and collars (**Figure 8**) in solvent. Inspect the axle for straightness, using a set of V-blocks and a dial indicator (**Figure 9**) Refer to **Table 1** for maximum axle runout. Actual runout is *one-half* of the gauge reading. Do not attempt to straighten a bent axle. Replace the part.

5. Refer to *Rim and Spoke Service* in this chapter for inspecting and truing the rim.

REAR WHEEL

Removal and Installation

1. Support the motorcycle so it is stable and the rear wheel is off the ground.

2. If the chain is tight, loosen the chain adjusters (**Figure 10**). The chain must be loose enough to be removed from the sprocket.

3. Loosen the rear axle nut, then remove the nut and washer from the axle (A, **Figure 11**).

4. Remove the chain from the sprocket.

5. Pull up on the rear wheel to take weight off the axle, then remove the axle from the left side of the swing arm. Lower the wheel and roll it out of the swing arm.

6. Remove the adjustment plate from the right side of the swing arm (B, **Figure 11**). On some models an adjustment plate is also used on the left side of the swing arm.

7. Remove the collars from the hub (**Figure 12** and **Figure 13**).

8. Inspect and/or repair the wheel and axle assembly as described in this chapter.

9. Reverse this procedure to install the wheel. Note the following:

   a. Apply grease to the axle, seal lips and collars (**Figure 14** and **Figure 15**).

   b. If the brake caliper was removed from the swing arm, install the caliper.

   c. Place the chain on the sprocket, then install the axle from the left side of the swing arm (**Figure 16**).

   d. Check that the index mark on the chain adjustment plate(s) (B, **Figure 11**) points up.

   e. Loosely install the washer and axle nut (A, **Figure 11**).

   f. Check chain adjustment as described in Chapter Three.

   g. Torque the axle nut.

   h. Check that the wheel spins freely and the brake operates properly.

Inspection

1. Inspect the seal (**Figure 17**) on both sides of the wheel. Check seals for:

   a. Hard or damaged rubber.

   b. Nicked or missing rubber at the seal lip.

   c. Grease or water seepage from the seal.

2. Inspect the bearings on both sides of the wheel. There are two bearings on the left side of the wheel. Check bearings for:

   a. Roughness. Turn each bearing by hand and check for smooth, quiet operation.

   b. Radial and axial play (**Figure 7**). Try to push the bearing in and out to check for axial play. Try to push the bearing up and down to check for radial play. Any play should be difficult to feel. If play is easily felt, the bearing is worn out. Always replace bearings as a set.

3. If damage is evident in the seals or bearings, refer to *Front and Rear Hubs* in this chapter for seal and bearing replacement procedures.

4. Clean the axle, nut, collars and adjustment plate (**Figure 18**) in solvent. Inspect the axle for straightness, using a set of V-blocks and a dial indicator (**Figure 9**). Refer to **Table 1** for maximum axle runout. Actual runout is *one-half* of the gauge reading. Do not attempt to straighten a bent axle. Replace the part.

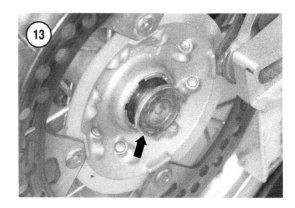

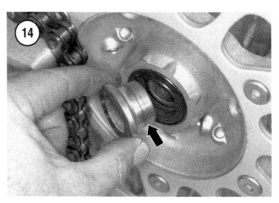

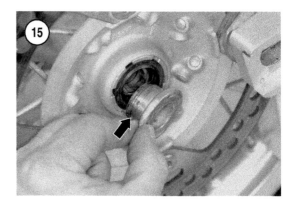

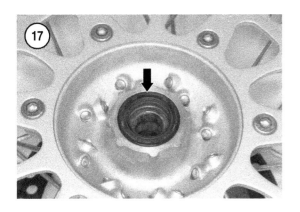

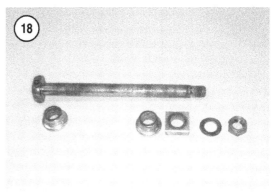

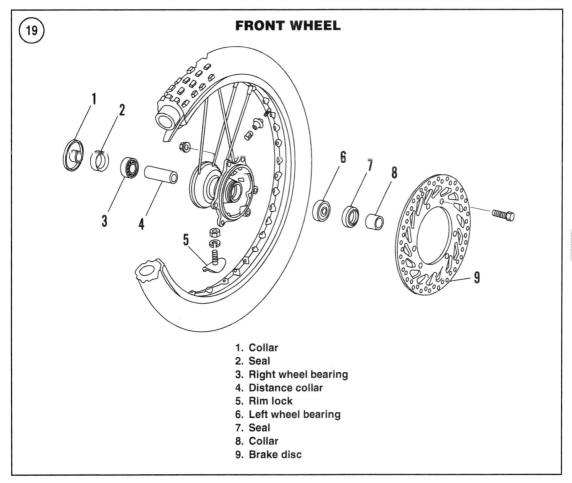

FRONT WHEEL

1. Collar
2. Seal
3. Right wheel bearing
4. Distance collar
5. Rim lock
6. Left wheel bearing
7. Seal
8. Collar
9. Brake disc

5. Refer to *Rim and Spoke Service* in this chapter for inspecting and truing the rim.

FRONT AND REAR HUBS

The wheel hubs contain bearings, seals and a distance collar. Inspect seals and bearings anytime the wheel(s) is removed. This section describes the removal and installation of seals and bearings. Procedures for servicing the front and rear hubs are essentially the same. Where differences occur, they will be described in the procedure.

Refer to **Figure 19** and **Figure 20** when servicing the front and rear hubs.

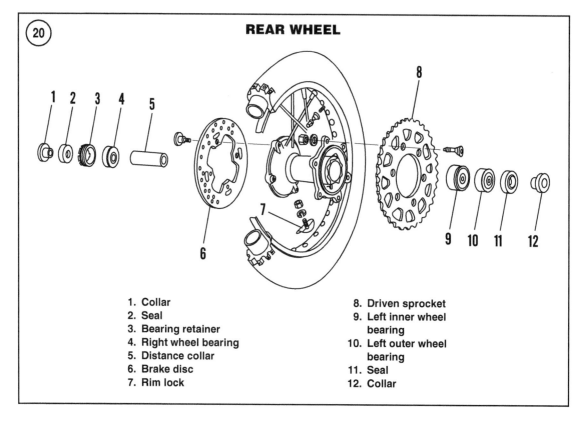

REAR WHEEL

1. Collar
2. Seal
3. Bearing retainer
4. Right wheel bearing
5. Distance collar
6. Brake disc
7. Rim lock

8. Driven sprocket
9. Left inner wheel
   bearing
10. Left outer wheel
    bearing
11. Seal
12. Collar

Inspection

The bearings can be inspected with the wheels mounted on the bike. With the wheels mounted, a high amount of leverage can be applied to the bearings to detect wear. Also, the wheels can be spun to listen for roughness in the bearings. Use the following procedure to check the bearings while the wheels are mounted. If the wheels must be dismounted, make the additional checks described in the wheel removal procedures in this chapter.

1. Support the bike with the wheel to be inspected off the ground. The axle nut must be tight. If the rear wheel is being inspected, remove the chain from the sprocket.

2. Grasp the wheel, placing the hands 180° apart. Rock the wheel up and down and side to side to check for radial and axial play. Have an assistant apply the brake while the test is repeated. Play will be detected in severely worn bearings, even though the wheel is locked.

3. Spin the wheel and listen for bearing noise. A damaged bearing will inconsistently sound rough and smooth. A severely worn bearing will sound consistently rough. In either case, replace the bearing.

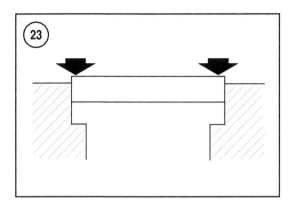

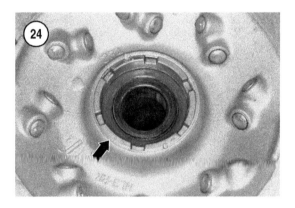

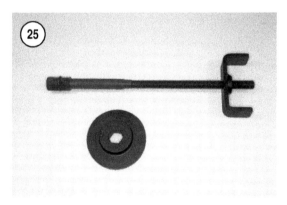

NOTE
If the disc brake drags and the bearing cannot be heard, remove the wheel. Place the axle in the wheel, then support the axle so the wheel spins freely.

4. If damage is evident, replace the bearings as a set. Always install new seals.

CAUTION
Do not remove bearings to check their condition. Bearing damage is likely to occur. The rear bearings are sealed

on both sides and cannot be serviced. Removed bearings must be replaced.

Seal Replacement

Seals are used to prevent the entry of moisture and dirt into the bearings. Always install new seals when the bearings are replaced.

CAUTION
In the following procedure, do not allow the wheel to rest on the brake disc. Support the wheel to prevent pressure being applied to the disc.

1. Remove the wheel as described in this chapter.
2. Pry old seals out of their recesses. Place a shop cloth under the tool to prevent damage (**Figure 21**). If a screwdriver is used to pry the seal, place a small block of wood under the tool so leverage can be applied. Avoid scratching the side of the bore.
3. Apply grease to the *new* seal, packing it into the inner lip.
4. Clean and lubricate the seal bore.
5. Place the seal *squarely* over the bore, making sure the manufacturer's numbers or marks are facing out.
6. Place a suitable-size driver or socket over the seal (**Figure 22**). The driver should seat against the outside diameter of the seal (**Figure 23**).
7. Carefully drive the seal into place.

Bearing Replacement

Two methods of bearing removal are provided in the following procedure. The first method uses a wheel bearing removal set and the second method uses common shop tools.

CAUTION
In the following procedure, do not allow the wheel to rest on the brake disc. Support the wheel to prevent pressure being applied to the disc.

1. Remove the seals as described in this section.
2. If repairing the rear wheel, remove the bearing retainer (**Figure 24**) from the right bore, as follows:

NOTE
*The bearing retainer removal wrench set (**Figure 25**) is available from a Honda dealership.*

11

a. Assemble the wrench set onto the wheel, as shown in **Figure 26** and **Figure 27**. Check that the tabs on the removal tool engage with the notches in the bearing retainer.

b. Use a wrench and turn the removal tool to unscrew the retainer from the bore (**Figure 28**).

3. Examine the bearings. Note the following:

   a. Make note of any visible manufacturer's marks on the sides of the bearings. The new bearings must be installed with the marks in the same direction. Mark each bearing, indicating its original location in the hub. The replacement bearings can then be matched and oriented correctly during installation.

   b. Determine which bearing is damaged the least. This bearing will be removed first. If repairing the rear wheel, remove the bearing from the right side of the hub first.

4A. Remove the bearing using the wheel bearing removal set as follows:

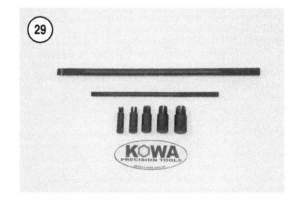

NOTE
*The tools described in this procedure are part of the Kowa Seiki Wheel Bearing Remover set (**Figure 29**). The set is available from K & L Supply Co., Santa Clara, CA.*

a. Select the appropriate-size remover head. The small, split end of the remover must fit inside the bearing race.

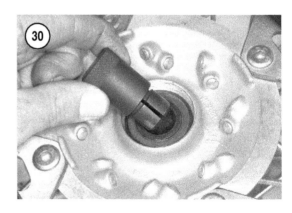

b. Insert the small end of the remover head into the bearing (**Figure 30**). Seat the remover head against the bearing (**Figure 31**).

c. Insert the tapered end of the driver through the back side of the hub (**Figure 32**). Fit the tapered end into the slot of the remover head (**Figure 33**).

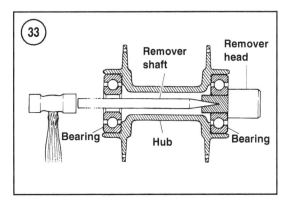

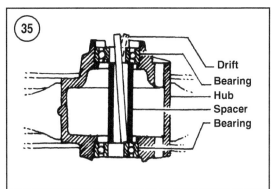

d. Position the hub so the remover head is against a solid surface, such as a concrete floor.

e. Strike the end of the driver so it wedges firmly in the remover head. The remover head should now be jammed tight against the inner bearing race.

f. Reposition the assembly so the remover head is free to move and the driver can be struck again.

g. Strike the driver, forcing the bearing and remover head from the hub (**Figure 34**).

h. Remove the driver from the remover head.

i. Remove the distance collar from the hub.

j. Repeat the procedure to remove the remaining bearing(s).

4B. Remove the bearing using a hammer, drift and propane torch as follows:

> *WARNING*
> *This procedure requires the use of a **propane** torch to heat the hub. Work in a well-ventilated area and away from combustible materials. Wear protective clothing, including eye protection and insulated gloves.*

a. Clean all lubricants from the wheel.

b. Insert a long drift into the hub and tilt the distance collar away from the bearing to be removed (**Figure 35**). If repairing the rear wheel, remove the bearing from the right side of the hub first.

c. Heat the hub around the bearing to be removed with a propane torch (**Figure 36**). Keep the torch moving and evenly heat the hub.

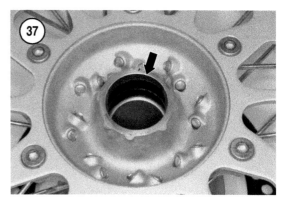

d. Turn the wheel over and tap around the inner bearing race. Make several passes until the bearing is removed from the hub.

e. Remove the distance collar.

f. Heat the hub around the remaining bearing(s). Drive out the remaining bearing(s), using a large socket or bearing driver that fits on the outer bearing race.

5. Clean and dry the interior of the hub (**Figure 37**). Inspect the hub for:

a. Cracks, corrosion or other damage.

b. Fit of the new bearings. If a bearing fits loosely in the hub bore, replace the hub. The bearings must be a driven-fit.

6. Inspect the distance collar (**Figure 38**) for:

a. Cracks, corrosion or other damage.

b. Fit. Check the fit of the collar against the back side of the bearings. It should fit flat against the bearings. Repair minor nicks and flaring with a file. Do not grind or shorten the collar. The collar must remain its full length in order to prevent binding of the bearings when the axle is tightened.

7. Before installing the new bearings, note the following:

a. Inspect the new bearings and determine which side faces out. This is usually the side with the manufacturer's marks and numbers. If a shield is on one side of the bearing, the shield faces out.

b. Apply grease (NLGI No. 2) to bearings that are not lubricated by the manufacturer or that are not sealed on both sides. Work the grease into the cavities between the balls and races.

c. Always support the bottom side of the hub, near the bore, when installing bearings.

8. Place a bearing *squarely* over the bearing bore (**Figure 39**). If repairing the rear wheel, begin in-

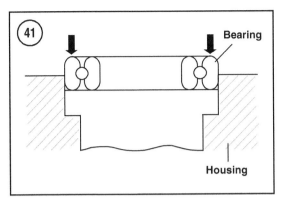

Bearing

Housing

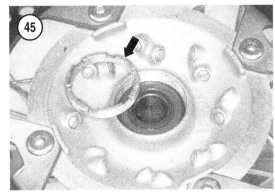

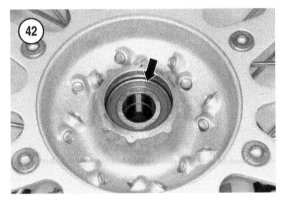

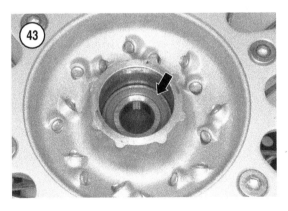

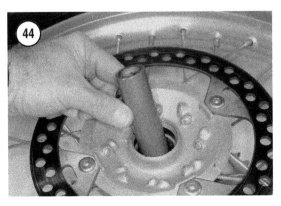

stallation with the inner bearing, on the left side of the hub.

9. Place a suitable-size driver or socket over the bearing (**Figure 40**). The driver should seat against the outside diameter of the bearing (**Figure 41**).

10. Press or drive the bearing, seating it in the hub. If repairing the rear wheel, repeat this step, seating the outer bearing (**Figure 42**) over the inner bearing (**Figure 43**).

CAUTION
Do not press or strike the bearing directly. Bearing damage will occur.

11. Turn the hub over and install the distance collar (**Figure 44**).

12. Press or drive in the remaining bearing, seating it in the hub.

13. If repairing the rear wheel, install the bearing retainer (**Figure 45**) into the right bore, as follows:

    a. Apply grease to the retainer, then finger-tighten it into the bore.

    b. Assemble the wrench set onto the wheel, as shown in **Figure 26** and **Figure 27**. Check that the tabs on the removal tool engage with the notches in the bearing retainer.

    c. Tighten the retainer to the specification in **Table 3**.

    d. Peen the edge of the retainer (**Figure 46**) to prevent it from backing off.

14. Install the seals as described in this section.

RIM AND SPOKE SERVICE

The rim and hub must be concentric to ensure good handling and prevent damage to the parts. When the bike is new, all spokes are tensioned equally and the rim and hub are aligned and concentric. As the bike is used, the spoke tensions become unequal and the rim may become damaged. When this occurs, the wheel develops radial (up and down) and lateral (side to side) runout. Wheel truing retensions the spokes, aligns the rim and hub, and makes the parts concentric. Regularly inspect and correct any problems with the wheel assembly.

Rim Inspection

Inspect the rims for flat spots, dents and warp. Also check the spoke holes for enlargement. The dent shown in **Figure 47** is common to this type of motorcycle, and causes the wheel to have excessive runout. Attempting to true wheels with large dents can result in hub and rim damage, due to the overtightened spokes. If the dent is minor and runout is minimal, the rider may find it acceptable to continue to use the rim.

Spoke Inspection

Inspect the spokes for damage and proper tightness. For new wheels, or wheels that have been rebuilt, check the spokes frequently. After the tensions stabilize, check the spokes as recommended in the *Maintenance and Lubrication Schedule* in Chapter Three.

When tightening spokes, always use the correct-size spoke wrench and do not exceed the torque recommendation in **Table 3**. The spoke wrenches shown in **Figure 48** grip the spoke on four sides (**Figure 49**). The spoke nipples can be rounded off or crushed if other types of tools are used. Do not attempt to true a wheel that has broken, bent or damaged spokes. Also, do not attempt to straighten bent spokes by excessive tightening. The spoke can crack the hub fitting and enlarge the rim hole.

In order to change spoke tension, spoke nipples must be able to turn easily. If a spoke is seized in its nipple, apply penetrating lubricant to the threads. If the spoke will not free itself or turn smoothly, replace the spoke and nipple.

Wheel Truing

Wheels can be trued with the wheel on or off the bike. Before truing a wheel, check the condition of the wheel bearings. Accurate wheel truing is not

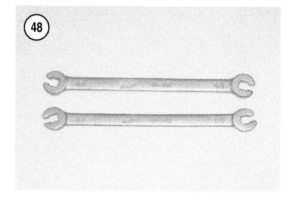

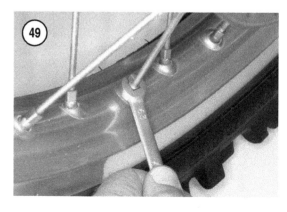

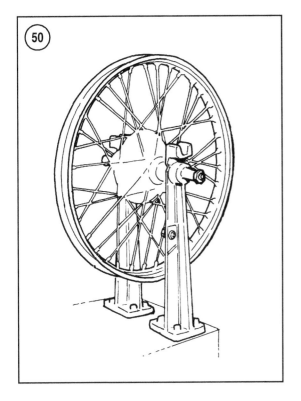

50

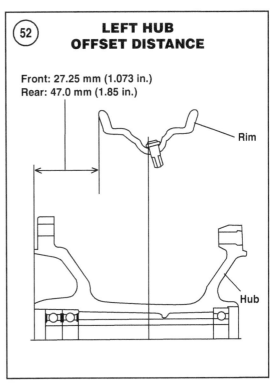

52

**LEFT HUB
OFFSET DISTANCE**

Front: 27.25 mm (1.073 in.)
Rear: 47.0 mm (1.85 in.)

Rim

Hub

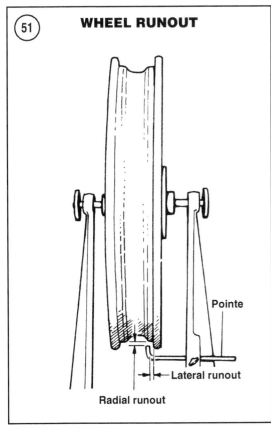

51

WHEEL RUNOUT

Pointe

Lateral runout

Radial runout

possible with worn wheel bearings. Refer to **Table 1** for wheel runout specifications.

If runout appears minimal, the wheel can be left on the bike to check runout. Raise the wheel so it is free to spin. Solidly hold a pointer against the fork or swing arm. While the wheel is turned, move the pointer toward or away from the rim until maximum runout is determined. The gap can be measured from the rim to the pointer. This is a general check and should only be used on rims that appear to be in good condition.

If the wheel needs major truing, mount the rim (tire and tube removed) on a truing stand, as shown in **Figure 50**. Then mount an adjustable pointer or dial indicator next to the rim to measure the runout in both directions (**Figure 51**). Place spacers on the axle to keep the rim from sliding along the axle.

Correcting lateral runout

When adjusting severe lateral runout, or when lacing new spokes to a rim and hub, the rim offset must be taken into account. The rim is offset from the hub by a specific dimension. **Figure 52** shows front and rear wheel offset. Maintain these distances when adjusting lateral runout.

To move the rim to the left or right of the hub, loosen and tighten spokes, as shown in **Figure 53**. The rim will move in the direction of the tightened spokes.

> *NOTE*
> *Always loosen and tighten spokes equally. Loosen a minimum of three spokes, then tighten the opposite three spokes. If runout is over a large area, loosen and tighten a larger number of spokes.*

Correcting radial runout

To make the rim concentric with the hub, loosen and tighten the spokes, as shown in **Figure 54**. The rim will move in the direction of the tightened spokes.

> *NOTE*
> *Always loosen and tighten spokes equally. Loosen a minimum of three spokes, then tighten the opposite three spokes. If runout is over a large area, loosen and tighten a larger number of spokes.*

DRIVE CHAIN

Refer to Chapter Three for drive chain cleaning, lubrication, adjustment and measurement. Refer to **Table 2** in this chapter for chain specifications.

When checking the condition of the chain, also check the condition of the sprockets, as described in Chapter Three. If either the chain or sprockets are worn, replace all drive components. Using new sprockets with a worn chain, or a new chain on worn sprockets will shorten the life of the new part.

When new, the bike comes with a standard chain and master link (no O-rings). The following procedure describes the removal and installation of a standard chain and master link, as well as an O-ring type chain with press-fit master link.

Removal and Installation

1. Support the bike so it is stable and the rear wheel is off the ground.
2. Shift the transmission into neutral.
3. Find the master link on the chain. Remove the spring clip (**Figure 55**) with a pair of pliers, then press the link out of the chain. Account for the

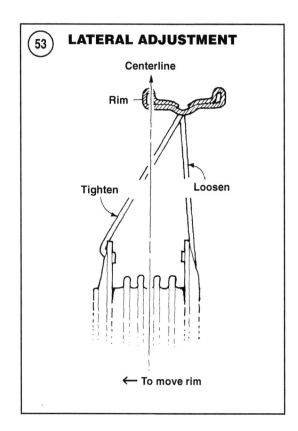

53 LATERAL ADJUSTMENT

Centerline

Rim

Tighten   Loosen

← To move rim

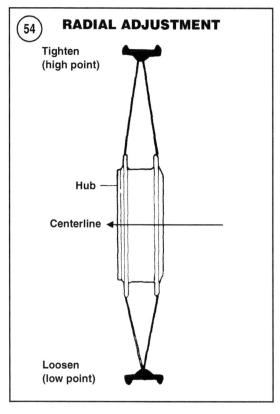

54 RADIAL ADJUSTMENT

Tighten
(high point)

Hub

Centerline

Loosen
(low point)

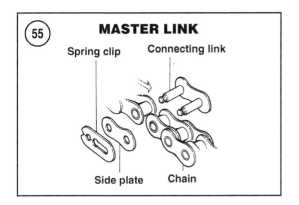

MASTER LINK

Spring clip   Connecting link

Side plate   Chain

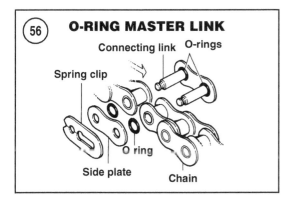

O-RING MASTER LINK

Connecting link   O-rings

Spring clip

O ring

Side plate   Chain

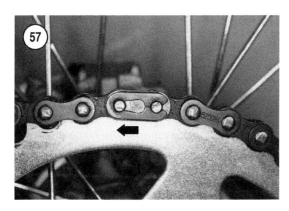

O-rings under the side plates (**Figure 56**) on O-ring chains.

NOTE
If the master link will not come apart after the spring clip is removed, the master link is probably a press-fit link. See Press-fit master link in this chapter for removal and installation procedures.

4. Remove the chain from the bike.

5. Clean and inspect the chain as described in Chapter Three.

6. Reverse this procedure to install the chain. Note the following:

   a. Install the chain and reassemble the master link. On O-ring chains, be sure to install the O-rings under both side plates.

   b. Install a *new* spring clip on the master link. The spring clip must be installed so the closed end of the clip points toward the direction of travel (**Figure 57**).

   c. Adjust the chain as described in Chapter Three.

Press-fit master link

Many chains are now fitted with press-fit master links. These links have side plates that are press-fitted into place, as well as a spring clip. This design prevents the chain from disassembling if the spring clip is jarred free. To remove and install this link, special tools are required.

1. To remove the master link:

   a. Remove the spring clip.

   b. Fit a chain breaker tool (**Figure 58**) over the side plate pin, then drive the pin out of the link.

2. To install the master link:

   a. Assemble the master link as shown in **Figure 59**.

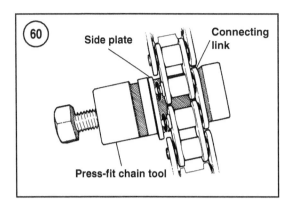

b. Fit a pressing tool (**Figure 60**) over the side plate, then press and secure the link into place. Work slowly when pressing the link. Overtightening the link will cause it to bind at the joint. The link is usually pressed sufficiently when the groove for the spring clip is visible.

c. After pressing the link, check for binding in the joint. Check that the spring clip will seat completely.

SPROCKETS

Check the condition of both sprockets and the drive chain as described in Chapter Three. If either the chain or sprockets are worn, replace all drive components. Using new sprockets with a worn chain, or a new chain on worn sprockets, will shorten the life of the new part.

Drive Sprocket Removal and Installation

1. Support the bike so it is stable and the rear wheel is off the ground.

2. Put the transmission in gear.

3. Remove the bolts, clamp and sprocket guard (**Figure 61**).

4. Remove the backing plate under the sprocket guard (**Figure 62**).

5. Loosen the sprocket bolt (A, **Figure 63**) by one of the following methods:

a. With the chain installed, apply the rear brake and loosen the bolt.

b. With the chain removed, hold the sprocket with a holding tool (such as a Grabbit) and loosen the bolt.

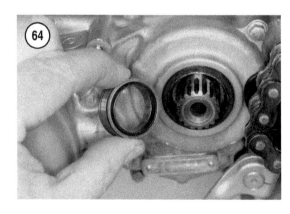

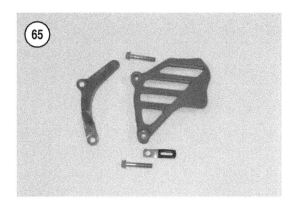

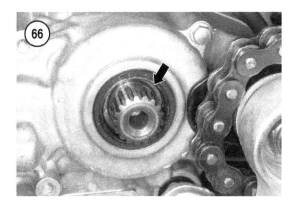

6. Remove the bolt, spring washer and sprocket from the shaft.

7. Remove the countershaft collar and O-ring (**Figure 64**).

8. Inspect the sprocket as described in Chapter Three.

9. Inspect the sprocket guard assembly (**Figure 65**) for cracks or other damage.

10. Clean and inspect the countershaft and seal cavity (**Figure 66**).

11. Reverse this procedure to install the drive sprocket. Note the following:

    a. Install a *new*, lubricated O-ring in the collar. Pack the collar with grease. Install the collar onto the countershaft (**Figure 67**), with the O-ring facing in.

    b. Install the sprocket with the flat side facing out (**Figure 68**).

    c. Install the spring washer (B, **Figure 63**) with OUTSIDE (stamped in washer) facing out.

    d. Tighten the sprocket bolt to the specification in **Table 3**.

    e. Adjust the chain as described in Chapter Three.

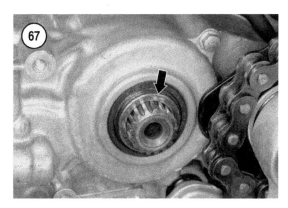

Driven Sprocket Removal and Installation

1. Support the bike so it is stable and the rear wheel is off the ground.

2. Remove the rear wheel as described in this chapter.

3. Remove the nuts, bolts and washers securing the sprocket to the hub (**Figure 69**).

4. Inspect the sprocket as described in Chapter Three.

5. Reverse this procedure to install the driven sprocket and rear wheel. Note the following:

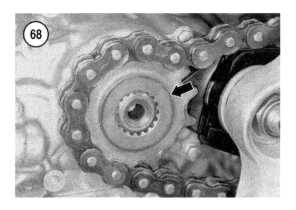

a. Tighten the bolts to the specification in **Table 3**. Tighten the bolts in several passes, working in a crisscross pattern.

b. Adjust the chain as described in Chapter Three.

TIRE CHANGING

Removal

NOTE
When changing a tire, work over a pad to prevent damage to the wheel assembly.

1. Remove the core from the valve stem and deflate the tire.

2. Loosen the nut holding the rim lock (**Figure 70**).

3. Press the entire bead on both sides of the tire into the rim.

4. Lubricate the beads with soapy water.

5. Insert a tire iron under the bead, next to the valve stem (**Figure 71**). Pry the bead over the rim, while forcing the bead on the opposite side of the tire into the rim.

6. Insert a second tire iron next to the first. While holding the tire with one iron, work around the perimeter of the rim with the second iron, prying the tire over the rim.

NOTE
If the inner tube is to be reused, be careful to not pinch the tube as the tire is being removed from the rim. Always replace the tube when a new tire is being mounted.

7. Remove the setting rubber (**Figure 72**) from the valve stem, then remove the inner tube from the tire. If necessary, reach inside the tire and pull the valve stem out of the rim hole.

8. Remove the nut, washer and rim lock from the wheel.

9. Stand the tire upright and pry the second tire bead over the rim (**Figure 73**).

Inspection

1. If the tire is to be reused, inspect the inside and outside of the tire for damage and objects that could cause a puncture.

2. Inspect the rim lock for damage.

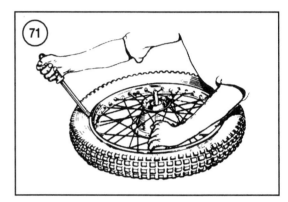

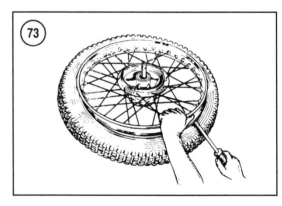

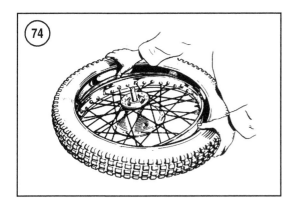

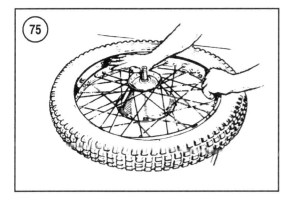

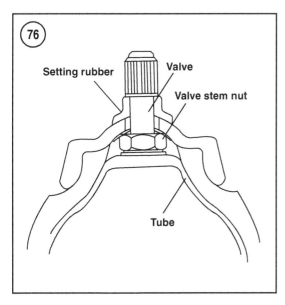

Setting rubber

Valve

Valve stem nut

Tube

3. Check that the spokes do not protrude through the spoke nipples.

4. Inspect the rim band for deterioration. If a new rim band is installed, place the roughest side of the band against the rim. If water is entering the rim, an alternative to the rim band is to wrap the rim with

two separate revolutions of duct tape. Punch holes for the valve stem and rim lock.

Installation

> *NOTE*
> *Installation will be easier if the tire is warm and pliable. This can be achieved by placing the tire in the sun or an enclosed vehicle.*

1. Sprinkle talcum powder around the interior of the tire casing. Distribute the powder so it is on all surfaces that will touch the inner tube. The powder minimizes chafing and helps the tube distribute itself when inflated.

> *NOTE*
> *Depending on the make and type of tire installed, check the sidewall and determine if it must be installed in a specific direction. A direction arrow is often embossed in the sidewall.*

2. Lubricate one of the tire beads, then push it onto the rim (**Figure 74**). When necessary, also work the tire from the opposite side of the rim (**Figure 75**).

3. Install the rim lock, lockwasher and nut. Do not tighten at this time. The rim lock must be over the edge of both tire beads when installation is completed.

4. Install the core into the valve stem, then insert the tube into the tire. Note that the valve stem nut goes to the inside of the rim (**Figure 76**). Check that the tube is not twisted as it is tucked into the tire.

5. Inflate the tube until it is rounded and no longer wrinkled. Too much air will make tire installation difficult and too little air will increase the chance of pinching the tube.

6. Lubricate the second tire bead, then start installation opposite the valve stem. Fit the rim lock over the tire bead, then work around the rim, hand-fitting as much of the tire as possible. If necessary, relubricate the bead. Before final installation, check that the valve stem is straight and the inner tube is not pinched. Use the tire irons to pry the remaining section of bead onto the rim.

7. Check the bead for uniform fit on both sides of the tire.

8. Lubricate both beads and inflate the tire to seat the beads onto the rim. Check the sidewall for a rec-

11

ommended seating pressure. If none is indicated, inflate the tire to 25-30 psi (172-207 kPa).

WARNING
If the tire does not seat at the recommended pressure, do not continue to over-inflate the tire. Deflate the tire and re-inflate to the recommended seating pressure. Relubricate the beads, if necessary.

9. Tighten the rim lock nut.
10. Bleed the tire pressure to 15 psi (100 kPa).
11. Install the valve stem cap.

Table 1 FRONT AND REAR WHEEL SPECIFICATIONS

Tire make/type	
Front	Dunlop K490G
Rear	Dunlop K695
Front tire size	80/100-21 51M
Rear tire size	110/90-19 62M
Tire pressure (front/rear)	100 kPa (15 psi)
Axle runout (front/rear)	0.20 mm (0.008 in.)
Rim runout (radial and lateral)	2.0 mm (0.08 in.)
Wheel hub to rim distance	
(offset at left side of hub)	
Front	27.25 (1.073 in.)
Rear	47.0 (1.85 in.)

Table 2 DRIVE CHAIN AND SPROCKET SPECIFICATIONS

Drive chain specifications	
Size	520
Type	Non-O-ring
Number of inks	114
Manufacturers/chain series	
(standard)	D.I.D. 520DM
	D.I.D. 520DMA2
	RK 520KZ6
Drive chain slack	25-35 mm (1.0-1.4 in.)
Drive chain length,	
wear limit (16 pitch/17 pins)	259 mm (10.2 in.)
Drive chain slider,	
thickness wear limit	5.0 mm (0.2 in.)
Drive chain roller,	
diameter wear limit	
1997	25 mm (0.98 in.)
1998	
Upper	25 mm (0.98 in.)
Lower	35 mm (1.38 in.)
1999	
Upper	25 mm (0.98 in.)
Lower	39 mm (1.54 in.)
2000-2001	
Upper and lower	25 mm (0.98 in.)
Stock sprocket sizes (front/rear teeth)	
1997	13/49
1998-2001	13/50

Table 3 WHEEL AND DRIVE TRAIN TORQUE SPECIFICATIONS

	N•m	in.-lb.	ft.-lb.
Axle pinch bolts	20	–	14
Axle nut (front)	88	–	65
Axle nut (rear)			
1997	93	–	69
1998-1999	108	–	80
2000-2001	127	–	94
Brake disc cover			
(front) bolts	13	–	9
Drive chain adjusting nut	27	–	20
Drive chain guide			
mounting nut	12	106	–
Drive chain roller bolt			
1997-2000	22	–	16
2001	12	106	–
Drive sprocket bolt	26	–	20
Driven sprocket nuts	32	–	24
Rear wheel bearing			
retainer	44	–	33
Rim lock	13	–	9
Spokes	3.8	34	–

11

CHAPTER TWELVE

FRONT SUSPENSION AND STEERING

This chapter provides service procedures for the front suspension and steering components. This includes the handlebar, steering head and fork. Refer to the tables at the end of the chapter for specifications, capacities, fork settings and torque requirements.

HANDLEBAR

Removal and Installation

The handlebar and controls must be tight and not move or pivot when pressure is applied. If the handlebar only needs to be repositioned, adjustment can be made by loosening the rear holder cap bolts. Tilt the handlebar to the desired position, then retorque the bolts.

> *NOTE*
> *Optional holders are available that can be rotated to offset the handlebar 3 mm rearward or forward. Always mark the holders before removing so*

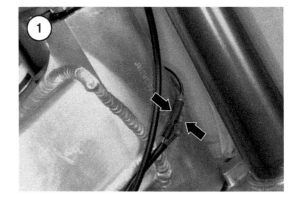

> *the matched positions of the holders are known.*

1. Support the bike so it is stable and secure.

2. Disconnect the engine stop button wires (**Figure 1**).

3. Remove the number plate from the handlebar, then remove the bolt and collar securing the plate to the upper fork bridge (**Figure 2**). Lift the lower tab on the plate out of the hole in the lower fork bridge.

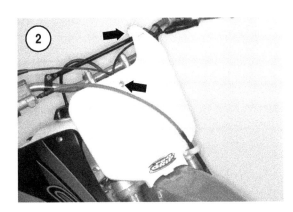

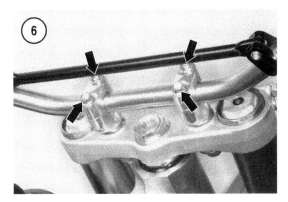

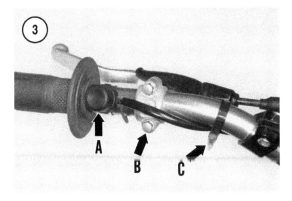

4. Remove the bands securing the engine stop button wires, then remove the button (A, **Figure 3**).

5. Remove the clutch lever clamp (B, **Figure 3**), then remove the lever and cable assembly.

6. Remove the holder clamp from the brake master cylinder (**Figure 4**), then remove the master cylinder and lever assembly.

CAUTION
Do not allow the master cylinder to hang by its hose. Keep the master cylinder in an upright position so fluid cannot leak out of the cap. This also prevents air from getting into the system. Wrap the master cylinder with a clean shop cloth, then secure it to the bike until the handlebar is reassembled.

7. At the throttle, loosen the housing clamp bolts (**Figure 5**). Turn the handlebar to create slack in the cable, then remove the throttle and cable assembly. If the throttle will not easily slide off the end of the handlebar, wait until the handlebar is removed from the bike. Do not allow the throttle cable to kink during removal.

8. If the handlebar will be replaced, remove the left grip. If necessary, insert a compressed air nozzle between the grip and handlebar. As air expands the grip, twist and pull the grip from the handlebar.

9. Remove the bolts from the holder caps (**Figure 6**), then remove the handlebar.

10. If necessary, for 1999-2001 models, the handlebar holders can be removed from the upper bridge as follows:

   a. Mark the front side of the holders.

   b. Remove the nuts, washers and bushings (**Figure 7**).

   c. Remove the holders (**Figure 8**).

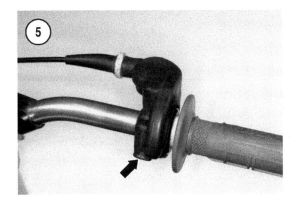

Inspection

1. Inspect the handlebar for cracks, bending or other damage. If the handlebar is aluminum, check closely where the handlebar is clamped to the fork, and at the clutch lever. If cracks, scores or other damage is found, replace the handlebar. Damage in these areas may cause the handlebar to break.

> *WARNING*
> *Never attempt to straighten, weld or heat a damaged handlebar. The metal can weaken and possibly break when subjected to the shocks and stresses that occur when riding the motorcycle.*

2. Inspect the threads on the mounting bolts and in the holders. Clean all residue from the threads. Replace bolts that are damaged or stressed.
3. Clean the handlebar, holders and caps with an aerosol parts cleaner. Use a stiff brush to clean the residue from the knurled areas on the handlebar. Use a soft brush on aluminum handlebars.

Installation

1. On 1999-2001 models, install the handle holders (**Figure 8**), if removed. Install as follows:
   a. Insert the bushings into the upper bridge.
   b. Install and finger-tighten the holders, washers and nuts. Check the marks on the holders to ensure they are both facing forward.
   c. Temporarily install the handlebar, holder caps and bolts. This will stabilize and align the holders so they can be tightened.
   d. Tighten the nuts to the specification in **Table 2**.
   e. Loosen the holder caps.
2. Slide the throttle and cable assembly over the right end of the handlebar, then position the handlebar in the lower holders. Install the holder caps, with the punch marks on the holders facing forward (**Figure 9**), then finger-tighten the two front bolts.
3. Standard position of the handlebar is when the punch mark on the handlebar aligns with the top of the holder (**Figure 9**). If desired, position the handlebar to the rider's preference.
4. When the position is established, tighten the front holder cap bolts to the specification in **Table 2**.

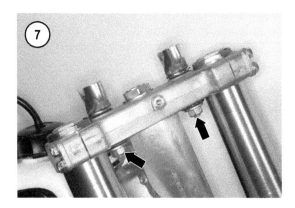

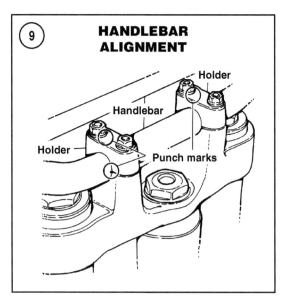

HANDLEBAR ALIGNMENT

Holder

Handlebar

Holder

Punch marks

5. Install the rear holder cap bolts, then tighten the bolts to the specification in **Table 4**. When installed, there should be a small gap between the holders, at the back.
6. Position the throttle housing, aligning the triangle on the dust cover (or punch mark on the hous-

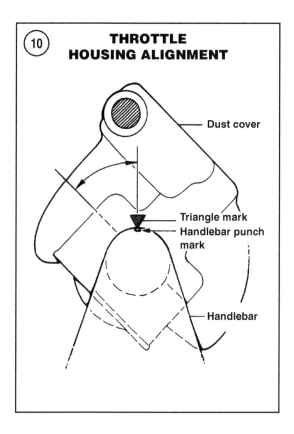

THROTTLE HOUSING ALIGNMENT

Dust cover

Triangle mark
Handlebar punch mark

Handlebar

ing) with the punch mark on the handlebar (**Figure 10**). Tighten the housing bolts to the specification in **Table 2**.

7. Install the brake master cylinder as follows:
   a. Align the master cylinder with the punch mark on the handlebar (A, **Figure 11**).
   b. Install the holder clamp (B, **Figure 11**) so *UP* and the arrow are facing up.
   c. Tighten the upper bolt first, then the bottom bolt to the specification in **Table 2**.

8. If removed, install the left grip. Before installing the grip, clean the handlebar and grip with solvent. Apply adhesive to the grip, then twist it into position on the handlebar.

9. Clamp the engine stop button (A, **Figure 3**) to the left handlebar. Connect the stop button wires (**Figure 1**).

10. Install the clutch lever assembly as follows:
    a. Position the clutch lever and clamp (B, **Figure 3**) next to the engine stop button.
    b. Align the lever bracket with the punch mark on the handlebar (A, **Figure 12**).
    c. Install the clamp (B, **Figure 12**) so the punch mark on the clamp faces up.

NOTE
The wire from the engine stop button must be routed over the top of the clamp.

11. Install the band (C, **Figure 3**).
12. Install and bolt the number plate into position (**Figure 2**).
13. Recheck the riding position and adjust the handlebar, if necessary. Turn the handlebar side to side and check for cable binding.

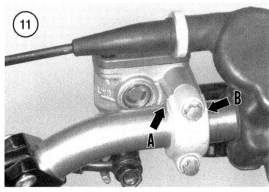

STEERING STEM AND HEAD

The steering stem pivots in the steering head on tapered roller bearings. The bearings are at the top and bottom of the steering stem. The inner races (mounted in the frame) and the lower bearing (mounted on the steering stem) should not be removed unless they require replacement. Lubricate the bearings as specified in Chapter Three. Before disassembling the steering head, perform the *Steering Play Check and Adjustment* procedures in this section. The checks will help determine if the bearings and races are worn, or if they only require adjustment.

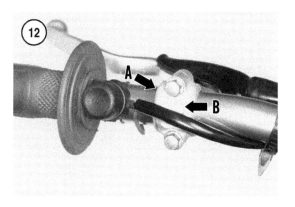

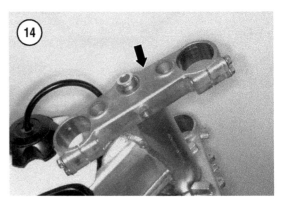

Disassembly

1. Remove the front wheel as described in Chapter Eleven.
2. Remove the front fender and hose guide.
3. Remove the handlebar as described in this chapter.
4. Remove the fuel tank breather hose from the steering stem, then remove the steering stem nut and washer (**Figure 13**).
5. Remove the fork legs as described in this chapter.
6. Remove the upper fork bridge (**Figure 14**).
7. While holding the steering stem, remove the steering stem adjust nut (**Figure 15**).

> *NOTE*
> *Remove the nut with a steering stem socket (part No. 07916-3710100) or a pin spanner wrench (part No. 07702-0020001). Order the tool from a Honda dealership.*

8. Lower the steering stem assembly out of the steering head (**Figure 16**), then remove the seal and bearing at the top of the steering head.

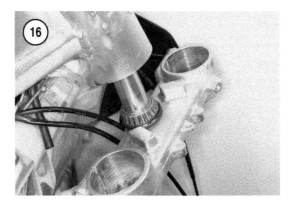

> *CAUTION*
> *The bottom bearing is pressed onto the steering stem. Do not attempt to remove the bearing unless it is to be replaced. Damage will occur during removal.*

Inspection

1. Clean the bearings and races with solvent.
2. Check the welds at the steering head for cracks or other damage. If damage is evident, have a qualified frame or welding shop make the repairs.

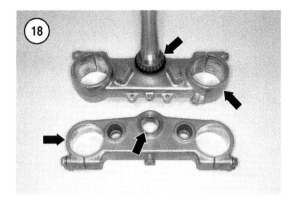

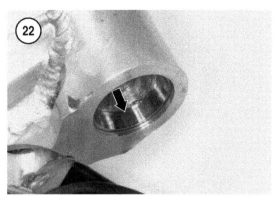

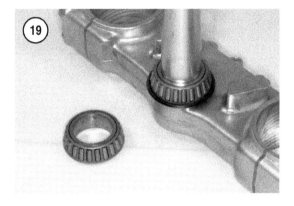

3. Inspect the steering stem nut, washer, adjust nut and seal for damage (**Figure 17**).

4. Inspect the steering stem assembly (**Figure 18**). Inspect the clamping and pivot areas for cracks or damage.

5. Inspect the bearings for pitting, scratches, corrosion or discoloration (**Figure 19**).

6. Inspect the bearing races in the frame for pitting, galling or corrosion. Compare the worn race in **Figure 20** with the new race in **Figure 21**. If a race is worn or damaged, replace both races and bearings as described in this section.

7. If the bearings will be reused, pack the bearings with waterproof bearing grease.

Outer Bearing Race Replacement

Only remove the bearing races from the frame when new races will be installed. When new races are installed, always install new bearings. Since the bearing races are recessed in the bores, installation is much easier using the Honda special tools. These are the bearing race installer (two required) (part No. 07VMF-KZ30100) and installer shaft (part No. 07VMF-KZ30200). These tools are used in the following procedure. A similar tool could be fabricated; however, the parts used as the installers must fit at the outside edge of the races and still be capable of entering the steering head bore.

1. Insert an aluminum drift into the steering head and position it on the edge of the lower race (**Figure 22**). Carefully drive out the race. To prevent binding, make several passes around the perimeter of the race. Repeat the procedure to remove the upper race.

2. Clean the race bores and inspect them for damage.

3. To install the lower race, perform the following:
   a. Place a new race squarely into the bore opening, with its wide side facing out.
   b. Assemble the tool as shown in **Figure 23**.
   c. Hold the installer shaft with a wrench and tighten the nut to seat the race.
   d. Remove the tool from the frame and check that the race is fully seated.
   e. Assemble the tool as shown in **Figure 24**. Note that the bottom race installer is seated in the lower race.
   f. Hold the installer shaft with a wrench and tighten the nut to seat the race.
   g. Remove the tool from the frame and check that the race is fully seated.
4. Lubricate the races with waterproof bearing grease.

Steering Stem Bearing Replacement

The steering stem bearing (A, **Figure 25**) is pressed into place. Perform the following steps to replace the bearing.

1. Thread the steering stem nut (B, **Figure 25**) onto the steering stem to protect the threads.

2. Remove the bearing and seal, using a hammer and chisel (**Figure 26**). To prevent binding, make several passes around the perimeter of the bearing.

> *WARNING*
> *Wear safety glasses when using the hammer and chisel.*

3. Clean and inspect the steering stem. If damaged, replace the steering stem.

4. Pack the new bearing and seal with waterproof bearing grease.

5. Slide the new bearing and seal onto the steering stem.

6A. To *press* the new bearing into place, perform the following:
   a. Place the steering stem and new bearing in a press, supporting the parts with two bearing drivers (**Figure 27**). Check that the lower bearing driver is seated against the inner bearing race and is not touching the bearing rollers.
   b. Press and seat the bearing onto the steering stem.

6B. To *drive* the new bearing into place, perform the following:
   a. Slide a bearing driver or long pipe over the steering stem, seating the tool on the *inner* bearing race (**Figure 28**).

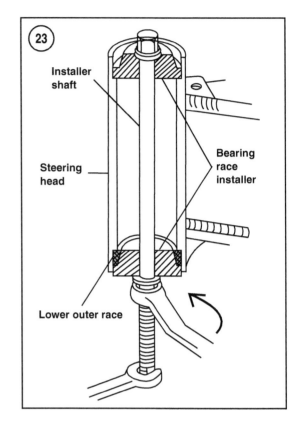

(23) Installer shaft — Steering head — Bearing race installer — Lower outer race

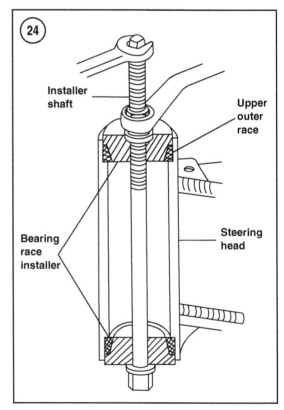

(24) Installer shaft — Upper outer race — Bearing race installer — Steering head

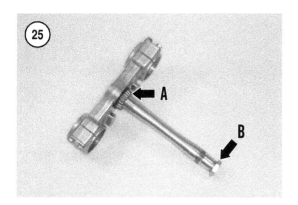

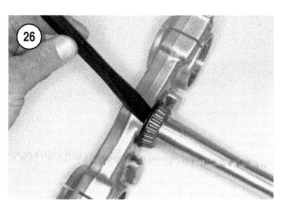

b. Drive the bearing onto the steering stem until it is seated.

Assembly and Adjustment

1. Check that the upper and lower bearing races are seated in the frame.

2. Check that bearings and races are lubricated with waterproof grease.

3. Guide the steering stem through the bottom of the frame (**Figure 16**).

4. Install the upper bearing into its race (**Figure 29**).

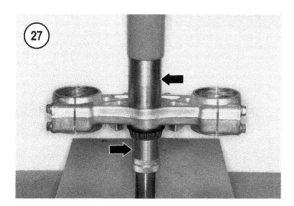

5. Install the bearing race seal (**Figure 30**).

6. Install and finger-tighten the steering stem adjust nut (**Figure 31**).

7A. To seat and torque the bearings using a torque wrench and spanner/socket (**Figure 32**), perform the following:

> *NOTE*
> *Refer to Chapter One for information concerning the use of torque wrench adapters.*

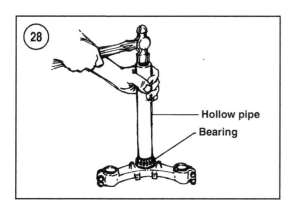

Hollow pipe

Bearing

a. Tighten the adjust nut to the specification in **Table 2**.
b. Turn the steering stem from lock to lock at least five times to seat the bearings.
c. Loosen and retighten the adjust nut to the specification in **Table 2**.
d. Check bearing play by turning the steering stem from lock to lock. The steering stem should pivot smoothly with no play, binding or roughness.

7B. If the tools in Step 7A are not available, seat and torque the bearings as follows:

a. Tighten the steering adjust nut with a spanner (**Figure 33**) to seat the bearings, then loosen the nut. Do not use excessive force when seating the bearings.
b. Retighten the adjust nut while checking for horizontal and vertical play. Stop adjusting the nut when play is eliminated in both directions. If properly tightened, the steering stem will pivot to the lock positions under its own weight, after an initial assist.

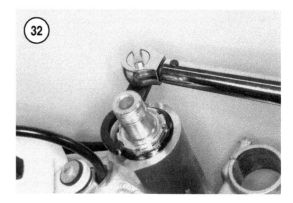

8. Install the upper fork bridge.

9. Install the washer and steering stem nut (**Figure 34**). Finger-tighten the nut.

10. Install the fork legs as described in this chapter. Do not tighten the lower bridge pinch bolts until the steering stem nut has been tightened. The lower bridge will move slightly as the nut is tightened.

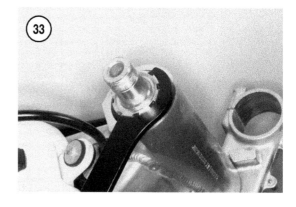

11. Tighten the steering stem nut (**Figure 35**) to the specification in **Table 2**.

12. Tighten the lower bridge pinch bolts to the specification in **Table 2**.

> *NOTE*
> *Because tightening the steering stem nut affects the steering bearing preload, it may be necessary to repeat the following steps until adjustment is correct.*

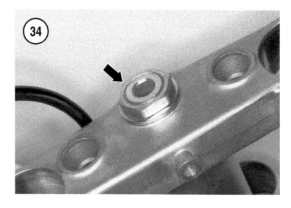

13. Check bearing play by turning the steering stem from lock to lock. If it does not turn smoothly and freely, readjust the bearing play as follows:

a. Loosen the steering stem nut, then slightly loosen the steering adjust nut.
b. Retighten the steering stem nut to the specification in **Table 2**.
c. Recheck play by turning the steering from lock to lock. If the adjustment feels good, position the fork so it points straight ahead.

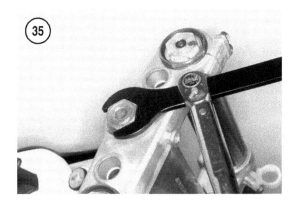

Have an assistant hold the bike, then grasp the fork tubes and firmly move them front to back several times. If there is play, but bearing adjustment feels good, the bearings and races are probably worn.

14. Install the handlebar as described in this chapter.

15. Install the front fender.

16. Install the front wheel as described in Chapter Eleven.

17. After 30-60 minutes of riding time, check the steering adjustment as described in *Steering Play Check and Adjustment* in this section.

Steering Play Check and Adjustment

Steering adjustment takes up any play in the steering stem and bearings and allows the steering stem to operate with free rotation. Excessive play or roughness in the steering stem makes steering imprecise and causes bearing damage. These conditions are usually caused by improper bearing lubrication and steering adjustment. Improperly routed control cables can also affect steering operation. Perform the following checks before disassembling the steering head. Also perform these checks after 30-60 minutes of riding time, after the steering head has been reassembled.

1. Support the bike so the front wheel is off the ground.

2. Turn the handlebar from lock to lock and check for roughness or binding. Movement should be smooth with no resistance.

3. Position the handlebar so the front wheel points straight ahead. Lightly push the end of the handlebar. The front end should fully turn to the side from the center position, under its own weight. Check in both directions. Note the following:
   a. If the steering stem moves roughly or stops before reaching the frame stop, check that all cables are routed properly.
   b. If cable routing is correct and steering is tight, the steering adjustment may be too tight. This condition can also occur if the bearings and races require lubrication or replacement. Perform Step 4 before loosening the steering adjustment in Step 5.
   c. If the steering stem moves from side to side correctly, perform Step 4 to check for excessive looseness.

4. Position the fork so it points straight ahead. Have an assistant hold the bike, then grasp the fork tubes (near the axle) and firmly move them front to back several times.
   a. If movement can be felt at the steering stem, tighten the steering as described in Step 5.
   b. If no excessive movement can be felt and the steering turns from side to side correctly, the steering is adjusted properly and in good condition.

5. Adjust the steering as follows:
   a. Loosen the lower bridge pinch bolts (**Figure 36**).
   b. Loosen the steering stem nut (**Figure 37**).

c. Tighten (to correct looseness) or loosen (to correct tightness) the steering adjust nut (**Figure 38**). Tighten the steering stem nut to the specification in **Table 2**, then recheck for play as described in this procedure. If necessary, readjust the steering stem nut.

> *NOTE*
> *Because tightening the steering stem nut affects the steering bearing preload, it may be necessary to repeat the adjustment steps several times. If proper adjustment cannot be achieved, then disassemble the steering stem and check the condition of the bearings and races.*

6. Tighten the lower bridge pinch bolts to the specification in **Table 2**.

FORK OIL CHANGE

The fork legs must be removed and partially disassembled to change the fork oil. Refer to the procedures in this chapter for removing, servicing and installing the fork legs.

FORK REMOVAL AND INSTALLATION

Removal

1. Support the bike so the front wheel is off the ground.
2. Remove the handlebar assembly as described in this chapter.

> *NOTE*
> *The handlebar assembly does not have to be completely disassembled. The handlebar must be removed so the fork cap (1997 models) or fork damper (1998-2001 models) at the top of each fork leg can be loosened. If the handlebar can be removed from the holders and secured out of the way, that will be sufficient for servicing the fork. On 1999-2001 models, the handlebar holders must also be removed.*

3. Remove the front wheel as described in Chapter Eleven.
4. Remove the brake caliper (**Figure 39**) as described in Chapter Fourteen.

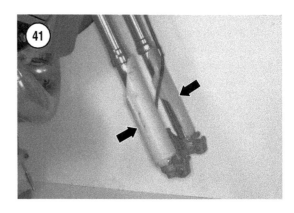

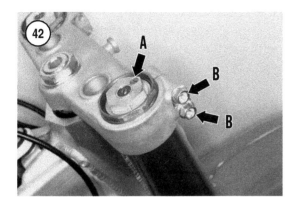

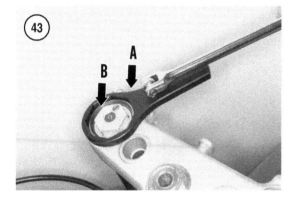

NOTE
When the caliper is removed, insert a spacer block between the brake pads. This will prevent the pads from being forced out of the caliper if the brake lever is accidentally operated. Support the caliper with a bungee cord or piece of wire. Do not allow it to hang by the hose.

5. Remove the brake hose from the fork protector clamp (**Figure 40**).

6. Remove the fork protectors (**Figure 41**).

7. Loosen the air release screw on each fork cap (A, **Figure 42**).

8. Loosen the upper bridge pinch bolts on each fork leg (B, **Figure 42**).

9A. On 1997 models, if the fork legs will be disassembled, loosen (do not remove) the fork cap on each fork tube.

NOTE
On 1998-2001 models, use a 50 mm locknut wrench to loosen the fork dampers. Adjustable or open-ended wrenches are not recommended as they will not adequately grip the thin hex surface on the fork damper. Refer to **Fork Tools** *under* **Fork Service** *in this chapter for a description of the proper tools.*

9B. On 1998-2001 models, if the fork legs will be disassembled, loosen the fork damper on each fork tube with a 50 mm locknut wrench (A, **Figure 43**). Do not loosen the fork cap (B, **Figure 43**).

10. Loosen the lower bridge pinch bolts (**Figure 44**), then twist and remove the fork tube from the upper and lower fork bridges. Repeat this step to remove the second fork tube.

11. Clean the fork tubes, fork bridges and clamping surfaces.

12. Remove and clean the pinch bolts. Replace damaged bolts.

12

Installation

CAUTION
Do not overtighten the fork tube pinch bolts in the following steps. Excessive tightening can permanently deform the tubes.

1. Install the left fork leg (with brake caliper mount) into the upper and lower fork bridges.

2A. On 1997 models, if the fork cap is loose, temporarily tighten the lower bridge pinch bolts (**Figure 44**) to the torque specification in **Table 2**. Then tighten the fork cap to the torque specification in **Table 2**.

NOTE
Before using a 50 mm locknut wrench to tighten the fork damper in Step 2B,

*refer to **Torque Adapters** in Chapter One.*

2B. On 1998-2001 models, if the fork damper is loose, temporarily tighten the lower bridge pinch bolts (**Figure 44**) to the torque specification in **Table 2**. Then tighten the fork damper with a 50 mm locknut wrench (**Figure 45**) to the torque specification in **Table 2**.

3. Position and tighten the fork leg as follows:
   a. Loosen the lower bridge pinch bolts and turn the fork tube so the air release screw (A, **Figure 42**) faces to the front of the motorcycle.
   b. Adjust the fork top end clearance in the fork bridge (**Figure 46**). On 1997 models, align the top surface of the upper bridge with the index groove that is 2 mm (0.1 in.) from the top of the fork tube. On 1998-2001 models, align the top surface of the upper bridge with the top edge of the fork tube.
   c. Tighten the lower bridge pinch bolts (**Figure 44**), then torque the upper bridge pinch bolts (B, **Figure 42**) to the specification in **Table 4**.
   d. Repeat Steps 1-3 for the right fork leg.

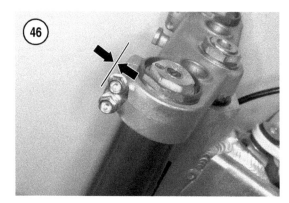

4. Tighten the air release screw on each fork (A, **Figure 42**).

5. Install the fork protectors (**Figure 41**). Apply threadlocking compound to the bolt threads.

6. Install the handlebar as described in this chapter.

7. Install the brake caliper (**Figure 39**) as described in Chapter Fourteen.

8. Install the brake hose into the fork protector clamp (**Figure 40**).

9. Install the front wheel as described in Chapter Eleven.

10. Make sure the gap in the wear ring (**Figure 47**) on each fork leg is facing rearward. Replace the wear rings when they are within 1.5 mm (0.06) of the fork tube. The wear rings prevent the fork protectors from contacting the fork tube.

11. If necessary, adjust the compression and rebound damping adjusters as described in this chapter.

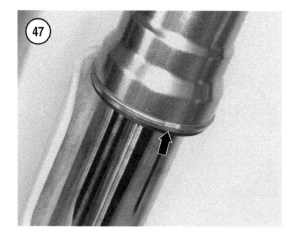

FORK SERVICE

A Showa 47 mm inverted twin-chamber cartridge fork with compression and rebound damping adjusters is used on all models. Sealed damper cartridges utilize separate air and oil chambers to prevent aeration.

While the front fork is typically trouble-free, it does require periodic service to replace the fork oil, inspect the bushings and check for spring fatigue and slider out-of-round. Fork adjustment problems can typically be traced to infrequent oil changes and sagged or incorrect weight fork springs.

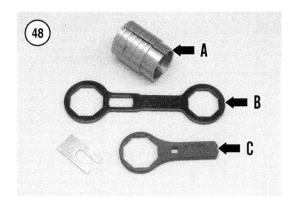

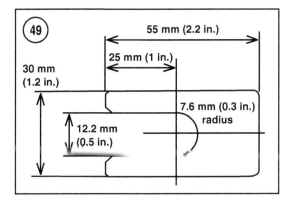

Fork Tools

The following special tools are required to disassemble and reassemble the fork tubes:

1. A 47 mm split fork seal driver (A, **Figure 48**) to install the fork seal and slider bushing. Motion Pro part No. (08-0138).

2. On 1998-2001 models, a 50 mm locknut wrench is required to loosen and tighten the fork damper. Adjustable or open-end wrenches are not recommended, as they will not adequately grip the damper and will round the hex-surfaces. Two types of wrenches are shown in **Figure 48**: the Motion Pro locknut wrench (B) (part No. 08-0236), and Honda locknut wrench (C) (part No. 07WMA-KZ30200).

3. A stopper plate tool (D, **Figure 48**) to hold the piston rod locknut when loosening and tightening the center bolt at the bottom of the slider. Make the tool from a 1 mm (0.039 in.) thick steel plate to the dimensions shown in **Figure 49**. Because of the high spring pressure exerted against the tool when under use, do not use a wooden tool.

Disassembly

Refer to **Figure 50**.

1. Depending on the service required, note the following:

   a. To change only the oil in the fork tube, perform Steps 2-8.

   b. To change only the oil in the fork tube and fork damper, perform Steps 2-17.

   c. To completely disassemble the fork assembly, perform Steps 2-24.

2. Clean the fork assembly and the bottom of the center bolt before disassembling the fork tube. Carefully check the fork tube and slider for visual damage.

3. Open the air release screw (A, **Figure 51**) to release any pressure from the fork assembly.

4. Turn the compression adjuster (B, **Figure 51**) counterclockwise to its softest setting. Count and record the number of clicks from its original position.

5. Turn the rebound adjuster (**Figure 52**) counterclockwise to its softest setting. Count and record the number of clicks from its original position.

6. If the fork damper will be removed, measure and record the length between the axle holder and the fork tube (not dust seal) surfaces shown in **Figure 53**.

NOTE
The standard length measurement is 311-315 mm (12.24-12.40 mm) on 1997-1999 models or 317-319 mm (12.48-12.56 in.) on 2000-2001 models. If the measured length is longer than this, the center bolt and locknut were installed incorrectly.

NOTE
*Two different fork cap/fork damper designs are used. On 1997 models, the fork cap (3, **Figure 50**) threads into the fork tube. On 1998-2001 models, the fork cap (3, **Figure 50**) threads into the fork damper (6), and the fork damper threads into the fork tube.*

7A. On 1999 models, hold the fork tube vertically and turn the fork cap (3, **Figure 50**) to remove it from the fork tube. Then slowly lower the fork tube until the dust seal bottoms against the slider.

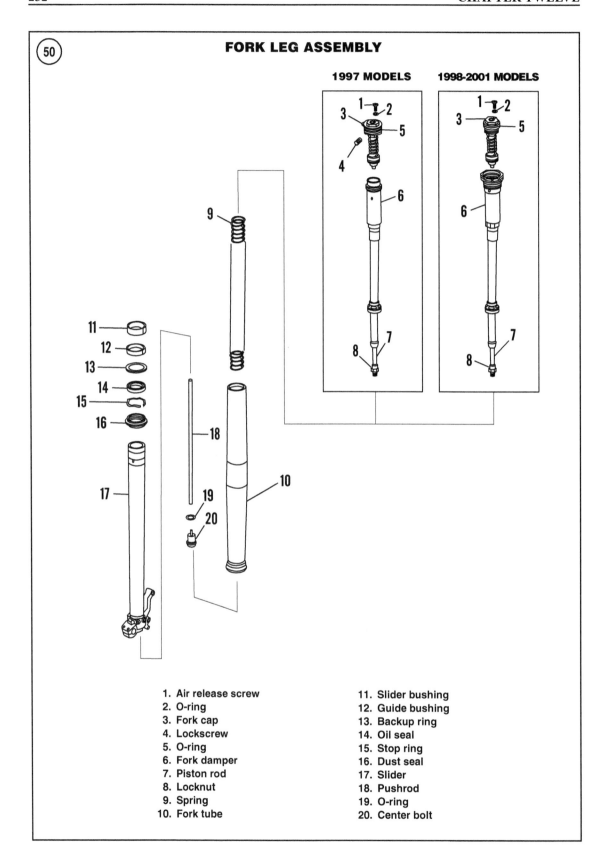

FORK LEG ASSEMBLY

1997 MODELS   1998-2001 MODELS

1. Air release screw
2. O-ring
3. Fork cap
4. Lockscrew
5. O-ring
6. Fork damper
7. Piston rod
8. Locknut
9. Spring
10. Fork tube
11. Slider bushing
12. Guide bushing
13. Backup ring
14. Oil seal
15. Stop ring
16. Dust seal
17. Slider
18. Pushrod
19. O-ring
20. Center bolt

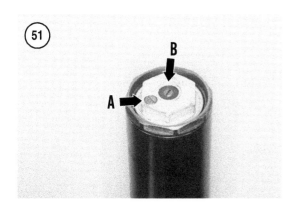

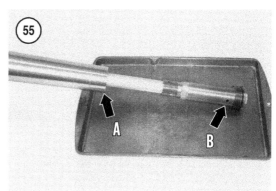

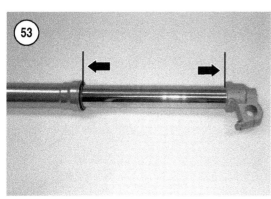

7B. On 1998-2001 models, hold the fork tube vertically and turn the fork damper with the 50 mm locknut wrench (A, **Figure 54**) to remove it from the fork tube. Do not loosen the fork cap (B, **Figure 54**). Then slowly lower the fork tube until the dust seal bottoms against the slider.

8. Hold the slider and pump the fork tube (A, **Figure 55**) to drain fork oil from the fork tube and through the hole in the fork damper (B).

NOTE
If the fork is being serviced to change only the fork oil in the fork tube, go to **Fork Oil Refilling and Fork Assembly** *in this chapter. To also change the oil in the fork damper, continue with Step 9. Refer to Steps 18-24 to remove the oil seals and bushings and complete fork disassembly.*

9. Temporarily install the fork cap (1997) or fork damper (1998-2001) into the fork tube (**Figure 56**) and tighten hand-tight.

10. Lock the axle holder in a vise fitted with soft jaws (A, **Figure 57**).

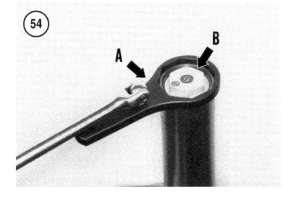

CAUTION
Do not overtighten the vise.

11. Loosen the center bolt (B, **Figure 57**) so that it is free from the slider.

CAUTION
Because of the large amount of spring pressure applied against the center bolt, have an assistant push on the fork cap when installing the stopper plate in Step 12.

12. Push on the fork cap to extend the center bolt and piston rod from the axle holder, then install the stopper plate between the axle holder and the locknut (**Figure 58**). Slowly release the piston rod/center bolt assembly until the stopper plate is held tightly between the parts.

13. Hold the locknut with a wrench (A, **Figure 59**) and loosen the center bolt (B).

14. Remove the center bolt (A, **Figure 60**) and the pushrod (B).

15. Push on the fork damper and remove the stopper plate.

16. Remove the fork damper and fork spring from the slider. Then remove the slider from the vise. See **Figure 61**.

17A. On 1997 models, remove the fork cap assembly from the fork damper as follows:

CAUTION
To prevent the piston rod from sliding into the fork damper where it cannot be retrieved, make sure the locknut (8, Figure 50) is installed on the piston rod.

   a. Using a 2 mm hex wrench, remove the lockscrew from the side of the fork cap.
   b. Turn the fork damper upside down and secure the fork cap in a vise with soft jaws. Do not overtighten the vise.

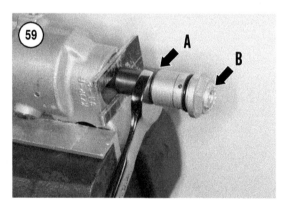

CAUTION
After mounting the fork cap in a vise, have an assistant stabilize the damper so that it does not pivot or fall out of the vise. This could damage the fork cap and fork damper.

   c. Hold the fork damper across its flats with a wrench, then turn the wrench to loosen the fork damper from the fork cap. When the fork

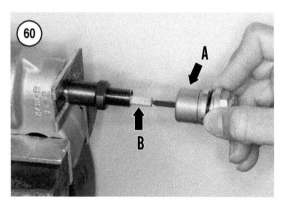

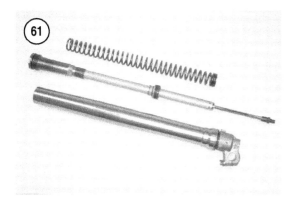

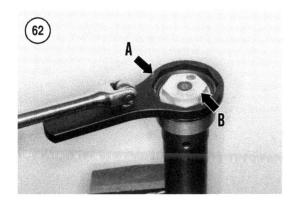

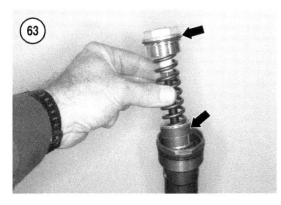

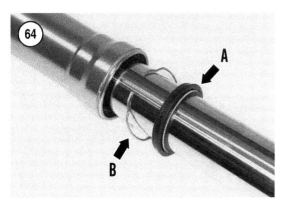

damper can be turned by hand, remove the fork damper from the vise.

d. Position the fork damper so that it is upright and remove the fork cap assembly.

e. Pump the piston rod (mounted on the bottom of the fork damper) to drain oil from the fork damper.

17B. On 1998-2001 models, remove the fork cap assembly from the fork damper as follows:

CAUTION
*To prevent the piston rod from sliding into the fork damper where it cannot be retrieved, make sure the locknut (8, **Figure 50**) is installed on the piston rod.*

a. Hold the fork damper across its flats in a vise with soft jaws. Do not overtighten the vise.

b. Hold the fork damper with the 50 mm locknut wrench (A, **Figure 62**) to help steady the assembly then loosen the fork cap (B) with a 6-point, 32 mm socket.

c. Remove the fork cap assembly from the fork damper (**Figure 63**).

d. Remove the fork damper from the vise and pump the piston rod (mounted on the bottom of the fork damper) to drain oil from the fork damper.

NOTE
*If the fork is being serviced to change only the oil in the fork tube and the oil in the fork damper, go to **Fork Oil Refilling and Fork Assembly** in this chapter. To complete fork disassembly, continue with Step 18.*

18. Carefully pry the dust seal (A, **Figure 64**) out of the fork tube.

19. Pry the stop ring (B, **Figure 64**) out of the groove in the fork tube.

20. Hold the fork tube and slowly move the slider up and down to check for roughness and binding. If the action is not smooth, inspect the slider and fork tube for damage.

21. There is an interference fit between the slider and guide bushings. To separate the fork tube from the slider, hold the fork tube and pull hard on the slider using quick in and out strokes (**Figure 65**).

Repeat as necessary to separate the parts (**Figure 66**).

22. Carefully pry the slot in the slider bushing (**Figure 67**) to spread and remove it. Do not pry the opening more than necessary.

23. Remove the following parts from the slider:
   a. Slider bushing.
   b. Backup ring.
   c. Oil seal.
   d. Stop ring.
   e. Dust seal.

24. Clean and inspect the fork assembly as described under *Inspection*.

Inspection

Replace parts that are out of specification or show damage as described in this section.

> *CAUTION*
> *Handle the bushings carefully when cleaning them in Step 1. Harsh cleaning can remove or damage their coating material.*

1. Clean all of the fork parts, except the fork damper, in solvent, first making sure the solvent will not damage the bushings or rubber parts. Then clean with soap and water and rinse with plain water. Remove all threadlock residue from the center bolt threads. Dry with compressed air.

2. Inspect the slider for:
   a. Nicks, rust, chrome flaking or creasing along the length of the slider (A, **Figure 68**). These conditions will damage the dust and oil seals. Repair minor roughness with 600 grit sandpaper and solvent. Replace the slider if necessary.
   b. Stress cracks and other damage at the axle holder (B, **Figure 68**).
   c. Check the axle holder bore inner diameter for dents or burrs that could damage the center bolt O-ring when removing and installing the bolt. Remove burrs with a fine grit sandpaper or a fine-cut file.
   d. Runout. Place the slider on a set of V-blocks (**Figure 69**) and measure runout with a dial indicator. Compare with the service limit in **Table 1**. The actual runout is 1/2 of the indicator reading.

3. Inspect the fork tube for:

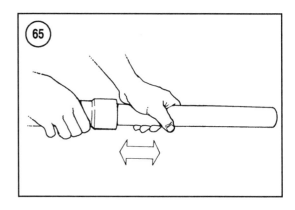

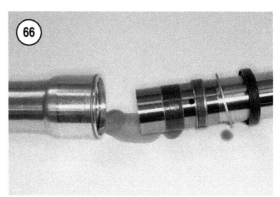

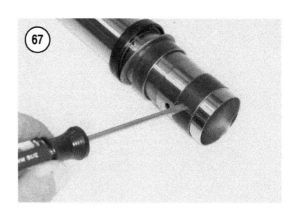

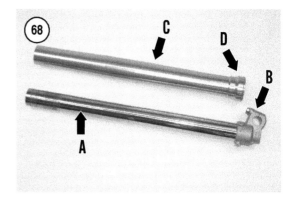

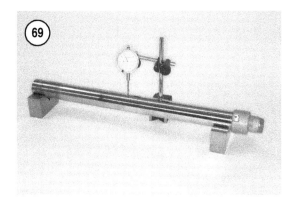

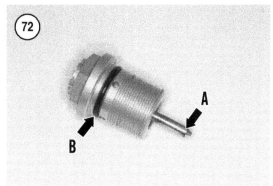

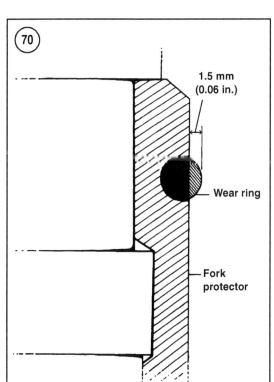

a. Damage and wear, particularly at the bushing and seal operating areas (C, **Figure 68**).

b. Damaged threads.

c. Wear ring condition (D, **Figure 68**). Replace the wear ring when it is within 1.5 mm (0.06) of the fork tube (**Figure 70**). The wear ring prevents the fork protector from contacting the fork tube during fork movement.

4. Check the fork cap assembly for:

a. Check the hex edges on the fork cap for rounding and other damage.

b. Damaged threads.

c. Worn or damaged bushings (A, **Figure 71**). Replace the bushings if necessary.

d. Operation of the compression adjuster. If the adjuster does not click when adjusting it, replace the fork cap assembly.

e. Spring fatigue or damage (B, **Figure 71**).

f. Worn or damaged O-rings (C, **Figure 71**, typical). Replace the O-rings if necessary. All of the O-ring installed on the fork cap assembly can be replaced.

g. Debris buildup on the piston and shim assembly (D, **Figure 71**).

> *CAUTION*
> *Do not disassemble the fork cap assembly (**Figure 71**). Refer service or adjustment to a qualified suspension specialist.*

5. Inspect the fork center bolt and adjuster rod for:

a. Damaged and debris buildup.

b. Damaged adjuster rod (A, **Figure 72**). The shoulders on the adjuster rod must be square for proper engagement with the pushrod.

c. Rebound adjuster operation.

d. Damaged threads.

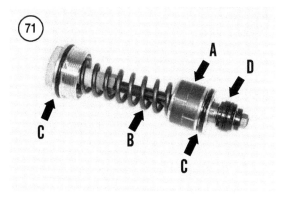

12

e. Replace the O-ring (B, **Figure 72**) if damaged.

> *NOTE*
> *Do not attempt to disassemble and service the center bolt. If damaged, replace it as a complete assembly.*

6. Check the guide (A, **Figure 73**) and slider (B) bushings for scoring, scratches and excessive wear. Excessive wear is indicated when the bushings are discolored or when the coating is worn through and the metal is visible.

7. Inspect the backup ring and replace if it is distorted on its inner edge.

8. Measure the fork spring free length with a tape measure (**Figure 74**) and compare to the service limit in **Table 1**. Replace the fork spring if it is too short. Replace the fork spring in both fork tubes at the same.

> *NOTE*
> *The fork springs require careful identification when replacing them. Identify the springs as described under **Fork Oil Refilling and Fork Assembly** in this chapter.*

9. Inspect the fork damper (A, **Figure 75**) and piston rod (B) for bending and other damage. Hold the fork damper and pump the piston rod to check for smooth operation. If the operation is not smooth, fill the damper with fork oil and repeat the check. If the operation is questionable, inspect the fork damper further during fork assembly when the fork damper is filled with oil and bled of air. Refer to *Fork Oil Refilling and Fork Assembly* in this chapter.

Assembly
(Fork Tube and Slider)

This section assembles the fork tube, slider, seals and bushings. Lubricate the fork components with the same fork oil used to refill the fork. See **Table 1** for the specified fork oil.

Refer to **Figure 50** when assembling the front fork.

1. Before assembly, make sure all worn or defective parts have been repaired or replaced. Clean all parts before assembly.

2. Install the wear ring into the fork tube groove (**Figure 76**).

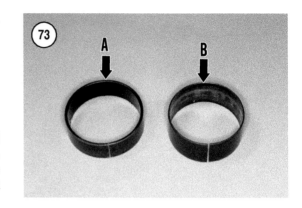

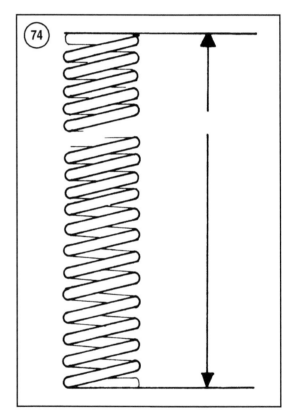

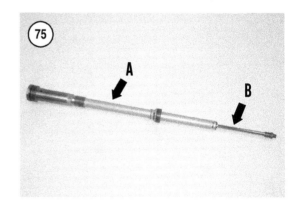

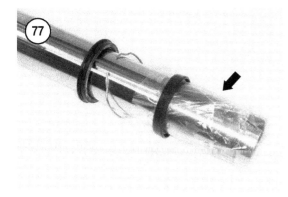

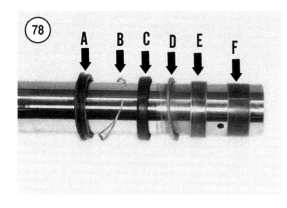

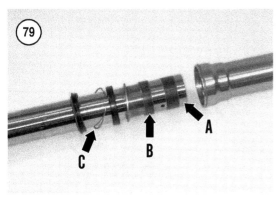

3. Cover the end of the fork tube with thin plastic (**Figure 77**) to prevent the bushing groove from tearing the seals during installation.

4. Lubricate the plastic cover installed in Step 3 and the fork seal and dust seal lips with fork oil.

5. Install the following parts on the slider:

    a. Dust seal (A, **Figure 78**). Install with the closed side facing down.

    b. Stop ring (B, **Figure 78**).

    c. Oil seal (C, **Figure 78**). Install with the manufacturer's marks (closed side) facing down. Remove the cover from the slider.

    d. Backup ring (D, **Figure 78**). Install with the flat side facing down.

    e. Guide bushing (E, **Figure 78**).

    f. Slider bushing (F, **Figure 78**). Spread the bushing only far enough to slip it over the slider. Seat the bushing into the groove.

6. Lubricate the guide and slider bushings with fork oil.

7. Install the slider (A, **Figure 79**) into the fork tube and stand the fork assembly upright with the axle holder facing up.

8. Install the guide bushing and backup ring as follows:

    a. Slide the guide bushing (B, **Figure 79**) into the fork tube. When it is sitting flush in the tube, slide the backup ring (C, **Figure 79**) down the slider and sit on top of the guide bushing.

    b. Assemble a split-type 47 mm fork seal driver over the slider. The narrow end of the driver should be facing the fork tube. Support the open end of the fork tube over a wooden block while holding the slider up with one hand. Then use the seal driver like a slide hammer to drive the guide bushing into the fork tube (**Figure 80**). When the sound of the seal driver changes, it indicates the backup ring is contacting the shoulder inside the fork tube and the bushing is fully installed. Turn the fork over and slide the backup ring away from the guide bushing to confirm that the bushing is positioned below the shoulder in the fork tube.

9. Install the oil seal as follows:

   a. Support the slider so its bottom end is facing up and slide the backup ring against the guide bushing.

   b. Slide the oil seal down the slider until it enters the fork tube. Check that the seal is seated squarely into the bore.

   c. Use the fork seal driver like a slide hammer (**Figure 80**) and drive the oil seal into the fork tube until the stop ring groove is visible above the seal.

10. Install and seat the stop ring (B, **Figure 64**) in the groove.

NOTE
If the stop ring will not seat completely in its groove, the oil seal is not installed deep enough into the slider. Remove the stop ring and repeat Step 9.

11. Slide the dust seal (A, **Figure 64**) down the slider and seat it into the top of the fork tube. See **Figure 81**.

12. Refer to *Fork Oil Refilling and Fork Assembly* in this chapter to fill the fork damper and fork tube and complete assembly.

Fork Oil Refilling and Fork Assembly

Because it is not possible to check and set the oil level on this fork, the fork tubes must be properly drained and filled to ensure equal oil capacity in both fork tubes. This procedure describes how to fill the fork damper and fork tubes with oil after rebuilding the fork tubes, during a routine fork oil change, or to adjust the fork by changing the front fork oil capacity. This procedure also completes fork tube assembly.

1. Note the following:

   a. Fork oil is added to the fork assembly in two separate places: fork damper and fork tube.

   b. **Table 1** lists the recommended fork oil.

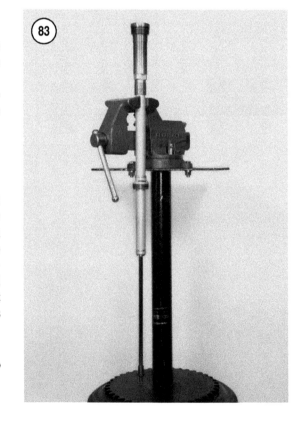

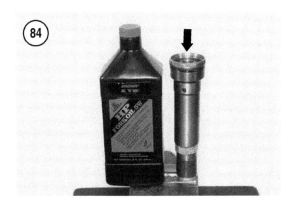

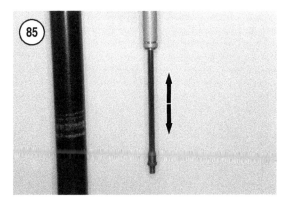

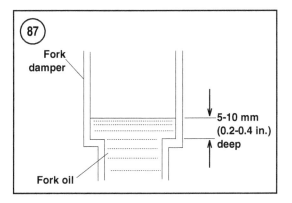

Fork
damper

5-10 mm
(0.2-0.4 in.)
deep

Fork oil

c. **Table 3** lists the oil capacity for the fork damper.

d. **Table 4** lists the oil level for the fork damper.

e. **Table 5** lists the different fork oil capacity specifications for the fork tube. Three oil capacity specifications are listed for the different rate fork springs (standard, softer and stiffer) available from Honda. Select the minimum, standard or maximum oil capacity for the installed fork spring (**Table 5**). All models were originally equipped with standard fork springs. When working on a used or unfamiliar motorcycle, the standard fork spring may have been replaced with a softer or stiffer spring. To identify the Honda springs, compare the spacing of the coil springs on the end of the springs (1997-1999), or the identification mark(s) (or no mark) found on the end of the springs (2000-2001) with the information in **Table 6**.

NOTE
If the fork damper was not removed, go to Step 12B to fill the fork tube with oil and complete fork assembly.

2. Check the fork damper and fork cap for cleanliness. The threads must be clean on both parts (**Figure 82**).

3. Support the damper so it is vertical and the piston rod can be fully extended (**Figure 83**). The vise must contact the damper at the wrench flats. Do not overtighten the vise.

4. Pour the recommended quantity of fork oil into the fork damper (**Figure 84**). See **Table 3**.

5. Slowly pump the piston rod (**Figure 85**) by hand several times to bleed air from the damper. On the last stroke, fully extend the piston rod (**Figure 83**).

6. Check and set the fork damper oil level. The oil level is the distance from the top of the oil to the top of the shoulder inside the fork damper. See **Figure 86** and **Figure 87**. See **Table 4** for the correct fork damper oil level.

7. Install the fork cap as follows:

a. Lubricate the fork cap bushings and O-rings (**Figure 88**) with fork oil.

CAUTION
Make sure the threads on the fork cap and fork damper are clean and dry. Oil remaining on these threads will cause an incorrect torque reading.

12

b. Carefully install the fork cap into the fork damper and tighten hand tight.

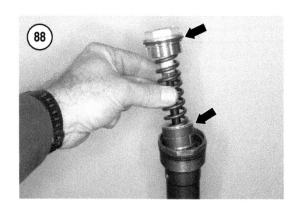

NOTE
If the fork cap is difficult to install, the oil level in the fork damper may be too high. Recheck the oil level.

8A. On 1997 models, tighten the fork damper onto the fork cap as follows:

a. With the fork cap threaded fully into the fork damper, turn the fork over and support the fork cap in a vise as described under *Disassembly* in this chapter.

b. Tighten the fork damper by turning it with a torque adapter at the wrench flats on the damper body. Tighten the fork damper to the torque specification in **Table 2**. If a wrench is used, tighten the fork damper securely.

c. Remove the fork damper from the vise.

d. Install the fork damper lockscrew (4, **Figure 50**) and tighten securely.

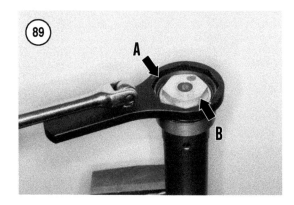

8B. On 1998-2001 models, tighten the fork cap into the fork damper as follows:

a. Support the fork damper in a vise (**Figure 83**) across its wrench flats.

b. Hold the top of the fork damper with a 50 mm locknut wrench (A, **Figure 89**) and tighten the fork cap (B) with a socket to the torque specification in **Table 2**.

9. With the fork damper held upright, slowly pump the piston rod a distance of 100 mm (3.9 in.) (**Figure 85**) several times. Do not exceed this distance.

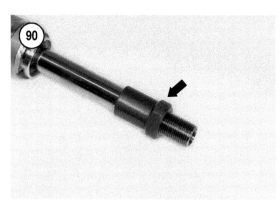

10. Remove excess oil from the fork damper spring chamber as follows:

a. Turn the locknut (**Figure 90**) so that it is fully seated on the piston rod.

b. Check that the compression and rebound adjusters are positioned at their softest position (both turned fully counterclockwise).

c. Lubricate the piston rod with fork oil.

d. Hold the fork damper so the locknut on the piston rod straddles a hold drilled in a block of wood (**Figure 91**). Do not allow the end of the piston rod to contact the wood. All of the pressure should be on the locknut.

e. Carefully pump the piston rod in a vertical motion, and for its full length. Do not allow the piston rod to move at an angle or it may bend.

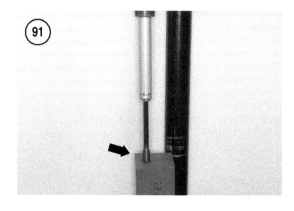

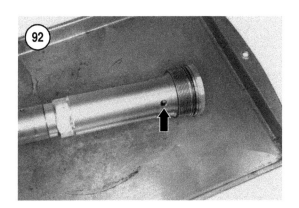

f. Place the fork damper on a flat surface and drain the excess oil from the hole in the damper (**Figure 92**).

g. Use compressed air to blow excess oil from the damper (**Figure 93**). If compressed air is not available, remove the air release screw (**Figure 94**) and invert the fork damper for 10 minutes, until all oil has drained. Reinstall and tighten the screw.

11. Check the fork damper for proper operation as follows:

a. Lubricate the piston rod with fork oil.

b. Check for smooth operation. Hold the damper so the locknut on the piston rod straddles a hole in a block of wood (**Figure 91**). Do not allow the end of the piston rod to contact the wood. All of the pressure should be on the locknut. Carefully pump the fork damper in a vertical motion, and for its full length. Do not allow the piston rod to move an angle, or the piston rod may bend. If binding is evident, check the piston rod for bending, scoring and other damage.

c. Check for piston rod extension. Place the damper on a flat surface. Carefully compress the piston rod in a horizontal motion, and for its full length (**Figure 95**). Release the piston rod when it is fully compressed. If the rod does not fully extend, air is in the damper. Bleed the damper again as described in this section.

d. Check for leaks. Wipe the piston rod clean, then lock the fork damper at its wrench flats in a vise with soft jaws (**Figure 96**). Do not overtighten the vise. Position the fork damper so the locknut on the piston rod straddles a hole in a block of wood (**Figure 91**). Do not

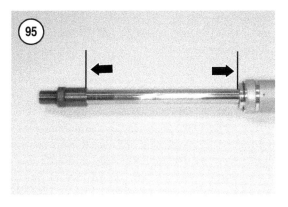

12

allow the end of the piston rod to contact the wood. All of the pressure should be on the locknut. Carefully compress the piston rod 200-250 mm (7.9-9.8 in.). Do not allow the piston rod to move at angle or the piston rod may bend. Add shims below the block of wood so the piston rod can be held in this position for 10 minutes. If leakage is evident, replace the fork damper assembly.

NOTE
Because the fork damper is installed inside the fork assembly, the oil level cannot be measured. Instead, the fork tubes are filled to a specific fork oil capacity. If the fork tubes were not disassembled and cleaned, the amount of oil that remains inside the fork tubes must also be considered when determining the oil capacity. Step 12A and Step 12B describe steps on how to determine the approximate amount of oil that remains inside the fork tubes after draining them. If the fork tubes were completely disassembled and cleaned of all oil, continue with Step 13.

NOTE
To determine the amount of oil that remains in the fork assembly after its initial draining, the fork assembly is inverted for a measured time period. During the time the fork is inverted, the ambient temperature in the work area must be monitored because it affects the oil flow (or how much oil remains in the fork tube); refer to **Table 7** *and* **Table 8**. *After reading through Step 12A and Step 12B, select a drain time specified in* **Table 7** *or* **Table 8** *for draining the fork tubes. Then cross-reference the ambient temperature to determine the approximate amount of oil that remains in the fork tube and add this to the total amount.*

12A. Record the ambient temperature in the work area. If the fork damper *was* removed from the fork assembly, but the fork slider and fork tube were not disassembled, turn the fork assembly upside down to drain oil from the fork tube for the amount of time and temperature selected in **Table 7**. For example,

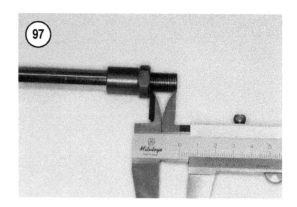

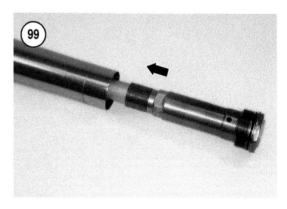

Table 7 shows that approximately 7 ml of oil will be left in the fork tube when drained for 20 minutes at 20° C (68° F).

12B. Record the ambient temperature in the work area. If the fork damper *was not* removed from the fork assembly, turn the fork assembly upside down to drain oil from the fork tube for the amount of time and temperature selected in **Table 8**. For example, **Table 8** shows that approximately 12 ml of oil will be left in the fork tube when drained for 20 minutes at 20° C (68° F).

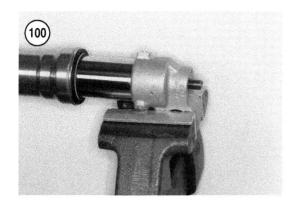

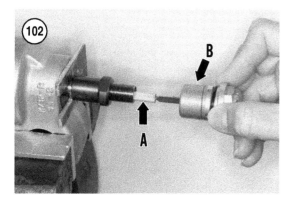

NOTE
Steps 13-27 are required only if the fork damper was removed from the fork tube.

13. Check that the locknut is seated on the piston rod, then measure the length of the exposed threads on the rod (**Figure 97**). There should be 15-16 mm (0.59-0.62 in.) of length exposed.

NOTE
The fork springs require careful identification because the spring rate de-

termines the amount of oil to add to the fork tube. Identify the spring and its spring rate as described in Step 14.

14. Before installing the fork spring, refer to **Table 6** to identify the spring as to whether it is a standard, softer or stiffer rate spring. Record the spring rate.

15. Install the spring (completely dry of all oil) into the fork tube (**Figure 98**).

16. Install the fork damper into the fork tube (**Figure 99**) but do not thread it in place.

17. Lock the axle holder in a vise with soft jaws (**Figure 100**).

CAUTION
Do not overtighten the vise.

18. Thread the fork cap (1997) or fork damper (1998-2001) into the fork tube. Do not tighten fully at this time.

CAUTION
In the following step, installation of the stopper plate will be easier if an assistant can pull on the locknut and piston rod, while the fork leg is compressed. This will also help minimize the chance of damaging the parts.

19. Push on the fork cap to extend the locknut and piston rod through the bottom end of the slider, then install the stopper plate between the axle holder and locknut (**Figure 101**).

20. Remeasure the exposed threads on the piston rod as described in Step 13 to make sure the locknut did not turn when the stopper plate was installed in Step 19. If necessary, turn the locknut until the length of the exposed threads is the same as that specified in Step 13.

21. Install the pushrod (A, **Figure 102**) into the piston rod until it stops, then turn and engage it with the adjuster in the fork damper.

22. Install the center bolt (B, **Figure 102**) by aligning its adjusting rod with the pushrod. Then thread the center bolt onto the piston rod by hand until it stops).

23. Measure the gap between the center bolt and locknut (**Figure 103**). The gap must be 1.5-2.0 mm (0.06-0.08 in.). If the clearance is incorrect, the locknut, center bolt or pushrod were incorrectly installed. Remove and reinstall the parts until the gap is correct.

12

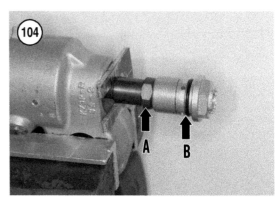

24. Turn the locknut (A, **Figure 104**) until it contacts the center bolt (B). Then hold the center bolt and tighten the locknut to the torque specification in **Table 2**.

25. Carefully remove the stopper plate from between the axle holder and locknut and allow the locknut and center bolt to move toward the slider.

26. Thread the center bolt (**Figure 105**) into the axle holder and tighten to the torque specification in **Table 2**.

27. Remove the fork tube from the vise and lay on a flat surface. Measure the length from the axle holder to the fork tube (not the dust seal) as shown in **Figure 106**. The measurements should be the same as follows: 311-315 mm (12.24-12.40 mm) on 1997-1999 models or 317-319 mm (12.48-12.56 in.) on 2000-2001 models. If the lengths are different, check the installation of the center bolt and locknut.

28. Add the correct amount of fork oil to the fork tube as follows:

   a. Loosen the fork cap (1997) or fork damper (1998-2001) and lower the fork tube away from the fork damper (**Figure 107**).

   b. Cross-reference the spring rate identified in Step 14 with the information in **Table 5** to determine the amount of oil to add to the fork tube.

   c. If the fork tubes were partially disassembled, subtract the amount of oil remaining in the fork tube (determined in Step 12A or Step 12B) from the total amount of oil to be added to the fork.

   d. Slowly pour the recommended type and quantity of fork oil into the fork assembly.

29A. On 1997 models, pull the fork tube up and hold it stationary, then thread the fork cap into the fork tube. Tighten the fork cap hand tight.

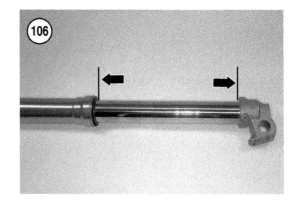

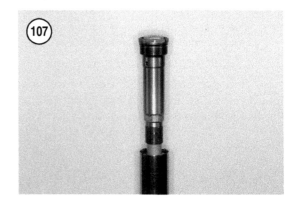

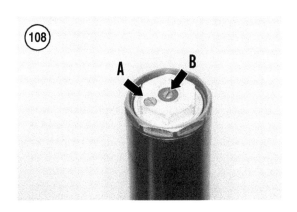

29B. On 1998-2001 models, pull the fork tube up and hold it stationary, then thread the fork damper into the fork tube. Tighten the fork damper hand tight.

30. Install the fork tube onto the motorcycle and tighten the fork cap (1997) or fork damper (1998-2001) as described under *Installation* in this chapter.

31. Reset the compression and rebound adjusters to the settings recorded during disassembly. If new settings are desired, adjust the fork as described in this chapter.

12

Table 1 STEERING AND FRONT SUSPENSION SPECIFICATIONS

Fork air pressure	0 kPa (0 psi)
Fork spring free length	
1997-1998	
New	491 mm (19.33 in.)
Service limit	483.6 mm (19.04 in.)
1999-2001	
New	493 mm (19.4 in.)
Service limit	486 mm (19.1 in.)
Fork slider runout limit	0.20 mm (0.0008 in.)
Fork top end clearance (standard)	
1997	2.0 mm (0.1 in.)
1998-2001	Align flush
Recommended fork oil	Pro Honda HP 5W fork oil or equivalent
Steering	
Caster angle	27°
Trail	113.8 mm (4.5 in.)
Travel	
Fork	315 mm (12.4 in.)
Axle	275.5 mm (10.8 in.)

Table 2 FRONT SUSPENSION TORQUE SPECIFICATIONS

	N•m	in.-lb.	ft.-lb.
Clutch lever holder bolts	9	80	–
Fork center bolt	69	–	51
Fork cap*			
1997	54	–	40
1998-2001	29	–	22
Fork damper*			
1997	118	–	87
1998-2001	54	–	40
Fork damper lockscrew (1997)	0.7	6	–
Fork damper piston rod locknut	22	–	16
Fork protector bolts	7	62	–
Fork tube pinch bolts			
Lower bridge	20	–	15
Upper bridge	22	–	16
Handlebar upper holder bolts	22	–	16
Handlebar lower holder nuts (1999-2001)	44	–	33
Master cylinder (front) holder bolts	10	88	–
Steering stem adjust nut	7	62	–
Steering stem nut			
1997-2000	147	–	108
2001	108	–	80
Throttle housing bolts	9	80	–

*See text for service procedure.

Table 3 FORK DAMPER OIL CAPACITY

	ml	U.S. oz..
All models	180	6.1

Table 4 FORK DAMPER OIL LEVEL

	mm	in.
All models	5-10	0.2-0.4

Table 5 FRONT FORK OIL CAPACITY AND SPRING RATES

	ml	U.S. oz.
1997		
Standard 0.40 kg/mm (22.40 lb./in.) fork spring		
Minimum	335	11.3
Standard	369	12.5
Maximum	430	14.5
Softer 0.38 kg/mm (21.28 lb./in.) fork spring		
Minimum	338	11.4
Standard	372	12.6
Maximum	432	14.6
Stiffer 0.42 kg/mm (23.52 lb./in.) fork spring		
Minimum	325	11.0
Standard	359	12.1
Maximum	419	14.2
(continued)		

Table 5 FRONT FORK OIL CAPACITY AND SPRING RATES (continued)

	ml	U.S. oz.
1998		
Standard 0.40 kg/mm (22.40 lb./in.) fork spring		
Minimum	326	11.0
Standard	375	12.7
Maximum	422	14.3
Softer 0.38 kg/mm (21.28 lb./in.) fork spring		
Minimum	329	11.1
Standard	378	12.8
Maximum	425	14.4
Stiffer 0.42 kg/mm (23.52 lb./in.) fork spring		
Minimum	316	10.7
Standard	365	12.3
Maximum	412	13.9
1999		
Standard 0.42 kg/mm (23.52 lb./in.) fork spring		
Minimum	318	10.8
Standard	373	12.6
Maximum	414	14.0
Softer 0.40 kg/mm (22.40 lb./in.) fork spring		
Minimum	329	11.1
Standard	383	13.0
Maximum	424	14.3
Stiffer 0.44 kg/mm (24.64 lb./in.) fork spring		
Minimum	324	11.0
Standard	379	12.8
Maximum	420	14.2
2000		
Standard 0.43 kg/mm (24.08 lb./in.) fork spring		
Minimum	328	11.1
Standard	386	13.1
Maximum	424	14.3
Softer 0.41 kg/mm (22.96 lb./in.) fork spring		
Minimum	333	11.3
Standard	391	13.2
Maximum	429	14.5
Stiffer 0.45 kg/mm (25.20 lb./in.) fork spring		
Minimum	322	10.9
Standard	380	12.9
Maximum	418	14.1
2001		
Standard 0.44 kg/mm (24.64 lb./in.) fork spring		
Minimum	337	11.4
Standard	383	13.0
Maximum	433	14.6
Softer 0.42 kg/mm (23.52 lb./in.) fork spring		
Minimum	334	11.3
Standard	380	12.9
Maximum	430	14.5
Stiffer 0.46 kg/mm (25.76 lb./in.) fork spring		
Minimum	332	11.22.
Standard	377	12.8
Maximum	428	14.5

* See text and Table 6 for spring identification.

12

Table 6   FRONT FORK SPRING IDENTIFICATION MARKS

Spring description and rate	Spring identification Coil alignment or scribe marks
1997	
Standard 0.40 kg/mm (22.40 lb./in.)	One closely wound coil at both ends
Softer 0.38 kg/mm (21.28 lb./in.)	Two closely wound coils at one end; one coil at opposite end
Stiffer 0.42 kg/mm (23.52 lb./in.)	Three closely wound coils at one end; one coil at opposite end
1998	
Standard 0.40 kg/mm (22.40 lb./in.)	One closely wound coil at both ends
Softer 0.38 kg/mm (21.28 lb./in.)	Two closely wound coils at one end; one coil at opposite end
Stiffer 0.42 kg/mm (23.52 lb./in.)	Three closely coils at one end; one coil at other end
1999	
Standard 0.42 kg/mm (23.52 lb./in.)	Three closely wound coils at one end; one coil at opposite end
Softer 0.40 kg/mm (22.40 lb./in.)	One closely wound coil at both ends
Stiffer 0.44 kg/mm (24.64 lb./in.)	Two closely wound coils at one end; one coil at opposite end
2000	
Standard 0.43 kg/mm (24.08 lb./in.)	No factory mark; aftermarket three scribe marks
Softer 0.41 kg/mm (22.96 lb./in.)	One scribe mark
Stiffer 0.45 kg/mm (25.20 lb./in.)	Two scribe marks
2001	
Standard 0.44 kg/mm (24.64 lb./in.)	No factory mark; aftermarket three scribe marks
Softer 0.42 kg/mm (23.52 lb./in.)	One scribe mark
Stiffer 0.46 kg/mm (25.76 lb./in.)	Two scribe marks

Table 7   AMOUNT OF OIL REMAINING IN FORK WITHOUT FORK DAMPER*

Temperature °C (°F)	Drain Time in Minutes						
	5	10	20	35	55	85	145
30° (86 degrees)	7.1	5.9	4.7	4.2	3.5	3.5	3.5
20°(68°)	10.6	8.2	7.1	5.9	5.6	4.7	4.7
10° (50°)	11.8	8.3	7.2	6.2	5.8	4.9	4.8
0 ° (32°)	12.9	10.6	9.4	8.2	7.9	7.1	5.9

*All units specified in milliliters (ml).

Table 8   AMOUNT OF OIL REMAINING IN FORK WITH FORK DAMPER INSTALLED*

Temperature °C (°F)	Drain Time in Minutes						
	5	10	20	35	55	85	145
30° (86°)	27	15.3	10.6	9.4	8.3	7.9	7.9
20° (68°)	29.4	16.5	11.8	10.6	9.4	8.2	8.2
10° (50°)	28.2	21.4	16.5	15.3	12.9	11.8	11.8
0°(32°)	30.6	22.4	18.8	16.5	16.5	15.3	14.1

*All units specified in milliliters (ml).

Table 9 STANDARD FORK SETTINGS

	Compression clicks out*	Rebound clicks out*
1997	9	8
1998	10	9
1999	10	12
2000	12	14
2001	11	14

*The numbers shown are the number of clicks out after the adjusters have been fully turned in (maximum damping force). Turning the adjusters out decreses damping force. Do not force the adjusters beyond their normal travel. Damage to the adjusters can occur.

CHAPTER THIRTEEN

REAR SUSPENSION

This chapter describes service procedures for the rear shock absorber, swing arm and linkage assembly. Refer to the tables at the end of the chapter for recommended suspension settings and specifications.

PRO-LINK SUSPENSION SYSTEM

The Pro-Link suspension includes the swing arm, single shock absorber and a two-piece linkage system. The lower end of the shock absorber is connected to the swing arm by the linkage system. The design of the linkage system combines with the spring and damper to provide good suspension performance over the operating range of the swing arm.

The function of the linkage is to vary the speed of shock absorber compression, depending on the position of the swing arm. This change in compression speed varies the *damping curve* of the shock absorber. Small bumps cause the swing arm to compress slightly, and the shock absorber provides a compliant ride. The damping curve is relatively flat

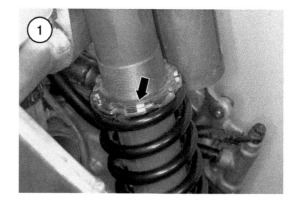

and soft under this condition. As riding conditions become more severe (large bumps), and swing arm travel increases, the same damping curve is no longer effective. The damping curve must rise in order to prevent *bottoming* of the suspension. To raise the curve, shock absorber speed must be *increased*, to raise hydraulic resistance (damping) in the shock absorber.

This increase in speed is achieved by the linkage system. During the transition from low to high swing arm movement, the linkage system pivots, in-

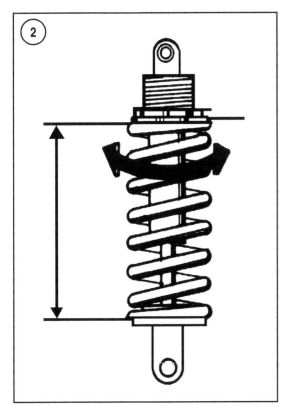

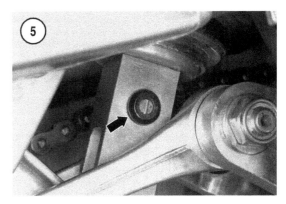

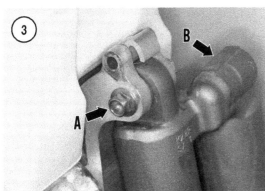

creasing its leverage on the shock absorber. This increases shock absorber speed, which results in a progressively firmer damping action.

SHOCK ABSORBER

The single shock absorber is a spring-loaded, hydraulically-damped unit with an integral oil/nitrogen reservoir. To adjust the shock absorber, refer to *Rear Suspension Adjustment* in this chapter.

Removal and Installation

Read all procedures before removing the shock absorber. If the bike has been modified, some disassembly procedures may not be necessary.

1. Support the bike so the rear wheel is off the ground.
2. Remove the seat and subframe as described in Chapter Fifteen.
3. If the shock absorber will be disassembled, loosen the spring locknut and adjuster nut (**Figure 1**) while the shock absorber is mounted. Measure and record the spring preload length (**Figure 2**) before loosening the parts. This will allow identical preload length to be reset during assembly.
4. Remove the upper mounting bolt (A, **Figure 3**).
5. Remove the lower mounting bolt (**Figure 4**)
6. Remove the shock absorber from the bike. Service the unit as described in this chapter.
7. Reverse this procedure to install the shock absorber. Note the following:
   a. Lubricate all bearings, seals and pivot bolts with molybdenum disulfide grease.
   b. Install the shock absorber so the reservoir (B, **Figure 3**) and rebound adjuster (**Figure 5**) are on the right side of the bike.

13

c. Tighten the bolts to the specification in **Table 3**.

Inspection

1. Inspect the shock absorber for gas or oil leaks.
2. Check the damper rod and clevis (A, **Figure 6**) for bending, rust and mounting hole wear.
3. Remove and inspect the spring (B, **Figure 6**) as described in this section.
4. Inspect the reservoir (C, **Figure 6**) for leaks or damage.
5. If the shock is leaking, or if it is time to replace the shock oil, refer all service to a Honda dealership or suspension specialist.

Spring Removal and Installation

1. Measure the spring preload length (**Figure 2**). Record the measurement.
2. Clean the threads on the shock absorber.
3. Mount the shock absorber in a vise with soft jaws.
4. Loosen the locknut (**Figure 3**) and back it away from the adjuster nut.
5. Loosen the adjuster nut until the spring is no longer preloaded.
6. Remove the stop ring, spring seat and spring.
7. Honda does not specify the spring free-length. If an aftermarket spring has been installed, measure the free length and compare the measurement to the manufacturer's specification. Replace the spring if it is shorter than the specification.
8. Inspect the stop ring, spring seat and spring for wear or damage.
9. Reverse these steps to install the spring. Note the following:
   a. Check that the spring seat is oriented correctly and seated against the spring.
   b. Set the spring preload length to the measurement recorded in Step 1, or to the specification in **Table 1**. If desired, the spring length can be adjusted to the preference of the rider. When making adjustments, each full turn of the adjuster nut changes the spring length by 1.5 mm (0.06 in.).

CAUTION
Make minor adjustments when adjusting spring length. If length is small,

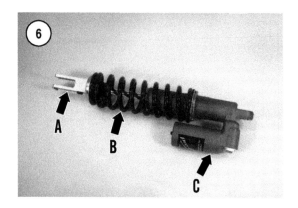

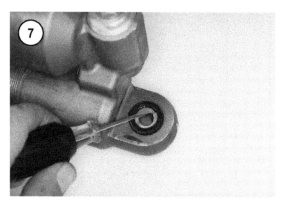

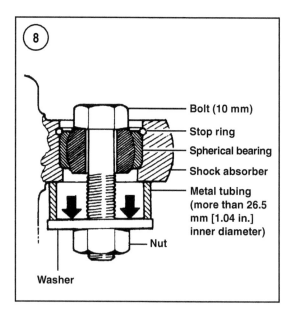

the spring may coil-bind when the shock nears full compression. This also overloads and weakens the spring. If length is too large, this can cause the spring locknut and adjuster to loosen.

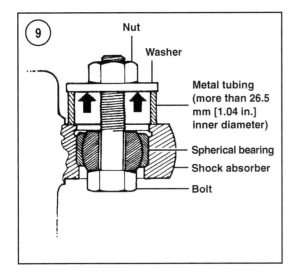

⑨

Nut

Washer

Metal tubing (more than 26.5 mm [1.04 in.] inner diameter)

Spherical bearing

Shock absorber

Bolt

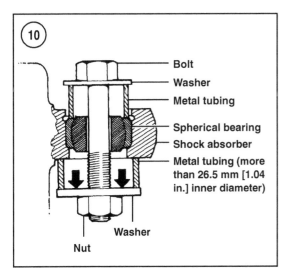

⑩

Bolt

Washer

Metal tubing

Spherical bearing

Shock absorber

Metal tubing (more than 26.5 mm [1.04 in.] inner diameter)

Washer

Nut

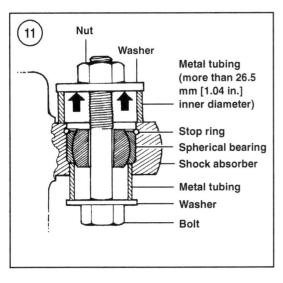

⑪

Nut

Washer

Metal tubing (more than 26.5 mm [1.04 in.] inner diameter)

Stop ring

Spherical bearing

Shock absorber

Metal tubing

Washer

Bolt

Bearing and Seals
Inspection and Replacement

To replace the bearing, a press may be used, or a tool can be made with a bolt, nut, washers, and two lengths of tubing or appropriate-size sockets. One tube/socket must fit against the bearing, but still be small enough to pass through the bore. The second tube/socket must fit against the shock absorber and be large enough to allow the bearing to enter as it is being extracted. A spherical bearing and seals are located in the upper mounting bore of the shock absorber.

1. Remove the seals from the bearing bores (**Figure 7**).

2. Pivot the bearing by hand and check for smooth operation. If the bearing is in good condition, proceed to Step 4. If roughness or play is detected, replace the bearing as described in the following step.

3. To replace the bearing without a press, use the tool as follows:

NOTE
The bearing is seated in a shouldered bore. The bearing can only be removed or installed from the side of the bore containing the stop ring.

a. Assemble the removal tool as shown in **Figure 8**. The bolt head should be on the same side as the stop ring. Hand-tighten the bolt so the head is centered against the bearing.

b. Tighten the nut until the bearing is drawn away from the stop ring, then remove the stop ring. Remove the tool.

c. Assemble the removal tool as shown in **Figure 9**. Tighten the nut and drive the bearing out of the bore and into the tubing. Remove the tool.

d. Clean and inspect the mounting bore. Check for cracks or other damage.

e. Lubricate the new bearing with molybdenum disulfide grease.

f. Fit the new bearing squarely over the bore. Assemble the installation tool as shown in **Figure 10**. Hand-tighten the nut so the driver is squarely against the outside of the bearing.

g. Tighten the nut and drive the bearing to the bottom of the bore.

h. Install a *new* stop ring. Remove the tool.

i. Assemble the tool as shown in **Figure 11**.

j. Tighten the nut and snug the bearing against the stop ring. Remove the tool.

13

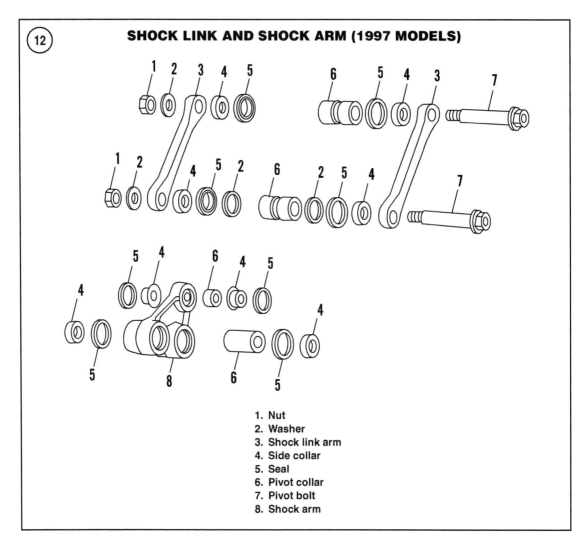

SHOCK LINK AND SHOCK ARM (1997 MODELS)

1. Nut
2. Washer
3. Shock link arm
4. Side collar
5. Seal
6. Pivot collar
7. Pivot bolt
8. Shock arm

4. Lubricate the seals with molybdenum disulfide grease.

5. Install the seals with the open side facing out.

6. Install the shock absorber as described in this section.

SHOCK LINKAGE

The shock linkage consists of the shock arm, shock link, pivot bolts, seals, collars and needle bearings (**Figure 12** or **Figure 13**). The shock link used on the 1997 model consists of two link arms, joined by bolts and pivot collars. The needle bearings at the shock link-to-frame joint are in the frame. The shock link used on 1998-2001 models is a one-piece link. The needle bearings at the shock link-to-frame joint are in the shock link. Both styles

of shock link operate identically. Since the linkage is often subjected to harsh riding conditions, disassemble and lubricate the linkage at the intervals indicated in Chapter Three.

Shock Link and Shock Arm
Removal and Installation

The shock link and shock arm may be removed for service without removing the swing arm. This procedure details the removal and separation of the shock link and shock arm assemblies. Refer to **Figure 12** or **Figure 13**.

1. Support the bike so it is stable and secure. The rear wheel must be off the ground.

2A. On 1997 models, remove the following:

  a. Brake pedal return spring.

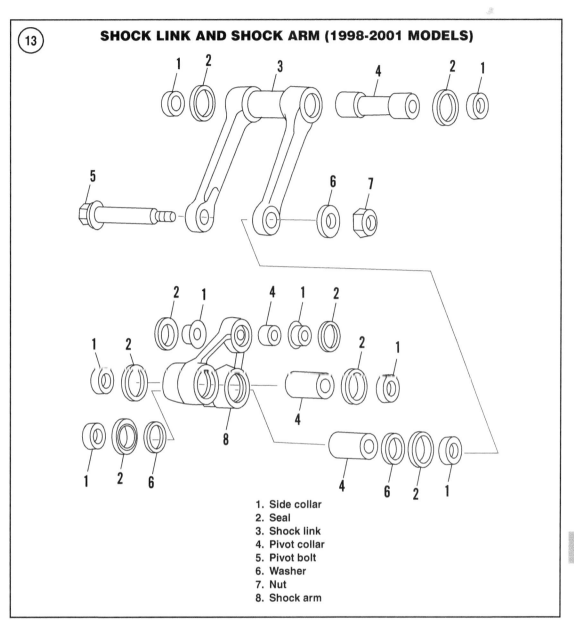

SHOCK LINK AND SHOCK ARM (1998-2001 MODELS)

1. Side collar
2. Seal
3. Shock link
4. Pivot collar
5. Pivot bolt
6. Washer
7. Nut
8. Shock arm

13

b. Hoses from hose clamp, at right side of shock link.

c. Left and right foot pegs.

2B. On 1998-2001 models, remove the chain roller (**Figure 14**).

NOTE
In the following steps, record the direction of all pivot bolts as they are removed. Pivot bolts must be installed in their original direction.

3. Loosen the pivot bolt (A, **Figure 15**) that secures the shock arm to the shock link. This bolt may be easier to loosen while the assembly is on the bike. It can be removed at the workbench.

4. Remove the pivot bolt (B, **Figure 15**) from the shock absorber and shock arm.

5. Remove the pivot bolt (C, **Figure 15**) from the shock link and frame.

6. Remove the pivot bolt (D, **Figure 15**) from the swing arm and shock arm.

7. Inspect and service the shock link and shock arm as described in this section. Refer to Chapter Three for detailed inspection of the drive chain roller.

8. Reverse these steps to install the parts. Note the following:

    a. Lubricate all bearings, seals and pivot bolts with molybdenum disulfide grease.

    b. Install pivot bolts in the direction recorded during disassembly.

    c. Lubricate bolt and nut threads before tightening.

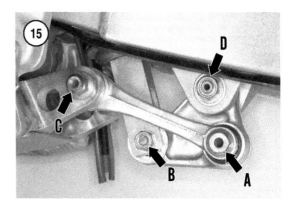

Shock Arm Inspection and Repair

Refer to **Figure 12** or **Figure 13**.

> *NOTE*
> *Handle the shock arm with care when the pivot collars are removed. The needle bearings are held in place only by the bearing grease. Keep any removed rollers with their respective bearing cage.*

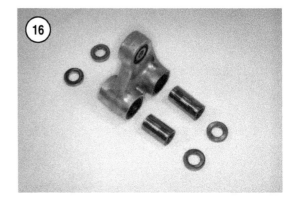

1. Remove the side collars and pivot collars from the bores shown in **Figure 16**.

2. Remove the two seals from both sides of the shock arm (**Figure 17**).

3. Remove the two washers (**Figure 18**) from the shock link/shock arm bore.

4. Remove the seals, side collars and pivot collar (**Figure 19**) from the remaining bore.

5. Remove the rollers from the bearing cages (**Figure 20**). Keep the sets of rollers identified with their respective bearing cage.

6. Clean and dry the parts.

7. Inspect the following:

    a. Inspect the shock arm for cracks, particularly around the bearing bores (**Figure 21**).

    b. Check all pivot bolts for scoring, wear and other damage.

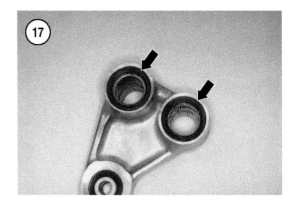

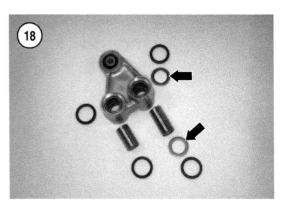

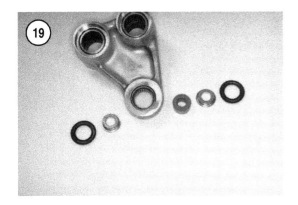

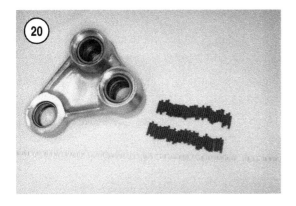

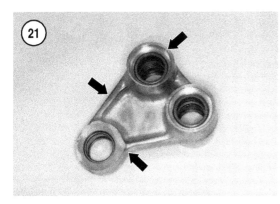

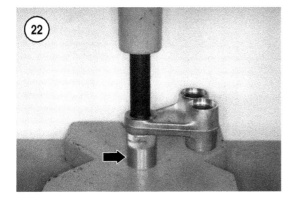

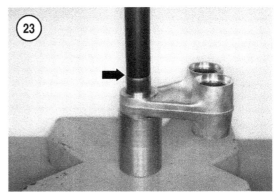

c. Check the seals for cracks, wear or other damage.

d. Check the pivot collars and side collars for cracks, scoring, wear or other damage.

e. Check the needle bearings for wear, play, flat spots, rust or discoloration. If the rollers are blue, overheating has occurred. Inspect the bearing cages for cracks, rust or other damage.

f. Lubricate the rollers and pivot collars with molybdenum disulfide grease, then assemble the bearings.

g. Insert the pivot collars into their respective bearings. The parts should turn freely and smoothly with no play. If play or roughness exists, replace the bearing as described in Step 8. When bearings are replaced in these parts, also replace the pivot collars. If the bearings are in good condition, go to Step 9.

8. Replace the needle bearing(s) in the shock arm as follows:

a. Support the part in a press so the bearing(s) can drop out the bottom of the shock arm (**Figure 22**).

b. Place a driver on the end of the bearing and press the bearing(s) out of the shock arm.

c. Clean and inspect the mounting bore.

d. Lubricate the new bearing(s) with molybdenum disulfide grease.

e. Refer to **Table 1** for the required depth to drive the bearing(s). The depth is required so the seals can be seated in both sides of the bore.

f. Fit the new bearing squarely over the bore, with the manufacturer's marks facing out. Fit a driver squarely against the end of the bearing (**Figure 23**). The driver must be capable

13

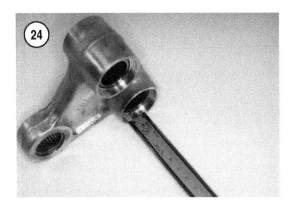

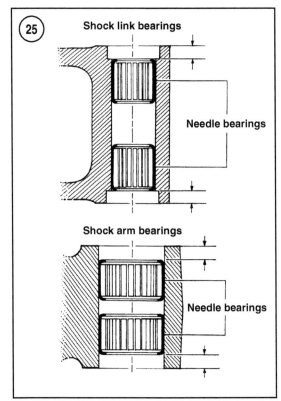

Shock link bearings

Needle bearings

Shock arm bearings

Needle bearings

of entering the bore to seat the bearing to the proper depth.

    g. Begin driving the bearing. After the bearing has entered the bore, frequently measure the bearing depth (**Figure 24**). Measure from the end of the bearing to the outside edge of the shock arm (**Figure 25**). Continue to measure and drive the bearing as required. If necessary, repeat substeps d-g for any remaining bearings.

9. Lubricate the bearings, seals, collars and washers with molybdenum disulfide grease.

10. At the shock absorber pivot:

    a. Assemble the stepped side collars and seals (**Figure 26**).

    b. Install the seals with the manufacturer's marks facing out (**Figure 27**).

    c. Install the pivot collar into the bearing, then install the seals and side collars into the shock arm.

11. At the shock link pivot, install the pivot collar, washers, seals and side collars into the shock arm. Install the seals with the manufacturer's marks facing out.

12. At the swing arm pivot, install the pivot collar, seals and side collars into the shock arm. Install the seals with the manufacturer's marks facing out.

13. Install the shock arm as described in this section.

Shock Link (1997) Inspection and Repair

When the shock link is removed, the bearings, seals and side collars at the frame pivot, remain in the frame. The pivot bolt and two shock link arms are the only parts removed at this connection. Use the following procedure to inspect the shock link

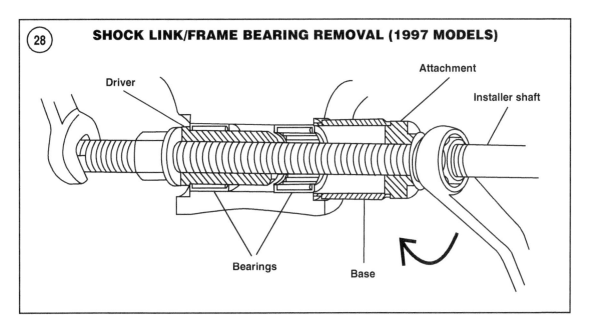

SHOCK LINK/FRAME BEARING REMOVAL (1997 MODELS)

(28)

Driver

Attachment

Installer shaft

Bearings

Base

arms and to replace the bearings and seals in the frame. Refer to **Figure 12**.

In the following procedure, special Honda tools are used to remove and install the bearings. These tools are the driver head (part No. 7946-KM40701), installer shaft (part No. 7VMF-KZ30200), 30 × 33 mm base (part No. 7VMF-KZ30300) and 22/30 × 34 mm installer attachment (part No. 7VMF-KZ30400).

A similar tool can be made with a threaded rod, nuts and washers. The driver head and base can be lengths of tubing or appropriate-size sockets. For the driver head, the tubing/socket must fit against the bearing, but still be small enough to pass through the bore. For the base, the tubing/socket must fit against the frame, and be large enough to allow the bearing to enter as it is being extracted.

1. Remove the side collars from the frame.
2. Remove the pivot collar from the bearing.

NOTE
Use care when the pivot collar is removed. The needle bearings are held in place only by the grease on the bearings. Keep any removed rollers with their respective bearing cage.

3. Remove the seals from both sides of the bore.
4. Remove the rollers from the bearing cages. Keep the sets of rollers identified with their respective bearing cage.
5. Clean and dry the parts.

6. Inspect the following:
   a. Inspect the shock link arms for cracks or bends, particularly along the length of the arms and around the pivot points.
   b. Check the pivot bolt for scoring, wear and other damage.
   c. Check the seals for cracks, wear or other damage.
   d. Check the pivot collar and side collars for cracks, scoring, wear or other damage.
   e. Check the needle bearings for wear, play, flat spots, rust or discoloration. If the rollers are blue, overheating has occurred. Inspect the bearing cages for cracks, rust or other damage.
   f. Lubricate the rollers and pivot collar with molybdenum disulfide grease, then assemble the bearings.
   g. Insert the pivot collar into the bearings. The collar should turn freely and smoothly with no play. If play or roughness exists, replace the bearings as described in Step 6. When bearings are replaced, also replace the pivot collar. If the bearings are in good condition, go to Step 7.
7. Replace the needle bearings in the frame as follows:
   a. Apply penetrating oil to the bearings and bores.
   b. Assemble the removal tool as shown in **Figure 28**. Hand-tighten the driver squarely against the bearing.

13

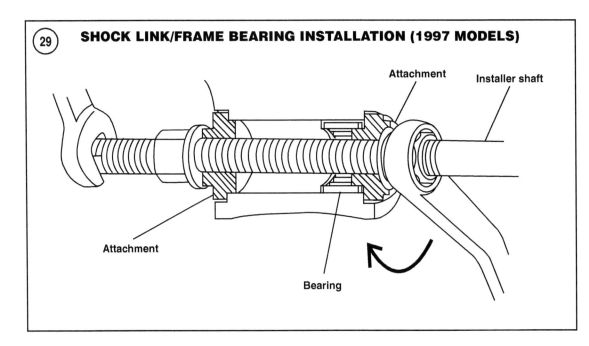

29 SHOCK LINK/FRAME BEARING INSTALLATION (1997 MODELS)

Attachment

Installer shaft

Attachment

Bearing

c. Use wrenches to hold the installer shaft and turn the nut. Drive the bearing out of the bore and into the base. Repeat for the other bearing. If necessary, disassemble the tool so the first bearing can be removed from the base.

d. Clean and inspect the mounting bores.

e. Lubricate the new bearings with molybdenum disulfide grease.

f. Refer to **Table 1** for the required depth to drive the bearings.

g. Fit a new bearing squarely over the bore, with the manufacturer's marks facing out. Assemble the installation tool as shown in **Figure 29**. Hand-tighten the driver squarely against the bearing.

h. Begin driving the bearing. After the bearing has entered the bore, frequently measure the bearing depth (**Figure 25**). Measure from the end of the bearing to the outside edge of the frame. Continue to measure and drive the bearing until it is properly located.

i. Remove the installation tool.

j. Repeat substeps g-i to drive the remaining bearing.

NOTE
When driving the second bearing, ensure that no pressure is applied to the first bearing.

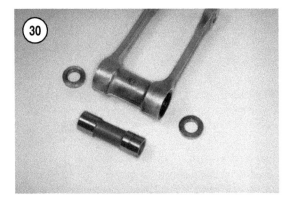

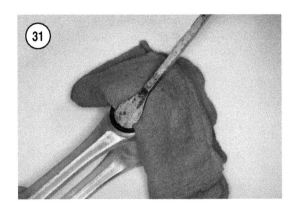

8. Lubricate the bearings, seals and collars with molybdenum disulfide grease.

9. Install the seals with the manufacturer's marks facing out.

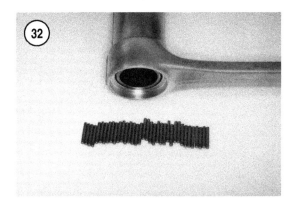

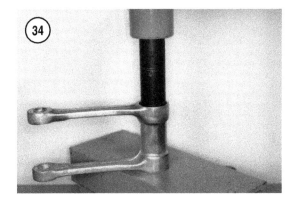

10. Install the pivot collar and side collars into the frame.

11. Install the shock link as described in this section.

Shock Link (1998-2001)
Inspection and Repair

Refer to **Figure 13**.

NOTE
Handle the shock link with care when the pivot collar is removed. The needle

bearings are held in place only by the bearing grease. Keep any removed rollers with their respective bearing cage.

1. Remove the side collars and pivot collar from the shock link (**Figure 30**).
2. Remove the seals from both bores (**Figure 31**).
3. Remove the rollers from the bearing cages (**Figure 32**). Keep the sets of rollers identified with their respective bearing cage.
4. Clean and dry the parts.
5. Inspect the following:
   a. Inspect the shock link for cracks or bends, particularly along the length of the arms and around the pivot points (**Figure 33**).
   b. Check the pivot bolts for scoring, wear and other damage.
   c. Check the seals for cracks, wear or other damage.
   d. Check the pivot collar and side collars for cracks, scoring, wear or other damage.
   e. Check the needle bearings for wear, play, flat spots, rust or discoloration. If the rollers are blue, overheating has occurred. Inspect the bearing cages for cracks, rust or other damage.
   f. Lubricate the rollers and pivot collar with molybdenum disulfide grease, then assemble the bearings.
   g. Insert the pivot collar into the bearings. The pivot collar should turn freely and smoothly with no play. If play or roughness exists, replace the bearings as described in Step 6. When bearings are replaced, also replace the pivot collar. If the bearing are in good condition, go to Step 7.
6. Replace the needle bearings in the shock link as follows:

NOTE
The bearing bores are stepped. Do not attempt to press the bearings out of the shock link. Bearings can be driven into the shock link with a press.

   a. Remove the bearings with a universal blind bearing puller.
   b. Clean and inspect the mounting bores.
   c. Lubricate the new bearings with molybdenum disulfide grease.
   d. Refer to **Table 1** for the required depth to drive the bearings.
   e. Support the shock link in a press (**Figure 34**).

13

f. Fit a new bearing squarely over the bore, with the manufacturer's marks facing out. Fit a driver squarely against the end of the bearing. The driver must be capable of entering the bore, to seat the bearing to the proper depth.

g. Begin driving the bearing. After the bearing has entered the bore, frequently measure the bearing depth (**Figure 35**). Measure from the end of the bearing to the outside edge of the shock link (**Figure 25**). Continue to measure and drive the bearing until it is properly located (**Figure 36**).

7. Lubricate the bearings, seals, collars and washers with molybdenum disulfide grease.

8. Install the seals (**Figure 37**) with the manufacturer's marks facing out.

9. Install the pivot collar and side collars into the shock arm.

10. Install the shock arm as described in this section.

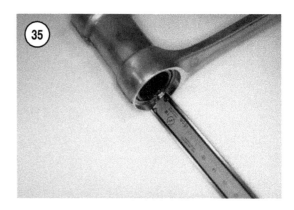

SWING ARM

Bearing Inspection

The swing arm bearings can be inspected with the swing arm mounted on the bike. Periodically check the bearings for play, roughness or damage.

1. Remove the rear wheel as described in Chapter Eleven.

2. Loosen the swing arm pivot nut, then retighten it to the specification in **Table 3**.

3. Remove the pivot bolt (A, **Figure 38**) from the shock absorber and shock arm.

4. Remove the pivot bolt (B, **Figure 38**) from the shock link and frame.

5. Separate the linkage so the swing arm action is only influenced by the swing arm pivot bolt.

6. Check the bearings as follows:

a. Have an assistant steady the bike.

b. Grasp the ends of the swing arm and leverage it from side to side. There should be no detectable play in the bearings.

c. Pivot the swing arm up and down, through its full travel. The bearings must pivot smoothly.

d. If there is play or roughness in the bearings, remove the swing arm and inspect the bearing and pivot assembly for wear.

7. Reinstall the pivot bolts and tighten to the specification in **Table 3**.

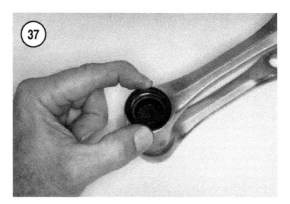

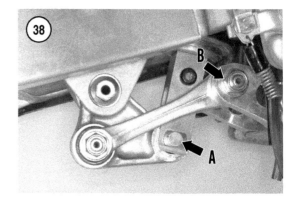

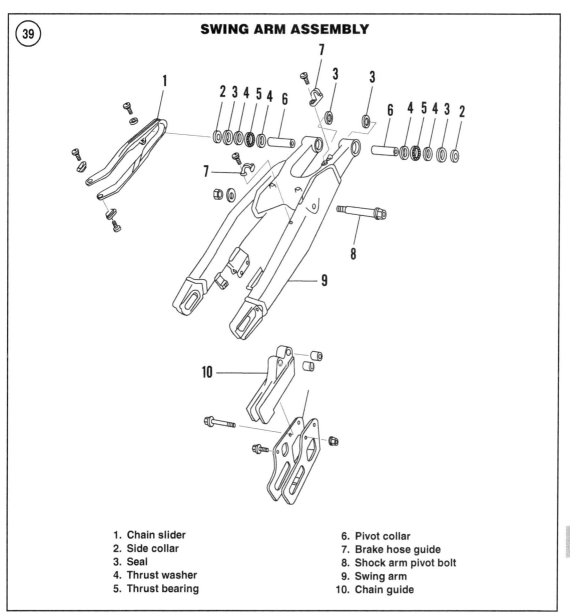

SWING ARM ASSEMBLY

1. Chain slider
2. Side collar
3. Seal
4. Thrust washer
5. Thrust bearing
6. Pivot collar
7. Brake hose guide
8. Shock arm pivot bolt
9. Swing arm
10. Chain guide

13

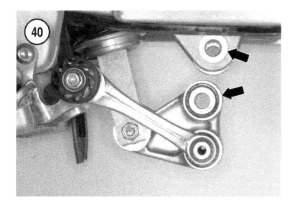

Removal and Installation

Refer to **Figure 39**.

1. Support the bike so it is stable and secure.

2. Remove the rear wheel and drive chain as described in Chapter Eleven.

3. Remove the pivot bolt from the shock arm and swing arm (**Figure 40**).

4. Remove the brake hose guides from the right side of the swing arm (**Figure 41**).

5. Slide the brake caliper (**Figure 42**) off the swing arm. Secure the caliper where it is out of the way.

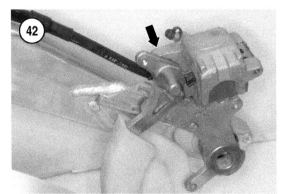

6. Remove the pivot bolt nut (**Figure 43**) from the left side of the frame.

7. Have an assistant hold the swing arm while the pivot bolt (**Figure 44**) is pulled from the swing arm. If a drift is used to drive the bolt out, avoid damaging the bearing assemblies.

8. Inspect and service the swing arm as described in this chapter.

9. Reverse these steps to install the swing arm. Note the following:

    a. Lubricate all bearings, seals and pivot bolts with molybdenum disulfide grease.

    b. Install the swing arm pivot bolt and shock arm pivot bolt from the *right* side of the bike.

    c. Tighten the bolts to the specifications in **Table 3**.

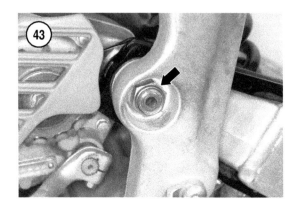

SWING ARM SERVICE

Disassembly, Inspection and Assembly

Do not intermix the left and right bearing assemblies. Install the parts in their original locations. Refer to **Figure 39**.

1. Clean the swing arm around both pivot points to prevent dirt from entering the bores.

2. Remove the pivot collar (A, **Figure 45**) and side collar (B) from the left side of the swing arm.

3. Pry the seals from both sides of the bore (**Figure 46**). Avoid damaging the bore with the pry tool.

4. Remove the two washers and thrust bearing (**Figure 47**).

5. Place the parts in a labeled container.

6. Repeat Steps 1-5 for the right side of the swing arm.

7. Wash and dry all parts so they can be inspected.

8. Inspect the removed parts for wear, scoring and seizure. The thrust bearing rollers must rotate

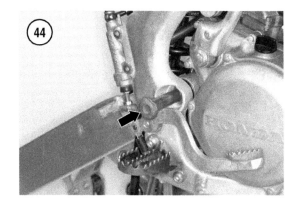

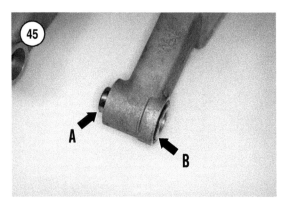

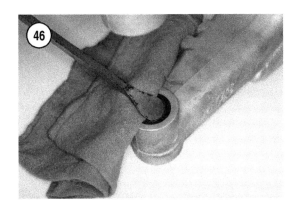

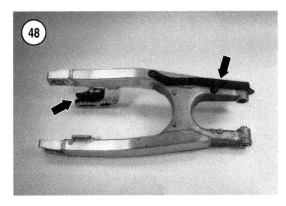

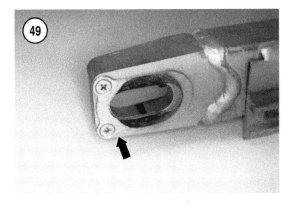

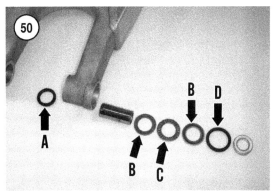

freely, but not fall from the bearing cage. Inspect the bearing cage for cracks.

9. Inspect the needle bearings in the swing arm pivots. Inspect as follows:

   a. Inspect the bearings for wear, play, flat spots, rust or discoloration. If the rollers are blue, overheating has occurred.

   b. Inspect the bearing cages for cracks, rust or other damage.

   c. Lubricate the pivot collars with molybdenum disulfide grease and insert them into their respective bearings. The parts should turn freely and smoothly with no play. If play or roughness exists, replace the bearing as described in *Swing Arm Bearing Replacement* in this section. Replace all bearings and pivot collars as a set.

10. Inspect the drive chain sliders (**Figure 48**) for wear and missing fasteners. The sliders prevent the chain from contacting the swing arm. Replace the sliders before they are completely worn through. Refer to Chapter Three for detailed inspections of the sliders and drive chain roller.

11. Inspect the axle wear plates (**Figure 49**) for wear or gouged surfaces.

12. Lubricate the bearings, collars, seals and washers with molybdenum disulfide grease.

13. Install the parts in the following order:

   a. Inner seal (A, **Figure 50**). Press the seal in with the fingers (**Figure 51**). The manufacturer's marks must face out.

   b. Washers (B, **Figure 50**) and thrust bearing (C). The bearing goes between the washers.

   c. Outer seal (D, **Figure 50**). Press the seal in with the fingers. The manufacturer's marks must face out (**Figure 52**).

13

14. Install the side collar (**Figure 53**) and pivot collar into both sides of the swing arm.

15. Install the swing arm as described in this chapter.

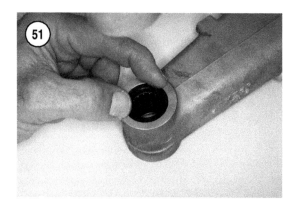

Swing Arm Bearing Replacement

Do not perform the following procedure until all seals, collars, thrust bearings and washers have been removed from the swing arm pivots. Refer to the disassembly procedures in this section for removing those parts. After replacing the swing arm bearings, return to the assembly procedures in this section to complete reassembly of the swing arm.

The following procedures describe removal and installation of the bearings, using a press or hand tools. Read both procedures to determine which method is most practical. If in doubt, take the swing arm to a dealership or machine shop to have the bearings replaced.

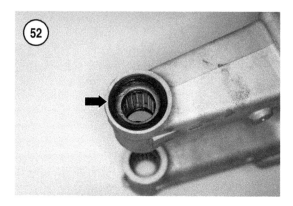

Press method

1. Support the swing arm in a press. Place the bearing bore over a large socket or similar tool (A, **Figure 54**) so the bearing can be driven out of the bore.

2. Pass a driver through the upper swing arm bore and to the lower bore (B, **Figure 54**).

3. Place a socket or driver (C, **Figure 54**) squarely against the bearing and press the bearing out of the arm. Turn the swing arm over and repeat the for the other arm.

4. Clean and inspect the mounting bores.

5. Lubricate the new bearings with molybdenum disulfide grease.

6. Fit the new bearing (A, **Figure 55**) squarely over the bore, with the manufacturer's marks facing out.

7. Place a socket or driver (B, **Figure 55**) squarely against the bearing and press the bearing into the arm (**Figure 56**). Turn the swing arm over and repeat for the other arm.

Hand tool method

In the following procedure, a swing arm bearing tool (Motion Pro part No. 08-0213) (**Figure 57**) is used. A similar tool can be made with a bolt, nut and washers. The driver can be a length of tubing or an

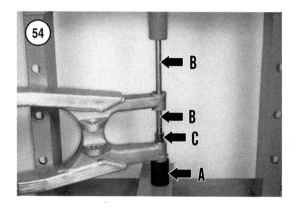

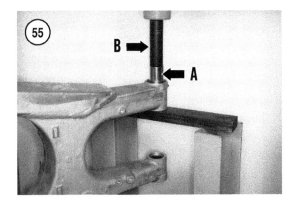

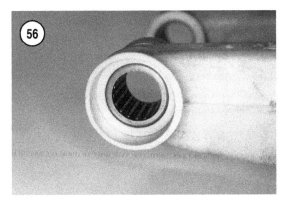

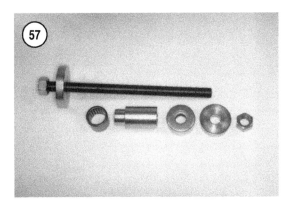

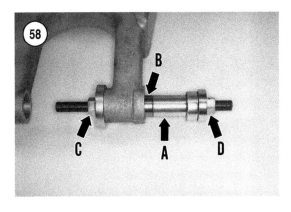

appropriate-size socket. The tubing or socket must fit against the bearing, but still be small enough to pass through the bore.

1. Remove the drive chain slider from the swing arm.

2. Support the swing arm so force can be applied to the bearings.

3. Apply penetrating oil to the bearings and bores.

4. Working with one bearing, heat the swing arm around the bearing with a propane torch. Keep the torch moving and do not overheat the swing arm. Heat the swing arm just enough to expand the bearing bore.

5. Pass a long driver through one swing arm bore and to the back side of the other bore.

6. Place a socket or driver squarely against the bearing. Drive the bearing out with a hammer and bearing driver. Repeat for the other arm.

7. Clean and inspect the bearing bores.

8. Lubricate the new bearings with molybdenum disulfide grease.

9. Assemble the bearing and installation tool as shown in **Figure 58**. Hand-tighten the nut until the driver (A, **Figure 58**) is squarely against the bearing (B). The manufacturer's marks on the bearing must face out.

10. Hold the inner nut (C, **Figure 58**) and turn the outer nut (D) to drive the bearing into the bore. Repeat for the other arm.

REAR SUSPENSION ADJUSTMENT

When making changes to the suspension settings, keep accurate records of all settings. It will be easier to analyze the changes so fine-adjustment can be achieved.

Shock Spring Preload Length Adjustment

Shock spring preload is determined by the length of the spring as it is mounted on the shock absorber. Spring preload can be adjusted with the shock absorber mounted on the bike.

1. Support the bike so the rear wheel is off the ground.

2. Remove the seat, side covers and subframe as described in Chapter Fifteen.

3. Refer to **Table 1** for the standard installed length.

13

4. Measure the existing preload length (**Figure 59**).

5. If the preload length is incorrect, perform the following:

    a. Clean the threads at the top of the shock absorber.

    b. Loosen the locknut above the adjuster nut (**Figure 60**), then turn the adjuster nut to change the spring preload length. When making adjustments, each full turn of the adjuster nut changes the spring length by 1.5 mm (0.06 in.). Tighten the locknut against the adjuster nut.

> *CAUTION*
> *Make minor adjustments when adjusting spring length. If the length is small, the spring may coil-bind when the shock nears full compression. This also overloads and weakens the spring. If the length is too large, this can cause the spring locknut and adjuster to loosen.*

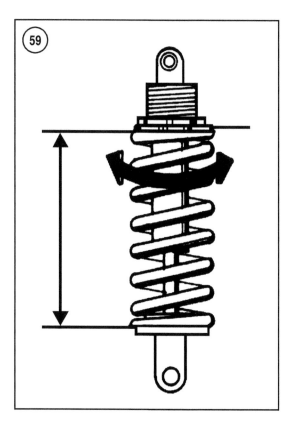

Rebound Damping Adjustment

Rebound damping controls the rate of extension of the shock absorber after it has been compressed. This setting has no affect on the compression rate of the shock. If rebound damping is set too slow, the rear wheel may bottom on subsequent bumps.

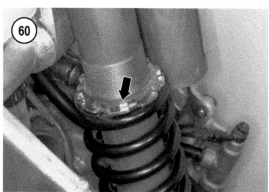

The rebound damping adjuster is located at the bottom of the shock (**Figure 61**). The standard setting for the adjuster is in **Table 2**. Set the adjuster as follows:

1. Turn the adjuster to the maximum hard position (clockwise). Do not force the adjuster beyond its normal range of travel.

2. Turn the adjuster counterclockwise while counting the number of clicks, as recommended in **Table 2**. When it is in the final position, check that the adjuster is seated in a detent and is not between detents.

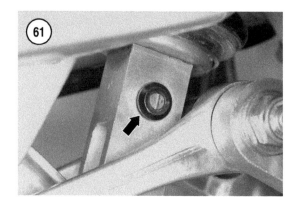

> *NOTE*
> *To decrease (soften) damping, turn the adjuster counterclockwise. To increase (harden) damping, turn the adjuster clockwise.*

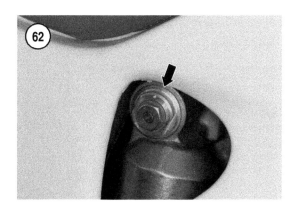

Compression Damping Adjustment

Compression damping controls the shock absorber compression rate, after hitting a bump. This setting has no effect on the rebound rate of the shock. There is a low and high-speed adjuster. The standard setting(s) for the adjuster(s) are in **Table 2**. The compression damping adjusters are located at the top of the shock reservoir (**Figure 62**). Set the adjusters as follows:

1. Turn the low-speed adjuster (slotted screw) to the maximum hard position (clockwise). Do not force the adjuster beyond its normal range of travel.

2. Turn the low-speed adjuster counterclockwise while counting the number of clicks, as recommended in **Table 2**. When it is in the final position, check that the adjuster is seated in a detent and is not between detents.

NOTE
To decrease (soften) damping, turn the adjuster counterclockwise. To increase (harden) damping, turn the adjuster clockwise.

3. Turn the high-speed adjuster (hexagonal ring surrounding the low-speed adjuster) to the maximum hard position (clockwise). Do not force the adjuster beyond its normal range of travel.

4. Turn the high-speed adjuster counterclockwise while counting the number of turns, as recommended in **Table 2**. When it is in the final position, check that the adjuster is seated in a detent and is not between detents.

NOTE
To decrease (soften) damping, turn the adjuster counterclockwise. To increase (harden) damping, turn the adjuster clockwise.

13

Table 1 REAR SUSPENSION SPECIFICATIONS

Rear suspension make/type	Showa Pro-Link
Rear wheel travel	318 mm (12.5 in.)
Shock absorber gas/pressure	Nitrogen @ 981 kPa (142 psi)
Shock arm bearing depths	
Swing arm bore	4.4-4.7 mm (0.17-0.19 in.)
Shock absorber bore	2.0-2.2 mm (0.08-0.09 in.)
Shock link bore	
1997-1999	6.5-7.0 mm (0.26-0.28 in.)
2000-2001	6.0-6.5 mm (0.23-0.26 in.)
Shock link bearing depth	
1997 (bearings in frame)	4.4-4.7 mm (0.17-0.19 in.)
1998-2001 (bearings in shock link)	4.4-4.7 mm (0.17-0.19 in.)
Shock spring preload length (standard)	
1997	269.8 mm (10.62 in.)
1998	267.7 mm (10.54 in.)
1999	267.4 mm (10.53 in.)
2000	254.6 mm (10.02 in.)
2001	257.9 mm (10.15 in.)

Table 2 STANDARD REAR SHOCK ABSORBER SETTINGS

	Low speed compression clicks out*	High speed compression turns out*	Rebound damping clicks out*
1997	8-11	2 3/4-3 1/4	9-12
1998	8-11	2 3/4-3 1/4	11-14
1999	8-11	2 3/4-3 1/4	11-13
2000-2001	7	2 1/4- 2 3/4	8-11

* The numbers shown are the number of clicks/turns *out* after the adjusters have been fully turned in (maximum damping force). Turning the adjusters out decreases damping force. Do not force the adjusters beyond their normal travel. Damage to the adjuster can occur.

Table 3 REAR SUSPENSION TORQUE SPECIFICATIONS

	N•m	in.-lb.	ft.-lb.
Drive chain guide mounting nut	12	106	–
Drive chain roller bolt			
1997-2000	22	–	16
2001	12	106	–
Shock arm (swing arm and shock link side)	79	–	59
Shock link (frame side)	79	–	59
Shock absorber mounting nuts (upper/lower)	44	–	33
Shock absorber spring locknut	88	–	65
Swing arm pivot nut	88	–	65

CHAPTER FOURTEEN

BRAKES

This chapter provides service procedures for the front and rear brake systems. This includes brake pads, master cylinders, calipers and discs.

Refer to Chapter Three for brake fluid level inspection, brake pad/disc inspection, and brake pedal and lever adjustment.

DISC BRAKE FUNDAMENTALS

The front and rear brakes are hydraulically actuated and therefore do not require cables and mechanical linkages to operate. When pressure is applied to the brake pedal or lever, the brake fluid is compressed in the brake line and pushes the brake pads against the brake disc. When pressure is relieved, the pads slightly retract from the disc, allowing the wheel to spin freely. As the pads wear, the piston(s) in the caliper extend, automatically keeping the pads adjusted.

A hydraulic brake system is not maintenance-free, nor indestructible. Observe the follow-

ing practices when maintaining or working on a hydraulic brake system.

1. Keep brake fluid off of painted surfaces, plastic and decals. The fluid will damage these surfaces. If fluid does contact these surfaces, flush the surface thoroughly with clean water.
2. Keep the fluid reservoirs closed except when changing the fluid.
3. Replace brake fluid often. The fluid absorbs moisture from the air and will cause internal corrosion of the brake system. Fresh fluid is clear to slightly yellow. If the fluid is obviously colored, it is contaminated.
4. Do not reuse brake fluid, or use new fluid that has been contaminated while in storage.
5. When rebuilding brake system components, lubricate new parts with fresh fluid before assembly. Do not use petroleum-based solvents. These can swell and damage rubber components.
6. Bleed the brake system whenever a banjo bolt or other connector in the brake line has been loosened.

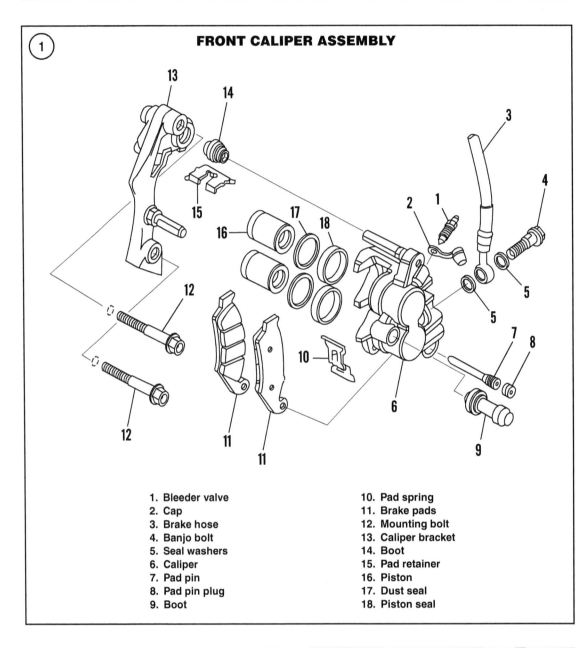

FRONT CALIPER ASSEMBLY

1. Bleeder valve
2. Cap
3. Brake hose
4. Banjo bolt
5. Seal washers
6. Caliper
7. Pad pin
8. Pad pin plug
9. Boot
10. Pad spring
11. Brake pads
12. Mounting bolt
13. Caliper bracket
14. Boot
15. Pad retainer
16. Piston
17. Dust seal
18. Piston seal

Air will be in the system and brake action will be spongy.

FRONT BRAKE PADS

Brake pad life depends on the riding habits of the rider and the type of material used to manufacture the brake pads. Replace the pads when they are worn or have been contaminated with oil or other chemicals. Refer to **Table 1** for the brake pad service limit. Always replace pads as a set.

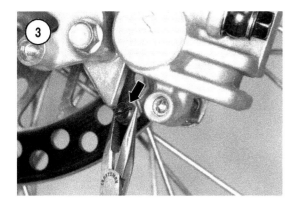

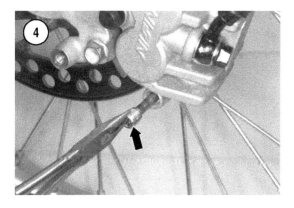

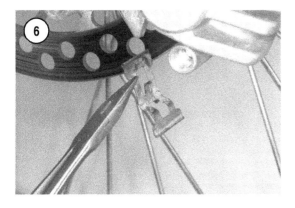

Removal and Installation

The brake pads can be replaced with the caliper mounted on the motorcycle. Refer to **Figure 1**.

> *NOTE*
> *If the caliper will be rebuilt, the pads can be removed and installed when the caliper is at the workbench. If desired, proceed to the **Front Brake Caliper** section in this chapter to remove, repair and install the caliper. Refer to this section to remove, inspect and install the pads.*

1. Remove the brake disc cover (**Figure 2**).

> *CAUTION*
> *In the following step, monitor the level of fluid in the master cylinder reservoir. Brake fluid will backflow to the reservoir as the caliper pistons are pressed into their bores. Do not allow brake fluid to spill from the reservoir, or damage can occur to painted and plastic surfaces. Immediately clean up any spills by flooding the area with water.*

2. Grasp the caliper and press it firmly toward the brake disc. This will push the caliper pistons down into their bores, creating room for the new pads.
3. Remove the pad pin plug (**Figure 3**).
4. Remove the pad pin (**Figure 4**).
5. Remove the brake pads (**Figure 5**).
6. Remove the pad spring (**Figure 6**).

> *NOTE*
> *Do not operate the brake lever with the pads removed. The pistons in the caliper can come out of the housing.*

7. Clean the interior of the caliper and inspect for leakage or damage. Also inspect for leakage at the fork seals. Fork oil will contaminate brake pads.
8. Inspect the pads and mounting assembly (**Figure 7**).
    a. Replace the pin, plug or spring if worn, corroded or damaged.
    b. Inspect the pads for contamination, scoring and wear. Replace the pads if they are worn to the wear indicator, located at the end of each pad.

14

c. If the pads are worn unevenly, the caliper is probably not sliding correctly on the slide pins. The caliper must be free to *float* on the pins. Debris buildup or corrosion on the pins can hold the caliper in one position, causing brake drag and excessive pad wear.

9. Seat the pad spring into the caliper (**Figure 8**). Check that the spring is oriented correctly.

10. Install the pads on each side of the disc, seating the pointed ends of the pads against the pad retainer (**Figure 9**).

11. Install the pad pin, guiding it through the holes in the pads. Tighten the pad pin to the specification listed in **Table 2**.

12. Install and tighten the pad pin plug to the specification in **Table 2**.

13. Operate the brake lever several times to seat the pads.

14. Check the brake fluid reservoir and replenish or remove fluid, as necessary.

> *NOTE*
> *If the caliper was rebuilt, or the brake hose disconnected from the caliper, bleed the brake as described in this chapter.*

15. With the front wheel raised, check that the wheel spins freely and the brake operates properly.

16. Install the brake disc cover (**Figure 2**).

FRONT BRAKE CALIPER

Removal and Installation

Use the following procedure to remove the caliper (**Figure 1**) from the motorcycle.

1. Remove the brake disc cover (**Figure 2**).

2. Determine if the system should be drained and the brake hose disconnected. Do one of the following:

    a. If the caliper will not be disassembled and serviced, proceed to Step 3. It is not necessary to drain the system or disconnect the brake hose.

    b. If the caliper will be disassembled and serviced, the caliper pistons can be pumped from the bores while the brake hose is connected and the system is filled with fluid. Do not remove the brake hose or drain the system at this time.

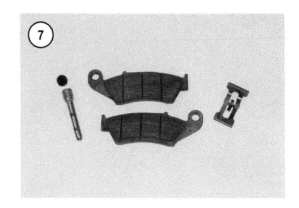

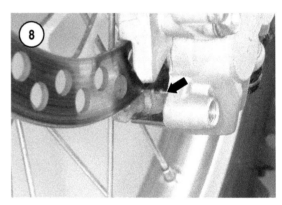

    c. If the caliper will be disassembled and serviced, the caliper pistons can be removed by using compressed air. Drain the system as described in this chapter. After draining, loosen the brake hose banjo bolt on the caliper (A, **Figure 10**). Leave the bolt finger-tight. It will be removed in a later step.

3. Remove the caliper mounting bolts (B, **Figure 10**), then remove the caliper from the fork.

4A. If the caliper will be left attached to the brake hose, but not disassembled and serviced:

    a. Attach a wire to the caliper and hang the caliper on the motorcycle. Do not let the caliper hang by the brake hose.

    b. Insert a small wooden block between the brake pads. This will prevent the caliper pistons from extending out of the caliper if the brake lever is actuated.

4B. If the caliper will be disassembled, using compressed air to remove the pistons:

    a. Remove the banjo bolt and seal washers from the brake hose. Have a shop cloth and container handy to catch excess brake fluid that drips from the hose.

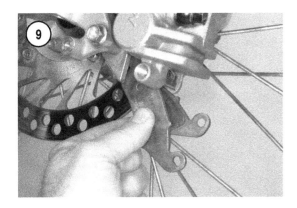

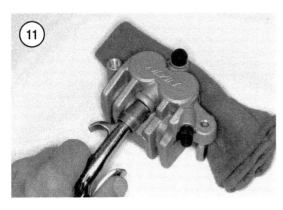

b. Wrap the hose end to prevent brake fluid from damaging other surfaces.

5. Repair the caliper as described in this chapter.

6. Reverse this procedure to install the caliper. Note the following:

   a. If the pads are already installed in the caliper, press the caliper pistons back into the caliper so the pads will clear the disc.

   b. Install the brake hose so the curve in the fitting points toward the wheel.

   c. Install *new* seal washers on the banjo bolt.

d. Tighten all bolts to the specifications in **Table 2**.

NOTE
If the caliper was rebuilt, or the brake hose disconnected from the caliper, fill and bleed the brake system as described in this chapter.

7. Operate the brake lever several times to seat the pads.

8. Check the brake fluid reservoir and replenish or remove fluid, as necessary.

9. With the front wheel raised, check that the wheel spins freely and the brake operates properly.

10. Install the brake disc cover (**Figure 2**).

Repair

Refer to **Figure 1**.

1. Remove the caliper as described in this section.

2. Remove the pad pin plug, pad pin, brake pads and pad spring as described in *Front Brake Pads*.

3. Separate the caliper bracket from the caliper.

4A. Perform this step if compressed air will be used to remove the pistons from the caliper bores.

   a. Place the caliper on a padded work surface.

   b. Close the bleeder valve on the caliper so air cannot escape.

   c. Place a strip of wood, or similar pad, in the caliper (**Figure 11**). The pad will cushion the pistons when they come out of the caliper. If necessary, place a strip of wood in the caliper to prevent either piston from fully coming out. Pressure can then be maintained in the caliper. When both pistons are equally pushed from the caliper, insert a narrower strip of wood and continue working the pistons out together.

WARNING
Wear eye protection when using compressed air to remove the piston. Keep fingers away from the piston discharge area. Personal injury can occur if an attempt is made to stop the piston by hand.

   d. Lay the caliper so the pistons will discharge downward.

   e. Insert an air nozzle into the brake hose fitting (**Figure 11**). If the nozzle does not have a rub-

14

ber tip, wrap the tip with tape. The nozzle must seal tightly and also not damage the threads.

    f. Place a shop cloth over the entire caliper to catch any spray that may discharge from the caliper.

    g. Apply pressure and listen for the pistons to *pop* from the caliper.

4B. Perform this step if hydraulic pressure will be used to remove the pistons from the caliper bores.

    a. Check the level of the brake fluid reservoir and fill if needed. Keep fluid in the reservoir during the removal process.

    b. Position the caliper over a drip pan. Have shop cloths on hand to wipe up spills.

    c. Slowly pump the brake lever while observing the pistons. The pistons must come out at the same rate. If necessary, place a strip of wood in the caliper to prevent either piston from fully coming out. Pressure can then be maintained in the caliper. When both pistons are equally pushed from the caliper, insert a narrower strip of wood and continue working the pistons out together.

    d. Continue to force the pistons out until they can be gripped and twisted out of the bores.

    e. Allow the brake fluid to drain from the system. Pump the lever to aid in draining.

    f. Remove the banjo bolt and seal washers from the caliper. Have a shop cloth on hand to wipe up excess brake fluid that drips from the hose.

5. Remove the dust seals and piston seals from the cylinder bores (**Figure 12**).

6. Remove the bleeder valve and cap from the caliper.

7. Remove the pad retainer (A, **Figure 13**) and rubber boots (B) from the caliper and caliper bracket.

8. Inspect the caliper assembly as follows:

    a. Clean and dry all parts to be reused. Use a wood or plastic-tipped tool to clean the seal grooves. Use clean brake fluid to aid in cleaning the pistons, bores and seal grooves.

    b. Inspect the cylinder bores (A, **Figure 14**) for wear, pitting or corrosion.

    c. Measure the outside diameter of the pistons (**Figure 15**). Refer to **Table 1** for the service limit.

    d. Measure the inside diameter of the caliper bores (**Figure 16**). Refer to **Table 1** for the service limit.

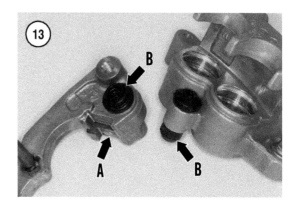

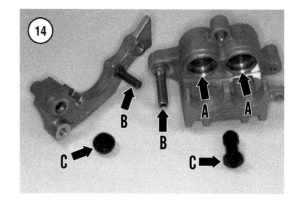

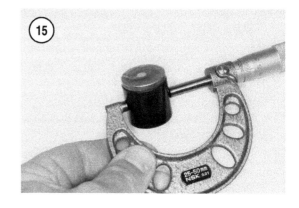

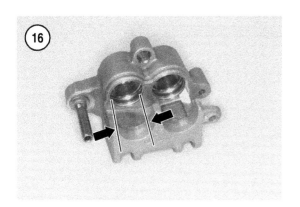

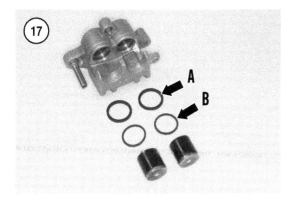

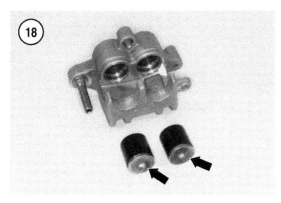

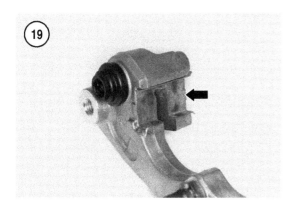

e. Inspect the slide pins (B, **Figure 14**) for wear, pitting or corrosion.

f. Inspect the boots (C, **Figure 14**) for deterioration.

g. Inspect the pad retainer for corrosion or damage.

h. Inspect the bleeder and cap. Check the threads and seat on the bleeder for corrosion and damage.

i. Inspect the pad pin plug, pad pin, brake pads and pad spring as described in *Front Brake Pads*.

NOTE
Use new brake fluid (rated DOT 4) to lubricate the parts in the following steps.

9. Install the *new* seals and pistons as follows:

a. Soak the dust seals and piston seals in brake fluid for 15 minutes.

b. Coat the caliper bores and pistons with brake fluid.

c. Seat the piston seals (A, **Figure 17**), then the dust seals (B) in the caliper grooves. The piston seals go in the back grooves.

d. Install the pistons, with the closed ends facing out (**Figure 18**). Twist the pistons past the seals, then press the pistons to the bottom of their bores. The pistons will not go straight into the bores.

10. Install and seat the boots (B, **Figure 13**). Apply silicone brake grease to the interior of both boots.

11. Seat the pad retainer into the mounting bracket (**Figure 19**).

12. Install the bleeder valve and cap.

13. Slide the mounting bracket and the caliper slide pins into the rubber boots (**Figure 20**).

14

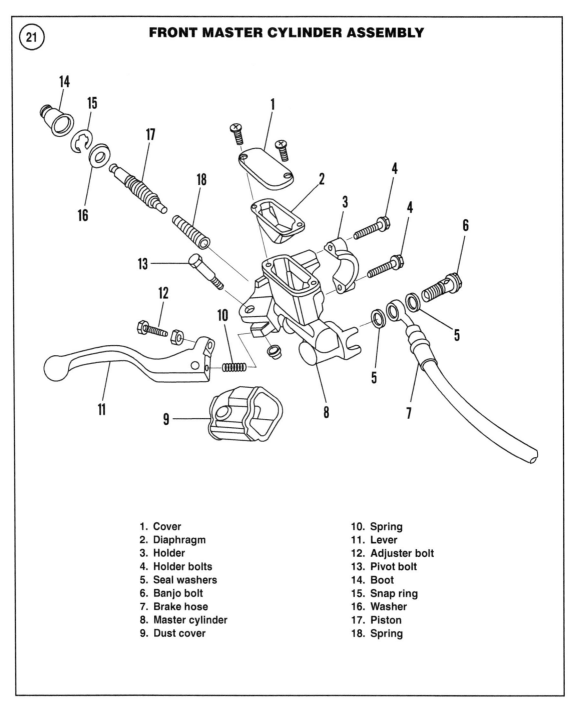

(21)   **FRONT MASTER CYLINDER ASSEMBLY**

1. Cover	10. Spring
2. Diaphragm	11. Lever
3. Holder	12. Adjuster bolt
4. Holder bolts	13. Pivot bolt
5. Seal washers	14. Boot
6. Banjo bolt	15. Snap ring
7. Brake hose	16. Washer
8. Master cylinder	17. Piston
9. Dust cover	18. Spring

14. Install the pad pin plug, pad pin, brake pads and pad spring as described in *Front Brake Pads*. The parts can be installed with the caliper either on or off the motorcycle.

15. Install the caliper as described in this section.

FRONT MASTER CYLINDER

Removal and Installation

Refer to **Figure 21**.

1. Cover and protect the fuel tank and area surrounding the master cylinder.

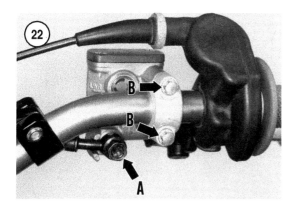

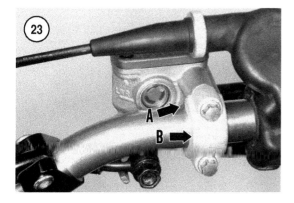

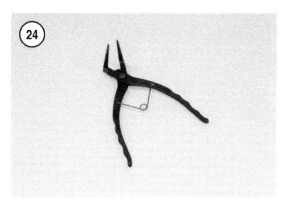

14

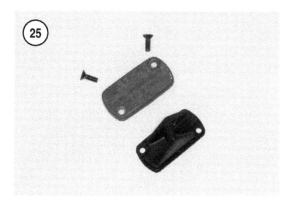

CAUTION
Do not allow brake fluid to splash from the reservoir or hose. Brake fluid can damage painted and plastic surfaces. Immediately clean up any spills, flooding the area with water.

2. Drain the brake system as described in this chapter.

3. Remove the brake hose banjo bolt from the master cylinder as follows:

   a. Remove the banjo bolt (A, **Figure 22**) and seal washers from the brake hose. Have a shop cloth and container handy to catch excess brake fluid that drips from the hose.

   b. Wrap the hose end to prevent brake fluid from damaging other surfaces.

4. Remove the bolts (B, **Figure 22**) securing the master cylinder to the handlebar, then remove the master cylinder and bracket.

5. Repair the master cylinder as described in this chapter.

6. Reverse this procedure to install the master cylinder. Note the following:

   a. Align the master cylinder with the punch mark (A, **Figure 23**) on the handlebar.

   b. The mounting bracket must be installed so the *UP* mark and the arrow (B, **Figure 23**) are facing up. Tighten the upper bolt first, then the bottom bolt.

   c. Install *new* seal washers on the banjo bolt.

   d. Tighten all bolts to the specifications in **Table 2**.

7. Fill the brake fluid reservoir and bleed the brake system as described in this chapter.

8. Check brake lever adjustment as described in Chapter Three.

Repair

NOTE
*The snap ring pliers (**Figure 24**) used in this procedure (Kowa Seiki part No. AKS-316-2010) have long arms that make snap ring removal easier, since the arms extend into the cylinder.*

1. Remove the master cylinder as described in this section.

2. Remove the cover and diaphragm (**Figure 25**), then wipe excess fluid from the reservoir.

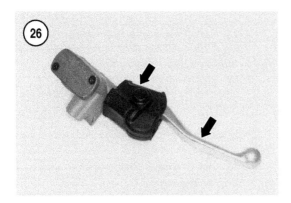

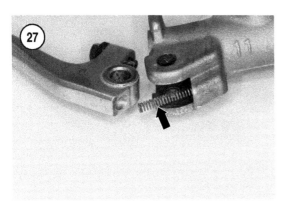

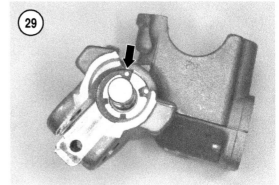

3. Remove the dust cover, pivot bolt, nut and lever (**Figure 26**). When removing the lever, remove the spring between the lever and master cylinder (**Figure 27**).

4. Remove the boot (**Figure 28**).

5. Remove the snap ring (**Figure 29**) from the master cylinder.

6. Remove the washer, piston and spring from the bore (**Figure 30**).

7. Inspect the master cylinder assembly (**Figure 31**) as follows:

    a. Clean all parts that will be reused with fresh brake fluid or isopropyl (rubbing) alcohol.

    b. Inspect the cylinder bore for wear, pitting or corrosion.

    c. Measure the inside diameter of the cylinder bore. Refer to **Table 1** for the service limit.

    d. Measure the outside diameter of the piston (**Figure 32**). Refer to **Table 1** for the service limit.

    e. Inspect and clean the orifices and threads in the reservoir (**Figure 33**). Clean with compressed air.

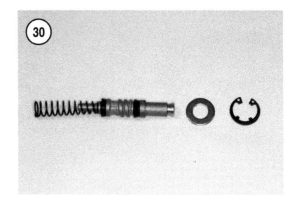

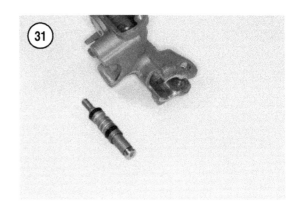

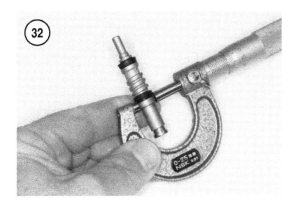

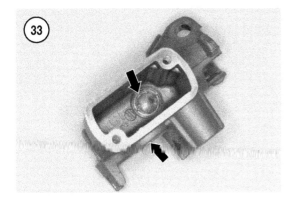

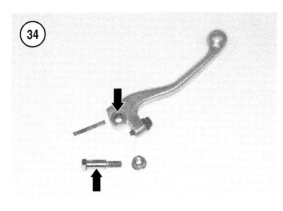

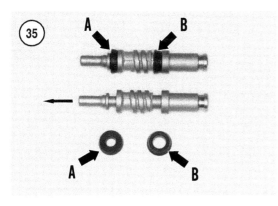

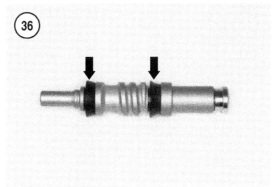

f. Inspect the brake lever bore and pivot bolt for wear (**Figure 34**). Replace the parts if they fit together loosely.

g. Inspect the diaphragm and reservoir cap for damage.

8. Assemble the piston, cups and spring as follows. **Figure 35** shows the piston cups, before and after assembly.

a. Soak the primary cup (A, **Figure 35**) and secondary cup (B) in fresh DOT 4 brake fluid for 15 minutes. This will soften and lubricate the cups.

b. Apply brake fluid to the piston so the cups can slide over the ends.

c. Identify the wide (open) side of the primary cup. When installed, the wide side of the cup *must* face in the direction of the arrow (**Figure 35**). Install the primary cup onto the piston.

d. Identify the wide (open) side of the secondary cup. When installed, the wide side of the cup *must* face in the direction of the arrow (**Figure 35**). Install the secondary cup on the piston.

e. The assembled piston should appear as in **Figure 36**. The wide side of both cups must face as shown.

f. Install the *small end* of the spring onto the piston.

9. Lubricate the cylinder bore and piston assembly with brake fluid.

10. Secure the cylinder in a vise so both hands are free to put the piston assembly into the cylinder. To prevent damage to the cylinder, temporarily thread a bolt and locknut into one of the cylinder mounting holes. Secure the cylinder with the bolt (**Figure 37**).

CAUTION
After the spring, piston and cups are in the cylinder, hold them in place un-

14

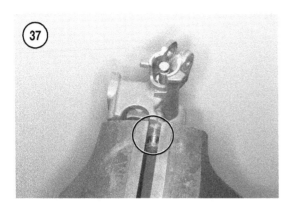

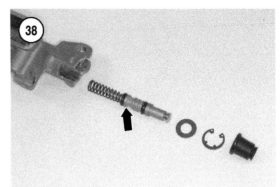

til the washer and snap ring are installed. Anytime the cups come out of the cylinder there is a chance of damaging the cup lips during the reinsertion process.

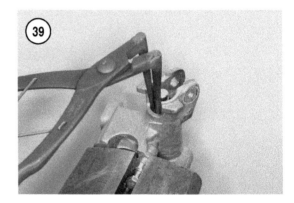

11. Insert the piston assembly (**Figure 38**) into the cylinder, carefully twisting the cups past the edge of the bore. The cup diameters are larger than the bore. Therefore, ensure that the lips do not fold back when entering the bore. Hold the assembly in place when it is fully in the bore.

12. Insert the washer into the cylinder, then lock it in place with the snap ring (**Figure 39**). The flat side of the snap ring must face *out* (away from the bore).

13. Remove the cylinder from the vise, then remove the bolt from the cylinder.

14. Apply silicone brake grease to the inside of the boot, then install the boot onto the piston (**Figure 40**).

15. Install the spring between the lever and master cylinder (**Figure 27**).

16. Apply silicone brake grease to the adjuster contact point (**Figure 41**), then bolt the lever to the master cylinder. Tighten the bolt and nut to the specification in **Table 2**.

17. Install the dust cover.

18. Loosely install the diaphragm and cap until the brake system is refilled.

19. Install the master cylinder as described in this section.

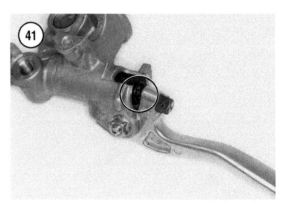

REAR BRAKE PADS

Brake pad life depends on the riding habits of the rider and the type of material used to manufacture the brake pads. Replace the pads when they are

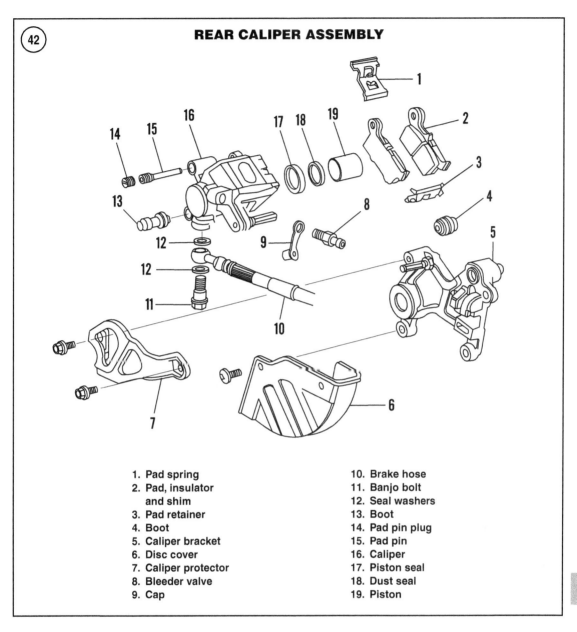

REAL CALIPER ASSEMBLY

1. Pad spring
2. Pad, insulator and shim
3. Pad retainer
4. Boot
5. Caliper bracket
6. Disc cover
7. Caliper protector
8. Bleeder valve
9. Cap
10. Brake hose
11. Banjo bolt
12. Seal washers
13. Boot
14. Pad pin plug
15. Pad pin
16. Caliper
17. Piston seal
18. Dust seal
19. Piston

worn or have been contaminated with oil or other chemicals. Refer to **Table 1** for the brake pad service limit. Always replace pads as a set.

Replacement

The brake pads (**Figure 42**) can be replaced with the caliper mounted on the motorcycle.

CAUTION
In the following step, monitor the level of fluid in the master cylinder

reservoir. Brake fluid will backflow to the reservoir as the caliper piston is pressed into its bore. Do not allow brake fluid to spill from the reservoir, or damage can occur to painted and plastic surfaces. Immediately clean up any spills, flooding the area with water.

NOTE
If the caliper will be rebuilt, the pads can be removed and installed when the caliper is at the workbench. If de-

*sired, proceed to the **Rear Brake Caliper** section in this chapter to remove, repair and install the caliper. Refer to this section to remove, inspect and install the pads.*

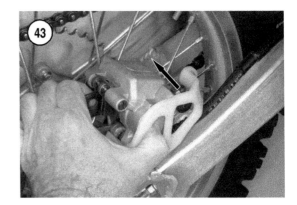

1. Grasp the caliper and press it firmly toward the brake disc (**Figure 43**). This will push the caliper piston down into its bore, creating room for the new pads.
2. Remove the pad pin plug (**Figure 44**).
3. Remove the pad pin (**Figure 45**).
4. Remove the brake pads (**Figure 46**). Check that the insulator (A, **Figure 47**) and metal shim (B) on the back of each pad is also removed.
5. Remove the pad spring (**Figure 48**).

NOTE
Do not operate the brake pedal with the pads removed. The piston in the caliper can come out of the housing.

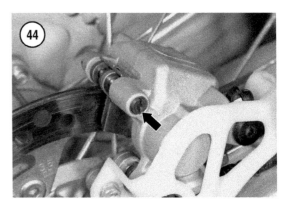

6. Clean the interior of the caliper and inspect for leakage or damage.
7. Inspect the pads and mounting assembly (**Figure 49**).
   a. Replace the pin, plug or spring if worn, corroded or damaged.
   b. Inspect the pad assemblies for contamination, scoring, wear and damage. Replace the pads if they are worn to the wear indicator, located at the end of each pad.
   c. If the pads are worn unevenly, the caliper is probably not sliding correctly on the slide pins. The caliper must be free to *float* on the pins. Debris buildup or corrosion on the pins can hold the caliper in one position, causing brake drag and excessive pad wear.

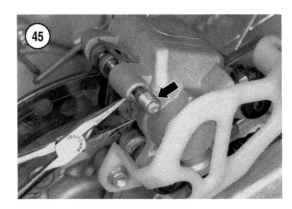

8. Install the pad spring into the caliper (**Figure 50**). Check that the spring is oriented correctly.
9. Assemble the pads. On the back side of the pad, install the insulator (A, **Figure 47**) and metal shim (B). The tab on the shim should fit over the pad.
10. Install the pad assemblies on each side of the disc, seating the pointed ends of the pads (**Figure 51**) against the pad retainer.
11. Install the pad pin, guiding it through the holes in the pads. Tighten the pad pin to the specification in **Table 2**.
12. Install and tighten the pad pin plug to the specification in **Table 2**.

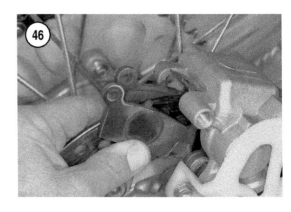

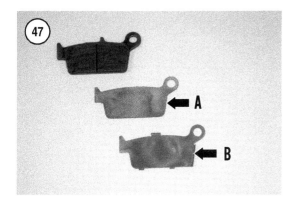

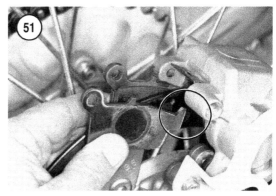

13. Operate the brake pedal several times to seat the pads.

14. Check the brake fluid reservoir and replenish or remove fluid, as necessary.

NOTE
If the caliper was rebuilt, or the brake hose disconnected from the caliper, bleed the brake as described in this chapter.

15. With the rear wheel raised, check that the wheel spins freely and the brake operates properly.

REAR BRAKE CALIPER

Removal and Installation

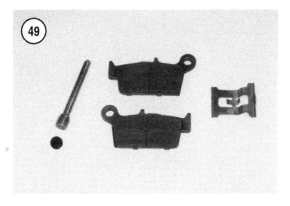

Refer to **Figure 42**.

1. Determine if the system should be drained and the brake hose disconnected. Do one of the following:

   a. If the caliper will not be disassembled and serviced, proceed to Step 2. It is not necessary to drain the system or disconnect the brake hose.

   b. If the caliper will be disassembled and serviced, the caliper piston can be pumped from the bore while the brake hose is connected and the system is filled with fluid. Do not remove the brake hose or drain the system at this time.

   c. If the caliper will be disassembled and serviced, the caliper piston can be be removed by using compressed air. Drain the system as described in this chapter. After draining, loosen the brake hose banjo bolt on the caliper (**Fig-**

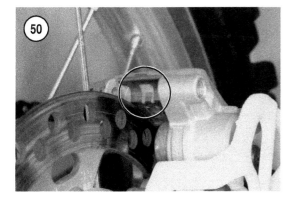

14

ure **52**). Leave the bolt finger-tight. It will be removed in a later step.

2. Remove the rear wheel as described in Chapter Eleven.

3. Slide the caliper off the swing arm (**Figure 53**).

4A. If the caliper will be left attached to the brake hose, but not disassembled and serviced:

   a. Remove the caliper from the caliper bracket (**Figure 54**).

   b. Attach a wire to the caliper and hang the caliper on the motorcycle. Do not let the caliper hang by the brake hose.

   c. Insert a small wooden block between the brake pads. This will prevent the caliper pistons from extending out of the caliper, if the brake pedal is actuated.

4B. If the caliper will be disassembled, using compressed air to remove the piston:

   a. Remove the banjo bolt and seal washers from the brake hose. Have a shop cloth and container on hand to catch excess brake fluid that drips from the hose.

   b. Wrap the hose end to prevent brake fluid from damaging other surfaces.

5. Repair the caliper as described in this chapter.

6. Reverse this procedure to install the caliper. Note the following:

   a. If the brake hose was disconnected, attach the hose and torque the banjo bolt while the caliper is off the motorcycle (**Figure 55**). There is not enough room to use a torque wrench after the caliper is mounted on the swing arm. Install *new* seal washers on the banjo bolt. Install the brake hose so it rests against the stopper cast into the caliper body (**Figure 56**).

   b. To install the caliper bracket onto the swing arm, align the tab on the bracket with the swing arm slide rail (**Figure 57**).

   c. If the pads are already installed in the caliper, press the caliper piston back into the caliper so the pads will clear the disc when the wheel is installed.

   d. Tighten all bolts to the specifications in **Table 2**.

7. Install the rear wheel as described in Chapter Eleven.

NOTE
If the caliper was rebuilt, or the brake hose disconnected from the caliper, fill and bleed the brake system as described in this chapter.

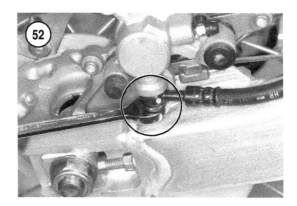

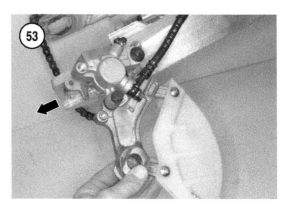

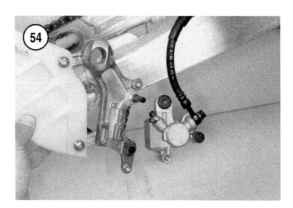

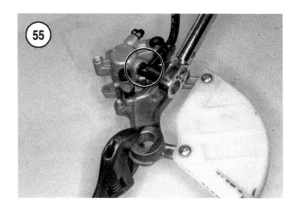

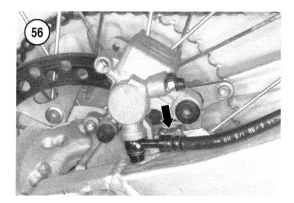

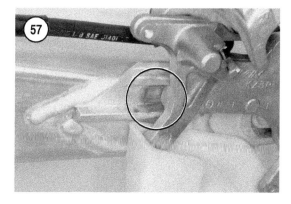

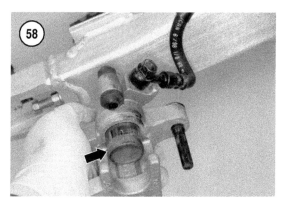

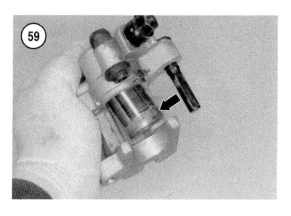

8. Operate the brake pedal several times to seat the pads.

9. Check the brake fluid reservoir and replenish or remove fluid, as necessary.

10. With the rear wheel raised, check that the wheel spins freely and the brake operates properly.

Repair

Refer to **Figure 42**.

1. Remove the pad pin plug, pad pin, brake pads and pad spring as described in *Rear Brake Pads*.

2. Separate the caliper bracket from the caliper.

3A. Perform this step if compressed air will be used to remove the piston from the caliper bore.

    a. Place the caliper on a padded work surface.

    b. Close the bleeder valve on the caliper so air cannot escape.

    c. Place a strip of wood, or similar pad, in the caliper. The pad will cushion the piston when it comes out of the caliper.

> *WARNING*
> *Wear eye protection when using compressed air to remove the piston. Keep fingers away from the piston discharge area. Personal injury can occur if an attempt is made to stop the piston by hand.*

    d. Lay the caliper so the piston will discharge downward.

    e. Insert an air nozzle into the brake hose fitting. If the nozzle does not have a rubber tip, wrap the tip with tape. This will allow the nozzle to seal tightly and prevent thread damage.

    f. Place a shop cloth over the entire caliper to catch any spray that may discharge from the caliper.

    g. Apply pressure and listen for the piston to *pop* from the caliper.

3B. Perform this step if hydraulic pressure will be used to remove the piston from the caliper bore.

    a. Check the level of the brake fluid reservoir and fill if needed. Keep fluid in the reservoir during the removal process.

    b. Position the caliper over a drip pan. Have shop cloths handy to wipe up spills.

    c. Slowly pump the rear brake pedal while observing the progress of the piston (**Figure 58**).

    d. Continue to force the piston out until it can be gripped (**Figure 59**) and twisted out of the bore (**Figure 60**).

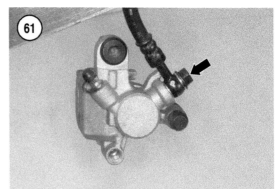

e. Allow the brake fluid to drain from the system. Pump the pedal to aid in draining.

f. Remove the banjo bolt and seal washers from the caliper (**Figure 61**). Have a shop cloth on hand to wipe excess brake fluid that drips from the hose.

4. Remove the dust seal and piston seal from the cylinder bore (**Figure 62**).

5. Remove the bleeder valve and cap from the caliper.

6. Remove the disc cover from the caliper bracket (**Figure 63**).

7. Remove the pad retainer (A, **Figure 64**) and rubber boots (B) from the caliper and caliper bracket.

8. Inspect the caliper assembly as follows:

a. Clean and dry all parts to be reused. Use a wood or plastic-tipped tool to clean the seal grooves. Use clean brake fluid to aid in cleaning the piston, bore and seal grooves.

b. Inspect the cylinder bore (A, **Figure 65**) for wear, pitting or corrosion.

c. Measure the outside diameter of the piston (**Figure 66**). Refer to **Table 1** for the service limit.

d. Measure the inside diameter of the piston bore (**Figure 67**). Refer to **Table 1** for the service limit.

e. Inspect the slide pins (B, **Figure 65**) for wear, pitting or corrosion.

f. Inspect the boots (C, **Figure 65**) for deterioration.

g. Inspect the pad retainer for corrosion or damage.

h. Inspect the bleeder and cap. Check the threads and seat on the bleeder for corrosion and damage.

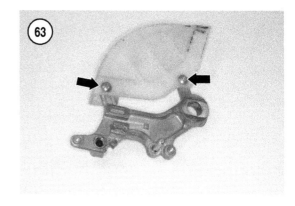

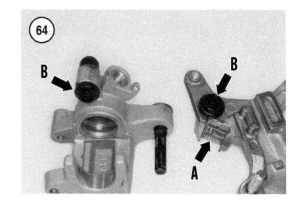

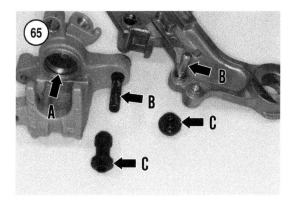

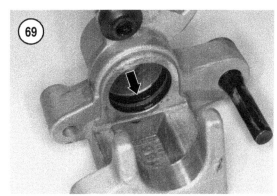

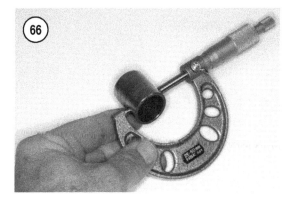

i. Inspect the pad pin plug, pad pin, brake pads and pad spring as described in *Rear Brake Pads*.

NOTE
Use new DOT 4 brake fluid to lubricate the parts in the following steps.

9. Install the new seals and piston as follows:

a. Soak the dust seal and piston seal in brake fluid for 15 minutes.

b. Coat the caliper bore and piston with brake fluid.

c. Seat the piston seal (A, **Figure 68**), then the dust seal (B) in the caliper grooves. The piston seal goes in the back groove (**Figure 69**).

d. Install the piston with the open end facing out (**Figure 70**). Twist the piston past the seals, then press the piston to the bottom of the bore. The piston will not go straight into the bore.

10. Install and seat the boots (B, **Figure 64**). Apply silicone brake grease to the interior of both boots.

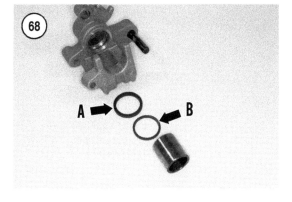

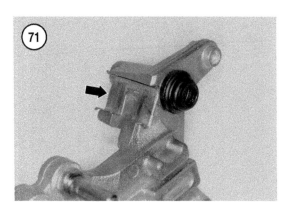

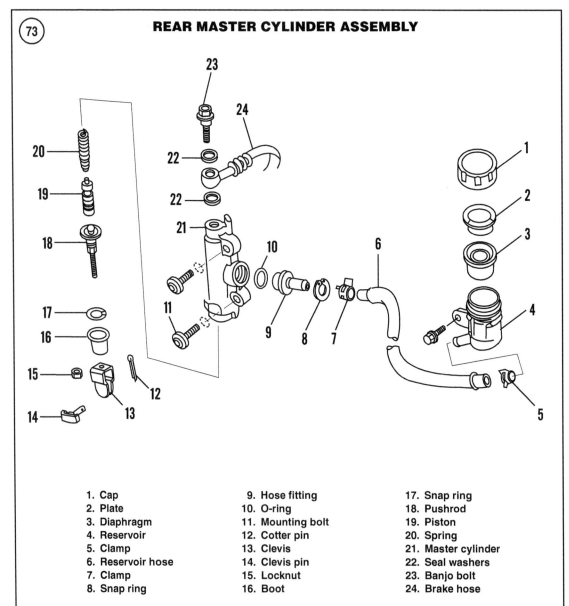

REAR MASTER CYLINDER ASSEMBLY

1. Cap	9. Hose fitting	17. Snap ring
2. Plate	10. O-ring	18. Pushrod
3. Diaphragm	11. Mounting bolt	19. Piston
4. Reservoir	12. Cotter pin	20. Spring
5. Clamp	13. Clevis	21. Master cylinder
6. Reservoir hose	14. Clevis pin	22. Seal washers
7. Clamp	15. Locknut	23. Banjo bolt
8. Snap ring	16. Boot	24. Brake hose

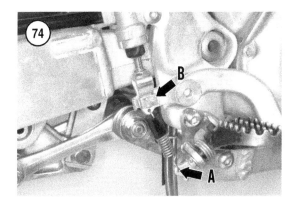

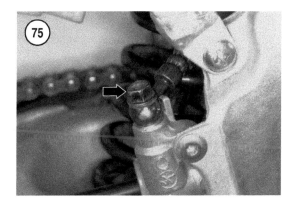

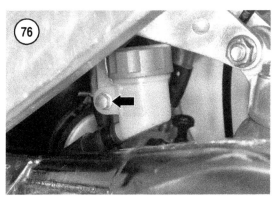

11. Seat the pad retainer into the mounting bracket (**Figure 71**).

12. Install the bleeder valve and cap.

13. Slide the mounting bracket and caliper pins into the rubber boots (**Figure 72**).

14. Screw the disc cover onto the mounting bracket. Apply threadlocking compound to the screw threads. Tighten the screws to the specification in **Table 2**.

15. Install the pad pin plug, pad pin, brake pads and pad spring as described in *Rear Brake Pads*. The parts can be installed with the caliper either on or off the motorcycle.

16. Install the caliper as described in this section.

REAR MASTER CYLINDER

Removal and Installation

Refer to **Figure 73**.

1. Drain the brake system as described in this chapter.

2. Disconnect the return spring on the brake pedal (A, **Figure 74**).

3. Remove the cotter pin and clevis pin (B, **Figure 74**), that secure the master cylinder clevis to the brake pedal.

4. Remove the brake hose banjo bolt from the master cylinder as follows:

   a. Remove the banjo bolt (**Figure 75**) and seal washers from the brake hose. Have a shop cloth on hand to catch excess brake fluid that drips from the hose.

   b. Wrap the hose end to prevent brake fluid from damaging other surfaces.

5. Remove the master cylinder and reservoir as follows:

   a. Remove the bolt (**Figure 76**) securing the reservoir.

   b. Remove the two bolts (**Figure 77**) securing the master cylinder.

   c. Remove the assembly from the motorcycle (**Figure 78**).

6. Repair the master cylinder as described in this chapter.

7. Reverse this procedure to install the master cylinder and reservoir. Observe the following:

   a. Install *new* seal washers on the banjo bolt.

   b. Install a *new* cotter pin on the clevis pin.

   c. Tighten all bolts to the specification in **Table 2**.

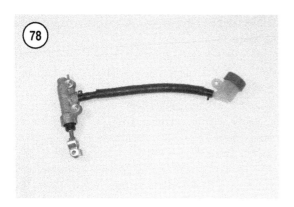

8. Fill the brake fluid reservoir and bleed the brake as described in this chapter.

9. Check rear brake pedal adjustment as described in Chapter Three.

Repair

> *NOTE*
> *The snap ring pliers (**Figure 24**) used in this procedure (Kowa Seiki part No. AKS-316-2010) have long arms that make snap ring removal easier, since the arms extend into the cylinder.*

1. Remove the master cylinder and reservoir as described in this section.

2. Remove the snap ring that retains the hose and fitting against the master cylinder. Remove the hose assembly and O-ring (**Figure 79**).

3. Loosen the locknut (A, **Figure 80**) from the clevis (B). Remove the clevis, locknut and boot from the pushrod shaft (**Figure 81**).

4. Remove the snap ring, recessed in the cylinder bore (**Figure 82**).

5. Remove the pushrod and snap ring.

6. Remove the piston and spring (**Figure 83**).

7. Remove the cap, plate and diaphragm from the reservoir.

8. Inspect the master cylinder assembly as follows:
   a. Clean all parts that will be reused with fresh brake fluid or isopropyl (rubbing) alcohol.
   b. Inspect the cylinder bore for wear, pitting or corrosion.
   c. Measure the inside diameter of the cylinder bore (**Figure 84**). Refer to **Table 1** for the service limit.
   d. Measure the outside diameter of the piston (**Figure 85**). Refer to **Table 1** for the service limit.

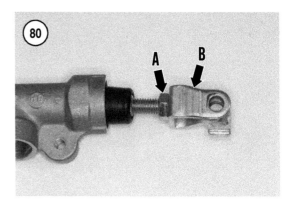

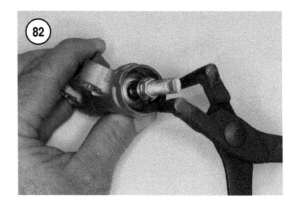

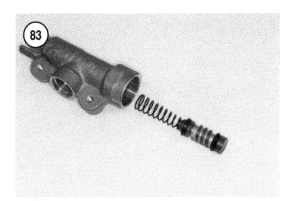

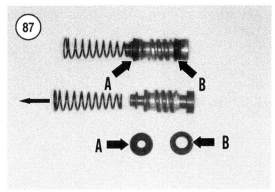

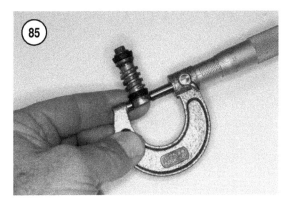

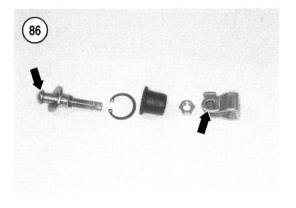

e. Inspect the pushrod and clevis assembly (**Figure 86**). Check the pushrod for straightness and wear at the contact point. Check that the pivot hole in the clevis is not elongated.

f. Inspect and clean the orifices and threads in the cylinder. Clean with compressed air.

g. Inspect and clean the reservoir.

h. Inspect the cap, plate and diaphragm for damage.

9. Assemble the piston, cups and spring as follows. **Figure 87** shows both an assembled and unassembled piston.

a. Soak the primary cup (A, **Figure 87**) and secondary cup (B) in fresh DOT 4 brake fluid for 15 minutes. This will soften and lubricate the cups.

b. Apply brake fluid to the piston so the cups can slide over the ends.

c. Identify the wide (open) side of the primary cup. When installed, the wide side of the cup *must* face in the direction of the arrow (**Figure 87**). Install the primary cup onto the piston.

d. Identify the wide (open) side of the secondary cup. When installed, the wide side of the cup *must* face in the direction of the arrow (**Figure 87**). Install the secondary cup on the piston.

e. The assembled piston should appear as in **Figure 88**. The wide side of both cups must face as shown.

f. Install the *small end* of the spring onto the piston.

10. Lubricate the cylinder bore and piston assembly with brake fluid.

11. Secure the cylinder in a vise so both hands are free to put the piston and pushrod assembly into the cylinder. To prevent damage to the cylinder, tempo-

14

rarily thread a bolt and locknut into the brake hose mounting hole. Secure the cylinder with the bolt (**Figure 89**).

> *CAUTION*
> *After the spring, piston and cups are in the cylinder, hold them in place until the pushrod assembly is installed. Anytime the cups come out of the cylinder there is a chance of damaging the cup lips during the reinsertion process.*

12. Apply a small amount of grease to the contact area of the pushrod.

13. Lubricate the cylinder bore, piston and cups with brake fluid.

14. Insert the piston and pushrod assembly (**Figure 90**) into the cylinder, carefully twisting the cups past the edge of the bore. The cup diameters are larger than the bore. Therefore, ensure that the lips do not fold back when entering the bore. Hold the assembly in place when it is fully in the bore.

15. Insert and seat the snap ring in the bore (**Figure 91**). The flat side of the snap ring must face *out* (away from the bore).

16. Remove the cylinder from the vise, then remove the bolt from the cylinder.

17. Apply silicone brake grease to the inside of the boot, then install the boot onto the pushrod (**Figure 92**).

18. Install the locknut and clevis onto the pushrod. Adjust the clevis so the pedal will be at standard height when the master cylinder is installed. Adjust as follows:

   a. Check that the pushrod is fully extended.

   b. Measure from the center of the cylinder mounting hole to the center of the clevis mounting hole (**Figure 93**). The distance should be 75 mm (2.95 in.).

   c. Turn the clevis in or out until the correct distance is achieved.

   d. Tighten the locknut against the clevis.

19. Attach the reservoir assembly to the master cylinder as follows:

   a. Lubricate a *new* O-ring with brake fluid (**Figure 79**) and install it into the cylinder.

   b. Seat the hose fitting into the cylinder, then lock it in place with the snap ring. Install the snap ring so the flat side faces out.

   c. Install the diaphragm and plate, then screw the cap onto the reservoir.

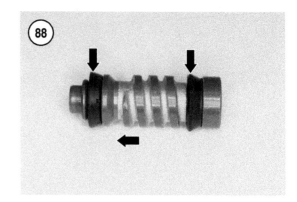

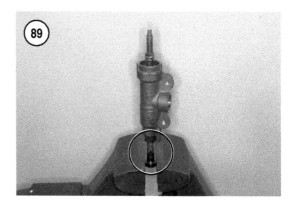

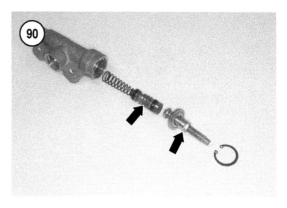

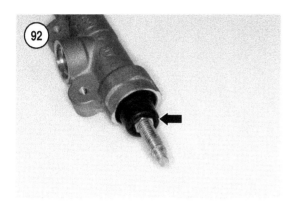

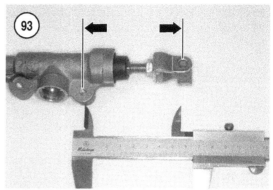

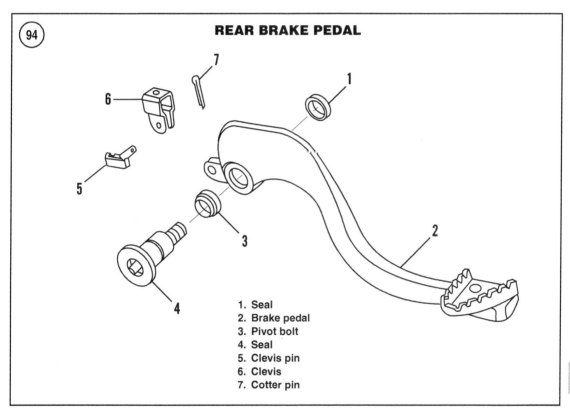

REAR BRAKE PEDAL

1. Seal
2. Brake pedal
3. Pivot bolt
4. Seal
5. Clevis pin
6. Clevis
7. Cotter pin

14

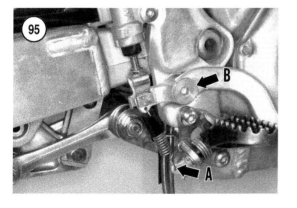

20. Install the master cylinder and reservoir as described in this section.

REAR BRAKE PEDAL

Removal and Installation

Use the following procedure to remove and install the rear brake pedal. Refer to **Figure 94**.

1. Disconnect the return spring on the brake pedal (A, **Figure 95**).

2. Remove the pivot bolt (B, **Figure 95**).

3. Remove the cotter pin and clevis pin (A, **Figure 96**), that secure the master cylinder clevis to the brake pedal.

4. Clean and inspect the parts as follows:

   a. Inspect the pivot bolt and bore for scoring, damage or the entry of water and dirt.

   b. If contamination has entered the bore, replace the seals (B, **Figure 96**), located on both sides of the pedal.

   c. Inspect the clevis pin and clevis. The pin must be a firm fit in the clevis.

5. Reverse this procedure to install the pedal. Note the following:

   a. Apply grease to the seals, bore and pivot bolt.

   b. Tighten the pivot bolt to the specification in **Table 2**.

   c. Check pedal height adjustment as described in Chapter Three.

   d. Install a new cotter pin.

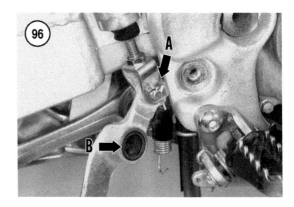

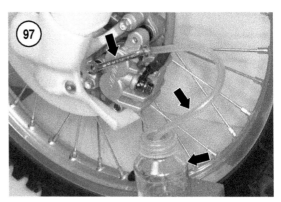

BRAKE SYSTEM DRAINING

To drain the old brake fluid from the system, use an 8 mm wrench, tip-resistant container and a length of clear tubing that fits snugly on the brake bleeder (**Figure 97**).

> *CAUTION*
> *Brake fluid can damage painted and finished surfaces. Use water to immediately wash any surface that becomes contaminated with brake fluid.*

1. If draining the rear brake, remove the caliper cover (**Figure 98**).

2. Attach one end of the tubing to the brake bleeder and place the other end into the container (**Figure 97**).

3. Open the brake bleeder (**Figure 99**) so fluid can pass into the tubing.

4. Pump the brake lever/pedal to force the fluid from the system.

5. When the system no longer drips fluid, close the bleeder.

6. Remove the cap assembly from the brake fluid reservoir and fill the reservoir to the upper level. Bleed the system as described in this section.

7. Install the caliper cover (rear brake only).

8. Dispose the used brake fluid in an environmentally safe manner.

BRAKE SYSTEM BLEEDING

Whenever the brake fluid is replaced, or if the brake lever or pedal feels spongy, bleed the brakes to purge all air from the system. Before bleeding the brakes, determine where the air is entering the system. Check all brake components for leakage, and fittings and hoses for deterioration, damage or looseness.

The brake system can be bled manually or by using a vacuum pump. Both methods are described in this section.

Manual Bleeding

To manually bleed the brake system, use an 8 mm wrench, tip-resistant container and a length of clear tubing that fits snugly on the brake bleeder (**Figure 97**). Bleeding the system is much easier if two people can perform the procedure. One person can open and close the bleeder while the other person operates the brake lever or pedal.

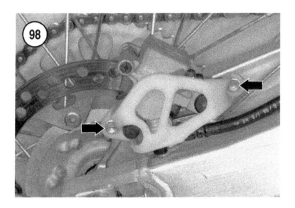

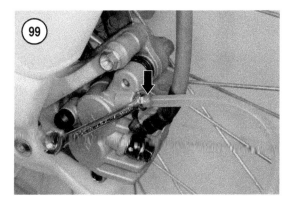

CAUTION
Brake fluid can damage painted and finished surfaces. Use water and immediately wash any surface that becomes contaminated with brake fluid.

1. If bleeding the rear brake, remove the caliper cover (**Figure 98**).
2. Attach one end of the tubing to the brake bleeder and place the other end into the container (**Figure 97**).
3. Fill the reservoir to the upper level with DOT 4 brake fluid.

CAUTION
Do not use brake fluid from an unsealed container. It will have absorbed moisture from the air and already be contaminated. Use DOT 4 brake fluid from a sealed container. Do not mix DOT 4 fluid with DOT 3 or DOT 5 rated fluids.

4. Apply pressure (do not pump) to the brake lever or pedal, then open the brake bleeder. As the fluid is forced from the system, the lever/pedal will travel its full length of operation. When the lever/pedal can move no farther, hold the lever/pedal in the *down* position and close the bleeder. Do not allow the lever or pedal to return to its *up* position before the bleeder is closed. Air will be drawn into the system.

NOTE
In the following step, release the lever/pedal slowly. This will minimize the chance of fluid splashing out of the reservoir as excess fluid in the brake line is returned to the reservoir.

5. When the bleeder is closed, release the lever/pedal so it returns to its *up* position. Check the fluid level in the reservoir and replenish, if necessary.

NOTE
During the bleeding process, the reservoir must contain fluid during the entire procedure. If the reservoir is allowed to become empty, air will be in the system and the bleeding process will have to be repeated.

6. Repeat Steps 4-5 until clear fluid (no air bubbles) is seen passing out of the bleeder.

NOTE
If small bubbles (foam) remain in the system after several bleeding attempts, close the reservoir and allow the system to stand undisturbed for a few hours. The system will stabilize and the air can be purged as large bubbles.

7. The bleeding procedure is completed when the feel of the lever/pedal is firm.
8. Install the caliper cover (rear brake only).
9. Check the brake fluid reservoir and fill the reservoir to the upper level, if necessary.
10. Dispose the used brake fluid in an environmentally safe manner.

Vacuum Bleeding

To vacuum-bleed the brake system, use an 8 mm wrench and a vacuum pump, such as the Mityvac pump shown in **Figure 100**.

CAUTION
Brake fluid can damage painted and finished surfaces. Use water and immediately wash any surface that becomes contaminated with brake fluid.

14

1. If bleeding the rear brake, remove the caliper cover (**Figure 98**).

2. Check that the banjo bolts are tight at the master cylinder and caliper.

3. Attach the brake bleeder to the bleeder valve (**Figure 100**). Suspend the tool with wire. This will allow the tool to be released when the fluid reservoir needs to be refilled.

4. Fill the reservoir to the upper level with DOT 4 brake fluid.

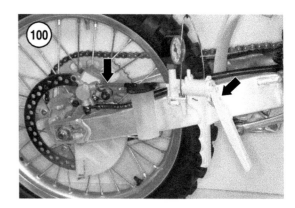

> *CAUTION*
> *Do not use brake fluid from an unsealed container. It will have absorbed moisture from the air and already be contaminated. Use DOT 4 brake fluid from a sealed container. Do not mix DOT 4 fluid with DOT 3 or DOT 5 rated fluids.*

> *NOTE*
> *During the bleeding process, the reservoir must contain fluid during the entire procedure. If the reservoir is allowed to become empty, air will be in the system and the bleeding process will have to be repeated.*

5. Pump the handle on the brake bleeder to create a vacuum.

6. Open the bleeder valve and draw the air and fluid from the system. Close the valve *before* the fluid stops moving. If the vacuum pump is equipped with a gauge, close the bleeder before the gauge reads 0 in. Hg. Replenish the fluid level in the reservoir.

7. Repeat Steps 5-6 until clear fluid (no air bubbles) is seen passing out of the bleeder. The bleeding procedure is completed when the feel of the lever/pedal is firm.

8. Install the caliper cover (rear brake only).

9. Dispose the used brake fluid in an environmentally safe manner.

BRAKE DISC

The condition of the brake discs and pads are often a reflection of one another. If disc scoring is evident, inspect the pads and disc as soon as possible. Visually inspect the discs and pads with the wheels mounted on the bike as described in Chapter Three. If damage is detected, perform the inspections described in this chapter.

> *NOTE*
> *Do not true a deeply scored or warped disc. The removal of disc material will cause the disc to overheat rapidly and warp. Maintain the discs by keeping them clean and corrosion-free. Use a solvent that is not oil-based to wipe grit that accumulates on the discs and at the edge of the pads.*

Thickness and Runout Inspection

1. Measure the thickness of each disc at several locations around its perimeter (**Figure 101**). Refer to **Table 1** for the service limit. Replace the disc if it is out of specification.

2. Measure disc runout as follows:

    a. Place a dial indicator on a stable surface and in contact with the disc (**Figure 102**).

    b. Zero the gauge.

    c. Turn the wheel and watch the amount of runout measured on the gauge.

    d. Refer to **Table 1** for the service limit. Replace the disc if it is out of specification.

NOTE
If the disc runout is out of specification, check the condition of the wheel bearings before replacing the disc. If the bearings are not in good condition, replace the bearings before disc runout is determined.

Removal and Installation

The discs are mounted to the hubs with bolts. Remove and install either disc as follows:

1. Remove the wheel from motorcycle as described in Chapter Eleven.

2. Remove the bolts (**Figure 103**) that secure the disc to the hub. There are six bolts at the front disc and four bolts at the rear disc.

3. Clean the threadlocking compound from the bolts and mounting holes.

4. Reverse this procedure to install the discs. Note the following:

    a. Install the disc so DRIVE (stamped on the disc) faces out.

    b. Apply threadlocking compound to the bolt threads.

    c. Tighten the bolts to the specification in **Table 2**.

Table 1 BRAKE SERVICE SPECIFICATIONS

	New mm (in.)	Service limit mm (in.)
Front disc brake		
Disc thickness	3.0 (0.12)	2.5 (0.10)
Disc runout	–	0.15 (0.006)
Pad wear indicator	–	1.0 (0.04)
Master cylinder inner diameter	11.0-11.043	11.05
	(0.4330-0.4347)	(0.435)
Master cylinder piston		
outer diameter	10.957-10.984	10.84
	(0.4314-0.4324)	(0.427)
Caliper bore inner diameter	27.0-27.050	27.06
	(1.0630-1.0650)	(1.065)
Caliper piston		
outer diameter		
1997-2000	26.90-26.950	26.89
	(1.0590-1.0610)	(1.059)
2001	26.681-26.894	26.853
	(1.058-1.059)	(1.057)
Rear disc brake		
Disc thickness	4.0 (0.16)	3.5 (0.14)
(continued)		

14

Table 1 BRAKE SERVICE SPECIFICATIONS (continued)

	New mm (in.)	Service limit mm (in.)
Rear disc brake (continued)		
Disc runout	–	0.15 (0.006)
Pad wear indicator	–	1.0 (0.04)
Master cylinder		
inner diameter	12.70-12.743	12.76
	(0.4999-0.5016)	(0.502)
Master cylinder piston	12.657-12.684	12.64
outer diameter	(0.4983-0.4993)	(0.498)
Caliper bore	27.0-27.050	27.06
inner diameter	(1.0630-1.0650)	(1.065)
Caliper piston	26.935-26.968	26.89
outer diameter	(1.0604-1.0617)	(1.059)
Brake fluid type	DOT 4	

Table 2 BRAKE SYSTEM TORQUE SPECIFICATIONS

	N•m	in.-lb.	ft.-lb.
Banjo bolts	34	–	25
Brake bleeder	5.4	48	–
Brake disc nuts (front)	16	–	12
Brake disc bolts (rear)	42	–	31
Brake disc cover (front)			
bolts	13	–	9
Brake disc guard (rear)			
mounting screws	6.8	60	–
Brake hose guide screws			
(rear) (2001 models only)	1.2	10	–
Brake pedal pivot bolt	25	–	19
Brake lever pivot			
bolt/locknut	5.9	52	–
Brake lever adjuster			
locknut	5.9	52	–
Caliper (front) mounting			
bolts	30	–	22
Caliper pin bolts (front)	22	–	16
Caliper pin bolt (rear)	27	–	20
Caliper (rear) bracket			
pin bolt	12	106	–
Master cylinder (front)			
reservoir cover screws	10.7	95	–
Master cylinder (front)			
holder bolts	9.9	88	–
Master cylinder			
pushrod locknut	17.2	–	13
Master cylinder (rear)			
mounting bolts	13	–	9
Pad pin	18	–	13
Pad pin plug	3	27	–

CHAPTER FIFTEEN

BODY

This chapter contains removal and installation procedures for the seat, side covers, radiator shrouds, fuel tank, fuel valve and subframe.

> *NOTE*
> *When removing or installing the bodywork, do not use excessive force. The bodywork is easily damaged.*

SEAT

Removal and Installation

1. Remove the rear bolt and collar (**Figure 1**) from both sides of the seat.

2. Lightly lift up on the rear of the seat and pull it away from the fuel tank and the tab on the subframe.

3. To install the seat, reverse this procedure and tighten the bolts to the specification in **Table 1**.

SIDE COVERS

Removal and Installation

1. Remove the seat as described in this chapter.

2. On 1997-1999 models, remove the front screw and collar (A, **Figure 2**) from both side covers.

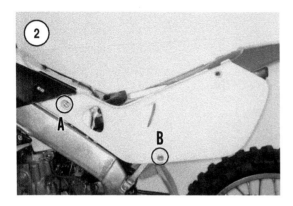

3. Remove the flange bolt and collar from both side covers (B, **Figure 2**).

4. To install the side covers, reverse this procedure.

RADIATOR SHROUDS

Removal and Installation

1. Remove the screws or bolts and collars that secure each shroud (**Figure 3**).

2. To install the shrouds, reverse this procedure.

SUBFRAME

Removal and Installation

1. Support the bike so it is level and stable.

2. Remove the seat and side covers as described in this chapter.

3. Loosen the band screw at the air filter (**Figure 4**).

4. Remove the upper subframe mounting bolt and the two lower mounting bolts (**Figure 5**).

5. Pull the subframe straight back and away from the bike.

> *NOTE*
> *If resistance is felt, check if the sealing rubber at the exhaust pipe and muffler connection is jammed (**Figure 6**).*

6. To install the subframe, reverse this procedure. Note the following:

    a. Insert all mounting bolts before tightening.

    b. Tighten the bolts to the specifications in **Table 1**.

Table 1 BODY TORQUE SPECIFICATIONS

	N•m	in.-lb.	ft.-lb.
Radiator shroud bolts	6	53	–
Seat bracket screw	6	53	–
Seat mounting bolts	26	–	20
Subframe mounting bolts			
Upper	30	–	22
Lower	41	–	30

15

INDEX

16

16

HONDA CR250R (1997-1998 MODELS)

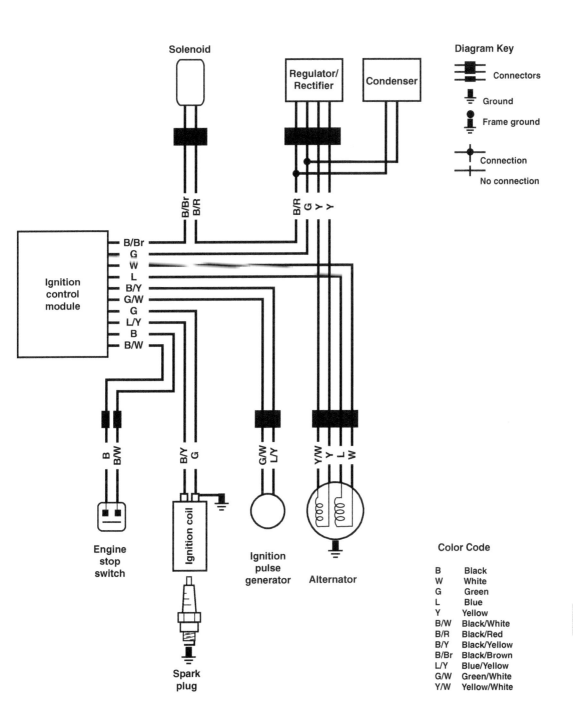

HONDA CR250R (1999 MODELS)

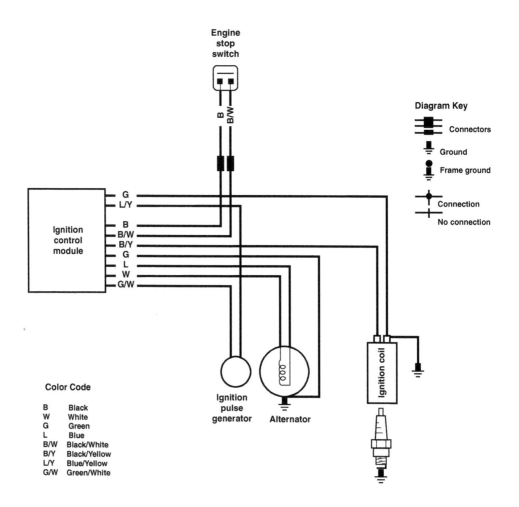

Diagram Key

Connectors

Ground

Frame ground

Connection

No connection

Engine
stop
switch

Ignition
control
module

Color Code

B   Black
W   White
G   Green
L   Blue
B/W   Black/White
B/Y   Black/Yellow
L/Y   Blue/Yellow
G/W   Green/White

Ignition
pulse
generator   Alternator

Ignition coil

HONDA CR250R (2000-2001 MODELS)

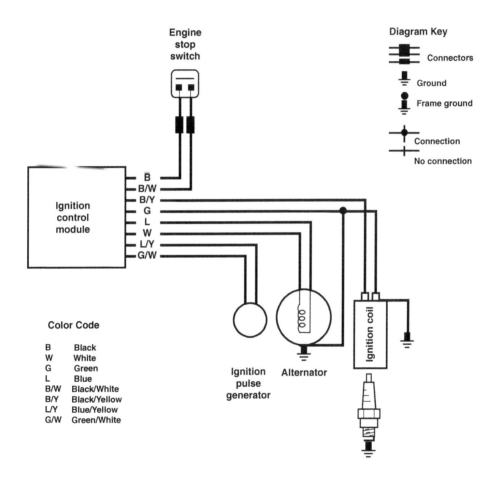

Engine stop switch

Diagram Key

Connectors
Ground
Frame ground
Connection
No connection

Ignition control module

B
B/W
B/Y
G
L
W
L/Y
G/W

Ignition coil

Ignition pulse generator

Alternator

Color Code

B	Black
W	White
G	Green
L	Blue
B/W	Black/White
B/Y	Black/Yellow
L/Y	Blue/Yellow
G/W	Green/White

17

NOTES

NOTES

NOTES

MAINTENANCE LOG

Date	Races	Type of Service

MAINTENANCE LOG

Date	Races	Type of Service